ENGLISH
VOICES

Also by Ferdinand Mount

NON-FICTION

The Theatre of Politics
The Subversive Family
The British Constitution Now
Communism (ed.)
Mind the Gap
Cold Cream
Full Circle
The New Few
The Tears of the Rajas

FICTION

Tales of History and Imagination
Umbrella
Jem (and Sam)
The Condor's Head

A Chronicle of Modern Twilight
The Man Who Rode Ampersand
The Selkirk Strip
Of Love and Asthma
The Liquidator
Fairness
Heads You Win

Very Like a Whale

The Clique

ENGLISH VOICES

Lives, Landscapes, Laments
1985–2015

FERDINAND MOUNT

**SIMON &
SCHUSTER**

London · New York · Sydney · Toronto · New Delhi

A CBS COMPANY

First published in Great Britain by Simon & Schuster UK Ltd, 2016
A CBS COMPANY

1 3 5 7 9 10 8 6 4 2

Simon & Schuster UK Ltd
1st Floor
222 Gray's Inn Road
London WC1X 8HB

www.simonandschuster.co.uk

Simon & Schuster Australia, Sydney
Simon & Schuster India, New Delhi

A CIP catalogue record for this book
is available from the British Library

Hardback ISBN: 978-1-4711-5597-0
eBook ISBN: 978-1-4711-5599-4

Typeset in Bembo by M Rules
Printed and bound by CPI Group (UK) Ltd, Croydon, CR0 4YY

'From this amphibious, ill-born mob began
That vain, ill-natured thing, an Englishman'

Daniel Defoe, *The True-Born Englishman*, 1701

CONTENTS

Introduction: The Amphibious Mob   xi

VOICES IN OUR TIME

Kingsley Amis: the craving machine   4
Alan Bennett: against splother   12
Muriel Spark: the Go-Away Bird   18
V. S. Naipaul: no home for Mr Biswas   24
Hugh Trevor-Roper: the Voltaire of St Aldate's   31
W. G. Sebald: a master shrouded in mist   39
John le Carré: spooking the spooks   46
Elias Canetti: the God-Monster of Hampstead   53
John Osborne: anger management?   61
Professor Derek Jackson: off the radar   70
Germaine Greer: still strapped in the cuirass   79

EARLY MODERNS

Rudyard Kipling: the sensitive bounder   89
George Gissing: the downfall of a pessimist   98
Virginia Woolf: go with the flow   106
Arthur Ransome: Lenin in the Lake District   114
E. M. Forster: shy, remorseless shade   124

Arthur Machen: faerie strains 131
Fred Perry: winner takes all 139
M. R. James: the sexless ghost 144
Wilfred Owen: the last telegram 152
John Maynard Keynes: copulation and
macroeconomics 157

DIVINE DISCONTENTS

Basil Hume: the English cardinal 165
The Red Dean 171
Charles Bradlaugh: the admirable atheist 180
Mr Gladstone's religion 190
The rise and fall and rise of Methodism 202

IN SEARCH OF ENGLAND

Pevsner in Berkshire 211
Oliver Rackham: magus of the woods 218
The last of Betjeman 225
Ronald Blythe: glory in the ruts 233
The suburb and the village 237
Mark Girouard and the English town 249

SOME OLD MASTERS

Thomas Hardy: the twilight of aftering 263
Charles Dickens: kindly leave the stage 271
Samuel Taylor Coleridge: a wonderful leaper 283
John Keats: what's become of Junkets? 290
Samuel Pepys: from the scaffold to Mr Pooter 298
Shakespeare at Stratford: the divine pork butcher 305

THE GREAT VICTORIANS

Sir Robert Peel: the first modern   318
Lord Palmerston: the unstoppable Pam   325
Walter Bagehot: money matters   335
Lord Rosebery: the palm without the dust   348
Arthur Balfour: a fatal charm   358

OUR STATESMEN

Margot, Asquith and the Great War   372
Churchill's calamity: day trip to Gallipoli   388
Oswald Mosley: the poor old Führer   399
Roy Jenkins: trainspotting lothario   412
Denis Healey: the bruiser aesthete   416
Harold Macmillan: lonely are the brave   423
Edward Heath: the great sulk   440
Margaret Thatcher: making your own luck   450

Notes and references   467
Acknowledgements   473
Picture permissions   474
Index   475

INTRODUCTION

The Amphibious Mob

The English have always had a fierce sense of themselves. As they waded up the beaches, our ancestors were apparently shouting 'Engla-Lond, Engla-Lond', as if the World Cup had already started. In King Alfred's day, women who adopted Danish hairstyles were attacked for being un-English. The Venerable Bede of Jarrow, in his *Ecclesiastical History of the English People,* finished as early as AD 731, laments the vices of his countrymen, notably sodomy, adultery and drunkenness, but also picks out their positives such as stoicism, telling the story of a fellow Tyneside monk bathing in a freezing river with blocks of ice all round him and someone calling from the bank that 'it is wonderful how you can manage to bear such bitter cold', to which the monk replies, like any true Geordie, 'I have known it colder.'

Further back still, according to the Roman historian Tacitus, our ancestors were already making their own suburbs, 'refusing to have their houses set together like the Romans and preferring to live apart, dotted here and there where spring, plain or grove has taken their fancy, each leaving an open space round his house'.

The point is not so much how accurate these stereotypes were but rather how, from very early times, observers were fascinated by the quiddities of the English.

Modern historians do not care for this kind of thing. In the eyes of scholars as diverse as Eric Hobsbawm, Ernest Gellner and Linda Colley, national identity is mostly an artificial construct. According to Benedict Anderson, national communities don't just grow, they have to be 'imagined'. From a very different viewpoint, Hugh Trevor-Roper claimed that 'Scottishness' was largely invented by Sir Walter Scott. Colley argues in her influential *Britons* that you can see unmistakable evidence through the seventeenth, eighteenth and nineteenth centuries of politicians and propagandists pushing the idea of Britishness, for fear that the Union might founder without this ideological buttressing. Even so, Colley does not deny that the idea of Britain was knocking around way before the union of Parliaments in 1707 and even before the union of the Scottish and English Crowns in 1603. And if Britishness is not quite such a latecomer as all that, Englishness is something else.

Patrick Wormald, that brilliant alcoholic depressive who lit up Anglo-Saxon history for all too brief a period before his early death, contends that a sense of Englishness was always present, as thick as the fog, as pervasive and pungent as the drains, long before the Norman Conquest and long after it, enduring through that conquest and then through all the twists and turns of the Reformation and Counter-Reformation: 'the onus probandi lies on those who would deny that such a sense remained embedded in the bulk of the English population throughout this long period. Unless a sense of English identity had penetrated towards the roots of society, it is very difficult to understand how it survived at all.' Wormald contends, not without passion, that 'there is evidence of a remarkably precocious sense of common "Englishness" and not just in politically interested circles. It is arguable that it is because "Englishness" was first an ideal that the enterprise launched by Alfred, his children and his grandchildren was so successful.'

In other words, the people in Wessex, Mercia and the rest were consciously and cussedly English for a long period before these territories were unified into a political realm called England, although that realm is itself remarkably ancient in both its boundaries and its monarchy, more ancient perhaps than any other significant realm in Europe, and more continuous if not unbroken in its duration. After the breaks – the Norman Conquest, the Commonwealth – the English simply re-emerged, not unaltered by the trauma but convinced that they were in essentials the same people they had been before.

This persisting sense of identity has rarely been bolstered by any feelings of racial purity. The English might think of themselves as different, but they have not gone in for myths of a unique genetic origin. English churchmen believed that mankind developed from a single common ancestor, the theory of monogenesis, as opposed to polygenesis, the belief that men originated in separate races and that, as a consequence, the differences between those races were ineradicable and important. The most notorious English racialist, Houston Stewart Chamberlain (1855–1927), found so little support for his theories in England that he made his career in Germany and took German citizenship. Pseudo-scientific racial theories never stood up to the facts of common observation in this country. An English crowd looks so diverse – tall, short, blond, dark, ginger, blobby, aquiline, eyes of every colour.

Quite early on, in fact, the English became proud of their mongrel heredity. Daniel Defoe's satire, *The True-Born Englishman* (1701), was an instant and lasting bestseller which went through forty editions in as many years. In it, Defoe mocks those of his fellow countrymen who object to foreign-born rulers such as William of Orange. Who, after all, were our ancestors? 'Auxiliaries and slaves of every nation' who had followed in the baggage train of the Romans, then the plundering Saxons and Danes, followed by waves of Picts, Scots and Irishmen, finishing up with the Norman heavies:

All these their barbarous offspring left behind
The dregs of armies, they of all mankind.
From this amphibious, ill-born mob began
That vain, ill-natured thing an Englishman.

As Jonathan Clark points out in *Our Shadowed Present*, the way the English usually described themselves was not 'true-born' but 'free-born'. Their heritage was not genetic but political. The 'amphibious mob' prided itself not on its ancient bloodlines but on its ancient liberties.

Of course they thought themselves not only different, but superior. Most nations do. But their claims to superiority were often tinged with self-mockery. In the heyday of Empire, the Victorian bourgeoisie guffawed at W. S. Gilbert's parodies of patriotic ditties:

He is an Englishman!
For he himself has said it
And it's greatly to his credit
That he is an Englishman!

Gilbert even asserts ironically that there is an element of choice in the matter:

In spite of all temptations
To belong to other nations
He remains an Englishman!

Nor have the English been conspicuously pleased with their nation and themselves, except perhaps under the first Elizabeth and in the high Victorian age. More often the dominant tone of English discourse is one of regret, of nostalgia rather than self-congratulation. In *Albion*, his vast sprawling enquiry into the origins of the English imagination, Peter Ackroyd identifies Bede as the first English writer, typically brooding on ruins and relics of the past and already, in the early eighth century, exuding that melancholy characteristic of these rainswept islanders. If there is a theme common to English writers from Bede to Betjeman, it is this regret for the past. The best has already come and gone and will not come again. Shortly after the Norman Conquest, a scribe charmingly known as the Tremulous Hand of Worcester sighs over the demise of Old English: nobody teaches the language properly any more, the people are lost and wrecked.

Only a gross imperialist like Cecil Rhodes would think of claiming that 'to be an Englishman was to draw first prize in the lottery of life'. In any case, it was always possible to buy a lottery ticket. In fact, from Disraeli onwards, paeans to Englishness have so often come from historians and political writers who are not English by descent. The philosopher Sir Isaiah Berlin, who was born in Riga and as a child witnessed the Bolshevik Revolution from his parents' apartment in St Petersburg, writes of the historian Sir Lewis Namier, born Ludwik Bernsztajn in Poland to a Jewish land agent who had converted to Catholicism:

> He was not disappointed in England. It took, as he had supposed, a humane, civilised and, above all, sober, undramatised, empirical view of life. Englishmen seemed to him to take account, more than most men, of the real ends of human life – pleasure, justice, power, freedom, glory, the sense of human solidarity which underlay both patriotism and adherence to tradition; above all they loathed abstract principles and general theories.

From almost everything that Berlin wrote and said, it is clear that these are Berlin's own sentiments too. It was, I think, his experience of England that helped to shape his crucial insight, that political theories and principles do not by nature fit neatly with one another and that wisdom consists in learning to live with the conflicts between them.

In the writing of English history, it has so often been incomers who have constructed the most vivid pictures of the way we were. Who has inked in our image of the Tudors more forcefully than G. R. Elton, Sir Geoffrey Elton, born Gottfried Rudolf Ehrenberg in Prague? In the introduction to his little book *The English* (1992), Elton touchingly records: 'I was well over seventeen years old when I landed in England on St Valentine's Day in 1939, and I knew virtually nothing of that country, not even its language. Within a few months it dawned upon me that I had arrived in the country in which I ought to have been born.'

What then are the characteristics of that country that were so immediately attractive to the young Ehrenberg? What makes or made it so enviable to be English, either by birth or by adoption? It is an inconvenient truth that just as our characteristics are not exclusive to us, neither are they unchanging. That sober, tolerant country which entranced Berlin, Namier and Elton had, three centuries earlier, been notorious for its sectarian ferocity and its terrible civil wars; one king had his head cut off, another was driven into exile. Fifty years later, the country was still being convulsed by violent uprisings in support of the exiled dynasty.

Neither our sexual mores nor our religious habits are constant, either. If the Victorians were pious and prudish, the Georgians were unbuttoned and tepid in their devotions. As for our supposed aversion to sexual display, what about Shakespeare's bawdry or the bare bosoms of Sir Peter Lely's beauties? English phlegm was unknown to the hot-tempered gallants of Restoration England. The stiff upper lip seems more like a by-product of Empire than an enduring feature of the English face; it crumpled terminally at the funeral of Princess Diana. In the 1930s, English bohemians fled their suffocating homeland, or 'Pudding Island' as Lawrence Durrell called it, for a climate where they could take their clothes off and let their hair down. Now foreigners flood into London, because it seems to them the least inhibited metropolis on earth.

Is there in fact any specific quality in life, or art or literature that we can pin down as intrinsically, enduringly and uniquely English? Ackroyd claims, for example, that the English have a special relationship to trees and hate seeing them cut down. Odd, seeing that we have cut down more of them than almost any other nation. Aren't the Germans rather more notoriously in love with their forests, even naming their gâteaux after them? One of the most famous lines in French nursery rhymes laments that 'we shall go no more to the woods, the laurels are cut down'.

Even where one can identify some cultural trait that appears idiosyncratically English, there always seem to be exceptions. The 'serpentine line of beauty' recommended by Hogarth certainly does apply to the English tradition in gardening – all meanders and no straight lines – but can you apply it to English architecture, the single unique style of which we happen to call perpendicular? Our Georgian terraces are anything but serpentine, certainly not when compared with the fantastic curlicues of Bavarian rococo. On none of these supposedly English qualities – understatement and modesty, sexual unease, or enduring love of the eclectic and the countryside, aversion to order and straight lines – can the English claim exclusive copyright.

But there are two ancient and continuing features of English culture which do have a solid claim to be peculiar and fundamental: the common law and the common language. The two are crucially interlinked, and between them, I would argue, are constitutive of Englishness.

At first sight it may seem bizarre that the most famous – and best – description of what the English common law does should come from a poem. But then it's a bizarre poem. It has no title. Alfred Tennyson simply begins with a question:

> You ask me, why, tho' ill at ease,
> Within this region I subsist,
> Whose spirits falter in the mist,
> And languish for the purple seas.

In other words, why the hell should he stay in England? And he answers himself with a paean to the liberty and tolerance of a country

> Where Freedom broadens slowly down
> From precedent to precedent.

The common law is not the creation of a single glorious revolution or a single brilliant legal mind. It is the deposit of ages, the outcome of legal battles yesterday and long ago, of judgments since refined, enlarged and sometimes revoked by generation upon generation of judges. Some of its principles have endured for centuries. Large parts of Magna Carta – and the judgments based on the Great Charter – remained law until the late nineteenth century. Even today we still have the clauses about not selling, denying or delaying justice and not imprisoning or dispossessing anyone 'save by the lawful judgment of his peers or by the law of the land'. The law against eavesdropping was part of English common law for nearly 600 years until it was tidied out of existence by the Law Commission in the 1960s – just when it was about to come in handy as a deterrent against phone hacking.

We cannot leave Tennyson's little poem without noting how, in typical English style, he undercuts his own grandiloquence in the final stanza:

> Yet waft me from the harbour-mouth,
> Wild wind! I seek a warmer sky,
> And I will see before I die
> The palms and temples of the South.

The English common law may be a fine thing, but the English poet is off to sun himself in San Remo.

The common law had from its beginnings a peculiarly intimate relationship with the English language, for one simple reason.

Right from the start, almost everything that mattered in Anglo-Saxon England was written in English: law, poetry, history, medical advice, especially law. Everywhere else in Europe, Latin was the language of learned men doing their business. Not in England. And nowhere else produced such an abundance of written law as England in the centuries before the Norman Conquest. As Nicholas Vincent points out in his study of Magna Carta, Anglo-Saxon England, though not Norman France, was 'a society already hard-wired with law'. Written codes of Anglo-Saxon law survive in numbers, perhaps from Ethelbert's day, more reliably from Alfred's. Elton was dazzled:

> Naturally, the laws being written down provide splendid information on the kind of society with which we are dealing. The first remarkable thing about them is the language in which they were originally composed. The kings and their advisers used the vernacular; unlike the rest of Western Europe they escaped the bureaucratic imposition of Latin.

And even though the Norman conquerors rewrote the laws in Latin and conversed in French, English re-emerged as the elite language in the course of the thirteenth century, in tandem with the development of the common law.

Elton points out that

> the fallow time proved to have been truly beneficial. Middle English is a distinctly more flexible language than Anglo-Saxon, grammatically simpler and with a markedly rich vocabulary including much borrowing from the temporary ascendancy languages. In this period the English language began its remarkable career as easily the most adaptable and most varied means of communication ever put together by man – much superior, it should be said, to Latin or even Greek, and far less hampered by rules than either French or German.

For two centuries, the English language went underground officially, while remaining the language of the people. And those two centuries were the making of it. The language of Chaucer may be hard for us to read today, but it is essentially our language, in its grammar and syntax, its turn of phrase and much of its vocabulary too.

And what a vocabulary it has. The English-French volume of my fat Harrap's dictionary contains 1500 pages; the French-English volume a mere 900. The endless mingling (or, if you prefer, smorgasbord, gallimaufry, hotchpotch, mishmash, mosaic, kaleidoscope or omnium-gatherum) of borrowings – from Latin and Greek and the Germanic languages, from the Norse tongues and from the Romance ones, the haphazard inflow of terms from Arabic and Hindi and Yiddish and every variety of pidgin – contrasts so strongly with the minimal rules of syntax and grammar, the relative absence of declensions and conjugations.

Unbounded richness and incomparable freedom. It's a rare combination, and one which often bewilders those who are learning English as a foreign language and who search in vain for clear structures to guide them. Anyone who has learnt another language to any degree of rigour will be aware how unusual English is in the way it shrugs off even those rules it does profess, so that it is near impossible to be told 'you can't say that'. That, after all, is why Voltaire famously could not get on with Shakespeare: 'he has neither regularity, nor propriety, nor art; in the midst of his sublimity he sometimes descends to grossness and in the most impressive scenes to buffoonery; his tragedy is chaos illuminated by a hundred shafts of light.' (Though we must remember that Voltaire's friend Alexander Pope thought much the same, for the reaction against Shakespeare's disorderliness was as much a matter of literary fashion as national difference.)

The ascent of English as the first truly global language, far outstripping Latin even in its heyday, is a story of our own time. English today is our most universal export and passport. But long before that extraordinary event, language had shaped almost everything about us, our freewheeling cast of mind, our indifference to verbal propriety, our taste for eccentricity and serendipity, our wacky humour. It is a vagabond language open to the seven seas, a language fit for an amphibious mob.

The English began with their language, and what they leave behind, long after their global empire has vanished and their global banks have gone bust, is their voices. The mongrel richness of the tongue generates an almost limitless individuality. With most of the people discussed in these pages you know who is talking after you have heard a couple of sentences. That may be what has sparked the English obsession with human quiddity, with what makes one person different from another, an obsession which so often turns English literature into life-writing and life-writing into literature in a way that can be unfamiliar and puzzling to speakers of other European languages. Nowhere else is the art of biography so revered; in France, by contrast, it is positively despised as no more than the higher gossip. But to us, telling the stories of English lives seems as good a way as any to tell the story of England.

That at least is my excuse for parcelling up a collection of portraits which take the life and the work together, melding quite unashamedly biography and critique. Most of the subjects are English or at any rate British by birth or residence, some carry other passports, but all are voices in our conversation, and voices that deserve to be celebrated. For the English, biography is phonography.

VOICES IN OUR TIME

M ild and easygoing, perhaps a little sluggish in the uptake:
that is how the English like to picture themselves. Com-
pared to other more 'excitable' nations, our minds and bodies
seem to us (I'm joining the selfie here) to have a low cruising
speed. Of the four medieval humours we identify with the phleg-
matic. In fact phlegm used to be our prime export to the colonies,
enabling the British to withstand the climate and the natives with
equal fortitude. If we are good at being tolerant, which too we
fancy we are, it is because it comes naturally to us, just as duck-
weed grows thicker where the stream runs slow.

So it's all the more of a shock to listen to those voices in our own
time which have most resounded in our ears. I'm talking here of
writers who were born between the outbreaks of the two world
wars and who have flourished in the half-century after 1945. You
might not think such diverse talents would share a common tone,
but they do, even if you only notice it when you read them one
after the other, just as a group medical inspection may bring out
certain shared defects in the recruits, such as overweight or fallen
arches. And it is a tone which is the opposite, a defiant, in-your-face
opposite of the traditional self-image of the English.

The writers who caught my attention are mordant, morose to

the point of sour, intolerant, impatient, unforgiving. Their wit does not play or caress, it bites. Nor are they slow-spoken. On the contrary, they are quick on the draw, partly because most of them are in a chronic state of suppressed rage. If you were choosing a medieval humour to sum them up, it would be the choleric or the bilious.

They vary in pace and temper, of course. Alan Bennett and W. G. Sebald have each perfected their peculiar strain of lugubrious lucubration, the Eeyore Tendency elevated to the condition of art. John Osborne and Kingsley Amis specialize in a high-voltage rant, which is more thoughtfully weighed and constructed than it seems. V. S. Naipaul and John le Carré pilot us through the deceptions, fractures and estrangements of the modern world. Hugh Trevor-Roper and Germaine Greer use feline bitchery to bolster their arguments about history and politics. But in one way or another, they are all angry.

When the Angry Young Men were first spotted as the coming thing, they were explained or explained away as an irruption of the grammar-school-educated lower-middle class into the previously genteel world of English letters. But even if the AYM were ever a group in any serious sense, which they weren't, the class explanation won't do. Young men from similar backgrounds, such as H. G. Wells and Arnold Bennett, had broken through after the Great War, and they had been genial upbeat characters.

The prevailing rancour, the sense of disappointment and disenchantment, the sense even of having been cheated, these were new. And they must surely have had something to do with the country's knackered, bankrupt, irremediably shabby and reduced state. We had come down in the world, and we lacked the means, the energy, the self-confidence to climb out of the crater. In *The Military Philosophers,* Anthony Powell describes the feeling of letdown at the thanksgiving service in St Paul's at the end of the war: 'everyone was by now so tired. The country, there could be no doubt, was absolutely worn out.'

In such a shattered city the only answer was the wrecker's ball.

Out of the ruins there comes an earsplitting series of blasts and wails, the scorching sound of strips being torn off and pretences being ripped away, and above all the sound of laughter. This must be the funniest bunch of writers ever to be working at the same time in England. The laughter is by turns derisive, vulgar, delicate, coarse, sublime, sour and very occasionally sweet. And it is irresistible.

What is marked too is the virtual absence of hope. There is no looking forward, only a vigilant raging against the present, and now and then a guarded, almost furtive looking back to the days, if not of innocence, of a life that was somehow more genuine: for Alan Bennett his parents' butcher's shop in Leeds, for V. S. Naipaul the carefree saunter along Miguel Street; for Hugh Trevor-Roper and Derek Jackson the headlong gallop across the hunting field; even, surprisingly, for Germaine Greer the simple life of an Italian village where women had a natural and honoured place, even if it wasn't anything like the place she wanted for them.

KINGSLEY AMIS:
THE CRAVING MACHINE

What is it about fruit? There is no more searing passage in the memoirs of Auberon Waugh than the bit when three bananas reach the Waugh household in the worst days of post-war austerity and Evelyn Waugh places all three on his own plate, then before the anguished eyes of his three children ladles on cream, which was almost unprocurable, and sugar, which was heavily rationed, and scoffs the lot. So in all the 900-odd pages of Zachary Leader's marvellous *The Life of Kingsley Amis* there is nothing that chills the blood more than the moment when Hilly Amis's eight-year-old son Jaime reaches for the one peach in a fruit bowl otherwise containing only oranges, apples and grapes and Kingsley shouts, in a voice described by his son Martin as 'like a man hailing a cab across the length of Oxford Circus during a downpour on Christmas Eve', 'HEY! That's my peach.'

Behind the sacred monster's mask lurks a monstrous baby, an insatiable craving machine. There is a line which appears in *Take a Girl Like You*, but which was also uttered by Kingsley himself as he and some friends pulled up at a fried-clam joint on the way to the Newport Jazz Festival: 'Oh good, I want more than my share before anyone else has had any.' Just as Kingsley would later tell the 'That's my peach!' story against himself, so he was constantly working his own episodes of unbridled selfishness into his fiction. In his last book, *The Biographer's Moustache*, the novelist tells his biographer, 'These days the public like to think of an artist as a, as a shit known to behave in ways they would shrink from.' To which the biographer, maddened by his subject, retorts at the end of the book, 'You're not a reluctant shit and certainly not an unconscious shit, you're a self-congratulatory shit.'

Amis was perfectly aware that he had, in the words of his poem 'Coming of Age', 'played his part so well / that he started living it, / His trick of camouflage no longer a trick.' He had worked up his public persona so effectively that he became a natural choice for an up-market fabrics campaign – 'Very Kingsley Amis, Very Sanderson'. Yet now and then he was plaintive about the costs of the impersonation. Why did he sit for twenty minutes in the bar at the Garrick and nobody come near him? His drinking partner, the naval historian Richard Hough, replied, 'Kingsley, doesn't it strike you that it could be because you can be so f***ing curmudgeonly?' Again, one is reminded of Evelyn Waugh sitting looking like a stuck pig in the bar at White's and glaring at each incomer, then complaining about nobody talking to him and the club going downhill.

The rage needed fuelling, of course. Throughout most of his later life, Amis was on a bottle of whisky a day, not to mention any available liqueurs, plus a ferocious assortment of drugs: Frumil for his swollen legs, verapamil for his heart, Brufen for pain, allopurinol for gout, Senokot and lactulose for constipation. The more he turned drink into a hobby like jazz or science fiction, the more he drank. Travelling through Mexico, he insisted on carrying with him a sort of mobile cocktail bar containing tequila, gin, vodka and Campari, plus fruit juices, lemons, tomato juice, cucumber and Tabasco. Wine was always a lesser interest though not a lesser intake. The first GP or General Principle of his book

On Drink is: 'Up to a point (i.e. short of offering your guests one of those Balkan plonks marketed as wine, Cyprus sherry, poteen and the like), go for quantity rather than quality.' I can't remember which Amis character it is who pats the fresh bottle that the waiter has just brought and murmurs happily, 'Nice and full.' Continuity of supply was a constant anxiety. He always liked to see where the next drink was coming from.

All this took its toll. As early as 1956 when he was only in his thirties, he was passing out cold after lunch or dinner, and in the 1970s often went upstairs to bed on all fours, though he never missed a morning at the typewriter. Yet it would be facile to imagine that it was the drink that somehow did for him morally. Like Waugh, he had a cruel streak long before he was seriously soused – it was an integral part of their comic genius. Both writers had fathers who were jovial, sentimental good sports. In Amis, as in Waugh, the savage gene skipped a generation. Kingsley's father, William Amis, had 'a talent for physical clowning and mimicry that made him, on his day, one of the funniest men I have known', but he also had 'a rowdy babyish streak in him which caused him, when perfectly sober, to pretend to be a foreigner or deaf in trains and pubs'.

In theory, not so very different from Kingsley's lifelong habit of delighting his audience with imitations of squawky radios and trains going through tunnels. It was his imitation in the quad at St John's College, Oxford, of a man falling down after being shot that made Philip Larkin, who had not met Amis before, think 'for the first time I felt myself in the presence of a talent greater than my own'. At Amis's memorial service, Martin played a tape of his father's celebrated party piece of FDR addressing his British allies over a faulty short-wave radio. The tape itself proved faulty, and so Martin relentlessly played it again – an episode straight out of a novel by either Amis. But William Amis's turns were all too often facetious – and for this, like Arthur Waugh, he was not to be forgiven, or not in his lifetime:

I'm sorry you had to die
To make me sorry
You're not here now.

Nor were the fits of howling and night terrors that woke
Kingsley in his later years a new development. As a young signals
officer, he had splashed on to the Normandy beachhead only a
month after D-Day – his first trip abroad – but he had always
been subject to what we now call panic attacks. From childhood
he had suffered screaming fits. When he was eighteen and the
City of London School had been evacuated to Marlborough, his
housemaster's wife had to comfort him in the middle of the night
when these fits woke him up. When his first wife Hilly was about
to have their third child, he was frightened to go to the callbox
by himself to summon the midwife and had to take Martin with
him. Martin was then aged four. After his second wife, the nov-
elist Elizabeth Jane Howard, left him, he was petrified of being
alone and his children had to organize a rota of Dadsitters. He
was so terrified of finding himself in an empty tube train that
when he and Jane were living out in Barnet, he would choose to
travel in the rush hour for his sorties to the Garrick Club.

This sensitivity was immediately obvious when you met him
and made him even more attractive. As the pictures in this gener-
ously produced biography show, he was dazzlingly handsome as a
young man and all his life he had a charming voice, hesitant but
not diffident, and somehow confidential as though he was talk-
ing to you alone. He seemed quite extraordinarily natural in a
way that made other people in the room seem loud or forced, and
as John Bayley, who met him first at Oxford, pointed out, 'The
natural Amis stayed with him all his life alongside the other one.'

Nor were these qualities superficial or put on. He was a tact-
ful consoler and capable of great generosity to people in trouble.
Although his household at Barnet already contained at least eight
assorted adults – they also entertained on a heroic scale – he

readily assented when Jane invited the dying C. Day-Lewis and his wife Jill Balcon to come and live with them, despite the fact that he didn't much like Day-Lewis and Jane had once had a brief fling with him.

Sometimes this generosity hardened into an ossified bar code: he was pernickety that everyone should stand his round and behave like a good fellow. It was an offence against the laws of hospitality to say to a lunch guest, 'Shall we go straight in?' There was no keener member of the 1400 Club at the Garrick, composed of those barflies who thought it poor form to sit down before 2 p.m. Like Richard Burton, he believed that 'the man who drinks on his own' was scarcely human.

But until his very last years his company still left a glow. And when he arrived in Swansea as a young lecturer with Hilly and their small children, they hit the place like a tornado, laying waste both the campus and the crachach in the Uplands district. Kingsley set about a programme of screwings that would have been enough to construct an ocean liner. Hilly followed in his wake, but hers was only a cottage industry in comparison with Kingsley's mass seduction. At Saturday-night parties he would ask every woman present to come outside and visit his greenhouse – an implausible pretext considering his well-advertised dislike of gardens and gardening – and one by one they would return dishevelled but with a wild, furtive triumph in their eyes.

Drink and sex were his passions. The extraordinary thing is that he could not believe that one might have an impact on the other. When his powers began to fail, he consulted a series of sex therapists (as well as regular shrinks to treat his night fears) and even consented, like the hero of *Jake's Thing*, to wear a 'nocturnal mensurator', a device for measuring penile tumescence. It never seems to have occurred to him that he might be suffering from an entirely normal case of brewer's droop.

Both in his letters to Larkin and to Robert Conquest, there is, it cannot be denied, a callous tone about his references to women.

To Larkin, for example: 'The only reason I like girls is that I want to f*** them.' When trying to reconcile Hilly: 'The successive application of tears and pork sword had brought hubby right back into the picture' – while at the same time denouncing Hilly (who was bringing up three children and doing everything for Kingsley without him lifting a finger in any direction) for 'her laziness, her continuous peevishness with the children, her utter lack of interest in anything whatsoever'. Soon he was able to report triumphantly, 'I have more or less got my wife back. As a consequence (though I can quite see how you can't quite see how this can be so), I have got my girlfriend back too.'

Nor did Elizabeth Jane Howard fare much better. When she eventually walked out on him, he explained to Larkin: 'She did it partly to punish me for stopping wanting to fuck her and partly because she realised I didn't like her much. Well, I liked her as much as you could like anyone totally wrapped up in themselves and unable to tolerate the slightest competition or anything a raving lunatic could see as opposition and having to have their own way in everything all the time.'

Well, it takes one.

Curious perhaps that he chose her in the first place. Many people found her affected and, though very beautiful, not all that easy to get on with. She did not herself deny that she was awkward and self-centred. To pursue her career as a writer, she had more or less abandoned her only child, her daughter by her first husband, the naturalist Peter Scott, but when married to Kingsley she worked night and day to look after the large, untidy household, drove him everywhere, dealt with all the repairs and accounts and acted as the most dutiful of stepmothers, all of which left little or no time for her own writing.

For someone who took such an intense interest in people's quirks, Kingsley often seemed indifferent to what people were actually like. He tolerated company at the Garrick Club that other members fled from. He would make regular excursions to Swansea to drink in the Bristol Channel Yacht Club with the solicitor Stuart Thomas, described by some as 'one of the most unpleasant men I have ever met' and eventually expelled from the Yacht Club on grounds of 'general horribleness'.

But then, as Zachary Leader points out, the desire to irritate and annoy animated Amis himself all his life, and hobnobbing with other curmudgeons was part of it. He liked to give offence in his books too, by putting in recognizable portraits of people he knew, like Peter Quennell's wife Marilyn or the old devils he drank with in Swansea. In embarking on a new project, for example his Ian Fleming pastiche *Colonel Sun*, he liked to think how much it would annoy intellectual lefties. Baiting was a pastime, ranking only slightly behind drink and sex. Nor did he restrict his venom to people who could stand up to him. He could be cruel to some shy stranger who made an ill-phrased remark or had an unfortunate laugh.

It was sometimes as though his reservoirs of sensitivity were concentrated on his writing. All his delicacy of touch went into the run of the sentence. Surprisingly, although Zac Leader is a professor of English literature rather than a biographer by trade (he also did an exemplary edition of the Amis letters), the one gap in this otherwise beautifully balanced, affectionate, unsparing and unfailingly accurate portrait is any discussion of Amis's style in its heyday. Rightly, Leader points out that late Amis can be almost as orotund and impenetrable as the late Henry James – a comparison which would have annoyed Amis greatly. Anthony Powell thought that in *The Folks That Live on the Hill*, for example, the determination not to be pretentious develops into a sort of pretentiousness.

But all memorable styles tend to become parodies of themselves in the end. And Amis's style is certainly memorable. To me it is one of the most original and infectious styles in twentieth-century English writing, comparable in its impact to that of Joyce or Hemingway, though not recognized as such, or not by academics, because of Amis's dislike of their carry-on. The way he writes

arises out of what Stephen Potter would call his ordinarychap-
manship, but it is only the starting point to declare, as Amis does
in what is taken to be the Manifesto of the Movement poets,
'Nobody wants any more poems about philosophers or paint-
ings or novelists or art galleries or mythology or foreign cities.'
What Amis does is not only to represent ordinary blokes and (less
successfully) blokesses but to catch the way their minds run on,
correcting their first thoughts, doubling back, trying to render
what exactly it is that they are thinking. More complicating still
is that Amis is at the same time setting down how the author is
trying to describe and then describe better, more exactly, more
vividly what the characters are doing or saying or looking like.
So that at its best you feel a thrilling sense of actually being there
as the text is being created. Amis was famous for liking unshowy
immediacy in books. All his life he preferred the sort of book
which began 'a shot rang out'. He hated writers like Bellow and
Nabokov for their distinguished style which 'usually turns out
in practice to mean a high idiosyncratic noise level in the writ-
ing, with plenty of rumble and wow from imagery, syntax and
diction'. Yet he was at pains to point out that immediate didn't
mean simple. *Paradise Lost* was the greatest poem in our language,
but it was difficult as well as being immediate. Amis was himself
engaged in something which was much more difficult than it
looked. When it works, a comic joy spreads over every page, even
when he is writing about death and decay as he is in *Ending Up* or
The Old Devils.

To the end Kingsley remained the spoilt only child who
believes that the universe ought to be organized for his benefit
and is furious whenever he discovers it isn't. 'You atheist?' the
Russian poet Yevgeny Yevtushenko asked him. 'Well, yes,' Amis
replied, 'but it's more that I hate Him' – resented the competi-
tion, I suppose. And it is this combination of indignation and
eloquence that puts him up there with Swift and all those other
monsters we hate to love.

ALAN BENNETT:
AGAINST SPLOTHER

'I've got great faith in the corner of the eye.' Alan Bennett is talking about the picture by the eighteenth-century Welsh artist Thomas Jones of some towels drying on a balcony in Naples. It is an utterly ordinary, unremarkable scene, a piece of background, but in its freshness, its irresistible thereness, it jumps off the wall. Jones only painted a handful of these little sketches, devoting the rest of his life to muddy historical paintings and pleasant but standard-issue landscapes. Alan Bennett by contrast has devoted his life to freezing the corner-of-the-eye moment, so that it seems not only touching and funny but somehow grand, far grander in fact than the bombastic rodomontades of high literature which by comparison come out looking like so much 'splother', to use the lovely word much employed by Walter and Lilian Bennett, Alan's mam and dad, to dismiss anything smacking of ostentation, pretension and fuss.

So it is that Bennett wants this huge collection of his writings over the past ten years to be thought of as occupying no loftier niche than those old children's annuals issued each Christmas by *Dandy* or *Beano* and packed with strip cartoons, stories and games. In such an easy-going format, his title sequence – essentially a memoir of his parents and his aunties Kathleen and Myra – stands out in all its laconic brilliance. *Untold Stories* is every bit as touching and funny as you would expect, but you are also left in no doubt about the, well, nobility is the only word for it, of the lives led by Mam and Dad, lives so restricted and inconspicuous by the world's standards. I have read nothing in recent fiction to rival the precision and power of the accounts of Mam's descent first into depression and then later into a dementia of sorts and, towards the end of the memoir, of finding Kathleen's body in the undergrowth beside the M6 after she had run away from Lancaster Moor Hospital.

When *Untold Stories* was serialized in the *Daily Telegraph*, a reader wrote in complaining that the description of how old ladies in such hospitals and care homes were neglected and so gently starved to death was exaggerated and unfair. As it happened, only a week later I read in *The Times* the report of a coroner's scorching criticism when precisely this had happened to a 91-year-old woman in a Manchester hospital. As I am writing this, another such case of slow starvation in a care home is reported in today's paper.

At the same time Bennett insists always upon his mother's jauntiness as soon as she has recovered her spirits. He never ceases to rejoice in the bravura of her denunciations: 'Tangerine! I wouldn't have tangerine curtains if you paid me.' Or of the blood-red figure of the Buddha that Aunty Myra brings back from the Far East: 'I don't care if it is a god, I am not having it on the sideboard with a belly-button that size.'

In fact, he shares Mam's distaste and unerring eye for the common. 'It would do as a definition of what's gone wrong in England in the last 20 years that it's got more common', and he remarks resignedly that 'it's a sign of my age that the shoe shops seem nowadays to be staffed by sluts, indifferent and unhelpful and with none of that matronly dignity'. He deplores the Dianafication of public emotion and, when he hears that the Queen is finally to broadcast to the nation after Diana's death, remarks sourly in his diary, 'I'm only surprised that Her Majesty hasn't had to submit to a phone-in.' When John Major sends the Stone of Scone up North in the vain hope of pacifying the Scots, Bennett comments that 'the Coronation Chair is left looking like an empty commode'. So, although he thinks of himself as a lifelong leftie, wants to see public schools abolished and worries about the future of the National Health Service, he emerges as an unregenerate small-c conservative, the grumpiest of grumpy old men. We catch him gorging himself on the journals of Anthony Powell and James Lees-Milne, his own diaries coming increasingly to resemble theirs, not least in his adoption of the elaborate Powellian participial clause moored alongside the main sentence. If encountered in someone else's book, the abysmal standard of proofreading in *Untold Stories* would certainly have provoked a tart comment (two publishers do not seem to be better than one). My favourite typo is Bennett's reference to an appointment with 'a complimentary health clinic in Harley Street'. Fat chance in that avenue of conspicuous extortion.

This appointment precedes the chemotherapy he undergoes for bowel cancer in 1997, an experience recounted in the closing piece, 'An Average Rock Bun' – according to the doctor, the size of the tumour in question. At the time, Bennett tells us, he refrained from talking about his illness, otherwise he might have died from embarrassment, but now that he is in the pink again (although the initial odds against survival were poor), he gives us a cheerfully uninhibited account of the whole business.

This is typical of his lifelong struggle with embarrassment. He backs in and out of the limelight, always just in time, he hopes, to escape looking pleased with himself, like some never-ending game of Grandmother's Footsteps. When the list of those who have turned down knighthoods is leaked to the newspapers, he finds himself noting how he is sometimes placed rather low down on the list of refuseniks and sometimes not mentioned at all. In the same way, he wouldn't want anyone to think that putting Mam's condition down to Alzheimer's was jumping on a bandwagon. He has a similar reaction when asked to appear on television after Gielgud's death: 'Reluctant to jump on the bandwagon, particularly when the bandwagon is a hearse.'

'Our Alan's like us, shy,' Mam would say, meaning it as a virtue. 'Sly' is Bennett's own verdict on himself. A bit of both, really. He is unashamed of his fastidiousness, content to have 'come out' (I cannot remember whether the inverted commas are mine or his or whether he uses the phrase at all) and delighted to have settled down with a partner who is half his age, but he still finds the uninhibited talk of all-male gatherings both tedious and embarrassing. Unashamed too of his long stretches of moony chastity when younger. Like Wilfred Thesiger in the desert, 'I could go for months, years indeed, on virtually no dates at all. No quarter could have been emptier than my twenties.' Yet of that decade and more of unrequited affection, he says in retrospect, 'It isn't an education which I would have elected to undergo, but nor do I wish it away, then or now.'

His unflinching watchfulness preserves him from easy slurping on remorse and regret. The illusion that he is some kind of cuddly national treasure cannot survive reading more than a couple of pages of this bumper compendium. He is about as cuddly as a Swiss army knife, old-fashioned in design and fits nicely in the pocket, but equipped with a ferocious variety of attachments for slicing through, gouging out and cutting down to size.

One by one, the tin gods are tapped and found hollow: 'Never comfortable with (and never unaware of) Saul Bellow's style, which puts an almost treacly patina on the prose'; 'I persevere with Sebald, but the contrivance of it, particularly his un-peopling of the landscape, never fails to irritate'; 're-reading Berenson I find him both intolerable and silly'. Ruminating on the famous shrinks who might have something to say about Mam's condition – R. D. Laing, Thomas Szasz, Freud, Oliver Sacks – he tends to find them posturing, if not irrelevant, and unhealthily drawn to patients who make a good story – 'mistake your wife for a hat and the doctor will never be away from your bedside'.

Even the merchants of literary gloom with whom he is sometimes bracketed do not escape. He finds Barbara Pym lowering to read, and in re-examining Larkin's verse, which he is often asked to give readings of (as though he were the nearest living substitute for the poet), he repeatedly discovers a cheap, hectoring note – 'the despair is too easy'. For all his well-advertised lack of airs and graces, Larkin has his own brand of splother.

I cannot think of another writer whose judgments are quite so steely, so genuinely unimpressed by reputation. But then in anything Bennett takes on there is a self-confidence which is nonetheless formidable because it is concealed under this carapace of modesty. It will be done his way or not at all. His plays, for example, offer only minimal homage to the gross contrivances of the stage; they explore an idea – a mad king, an old-fashioned schoolmaster – in a discursive, dwelling style which doesn't seem to be going anywhere much. According to the conventional preconceptions, this ought to be box-office poison, but never is. *Talking Heads* deliberately affronts the telly producer's taboo – that the viewer cannot tolerate prolonged exposure to a single face and voice. The irony is that, although this concentration is just how the playlets make their remarkable effect, one does miss something and that something is Bennett's own voice, those kindly, tired, gravelly tones, so thoughtful, so eternally self-critical, for it is that voice which redeems his characters from condescension and caricature.

Untold Stories, for its part, says boo to the notion that a serious writer's anthology should be a ruthless culling of his best work. This is a Christmas allsorts, jam-packed with delights. Only the reminiscences of theatrical productions are for me as tedious as I always find such things, no matter what the play or the players. I would not cross the road to hear William Shakespeare himself telling the story of *Twelfth Night*'s first night. The rest of it – the rambles round art galleries and out-of-the-way medieval churches, the acerbic commentaries on modern life, the vivid recollections of the Leeds of his youth – is pure pleasure, a marvellous meander you dread to see the final bend of. Even so, I might be tempted to lift out 'Untold Stories' from *Untold Stories* and preserve it separately for the nation, because it is something else, a work of art, and without a drop of splother in it.

MURIEL SPARK:
THE GO-AWAY BIRD

There is no plaque yet on No. 13 Baldwin Crescent, otherwise known as 'Dunedin'. There ought to be. For on the top floor of this shabby yellow-brick house, hidden away between the Camberwell New Road and gloomy Myatt's Fields, Muriel Spark wrote most of the four or five novels for which we'll remember her. She was as happy in leafy, run-down Baldwin Crescent as she ever had been or was to be in her long, tense, proud, unforgiving life. She did, it is true, make an excursion to her childhood Edinburgh home to reimmerse herself in the speech of Morningside while she wrote *The Prime of Miss Jean Brodie* in four weeks. But all her other masterpieces – *Memento Mori, The Ballad of Peckham Rye, The Bachelors* and much of *The Girls of Slender Means* – were written within a glorious period of only five years in her two attic rooms in Camberwell. After she left, she never lived in Britain again.

Because she was so stunningly original and burst upon the leaden post-war scene with such a delicious sizzle, as though this was the first time we could afford proper fireworks again, it is easy to forget how beautifully rooted in their settings those early books are. She had only just begun writing novels at the age of thirty-nine, having thought of herself till then as a poet. Yet in a few masterly lines she gets up for us the clapped-out pubs and factories of Peckham and the boozy gangs wandering across the Rye as indelibly as she does the corridors of Marcia Blaine School for Girls and the Princess May of Teck Club, based, quite closely, on her times at James Gillespie's High School for Girls and the Helena Club in Lancaster Gate respectively. She was a realist before she was a surrealist. As Fleur Talbot, her alter ego novelist heroine in *Loitering with Intent*, says: 'When I first started writing, people used to say my novels were exaggerated. They never were exaggerated, merely aspects of realism.'

When her books ran thin, as they began to do all too soon after her golden flowering, it was because they no longer had much solid ground to take off from. These later stories were derived not from life but from the glossies and newspapers and film mags. They became as insubstantial and shadowy as those late paintings by Sickert that he worked up from newspaper photographs.

It is hard to read the early novels without an inappropriately seraphic smile breaking out on one's face like the ghoul at the weepie in the Charles Addams cartoon. By contrast, I find her later books strangely hard to get through, though they are just as short, 50,000 words or so. It is like trying to operate an apparently simple gadget which has been supplied without some vital part though you cannot identify what it is. Those little macabre jumps into the future no longer take your breath away: 'She will be found tomorrow dead from multiple stab wounds.' The little nudges to the reader are no longer so winning: 'Who knows her thoughts? Who can tell?' Even the most devoted fan may feel like whispering 'Who cares?'

I cannot help feeling that her exile from her material was part of the trouble. By then she was too famous for anyone to tell her anything. In any case, she was never one to admit error, except in her choice of men ('I was a bad picker'). On the contrary, she claimed grandly that 'it was Edinburgh that bred within me the condition of exiledom. It has ceased to become a fate, it has become a calling', the calling of the real artist, just as it had been the calling of other high priests of modernism, such as Eliot, Joyce and Auden.

Yet it is also true that she simply could not get on with people and places for very long. As Martin Stannard shows in this massive biography, which is simultaneously inspiriting and dispiriting, for years 'her only intimate relation to other human beings had been with her readers'. After leaving London, she moved between New York and Rome, travelling all over the place in between, accompanied by an ever-changing cast of gay cavaliers, some kind-hearted and solicitous for her welfare, others catty and freakish like the bizarre Baron Brian de Breffny, a Mormon genealogist who was the son of a London cabbie or possibly bookie. She never liked to warm her hands too long at any one camp fire.

But her gay friendships lasted better than most of those with her fellow writers. Ved Mehta said 'She went through people like pieces of Kleenex'. In Muriel's own brief and sunny memoir, *Curriculum Vitae*, she claims that 'I am a hoarder of two things: documents and trusted friends'. In reality, by the end she had accumulated a mountain of paper recording every transaction in her life but scarcely a single old friend, except her charming and level-headed companion Penelope Jardine, in whose Tuscan priesthouse she lodged for her last twenty years and more, only once or twice threatening to decamp or at least to stop paying her share of the expenses. Her devoted publisher, Alan Maclean, she eventually wrote off as 'an indescribably filthy liar'. Of the poet and critic Derek Stanford, a queer fish admittedly but the only man she seriously loved and wanted to marry, her closing words were 'I hate the man's guts'. Her conversation became as brittle as her books, snapping off a topic the moment she tired of it, leaving her audience with a feeling of inadequacy.

At her death in April 2006, she was brewing up for a monster row with Stannard, describing the draft of his biography as 'based on negative rhetoric and terribly mean and hostile and very poorly written'. In fact it is perfectly well written, sometimes rather witty and painstakingly based on all the documents she gave him the run of. The worst you could accuse him of is now and then flinching from Muriel's own plain speech. He refers, for example, to her 'street-slang annotation' on an enquiry from a reader and her 'scribbling something uncomplimentary' on a whingeing letter from Stanford, without spelling out what she actually wrote.

Above all, Stannard demonstrates with unfailing sympathy why she armed herself with such an adamantine carapace. She had come through a terrible mixture of relentless poverty, recurrent bad luck and dogging ill health. She needed all the defences she could muster to protect her reputation and her self-confidence. Her father, Barney Camberg, was a fitter and mechanical engineer at the North British Rubber Company all his life. As a member of the kingly tribe of Cohens, he went first into the synagogue, but he was looked down on for not being in business like the rest of the Edinburgh Jewish community.

Muriel described herself as a Gentile Jewess, which was to lead to a literally blood feud with her only child Robin, who insisted on being barmitzvahed, claiming that he was fully Jewish because his grandmother, Barney's wife Cissy, was also Jewish by maternal descent. Muriel fiercely disputed this. Stannard does his best to unravel the truth of the matter. But whichever of them was right, it scarcely excuses Muriel's festering contempt for her son or her eventually cutting him out of her will at the end of her life, just as she had cut him out at the beginning by leaving him behind in Rhodesia at the age of five when she fled her mad and violent husband, Solly Spark. She had married Solly at the age of nineteen to get away from her family, scarcely knowing him and soon wishing she never had. Quoting the title of her famous story, Muriel remarked, accurately enough, 'I was really myself a Go-Away Bird'. She diagnosed herself as not the marrying type. As Stannard puts it nicely, her pram was always to remain in someone else's hall.

When she went to Edinburgh in later years, she stayed, not with Cissy and Robin, but with the high sheriff or at the North British Hotel. On her last visit, she did not bother to see her son who was only a ten-minute walk away. Robin's life was nothing to be ashamed of. He had risen in the Civil Service to become chief clerk to the Scottish Law Commission, then resigned to become a well-regarded painter. But Muriel would concede nothing to him: he was only stoking up the row about their Jewishness because he wanted publicity for his lousy paintings which he couldn't sell.

Not that she found life much easier back in London when she first set up as an independent woman earning her own living. She was turfed out of her job at the Poetry Society by a claque of querulous poets. Publisher after publisher whom she worked for or submitted work to went bust, and one went to prison. She was outstandingly industrious and competent – the publisher Peter Owen described her as 'the best bloody secretary I ever had'. But nothing much went right for her, certainly not the weak and cowardly men she fell in with. Like Evelyn Waugh, she began to suffer from hallucinations, and for the same reason, addiction to chloral in his case, Dexedrine in hers (Waugh became a loyal admirer and told her he thought *The Comforters* was much better than *Pinfold*). After reviewing *The Confidential Clerk*, she got it into her head that T. S. Eliot was sending her threatening messages, encoding them in the theatre programme and in the play itself, and then going on to pose as a window cleaner to spy on her friends.

A little earlier, she had been baptized and confirmed, first as an Anglican, then as a Catholic, and she began the practice of retiring now and then to places of retreat like Allington Castle to restore her balance. At one point, she thought of becoming a nun. The Church remained a comfort and an anchor to her, a bulwark against the materialist philistines, although the joy that she had experienced on first reading Newman's *Apologia* inevitably dried up a bit. Towards the end of her life she rarely went to church, except at Easter. She was, notoriously, more interested in theology than in morality. But she denied that her books were amoral or inhuman. They were simply true to life as everyone knew it really was but did not like to say. 'I love all my characters; when I'm writing about them I love them most intensely, like a cat loves a bird.'

Certainly no writer could have been in person more like her books: exuberant and stony-hearted, switching without any sort of notice from charming and flirtatious to chilly and dismissive. You never knew where you were with her, and that's how she liked it. She picked up the trick from Dame Edith Sitwell, whom she greatly admired as another woman who didn't give a damn about anyone or anything except art and the Catholic Church: 'My dear, you must acquire a pair of lorgnettes, focus the glasses on that man and sit looking at him through them as if he were an insect. Just look and look.'

And she did. It was just about the only piece of advice she ever took from anyone.

V. S. NAIPAUL:
NO HOME FOR MR BISWAS

Does man qualify as a migratory species? Or are human migrations too random, violent and erratic? Seen from some more placid planet which counts in centuries, Earth must look like one long rush hour: empires waxing and waning, Goths and Vandals sweeping across the steppes, Vikings and Normans across the seas, pioneers, pilgrims, settlers, convicts, slaves and indentured labourers all moving vast distances under varying compulsions.

Yet in literature, migration does not crop up all that often. There are plenty of books about strangers arriving and unsettling established communities; there are also books set in imperial or colonial worlds, about the struggle to convert or dominate alien lands and alien peoples. But there is rather less writing of quality about the experience of being unsettled. Even writers who use a foreigner to represent The Outsider tend to use him mainly for un-local colour; Joyce chooses Bloom for *Ulysses*, not because he is interested in what it was like to be Jewish in Dublin at the turn of the century but because he is interested in Dublin and in being Irish at the turn of the century.

Perhaps this is not so odd: writers like to write about substance not absence. The gaps in the substance are to be deplored, not explored; gappiness is a testing, elusive kind of subject. And then there is the political aspect. To describe the unsettled individual and the half-made society, or the immigrant society mimicking some other society, is not the way to easy popularity. How much more attractive to celebrate the rich diversity of English life, or to hymn the struggles of Azania to realize itself as a nation. Writers, especially in the twentieth century, have stood in an extremely uneasy relationship towards both nationality and socialism; the better ones tending to fall for fascism, the less good being equally deluded about communism; both sorts ill at ease with the Immigrant – the pro-fascists tending to brutish abuse (Pound, Eliot and co.), the pro-socialists pretending that nationality was a trivial accident which time and revolution would dissolve.

V. S. Naipaul's work is therefore remarkable in several ways; that he has written first and last, for nearly thirty years, about unsettled individuals and unsettled societies – which, after all, comprise a large proportion of the world's population – without at any point deviating into the sentimental or the didactic, and without falling for any of the comfortable cure-alls that will soothe or explain away the realities: not religion, or socialism, or capitalist development, or indeed political enthusiasm of any sort. He never fails to take careful aim. His scorn withers its victims without parching the surrounding landscape; his pity for the helpless and the bewildered does not drench the continent; and his capacity for farce is reined in, sometimes too much so for the reader who is constantly hoping for every page to be as funny as the funniest pages of *A House for Mr Biswas*. There is a continuing fineness of discrimination at work, an unwavering seriousness of purpose; temptations to take the easy scores are always resisted. This all makes him sound dry and getting drier; yet there is a glorious free swing about his late-ish masterpiece, *A Bend in the River* – a triumphant proof that he has not lost the art of letting go.

Finding the Centre is a relaxation of another sort. In these two 'personal narratives', Naipaul deviates from his usual retiring, almost mannered impersonality to offer what he calls a 'Prologue to an Autobiography', followed by a piece – 'The Crocodiles of Yamoussoukro' – which shows the writer 'going about one side of his business' in a manner which has become familiar to us; here Naipaul is in the Ivory Coast, but the technique is the same as that which he has practised in India, the West Indies, the Middle East, the Congo and elsewhere:

> To arrive at a place without knowing anyone there, and some-
> times without an introduction; to learn how to move among
> strangers for the short time one could afford to be among them;
> to hold oneself in constant readiness for adventure or revelation;
> to allow oneself to be carried along, up to a point, by accidents;
> and consciously to follow up other impulses – that could be as
> creative and imaginative a procedure as the writing that came
> after.

Naipaul finds this kind of travel-work glamorous. He also finds it demanding and exhausting (to the rooted homebody, it sounds a bit bleak too). Yet if the process uses him up, he also uses up the place:

> I travel to discover other states of mind. And if for this intellec-
> tual adventure I go to places where people live restricted lives,
> it is because my curiosity is still dictated in part by my colonial
> Trinidad background. I go to places which, however alien, con-
> nect in some way with what I already know. When my curiosity
> has been satisfied, when there are no more surprises, the intel-
> lectual adventure is over and I become anxious to leave.

I was reminded of the life of a professional player of some highly lucrative sport, tennis or golf perhaps: the same round of hotels and airports; the same kind of meetings with the hangers-on and the officials connected with the game, the equivalent of the expatriates and diplomats of whom Naipaul sees a good deal, and who are usually very helpful to him; and also the same need to keep one's game in good shape, not to go slack or go native, and to stick to the orange juice. As the player has to practise to retain the pure arc of his swing, so Naipaul has to keep his rootlessness in trim. When the game is over, the player moves on.

This kind of wilful detachment makes some readers uncomfortable; it sticks out so flagrantly against the general mucking-in and joining-up.

David Hare's play *A Map of the World*, not one of his best, stars Roshan Seth as an author who is unmistakably modelled on Naipaul – witty, fastidious, uncompromising. The character is not treated wholly unfairly – although, towards the end, the play, like many plays, loses its way – and is given the best lines, certainly better than those given to the other rather disillusioned characters who are milling around the milieu of the same Third World conference. Still, the impression is left that a writer, or indeed any person, who does not associate himself wholeheartedly with the struggles of the Third World is a dubious character or, at the very least, poses a moral question.

This familiar misunderstanding about literature is widely shared by politicians and public persons of all sorts. The fallacy is that political commitment indicates warmth and humanity, while detachment is the sign of a cold fish and a dead soul. Yet what could be colder and deader than to shovel so many ill-assorted and ill-used beings into some huge makeshift bin of ideology or nationality? By paying attention to them as individuals, the author gives proper value to the diversity and poignancy of their experience; to say that he immortalizes their plight is not to say that he is indifferent to it.

Sometimes the only thing shared by such people is a sense of loss. Even those who prospered in the West Indies, like Naipaul's grandfather, often continued to think of India as the real place and Trinidad as 'the interlude, the illusion'. When the SS *Ganges* arrived at Calcutta in 1932 with a thousand unhappy Indians who had served out their indentures in Trinidad, the ship was stormed by hundreds of other Indians who had been previously repatriated and now wanted to be taken back to Trinidad.

This autobiographical fragment is dominated by the story of Naipaul's father, a story which he fully discovered only in 1970, seventeen years after his father's death. An English journalist, Gault MacGowan, brought out to modernize the *Trinidad Guardian*, had encouraged Naipaul's father to become a sprightly reporter writing in an up-to-the-minute Fleet Street style. Then MacGowan left the island, Naipaul's father was reduced to a stringer, fell ill and had a nervous breakdown lasting years, becoming a listless wanderer, dependent on his wife's family. What had happened? From press cuttings Naipaul pieced the story together: his father had written a report mocking the superstition of local Hindus who were sacrificing goats to guard their cattle against paralytic rabies instead of having them vaccinated; he received an anonymous threatening letter in Hindi ordering him to perform the very same ceremony which he had criticized or he would die within a week. After blustering defiance in the columns of the *Guardian*, he then yielded to his terror, less of divine retribution than of the violent feuding gangs on the island, and performed the ritual sacrifice. His image of himself as a modern-minded, rational man collapsed. Caught between the borrowed ways and the inherited ways, the new home and the old home, the present and the past, life is an endless series of catches; there is no permanent lodge or purchase, no home for Mr Biswas.

In the Ivory Coast, celebrated as the most successful former colony in black Africa, Naipaul finds something different: a glimpse of an African Africa, an Africa which 'has always been in its own eyes complete, achieved, bursting with its own powers'. Something like this, a similar religious feeling, was, fleetingly, at the back of many of the slave revolts in the Caribbean. The idea of African completeness endures in various Caribbean religious cults;

and touches the politics of the region. Many of the recent political movements in the black Caribbean have had a millenarian, ecstatic, purely African side. Naipaul rather indulges this feeling, finding in the feeding of the crocodiles round the president's palace not only a tourist sight but also a sinister, mysterious rite touched with the magic and power which the president doubtless intended it to have. For Africans, we are told, the real world is the world of the night, the world of ghosts and magic; the world of the day, the Western world, seems rather childish to them; and when the Europeans go, their world will go with them.

Here I think Naipaul strains for effect a little. After all, a Chinese official touring Britain who strayed off the M4 and lost his way and found himself watching Lord Bath's lions being fed, then took refuge from the weather in a tin hut with a cross on its roof and there happened to find an old man in a long robe mumbling in Latin and placing small fragments of bread on the tongues of his followers – such a highly rational person might well feel somewhat uneasy as the West Country rain drummed on the corrugated iron roof. The idea of spiritual completeness is not confined to Africa. Country people almost everywhere have, or used to have, much the same feelings of amused superiority as they contemplated the childish scurryings of townees with their childish fads. The sight of a stain on the wall of a modern flat in Abidjan where the rain has penetrated reminds the narrator of something an expatriate has said to him earlier: 'Africa seeps through'. But in that sense, England seeps through too. So do most places. In 'The Crocodiles of Yamoussoukro' we have in fact been quietly, unconsciously carried over the border which divides reporting from creating, the setting down of experience from the working up of material, journalism from art. Yet the working up of mumbo jumbo (in the strict sense of that term) is essential to Naipaul's narrative; for the mumbo jumbo is the background to the people he is really dealing with – the expatriates, the marginal, the displaced, the half-Europeans; this mixture of excitement and fear is what lures them to the edge of the jungle and keeps them there. It is their story which is to be told.

And storytelling is the driving force of Naipaul's work: 'any attempt at narrative can give value to an experience which might otherwise evaporate away.' It is precisely the inconsequential which most needs consequences; the story that has no point or twist which most needs a beginning, middle and an end. The narrative impetus dignifies, sharpens, intensifies effects, whether of pathos or humour. Narrative and simplicity. How beautifully and clearly Naipaul starts his autobiographical fragment by telling the story of how he wrote *Miguel Street*, a collection of Trinidad tales which has the carefree fluency of so many of his first books: he was sitting in a gloomy office in the BBC; he describes the room and he sets down the first sentence he tapped out on the old typewriter and the magical feeling of having written it: 'Every morning when he got up Hat would sit on the banister of his back verandah and shout across, "What happening there, Bogart?"'

I read *Miguel Street* years ago; that first sentence brings it all back in a rush, and to recall the rush of pleasure is to present as moral a justification as any, if justification were needed, which it isn't.

HUGH TREVOR-ROPER:
THE VOLTAIRE OF ST ALDATE'S

Ah Oxford! Welcome to the City of Dreadful Spite, otherwise known as Malice Springs, the permanent Number One on the Bitch List. Not since the vituperative pamphleteers of the English Civil War has there been a community so dedicated to character assassination as the dons of Oxford. Living on the same staircase, dining side by side, night after night, term after term, dries up the milk of human kindness. Here is Hugh Trevor-Roper, Regius Professor of Modern History for twenty-three years, describing C. S. Lewis, a Fellow of Magdalen College for nearly thirty:

> Envisage (if you can) a man who combines the face and figure of a hog-reeve or earth-stopper with the mind and thought of a Desert Father of the fifth century, preoccupied with meditations of inelegant theological obscenity: a powerful mind warped by erudite philistinism, blackened by systematic bigotry, and directed by a positive detestation of such profane frivolities as art, literature and (of course) poetry: a purple-faced bachelor and misogynist, living alone in rooms of inconceivable hideousness, secretly consuming vast quantities

of his favourite dish – beefsteak-and-kidney-pudding; periodically trembling at the mere apprehension of a feminine footfall; and all the while distilling his morbid and illiberal thoughts into volumes of bestselling prurient religiosity.

But the vitriol flows both ways. Here is the classical scholar Sir Maurice Bowra, Warden of Wadham for thirty-two years, writing to Evelyn Waugh in 1947: 'Trevor-Roper is a fearful man, short-sighted, with dripping eyes, shows off all the time, sucks up to me, boasts, is far from poor owing to his awful book [*The Last Days of Hitler*] on every page of which there is a howler.'

In Oxford, popular success in the outside world is the unforgivable sin. Thus for Trevor-Roper the bestselling A. L. Rowse is 'typical of modern Oxford historians. There is neither breadth nor depth in him. He is provincial – a good provincial journalist.' Later in this selection of his letters to the great art historian Bernard Berenson, he describes Rowse as 'a Cornish peasant with the character of a mediaeval village usurer'.

On and on it goes. Herbert Butterfield was 'a very undistinguished historian', while the great refugee classicist Eduard Fraenkel was 'a German of the most boring kind'. Berenson would no doubt be delighted to hear that the mesmerizing Slade lecturer on art, Edgar Wind, was 'a charlatan of something akin to genius', and Arnold Toynbee was 'the Apostle of the Half-Baked'.

Even Trevor-Roper's friends sometimes wearied of this relentless battering. The publisher Hamish Hamilton wrote to Berenson after a weekend with the Duchess of Buccleuch, 'Hugh Trevor-Roper was there, and we found ourselves wondering if one so young and gifted ought to spend quite so much time hating people. He has hardly a charitable word for anyone, and seems to relish the discomfiture even of those he is supposed to like.'

Although not much of a one for introspection, Trevor-Roper could identify clearly enough the influences that had put lead in his bludgeon. He found his father, a workaholic physician, aloof and unresponsive. His mother, from a Belfast linen family, was cold, humourless and snobbish. 'Ours was a grim household without warmth, or affection, or encouragement, or interest.' Until extreme old age, he retained a weirdly boyish skin – the impression of youthful irresponsibility heightened by the chuckles that would break out at the news of some comical mishap to a butt or rival. His Christ Church friend, the economist Roy Harrod, claimed that Trevor-Roper had once undergone extensive cosmetic surgery after a riding accident or car smash (I forget which) but that sometimes, in the light cast obliquely by the candles in Christ Church Hall, it was possible to catch a glimpse of the old face underneath, twisted and wrinkled by years of backbiting.

His gestures were awkward, as though he had only just learnt them, and he appeared stiff and uneasy beside his exuberantly gay brother Pat, a distinguished and convivial eye surgeon, so convivial in fact that one sometimes trembled for the first patient of the morning after – not that Hugh was much beside him, for like Berenson he shied away from the claims of family life. When at the age of forty he married Field Marshal Haig's daughter Alexandra ('Xandra'), who was seven years older, he grumbled constantly about how her three children interfered with his timetable. Nor did Alexandra receive much of a welcome from the Berenson ménage at I Tatti. The sage recorded in his diary, 'Youngish woman with wooden angular profile, Celtic blonde colouring, fairly good figure, no interest or talk to entitle her to frequent us or to be travelling with Hugh.' His judgment after a later visit by the Trevor-Ropers was barely less chilly: 'She looked haggard and years older than Hugh, but very well dressed and is not by any means as stupid and dazed as she looks.'

Berenson was eighty-two when they first met in July 1947; Trevor-Roper only thirty-three. They could not therefore enjoy that instinctive understanding which irradiates the correspondence of people who were young together, like Kingsley Amis and Philip Larkin or Evelyn Waugh and Nancy Mitford. What they shared were conservative sympathies in culture and politics, a reverence for the liberalism of Erasmus and Burckhardt, a distaste for organized religion in general and the Roman Catholic Church in particular, and above all a taste for gossip, though one sometimes wonders when Trevor-Roper is retailing a titbit about some Fellow of Merton or Belgravia hostess whether Berenson had a clue who he was talking about. Berenson himself admitted, 'I have but a tangential relationship to my younger friends; they do not think of me as one of themselves.'

So to some extent these letters are a performance to entertain an old man, comparable to, though much richer and cattier than, Rupert Hart-Davis's letters to George Lyttelton. They are superbly edited. Richard Davenport-Hines's introduction is so crisp and perceptive that it sometimes makes the actual letters seem a little plodding. His footnotes, too, are an unobtrusive delight, inform- ing us for example that Berenson's sister Senda Abbott introduced basketball as a team sport for women and that Randal, 8th and last Earl of Berkeley, was 'a world expert on osmosis and the only man at that time to be simultaneously a Fellow of the Royal Society and a Master of Foxhounds'. I like the 'at that time', as though at other periods there might have been half-a-dozen chaps who had brought off the double.

It is to a footnote, too, that we owe the information that at lunch at I Tatti, Thomas Pakenham, then aged nineteen or twenty, 'asked loudly and inconveniently how the money had been made to pay for such grandeur'. The answer to that interesting question is given here. The unstoppable art dealer Joseph Duveen began by paying Berenson a commission of 10 per cent on the sale price of paintings for which BB had provided an attribution. These huge pourboires netted more than $80,000 in 1909 alone. Berenson lamented, 'I have become a society-lounger and money-grubber and God knows what, I do not like it at all and mean to wrench myself away as soon as possible.' But far from wrenching away, he ratcheted up his fee to an almost incredible 25 per cent and remained in cahoots with Joe Duveen until 1937, and then after the war transferred his services to Georges Wildenstein.

Imprisoned in this dubiously acquired splendour (for how could he not bend just a little to Joe's insistence that this one really was a Titian or a Bellini?), he envied what he saw as Trevor-Roper's insouciant independence amid the dreaming spires, just as Trevor-Roper longed for the grace and calm of I Tatti's fountains and cypresses, hating Oxford's squabbles and intrigues, which so consumed his energies. The dreary company of embittered old men was at odds with the Oxford he liked to believe in, 'a gay sceptical tolerant enquiring unshockable world'. 'I made a careful computation the other day which satisfies me that there are in this university only 19 intelligent people, of whom six are hermits or otherwise unsuitable for social life and eight are so social that they can never be found, always being in Paris, London or some such place.' And their idleness was often on a heroic scale, fully matching the sloth of Oxford professors in the days of his hero Edward Gibbon: 'We now have in this university seven professors of history, only one of whom has ever written so much as one book on a historical subject, and two of whom have never even committed so much as a single antiquarian review.'

For both men, conversation was the thing. In Berenson's words, 'the give and take of talk has been from my earliest years and remains the crowning joy of my life'. He thought Trevor-Roper a good talker, a fine historian, but above all a superb letter-writer. Davenport-Hines calls him 'the greatest letter-writer of his generation, a letter-writer whose irony, grace and knowledge make him the twentieth-century equivalent of Madame de Sévigné or Horace Walpole'. After *The Last Days of Hitler*, Trevor-Roper's second post-war masterpiece was, we are told, his correspondence.

On the evidence of this volume I don't quite think so, although his enormous correspondence with friends of his own age might give a different impression. Certainly his judgments of character are often piercing, and his vignettes can be terrific; for example, his description of calling on Jan Masaryk, the Czech foreign minister, a few weeks before the communist coup in Prague after which Masaryk threw himself or was thrown out of the window of his ministry:

> He was alleged to be ill, but I think it was an illness of convenience, for he seemed in excellent form when I found him, lying in bed in a vast and luxurious apartment of the Czernin Palace. He was writing private letters in violet ink and reading Gogol's *Dead Souls*, and the elaborate canon of the bells of the Capuchin Loreto drifted in through the curtains, and he made elaborate jokes in brisk brogue, and all the time he was leaving the foreign policy of Czechoslovakia to his communist under-secretary.

But the repeated use of 'lower-middle-class' as a pejorative epithet, indeed the whole faintly camp apparatus of snobbery, becomes wearisome. And the mock-heroic accounts of those Lilliputian Oxford sagas – the election of the professor of poetry, the battle to install Macmillan as chancellor of the university – do drag on a bit. They are more amusingly told in the cod seventeenth-century despatches which Trevor-Roper contributed to the *Spectator* under the byline of 'Mercurius Oxonensis'. On each page there is some arresting thought or phrase, and I turned each page eagerly, but something is missing; not so much the occasional patch of human warmth, though that would be nice, as the unguarded confidence, the stray glimpse into the soul. Even the famous Gibbonian irony sometimes sounds a little forced. In its insidious way, ultimately Oxford got to him. Gibbon, after all, lasted only fourteen months at Magdalen – 'the fourteen months the most idle and unprofitable of my whole life'. Trevor-Roper stayed there nearly half a century.

He remains inimitable, I think, not so much as a letter-writer but as the author of short, telling historical essays which transform the way we look at a subject; and inimitable, too, as a frondeur who cannot see a fallacy without setting out to expose it, or a fraudulent claim without stamping on it with both feet. He was the greatest debunker of his age. *The Last Days of Hitler* remains a masterpiece of contemporary history, never equalled or supplanted, not merely because of its high narrative verve and the acute brilliance of its portraits of the ghastly dramatis personae, but because it established once and for all what actually happened. After it was published, no one could seriously maintain that Hitler was still alive and had been spirited away to Moscow or Buenos Aires.

Trevor-Roper's relentless pursuit of his victims may sometimes look like sheer malice: for example, in his campaign to convince Fernand Braudel and the other Annales historians (whom he greatly admired) that as a historian Lawrence Stone was a charlatan. But I do think that Stone was, if not a charlatan, at best perniciously mistaken about sixteenth- and seventeenth-century social history, and, since he was so fashionable on both sides of the Atlantic, only the most hard-driving campaign had any chance of unseating him.

Again, when Count Bernadotte, the UN mediator in Palestine, was assassinated by the Stern Gang in 1948, he achieved the status of a martyr-hero. It was a thankless task, but one which Trevor-Roper undertook with his usual relish, to prove that it was Himmler's masseur Felix Kersten and not Bernadotte who had been primarily responsible for rescuing 20,000 prisoners from Nazi concentration camps, and that in fact Bernadotte, as an official of the Red Cross, had been responsible only for arranging the transport and, what's more, had initially refused to take any Jews, confiding to Himmler that he shared his racial views.

In a small way, I once saw Trevor-Roper in action on one of these skirmishes. He had lighted upon an infinitely obscure organization called the Society for Anglo-Chinese Understanding, which had become a communist front, broadcasting reports of Chairman Mao's bottomless benevolence and allegiance to high liberal principles and kept going by the usual stage army of stooges led by the famous Cambridge scientist Joseph Needham. Hugh assembled a rival stage army of capitalist stooges, including me, and I can still remember his mad gleam of triumph at SACU's ill-attended AGM as our lot took control. Zero tolerance for the intolerable was his motto. Appeasers beware, from Munich to Mao. He was the Voltaire of St Aldate's.

All this – the battling with *l'infâme*, the canvassing of rural deans to vote this way, or that, the dining with duchesses, and, of course, the incessant correspondence – took up time which soberer spirits said should have been devoted to composing major historical works. Although he published any number of reviews, essays and pasquinades, although he travelled everywhere and met everyone, was he not ultimately vulnerable to the same charge as those other Oxford historians he derided for failing to put something substantial together? Would he not have done better to settle down in real scholarly seclusion rather than fritter his time and his reputation in authenticating forged Hitler diaries for Rupert Murdoch or, as Master of Peterhouse, Cambridge, in his late sixties, trying to quell a bunch of dons who made his old Oxford enemies look positively sweet-natured and ingenuous? Whatever became of his major work on the rule of Robert Cecil? Or of his vast book on the Puritan Revolution (he wrote 600 pages, tore them up, rewrote them and then what?)? Or of his life of Cromwell in three volumes?

Well, we miss them all, but I don't think we miss their effects, because, by and large, the causes for which he battled with such ferocious glee have come out on top, in the Cold War no less than in the English Civil War. In politics as in historiography, the Marxists and the marxisants have been routed. It is easy to forget how their premises and arguments were once taken for granted and how quirky and perverse seemed those who spoke out against them. But then looking quirky and perverse was something Hugh Trevor-Roper never minded.

W. G. SEBALD:
A MASTER SHROUDED IN MIST

At the end of the 1960s, three young lecturers arrived at the University of East Anglia: Malcolm Bradbury, Lorna Sage and, from south Germany by way of Manchester, W. G. Sebald, always known as Max. All three were to spend the rest of their lives teaching there, and they all died rather young within about a year of one another. Each produced at least one memorable book, Bradbury's *The History Man,* Lorna Sage's *Bad Blood* and Sebald's *The Emigrants.* Each had a huge knowledge and understanding of literature of all kinds. These reservoirs of sympathy did not, however, extend very far into human relations. As is not unknown among academics cooped up together for years on end, they did not get on. For Lorna at least, this antipathy became as pleasurable a drug as the cigarettes which fed her emphysema. It was impossible to be in her company for five minutes without her exploding into gurgles of indignation about the latest tiresomeness of Malcolm or Max. This puzzled me, as both her colleagues seemed quite affable, positively genial in the case of Bradbury and mild, even shy in the case of Sebald. Yet her irritation did alert me to the possibility that Sebald might not be quite as easy to pin down as he seemed.

This is not, as some critics have said, because his writing is hard to categorize. On the contrary, Sebald's style of atmospheric rumination – part autobiographical, part anecdotal and historical – has long been a well-loved genre in European writing. Indeed he quite often glances back to his predecessors: Rousseau's reveries, Sterne's ramblings, Sir Thomas Browne's *Urn Burial* and Burton's *The Anatomy of Melancholy*. Sebald's half-dozen prose works, all published in the last ten years of his life, are not essays exactly and they are certainly not novels, although Sebald's *Austerlitz* is couched in that form. Sebald himself said 'My medium is prose, not the novel.' For quite a few writers today, he is now acknowledged as 'probably the greatest intellect and voice of the late 20th century', to quote Antony Beevor, or 'the most significant European writer to have emerged in the last decade', in the view of one *TLS* reviewer. 'Is literary greatness still possible?' Susan Sontag asks and immediately replies that 'one of the few answers available to English-language readers is the work of W. G. Sebald'.

Yet among German-language readers (and despite living in England for over thirty years, Sebald almost always wrote in his native German) there is a dissenting minority. I recall a professor of literature at Frankfurt becoming almost apoplectic at the mention of 'that charlatan'. Certainly Sebald's prose seems to me to have rather less impact in the original, its atmospherics somehow less seductive. At a public reading in the Queen Elizabeth Hall not three months before he was killed in a car crash in December 2001, Sebald read from *Austerlitz*, which was published that autumn, while his translator, Anthea Bell, read her English version. It was not, I think, just Sebald's rather drowsy delivery that made the German sound a little flat, even laboured, while the English did have an alluring strangeness, perhaps just because it was, so to speak, double distilled through translation from the German of a German who had lived almost all his adult life in England without becoming in the least English.

Jacques Austerlitz is a Czech Jew who is brought over as a small

child on a Kindertransport and brought up by a grim minister
and his desperate wife in the slatiest reaches of North Wales to
know nothing of his origins and to call himself Dafydd Elias.
The passage that Sebald and Anthea Bell read describes his escape
from this deadly couple into the outlandish delights of his school
friend's home, Andromeda Lodge, with its eccentric uncles, its
moths and cockatoos and carrier pigeons and its heart-stopping
views of the Mawddach Estuary. These are among the most vivid
and poignant pages Sebald ever wrote. The paradox is that they
are also the closest to conventional fiction.

By contrast, Sebald's more openly autobiographical wander-
ings sometimes exude, to me at least, a curious off-putting tang,
rather like a whiff of disinfectant blowing into a concert hall.
Whether he is in East Anglia or Belgium or the Black Forest,
the W. G. figure, as we might call him, trudges disconsolately
through unvisited museums and down-at-heel zoos, eats solitary
and usually vile meals in grimy railway refreshment rooms and
out-of-season resorts, alternately disheartened by the irremediable
decay and the brash vulgarity that he finds everywhere. Always
he sees the legions of the dead flocking around him, and in his
frequent bouts of paralysis and depression the hard edge of things
appears to flicker and fade until it begins to merge with the ghosts
of the past. He embarks on these low-spirited excursions for rea-
sons that he tells us he cannot recall, sometimes to escape from
difficulties in his life that he finds too painful to rehearse.

This anonymous being seems to correspond in many particu-
lars to Professor Sebald of UEA. Yet he is, as it were, disembodied
and free to float among his ghosts. In his estrangement from the
material world and its inhabitants, both usually depicted as coarse
and gross, W. G. is of course the epitome of the modern writer,
which is partly why so many modern writers find him so irre-
sistible and discern in his writing a depth of focus which makes
other treatments of the sufferings of the twentieth century and the
Holocaust in particular seem superficial.

For all his deliberate pace and discursive method, Sebald does pull you along in an almost hypnotic fashion. And that is a great virtue. Yet I wonder about the profundity. Reading him, even going quite slowly, I get more a sensation of glancing or skimming rather than of being dragged deeper into things. Even his most memorable images and encounters leave behind an impression that tends to be sketchy and evanescent. For one thing, these carefully oblique reflections on the horrors of our time draw much of their material and their force from first-hand accounts of them that are plainer and more direct, such as the poet H. G. Adler's recollections of Theresienstadt, not to mention Primo Levi's of Auschwitz.

One cannot help noticing too the calculated efforts to tug at the reader's heartstrings. The most blatant examples are the smudged black-and-white photos with which he peppers his peregrinations: pictures of deserted factories, peeling doorways, long-dead relatives in old-style clothes or fancy dress. These fragile shards of the past, to pastiche the Sebaldian style, remind me rather of those short-lived editions of old Dennis Wheatley crime mysteries which came fully equipped with a used book of matches, a piece of bloodstained cloth, a crumpled feather and other clues stuck into their pages to stimulate the sluggish imagination. I cannot help feeling that this kind of Shardenfreude is as crude as the methods employed in what Sebald would no doubt call, in his old-fashioned way, a house-maid's novelette.

Certainly it would be unfair to judge Sebald on the strength of *Campo Santo*, which is a collection of posthumous leavings: four little sections from a never-completed book on Corsica, half-a-dozen literary essays, mostly on German writers such as Kafka and Peter Handke, and a few final morsels on subjects as diverse as mackerel, Sebald's early musical experiences and Bruce Chatwin and the collector's instinct. Beginners should start instead with *Austerlitz* or *The Emigrants*.

At the same time, precisely because these are scraps and sketches, not fully finished, something worrying does begin to show through the thin, unvarnished texture. And that something is banality.

The opening piece, 'A Little Excursion to Ajaccio', describes, in Sebald's usual charming fashion, a visit paid on an idle whim to the Napoleon museum, where the slightest relic of the Emperor is preserved and the elderly attendants all look like members of the Bonaparte family. Towards the end of the piece, Sebald branches out into his familiar descant upon the transience of things. Neither of Napoleon's parents, he says, 'can of course have dreamed that the children at the dining table with them daily would eventually rise to the ranks of kings and queens, or that the time would come when the most hot-tempered of them ... would wear the crown of a vast empire extending over almost the whole of Europe'. No indeed. In the next sentence, equally typically, Sebald shifts from this local rumination to the universal: 'But what can we know in advance of the course of history, which unfolds according to some logically indecipherable law, impelled forward, often changing direction at the crucial moment, by tiny imponderable events?' etc., etc.

Now this might simply be Sebald on an off day. Such thoughts are liable to swim into one's head on a hot Corsican afternoon, not to be recognized, then or alas later, as thoughts that other people have thought roughly a million times before.

But then take the next piece, the title essay 'Campo Santo'. Sebald wanders through an abandoned graveyard. What does he notice? 'Another striking feature of the design of the Piana graveyard ... was the fact that in general the dead were buried in clans, so that the Ceccaldi lay beside the Ceccaldi and the Quilichini beside the Quilichini.' Once we have recovered from this startling observation, which could be replicated in almost any cemetery anywhere, he moves on to note that the better-off corpses in Piana have larger tombs with pediments and sarcophagi, while the poorest have only a metal cross stuck in the bare earth. Well, now, there's a thing.

Then – and this too is typical – Sebald does produce some genuinely fascinating material about Corsican burial customs. This material is drawn from his UEA colleague Stephen Wilson's study of nineteenth-century Corsican feuds. Until quite recently, it seems, most Corsicans shunned public cemeteries and buried their dead on their own land in an olive grove or under a chestnut tree so that the dead might continue to watch over their property. Looking back at other essays in, for example, *The Rings of Saturn*, one cannot help noticing the same phenomenon: the relative ordinariness of Sebald's own observations which are then tricked out by his magpie's gift of picking up brilliant insights and anecdotes from other writers.

Sebald also deploys, too often for comfort, the device of linking together odds and ends about famous people in order to impart an air of imaginative profundity. In one piece here, he describes going to bed during a thunderstorm and dreaming of how, when Verdi was dying, the people of Milan put down straw outside his house to muffle the sound of horses' hooves. Then the storm outside his window makes him think of a thunderstorm that Wittgenstein saw as a boy of six from the balcony of his family's summer home. Neither of these fragments of memory is doing any real work. Putting down straw in order not to disturb the dying was common practice over most of Europe at the time and it being Verdi who is dying contributes nothing, just as there is no extra philosophic depth added to the passage by it being the boy Wittgenstein who saw the storm. This is celebrity tourism dressed up as literature. In the literary essays collected in *Campo Santo*, Sebald's gift for quotation becomes a generous and unassuming trait. He is able to show us the best of Nabokov, for example, the wonderful image from *Speak, Memory* of the author's father being tossed up in the air as an act of homage from his grateful peasantry.

But in the political and psychological reflections one cannot help feeling that Sebald is doing little more than recycling (with due acknowledgment) the earlier insights of others, without adding

much of his own to, for example, Alexander and Margarete
Mitscherlich's theory of the 'inability to mourn' in post-war Ger-
many. Indeed, he readily acknowledges his debt to those writers
who have taught us that an unpretentious factual account of what
happened is the best way to resist the human tendency to suppress
painful or shameful memories in order to 'get on with our lives'
or 'move on'.

What Sebald says is not untrue or ignoble or unfelt or not
worth repeating. It is just that it is hard to detect much original-
ity or creative energy there. He does not have one of those minds
which cannot tick over for five seconds without throwing off
something fresh and sharp. There is not the effortless bubbling up
you find in the prose of, to take a random bunch, Ruskin, D. H.
Lawrence, Edmund Wilson, John Berger, V. S. Pritchett or Philip
Larkin.

What you have instead is a tone, a wistful, misty strange-
ness which covers the most familiar objects in an alluring fog,
making them seem alien, unsettling and unsettled, pregnant with
melancholy and memory. And it is part of Sebald's enchantment
that when we come to touch his conclusions they are so reas-
suringly familiar. Rather like Molière's Monsieur Jourdain, we
are delighted to discover that what we had always thought turns
out to be literature. And so it is, I think, with Sebald himself.
Through the mist one seems to see a prophetic figure engaged on
some mysterious and significant mission. But when the mist clears
one sees only an elderly gentleman with a moustache poking at
the brambles with his walking stick.

JOHN LE CARRÉ:
SPOOKING THE SPOOKS

When we first meet Maxie – he has no other name – he is wearing a crumpled tropical suit with a sleeveless Fair Isle jersey and a sun-bleached khaki canvas bag swinging from his shoulder. He has come on his pushbike to a house off Berkeley Square full of tycoons and chandeliers and he is cursing because the bike has got a puncture. With his manic stride, his faraway blue eyes and haywire mop of sandy hair, he has the slovenly self-confidence that says Special Forces, the unnerving indifference to what others may think of him that goes with a man who is capable of anything. Mr Anderson, who is high up in a very secret bit of the Ministry of Defence, says, 'Maxie is, I am told, a genius in his field.' What is his field? Maxie himself explains that he has come to sort the Eastern Congo, 'to bring sanity back to a f**king madhouse'.

Maxie is John Buchan's Sandy Arbuthnot reborn, the wandering soldier of fortune who is at home in a tight spot anywhere in the world. Only, this being the start of the twenty-first century, the type is now terribly degraded, past redeeming. While Sandy was graceful and charming in half-a-dozen languages, Maxie says f**king every second word, can speak only fractured French and

wants to ferry in a bunch of hoodlums from South Africa in heli-
copters painted white with UN markings, the mercs (not cars,
stupid) to be armed with Kalashnikovs and Gatling machine-
guns. Nice to see Gatling still in business, a hundred years after
Sir Henry Newbolt's sitrep from an earlier small war: 'The
Gatling's jammed and the colonel dead.'

There is not much chance here of anyone playing up and
playing the game, for these dogs of war are the lowest type of
mongrel, less in the tradition of Buchan's *Greenmantle* than of
Conrad's *Heart of Darkness*, from which le Carré takes his epi-
graph: 'The conquest of the earth, which mostly means the taking
it away from those who have a different complexion or slightly
flatter noses than ourselves, is not a pretty thing when you look
into it too much.'

Le Carré shows no sign of slowing up or losing touch. If he has
altered at all in the half-century since *The Spy Who Came in from
the Cold*, it is only that his vision has grown darker and his quarrel
with the old English elite bitterer. Nine-tenths of the characters
in *The Mission Song* are utterly corrupt, either slimy-cynical cor-
rupt or brutal, apply-electrodes-to-your-privates corrupt.

The only exceptions are the innocent narrator Bruno Salva-
dor and his girlfriend Hannah, a Congolese nurse working in
London, who is luscious and saintly (le Carré's women tend to
come in three sizes: saints, good sorts and nymphos – which is an
improvement on some notable American novelists, who offer only
one model, the unmitigated bitch). Salvo is a half-caste, a Métis,
a zebra, the son of a randy bog-Irish missionary and a Congolese
village woman. He grows up with a mynah-bird ear and a jack-
daw memory, fluent in half-a-dozen languages of the Congo, not
to mention English, French and Swahili, wins a first at SOAS
and becomes a superb interpreter, promiscuously translating for
anyone who will hire him – global slush funds, prisons, hospitals,
immigration authorities and the murkier regions of government,
which is how he becomes a naive and at first utterly deceived

witness of Maxie's plot, which is hatched between certain very interested parties on a mysterious island somewhere near Denmark.

The opening passages in which Salvo tells us about his early years have a jaunty-sad brilliance about them. They are as irresistible as any of V. S. Naipaul's portraits of dispossessed characters scratching around the world. I read these pages with such pleasure and at such a gallop that when the book settled down into the iron disciplines of the suspense novel, I was going much too fast and missed half the subtleties of the plot and had to reread the last 200 pages with the concentration they deserved. Paradoxically, high-popular novels require much closer attention than highbrow fiction. The narrative pace is so relentless, because, like *Just a Minute*, the genre forbids hesitation, repetition or deviation. You may not lose much by letting your eyes blur over a couple of pages of Proust or Joyce, or indeed of Ben Okri and Salman Rushdie, but you speedread le Carré at your peril.

I do not mean that *The Mission Song* is full of twists exactly, more that the thread is twisted ever tighter on the same spool. The real surprise ending would be if the coup came off and Mr Anderson of the MoD turned out to be awfully decent and far-sighted. It does not diminish our pleasure at all that we know from the moment we meet Salvo's hero, Lord Brinkley of the Sands, the billionaire entrepreneur and champion of Africa, that he will turn out to be a rotter – a bit like Tiny Rowland though not so manic. Nor do we for one moment believe Mr Anderson when he tells Salvo, 'You're going to meet some of these ruffians in the flesh and do a little bit of good for your country while you're about it.' Mr Anderson may have an avuncular north-country burr and sing in the Sevenoaks Choral Society, but we are fully aware that the intentions of HMG are corrupt, too, and her servants can maintain their moral self-esteem only by keeping at arm's length the chaps like Maxie who do the dirty work.

What never fail in *The Mission Song*, as usual in le Carré, are the more than incidental pleasures. There is, for a start, the fanciful language of the spook's tradecraft, those playful euphemisms which cover up the horror. The contract which is to carve up the Eastern Congo between the local warlords and the far-off grasping investors is described as 'agricultural' – meaning that it covers all the minerals you can think of, from gold and diamonds to the stuff that makes uranium – and the equipment that the anonymous syndicate is to furnish is listed as shovels, pickaxes, scythes and wheelbarrows, by which is meant guns, rocket-propelled grenades and helicopters.

Like Salvo, le Carré has a mynah's ear for dialogue, from the breezy philosophizing of Maxie à la John Aspinall – 'no point hanging around the back of the herd when your time's up' – to the hypnotic, hectoring discourse of the Mwangaza, the incorruptible Enlightener, who is to chase out the rascals and liberate the Eastern Congo but who has, alas, already cut a deal with the rascals in Kinshasa while he was still in his ten-million-dollar villa in Spain with plasma TV screens in every toilet.

Half a century ago, before he became John le Carré and was still teaching me German at Eton College, David Cornwell was already in full command of that gift which goes beyond mere mimicry. He would tease the yobs in the back row of the class and cow them into bemused acquiescence by catching not merely the accents of their insolent drawl but the spoiled arrogance behind it. He was the most brilliant of teachers, crisp, imaginative, authoritative, but also sensitive to both the potential and the limits of his pupils.

And he is a teacher still. No other modern writer I can think of has such a hard didactic streak running through his most playful passages. His own rackety upbringing – his fraudster father in and out of jail, his mother disappearing from his life for years – has given him an implacable sense that actions have consequences and extravagances will have to be paid for by someone. And the links of the chain run on remorselessly across enormous distances. As the Mwangaza is belabouring the fat cats who have stolen the

People's Portion and Salvo is rendering his words with his usual mellifluous agility, the interpreter still finds time to reflect on the desperate shortage in Britain of PlayStation toys at Christmas a couple of years back. This was caused not by the incompetence or malevolence of the manufacturers or distributors but by the genocide that had engulfed the Eastern Congo, thereby interrupting the supply of the mineral coltan, which provides a tiny but essential speck in every cellphone and electronic gizmo.

Both in his books and in the public prints, le Carré remains the flintiest of controversialists, giving no quarter to the ungodly from Rushdie to George W. Bush. Not for the first time, it is the ugly Americans who really get it in the neck, making Graham Greene's efforts in the same line seem positively half-hearted. In *The Mission Song*, ghastly as the local warlords are, a far more sinister threat to the Eastern Congo is posed by the Union Minière des Grands Lacs, a ruthless conglomerate which is ultimately controlled by 'a *Who's Who* of American corporate and political power, A-list neoconservatives'. The true heart of darkness now is to be found at the HQ of Bechtel or Halliburton.

In literary circles, preaching went out of style with George Eliot, or at the latest with E. M. Forster and D. H. Lawrence. These days we esteem novels for their multivocal ambiguity, their crosscutting and undercutting, for being ludic and parodic and subversive, in short for being so complicated you could not possibly extract anything so kitsch as a message out of them before they disappear up their own ironies. Messages are for politicians and other merchants of the banal.

Yet le Carré's undiminished anger is as bracing as an east wind. It is provocative in the true sense of that overworked adjective. Almost every book of his makes me want to argue in a way that other modern novels don't. Is spying really any more deforming as a profession than soldiering or being a lawyer or policeman, let alone a politician or a journalist? And if le Carré's novels really persuaded you that it was, would so many spooks be such fans of his, just as senior civil servants adored Sir Humphrey and lawyers love John Grisham (there's a fortune awaiting the novelist who can come up with a page-turner about creative accounting)? Aren't the Arabs just a little too noble in *The Little Drummer Girl*, and isn't there just a whiff of an international Jewish conspiracy in the final pages of that enthralling novel? Are the big pharmaceutical companies quite so Machiavellian as depicted in *The Constant Gardener*? Ever since Harry Lime started cutting penicillin, Big Pharma has been a convenient villain, but would life expectancy in the Third World have improved so quickly without it?

Perhaps my habit of rebelling against the message is a rare and shameful quirk. Perhaps I am the only reader of *Middlemarch* who actually wants Mr Casaubon to discover the key to all mythologies so he can say snubs to that annoying Dorothea. Perhaps I am the only reader of *Lady Chatterley's Lover* to identify with Sir Clifford. So it may be that I shall be the only reader of *The Mission Song* who has a sneaking hope that Maxie's plot actually succeeds and the Mwangaza is parachuted into power ahead of the elections. Poor Salvo complains that the Congo is a land dying of neglect by the outside world, a country in which 4 million dead can finish up 'on page 29, next to the quick crossword'. So is intervention always hopelessly misguided? After all, as I am writing this review, I read reports in the newspapers, on page thirty-one of *The Times* for example, of bodies littering the streets of Kinshasa as fierce fighting breaks out in advance of the second round of presidential elections. Might not a tiny coup have forestalled the anarchy?

But of course such a shameful thought is total fantasy, and it is part of le Carré's cunning to have lured me into thinking it. To see that no good could ever have come of such an intrinsically squalid enterprise, you have only to look at the real-life counterpart of Maxie's little caper, the aborted coup in Equatorial Guinea (Sir Mark Thatcher prop.), and to watch the real-life Maxie,

Simon Mann, the son and grandson of England cricket captains, being led away in irons, filthy, dishevelled and disgraced. And to those who fondly believe that HMG could never get mixed up in such a disreputable business, we need only recall the warm enthusiasm expressed by Our Man in Sierra Leone for the latest regime change there. This is darkness visible, and it is John le Carré's abiding mastery to make us see it even if we would rather not.

ELIAS CANETTI:
THE GOD-MONSTER
OF HAMPSTEAD

Some quite bad writers have won the Nobel Prize in Litera-
ture. Pearl Buck is the most notorious. So have some great
men who are better known for other, not strictly literary endeav-
ours, such as Churchill and Sartre. Many more laureates have
written in small-circulation languages which you wonder if the
judges are qualified to judge.

But I can think of only one Nobel literary laureate of whom
you might be tempted to ask: what exactly has he won it for?
When Elias Canetti was awarded the Nobel in 1981, he had pub-
lished only a scattering of assorted things, mostly rather slight:
three farces, a travel book, a few essays, one novel published
forty-five years earlier, two-thirds of an autobiography (his most
evocative and attractive work), plus what I suppose might be
described as a work of popular social anthropology, *Crowds and
Power*.

Yet nobody much at the time gainsaid Canetti's claim to the
Nobel. For it was tacitly (and sometimes openly) agreed that his
supreme work of art was himself. When he arrived in England,
as Jeremy Adler remarks in his introduction to *Party in the Blitz*,

a posthumous montage of Canetti's writings about England, 'initially he did not owe his reputation to his publications but rather to the force of his personality'. And that remained the case even as his fame grew. For his lover Iris Murdoch, he was the magus, both the subject and the dedicatee of her second novel, *The Flight from the Enchanter*. Her husband, John Bayley, less enchanted by Canetti, particularly by his cruelty to Iris, christened him the God-Monster of Hampstead. Canetti himself says, 'My chief trait, much my strongest quality, which has never been compromised, was the insistence on myself . . . It may be a sort of virtue.' Or it may not.

This self-centredness reaches marvellous heights in his contempt for other living writers. T. S. Eliot was a 'miserable creature'. Kathleen Raine was a tedious whinger who committed the unforgivable sin: 'Not for a moment did she see me as a writer, the little she was able to read of mine struck her as tasteless, though she was careful never to tell me so. I, however, always knew it, and thought with some satisfaction how little her poems did for me.' As for Iris, 'she has not one serious thought . . . Everything I despise about English life is in her . . . I don't think there is anything that leaves me quite so cold as that woman's intellect.' Except perhaps her body – which he nonetheless took advantage of whenever she offered it. His descriptions of their lovemaking are so chilling that you have to read them twice to make sure you have read them properly.

There is one shining exception to these bilious denunciations of his literary contemporaries and supposed friends and lovers: the great Chinese scholar-translator Arthur Waley. No prizes for guessing why. Waley was the only man in England who had read Canetti's novel before the war and loved it.

At times, Canetti reminds me disgracefully of the Russian novelist Vladimir Brusiloff in 'The Clicking of Cuthbert': 'No novelists any good except me. Sovietski-yah! Nastikoff-bah! I spit me of zem all. No novelists anywhere any good except me. P. G. Wodehouse and Tolstoi not bad. Not good, but not bad.' He was born in 1905 into a cultivated Sephardic family of a line long settled in Turkey but more recently in Bulgaria. En famille, he and his wife Veza spoke Ladino, the Spanish dialect amazingly preserved among Jewish families expelled from Spain four centuries earlier. But English was the first language he learnt to read in, though he always wrote in German, and he first came to England in 1911, to Manchester, where his father died of a stroke the day after his wife had told him she had fallen in love with her doctor – a crucial trauma in Canetti's life and movingly recounted in his first memoir, *The Tongue Set Free*. After fleeing the Nazis, he and Veza finally settled in Hampstead in February 1939, amid the large refugee community which at that time constituted nearly half the borough's population. Apart from a brief intermission in Chesham Bois during the Blitz, they lived there until Veza's death. In his last years he moved to Zürich with his second wife, where he died in 1994.

Throughout the war and for some time afterwards, he was deeply admiring of the fortitude and tolerance of the English, and he became a British citizen. In 1951 he declared, 'I now feel completely at home in England, especially in London. I can now become an Englishman with a good conscience.' But this fellow feeling curdled with the passage of time. He began to detect 'a smell of weakness' in the English. He had come to loathe the insipidity of their conversation, the coldness of their manners, their awful stodginess. Even their famous tolerance was linked to their *Gefühlsimpotenz*. Above all, he loathed their parties, those appalling *Nichtberührungsfeste*. Professor Adler calls this term utterly untranslatable, but I think 'non-contact sports' will do quite nicely. These post-war gatherings in Hampstead or Chelsea or Kensington struck him as 'senseless and heartless, every bit in keeping with such cold people'. There was no touching, no intimacy, no curiosity. Adler points out that Canetti failed to take in (or did not live long enough to see) the kissing, hugging, crying, confessing post-Diana England. One can, however, be sure that he would have abominated that too.

Canetti's portrait of England is frozen in time, as most such portraits of national character tend to be. It took me a while to think what it most closely recalled. Then I realized that it was just like *The British Character*, that series of drawings by Pont of *Punch* first collected in book form in 1938. There they all are, the qualities first admired and then denounced by Canetti: Refusal to Admit Defeat, Importance of Not Being an Alien (the squat, underdressed Continental amid the horse-faced English in white ties even bears an eerie resemblance to the younger Canetti), Love of Keeping Calm, Absence of the Gift for Conversation, Importance of Not Being Intellectual and, above all, Reserve.

The actual party in the Blitz took place in Roland Penrose's house in Downshire Hill. It was a lascivious, unbuttoned affair, not at all a *Nichtberührungsfest*. On each floor there were couples embracing and dancing, while down in the basement sweating firemen were passing out buckets of sand to protect the houses that were burning in the neighbourhood. The firemen and the dancers seemed quite oblivious of each other. One can imagine one of Pont's furiously crowded, smoky, crosshatched drawings depicting the scene, entitled no doubt The Blitz Spirit.

This then is a period piece which suffers from being written at the end of Canetti's life, half a century after the period it describes. It is assembled from a jumble of shorthand manuscripts, notes and diaries, although it excludes (wrongly, I think) those passages that Canetti explicitly classified as 'Diaries' and stipulated were not to be published until thirty years after his death. So the book has a thin, spatchcocked feel. Adler candidly tells us that there was some discussion as to whether the book should have been published at all. Moreover, Canetti himself in extreme old age confesses, 'When I talk about England, I notice how wrong it all is.' Wrong quite often in details. He speaks of a Church of England clergyman who begins to doubt the Thirty-Seven Articles of his Faith. He admires Bertrand Russell for nobly declining the dukedom of Bedford. He tells us equally breathlessly and erroneously that Enoch Powell was one of only two Tory MPs from humble backgrounds and had distinguished himself by his bravery as a brigadier in Montgomery's Desert Army. No doubt Powell would have, given half a chance, but in fact he served out the war as a staff officer of Widmerpoolian assiduity.

For all that, Canetti's description of Enoch discoursing unstoppably on Dante and Nietzsche at a staid Tory soirée has a bite and vivacity to be found in others of his vignettes of English intellectual life, of dinner with Bertrand Russell with his 'goatish chuckle', of visiting that tragic Professor Branestawm figure, Geoffrey Pyke, who almost persuaded Mountbatten to build battleships out of blocks of ice, to be known as Pykrete.

These portraits achieve that pithy, abrupt quality that Canetti so admired in Aubrey's *Brief Lives*. And for them alone *Party in the Blitz* was well worth publishing, even though it is spoiled by Canetti's irrepressible habit of generalizing from insufficient evidence. For instance, he repeatedly curses the English obsession with saving time, giving as his prime example the Labour politician Douglas Jay saying to a woman, 'I've got five minutes' before taking off his trousers. But that is surely the impatience of lustful politicians the world over. Why else is President Chirac nicknamed 'Fifteen-minutes-including-the-shower'? Marlene Dietrich claimed that JFK fitted her into a half-hour slot. Mussolini too was no slouch, given any convenient flat surface to lay a woman on.

In the end, Canetti only seems to like people in England to the degree that he can identify them as not English, for example, the historian C. V. Wedgwood, who, he says, had none of the sluggish reserve of so many English people, her dark looks, warmth and quickness coming from her Celtic ancestors. Of course, 'I do not think much of her own writings, she was unoriginal, had no ideas of her own about anything', and – this was the limit – she adored Mrs Thatcher (Canetti never quite abandoned his leftist politics, though he kept his pre-war association with Brecht rather dark). However, Veronica could be forgiven much because she was an enthusiast for Canetti's novel, persuaded Jonathan Cape to publish it and volunteered to translate it herself.

And it is her translation which Harvill has used in reissuing, for Canetti's centenary, *Auto da Fé* as it was called when it came out in Britain in 1947. The book was first published in 1936 as *Die Blend-ung – The Blinding* or *The Deception* – and later in the US as *The Tower of Babel*, this variety of titles suggesting a smidgeon of uncertainty as to what the book was actually about. Veronica Wedgwood's transla-tion is stilted and clumsy and now and then, I think, mistakes the sense. I doubt whether this matters. Even if Englished by a master craftsman like Michael Hofmann (who has done *Party in the Blitz* beautifully), *Auto da Fé* would still be unendurable.

I do not mean that it is impossible to be carried along for a few pages by Canetti's prose, which is never less than lucid and fluent. It is just that the story is at the same time so whimsical and so crass, its allegorical subtext so leaden and brutish that it subverts its own subversion, or, to put it less politely, disappears up itself. A dis-tinguished Sinologist, Peter Kien, who lives a crazy, reclusive life obsessed by his enormous library, is tricked out of his inheritance by, among others: his housekeeper, later wife, a lubricious, greedy peasant woman; an evil, chess-playing, hunchbacked dwarf; and a lecherous blind man. From time to time he is abused and beaten up by a crowd of Bosch-like lumpenproles. And all this happens over and over again, quite relentlessly, for nearly 500 pages.

The blurb claims that *Auto da Fé* still 'towers as one of the greatest novels of the 20th century'. I find it hard to believe that it towered as one of the greatest novels of 1936. The epithet 'Kaf-kaesque' will no doubt be trotted out for the occasion. But if Kafka had treated the theme, he would have done it in twenty light, haunting, allusive pages which would have left the reader dangling in an exquisite uncertainty. Another point much insisted on by Kafka's compatriot Milan Kundera is that Kafka manages in some mysterious way to be very funny. *Auto da Fé* is no joke.

Those drawing up the Nobel citation obviously had some

difficulty deciding precisely what Canetti was on about, referring cautiously to 'his broad outlook' and 'his wealth of ideas'. In fact, I think that his outlook was quite narrow and his governing idea was a relatively simple one. In all his work he is haunted by the fear of the crowd.

In *Crowds and Power*, he purports to offer a typology of crowds, dividing them up into the open crowd, the closed crowd, the baiting crowd (or lynch mob), the lamenting crowd (or cortège), the flight crowd (or panic-stricken mob), the feast crowd and so on. Then he moves on to draw analogies between these modern types of crowd and the war packs of the Amazonian Indians, the rain dances of the Pueblo Indians, the kangaroo hunts of the Australian Aborigines, the Bushmen, etc. Except that he does not actually draw such analogies, but for the most part merely displays his examples alongside one another, leaving readers to draw their own conclusions. These examples are collected from a wide variety of sources – the book took more than twenty years to write, but despite this long gestation it is remarkably free from analytical thought. Large parts of it read like an up-market version of Desmond Morris's books in which the behaviour of chimps and hyenas is assumed to throw important light on human behaviour, but only by a loaded reasoning that selects only those features of animal behaviour that resemble human behaviour and discards those that do not.

'The crowd is the same everywhere,' Canetti asserts, 'in all periods and cultures; it remains essentially the same among men of the most diverse origin, education and language. Once in being, it spreads with the utmost violence. Few can resist its contagion.' This sweeping thesis is assumed throughout the book but never proved. Nowhere does Canetti bother to refute the possibility that evolution or history might have modified crowd behaviour. Nor does he offer proof that violence, panic or persecution is confined to men acting in crowds. Yet surely people also fight, lynch, murder, persecute, take fright, feast, mourn and hunt in ones and twos and fours and dozens, according to time, circumstance and convenience.

Crowds and Power is in no sense a rational enquiry. It is a violently tendentious tract, inspired, like *Auto da Fé,* by the ghastly experiences of the mob which, quite understandably, obsessed the European intellectual in the 1930s. Although not actually published until 1960, it belongs on the same shelf as Ortega y Gasset's *The Revolt of the Masses* (1929). You can find this fear of the masses almost anywhere you look in the highbrow English literature of the period, in Virginia Woolf, D. H. Lawrence, Aldous Huxley.

It would of course be possible to argue the precise contrary, that, then as now, it is small vanguards of pseudo-intellectuals, usually armed with some debased ideology, who inject the real poison and that crowds are a neutral phenomenon capable of just as wide a range of behaviour as individual human beings. But that is not what the intellectual wishes to believe. For him the only hope lies in the solitary, unillusioned mind, that is, in himself.

Need we look further for an explanation of the huge success that Canetti enjoyed in his later years? He was indeed a writer of some grace, wide learning and considerable critical acuity, and he had paid close attention to the terrible events of the century he nearly spanned. But none of this would have elevated him to the status of magus. What he illustrated as much by his life as by his work was that a solitary intellectual, without friends or funds or even a country to call his own, could come out on top, that the life of the mind was the life that mattered. What did the trick was his appeal to the self-esteem of intellectuals everywhere. He raised them above the dangerous, dull-witted crowd, and they in turn raised him.

JOHN OSBORNE:
ANGER MANAGEMENT?

The heart starts to sink on the very first page, page xiii to be precise, because this is still the preface: 'When I began work on Osborne's biography, hoping for the best, I asked his wife Helen, "What does no one know about your husband?"' Already you can see the gleam in the biographer's eye, the headline on the review front: Angry Playwright's Other Life, Secret Shame of John Osborne. By page xiv we have sunk lower: 'What caused his depressions would send me in time on an obsessive search for the one explanation of Osborne's torment and fury that might account for everything – "the Rosebud Theory".' So the Fleet Street sleuth is also a Hollywood shrink – Geoffrey Levy meets Orson Welles and the analyst comes too.

Helen Osborne was the Katharine Parr in The Five Wives of John Osborne – divorced, died, died, died, survived. The middle three – Mary Ure, Penelope Gilliatt and Jill Bennett – were also divorced, and all three more or less killed themselves by drink and drugs. Helen was the only one to take his name. She endured his tantrums and his glooms, coped with his drink and diabetes, matched him joke for joke and glass for glass. In this scene of carnage as full of corpses as the end of Hamlet, she alone, the chain-smoking, wisecracking Widow of Oz, as she styled herself, was left to tell the tale. Except that she didn't and John Heilpern did. Which is a pity.

No human being in recorded history stands in less need of further revealing than John Osborne. To say he wore his heart on his sleeve is a genteel understatement. He flayed himself alive in public at regular intervals. Even before the first word is spoken in *Look Back in Anger*, the stage directions describe Jimmy Porter in precise terms which fit his creator as near as dammit:

> He is a disconcerting mixture of sincerity and cheerful malice, of tenderness and freebooting cruelty; restless, importunate, full of pride, a combination which alienates the sensitive and insensitive alike. Blistering honesty, or apparent honesty, like his, makes few friends. To many he may seem sensitive to the point of vulgarity. To others, he is simply a loudmouth. To be as vehement as he is is to be almost non-committal.

Osborne himself was the understudy for Jimmy Porter in the first, never-to-be-forgotten production at the Royal Court in 1956. And he went on rehearsing the part for the rest of his life, enchanting, torturing and eventually freezing out any man, woman or child within range. His obsession with loyalty (to be shown to him, not by him of course), the difficulty of knowing when he was being serious and when he wasn't (he didn't know himself half the time), his mourning for his sweet, hopeless father who died when he was ten – all these things are in the play which he wrote when he was twenty-six.

His grand tirades too commuted easily between the life and the stage. Unfortunately for his nearest and dearest he could only practise with live ammunition. Jimmy's needling of Alison in *Look Back in Anger* as 'the Lady Pusillanimous' is a mild echo of his invective against his first wife Pamela Lane, whom he was just splitting up from: 'That bitch, that pusillanimous, sycophantic, snivelling, phlegmish yokel, that cow – fortunately I've ceased to care what happens to her' – which didn't stop him sleeping with her now and then after he had remarried, nor from supporting her financially for years afterwards.

Even in mid-rant there was a part of him which knew perfectly well how ghastly he was being and which could not help advertising his knowledge with a wicked glee. He left his lover Jocelyn Rickards for Penelope Gilliatt by simply stepping out of the taxi as it stopped at the Chesham Place lights and saying, 'I'm sorry, my darling, I'm going to behave rather badly again.'

The most chilling example is the letter he wrote to his only child, his daughter Nolan (by Penelope Gilliatt) then aged sixteen, casting her out of his home and his life. He never saw her again, cut her out of his *Who's Who* entry and refused to acknowledge her children. Her only offence, as far as one can tell, was to watch *Top of the Pops* and to have a boyfriend. For this he denounced her as 'almost uniquely cold-hearted', 'criminally commonplace', etc. Yet in the middle of this evacuation of senseless bile he cannot resist telling her to look up the first act of *King Lear*: 'How sharper than a serpent's tooth it is to have a thankless child.' He knows perfectly well that he is Lear and she is Cordelia and he wants to tell everyone and take a copy for the record to be deposited with the rest of his papers in the Harry Ransom Center at Austin, Texas.

So Osborne does not exactly keep things to himself. The real Osborne is about as hard to track down as the real M25. In any case, he also published two volumes of autobiography, *A Better Class of Person* and *Almost a Gentleman*. These two caustic and evocative memoirs have recently been reissued by Faber in one volume, under the title *Looking Back: Never Explain, Never Apologise*, and given away at £14.99. When a biographer's subject has already written his own life, an uneasy relationship arises. Naturally the biographer must ceaselessly raid the material, but he has to be wary too, because the horse's mouth represents dangerous competition. So Heilpern, like other biographers in this bind, refers as little as possible to the Osborne self-lives and mentions only fleetingly the stir they made when they came out, provoked mostly by the author's merciless portrait of his mother, Nellie Beatrice, as a feckless, ignorant harridan.

Nor is it as if people who knew him well were puzzled by him. Sir Simon Bland, the retired courtier who lived next door to Osborne in Kent, could see just as well as Harold Pinter that, in Pinter's words, 'the great thing about John Osborne was that he was a piss-taker. He just liked to take the piss out of everybody, including himself.'

But Heilpern insists on constructing a dark psychological narrative, according to which Osborne's early struggles and deprivations created this tempestuous mixture of aggression and depression, of guilt and vainglory. This is only half-convincing. Alec Guinness, for example, had a similar early life: a drunken, raging, ill-educated mother whom he loathed but supported for the rest of her long life, an absent father, education at dim, fee-paying schools paid for by mysterious distant funds, painful early failures as an actor. Yet the adult persona he constructed could not have been more different: bland, exquisitely courteous, totally self-concealing. The only things Guinness had in common with Osborne were his dedication to his art and his generosity with the torrents of cash that came his way.

Readers should be warned too that it is uphill work trekking with Heilpern. He carries out his obsessive quest largely, and in my view fatally, through a series of interviews of the sort he used to do for the *Observer*. So when we come to Osborne's early days on two trade periodicals, *Gas World* and *The Miller*, Heilpern makes us trudge all the way to Toronto to meet Osborne's old editor, Arnold Running, 'still a fine-looking man with his full head of hair and grey beard hinting at the bohemian. He looked alert and welcoming, peering at me with his glasses perched on the end of his nose. His wife Pamela, formerly one of the leading breeders of wire-haired fox terriers in Canada, came bustling into the sitting room with coffee and cakes.'

After a page or two more of this sort of thing, what we learn is that John was a nice young man who had left-wing views and copied words out of dictionaries. Heilpern tells us too that Osborne's early collaborator and landlord Anthony Creighton is 'now 74, tanned from the sun, and dressed informally in a checked shirt, neat corduroys and sturdy walking shoes'. Do we really care how sturdy his walking shoes are or where he gets his tan from? All we wish to know, or all that Heilpern wants us to wish to know, is whether when he and Osborne shared a houseboat their passionate friendship led to sex. Yes, Creighton told the *Evening Standard*. Er no, he now tells Heilpern. My guess would be somewhere in between, but since we already know that Osborne has sex with anything that isn't nailed down, I'm not greatly excited either way. Still, it's more interesting than the wire-haired fox terriers.

But I do wish Heilpern would take a little more trouble. Did Osborne and his first wife rent a room from Creighton at 35 Caithness Road (page 124), or 53 Caithness Road (page 146), or even 14 Caithness Road (*A Better Class of Person*, page 247)? He constantly expresses wonder that Osborne should spend so much time reading 'fat dictionaries' (dictionaries are always 'fat' or 'solid' in this book, just as Belgravia is 'exclusive' and respectability is always 'bourgeois', subjects are 'thorny' and any university you have ever heard of is 'prestigious'). But a little recourse to the dictionary might have helped Heilpern to spell some of the longer words like 'dilettante' and 'philoprogenitive' (the ones that spellcheck doesn't help you with). I suspect that one of Osborne's ancestors was a billiard-marker, not a 'billiard-maker'. The great Education Act was passed in 1944, not 1945. Edwin Landseer (died 1873) is not best described as 'beloved Edwardian portrait artist of stags and pedigree dogs'. Heilpern repeatedly uses 'disinterested' when he means 'uninterested'. Penelope Gilliatt, we are told, 'sends her staff in search of out-of-season quail and spatchcock', as though spatchcock were an esoteric breed of grouse instead of merely a method of cooking the fowl. We are told too that Faith, Osborne's sister who died in infancy, was christened at St Martin-in-the-Fields by 'the Reverend Dick Sheppard, the England star cricketer'. In fact, David Sheppard, the great batsman, later Bishop of Liverpool, was in the womb at the time, so not doing much batting or baptizing yet. Dick Sheppard was famous too but as a preacher and founder of the Peace Pledge Union – a fact not entirely irrelevant, since Osborne grew up to support CND and join the Committee of 100.

Which brings us to Heilpern's supposed great Rosebud discovery: that Faith died of TB not when Osborne was two, as he always believed, but when he was only three months old. According to Heilpern, his recurrent despair can be explained because he was born into a household that was shadowed by intolerable grief. A moment's thought is enough to see that the discovery adds very little to what we already know. If anything, John would have been more, not less conscious of the agony of the bereavement if it had happened when he was two. But whatever the date, the pain of Faith's death would never have left his parents, as Osborne makes clear at the end of the chapter about their marriage in his autobiography.

Heilpern's little errors might be less annoying if the surrounding prose were not so indigestible – like finding withered raisins in a stodgy pudding. He seldom reaches for a metaphor without mixing it. Osborne's treatment of Mary Ure 'unhinged her core of fragility'. Pleasure in silly things is 'the safety-valve of the buttoned-up British'. Adjectives get disastrously transferred from subject to predicate. So Mary Ure 'took the slavish advice of a New York gynaecologist' and 'took solace in her infatuated love affair with Robert Shaw'. Some sentences are so stomach-curdling that you have to stop and take a deep breath before carrying on. Of Osborne's local town in Kent, Heilpern says, 'Ye Olde High Street in Edenbridge still looks as if Miss Marple might suddenly appear bustling along it solving crimes.' As a discriminating stylist, or 'mature wordsmith' as Heilpern puts it, what Osborne would have done with this book does not bear thinking of.

At least Heilpern does give proper room to the epoch-making first night of *Look Back in Anger*, 'the only play in the history of theatre to have a birthday' (the French might argue about the first night of Victor Hugo's *Hernani*, but that just shows the league we are in). When Binkie Beaumont walked out in disgust at the interval, it was a defining moment. But it did not seem like that at the time. Every established theatre manager and agent had rejected the play. The first-night critics mostly found it a putrid and boring production, with the glowing exception of Derek Granger in the *FT* who saw that it was 'arresting, painful and sometimes astonishing'. Only when Kenneth Tynan and Harold Hobson weighed in the following Sunday did the play's reputation really take off. Even then, there had to be an eighteen-minute extract on BBC TV before young people began flocking to the Royal Court.

The term 'Angry Young Man' is attributed here to George Fearon, the English Stage Company's press officer, who told Osborne, 'I suppose you're really an Angry Young Man.' But Heilpern does not give the whole story. The phrase was already in the air after a recent novel of that title by Leslie Paul. And what Fearon went on to say later was, 'We decided then and there that henceforth he was to be known as that.' In other words, it was a marketing ploy, and though Osborne later complained that it had become a millstone round his neck, that did not stop him buying the AYM1 number plate for his first sports car.

Posterity likes to unpeel labels. We are now told how diverse all the supposed Angry Young Men were in reality. Amis for one, Heilpern tells us, 'refused to be buttonholed in their company' (I think he means pigeonholed. Oh God what a book this is). Yet looking back, I can't help thinking that the unleashing of some pent-up rage does seem to be common to that generation. This is how they startle, Osborne and Amis and Larkin and Pinter too: the sudden explosion of anger in polite society, the obscenity in the iambic, the lava spouting out of the dining-room table. The rage is always lurking, rage against the deceitfully bland, the manipulative evasion, against all feeling-suppressants, the rage occasionally over-blowing into sheer flatulence, like that great expulsion of wind, *Damn You, England*, composed beside Tony Richardson's pool in the South of France.

This does not mean that they congregated and drew up mani-festos. Each had his own private kingdom of anger. They no more formed lasting alliances than do extreme nationalist movements in different countries. In that Olympus of Grumpy Old Men, the 1400 Club (reserved for those members of the Garrick Club who cannot abide sitting down to lunch before 2 p.m.), Amis and Osborne refused to address each other directly, and would speak only through third parties.

There is something else they have in common too and Osborne has in abundance, which is an ear for ordinary speech, for its loops and repetitions and jumps and hesitations, its sudden flaring up and dying down again into banal set phrases. In his best four or five plays, *The Entertainer* and *Inadmissible Evidence* especially, there is an almost magical flow to the monologues as well as to the con-versations which manages to be both wholly original and utterly down-to-earth. That is the real break with the theatre of Coward and Fry and even Rattigan. And when Osborne revivals come across as dated, as people now and then complain, it is usually because the actors have forgotten how people talk.

The sad thing is that the gift doesn't last. 'We theatre scribblers average about a dozen years or so,' Osborne said gloomily. 'Nobody ever wrote a great play after the age of 40.' The ear dulls, the suc-cessful playwright floats away from his original material on a tide of champagne and ties up at the port of Thespia, where they speak a different language.

The conventional line is also to chart a falling away from Jimmy Porter in his radical rage inveighing against the church bells to Squire Osborne on his knees in the parish church with a 'Save the Book of Common Prayer' sticker in his back window. Can this be the same person who vehemently refused to be confirmed and was sacked from school for knocking down Mr Heffer the headmaster? Well, yes, it can. Perceptive critics like Harold Hobson (who looks better and better in hindsight) spotted from the start the elegiac note in all Osborne's plays. Even in his early thirties he was singing old music-hall songs with John Betjeman, and, though it is hard to imagine in that sea of booze, when he was married to Penelope Gilliatt, prayers were sometimes said after dinner in Chester Square.

In fact, the only time I clapped eyes on Osborne was in church, at a confirmation service in a dimly lit side chapel in Westminster Abbey, or rather I think it was a combined baptism and confirmation for those who had somehow missed out on the first leg, including John Osborne's much-loved godson, Ben Walden, later a good actor and one of the few people he never quarrelled with. Just before it started, in stalked this tall, reddish-grizzled man in a huge green overcoat with complicated flaps. He looked like an old-style actor-manager who had been transported from some other time, the time of Sir Henry Irving perhaps or even the Crummleses, and had been left stranded by the time machine. He was absurdly stagey, exuded melancholy from every flap, no flincher from the glass or from anything else. He looked magnificent, terrible but magnificent.

PROFESSOR DEREK JACKSON:
OFF THE RADAR

In all the history of second-guessing in warfare, the Window affair is one of the most extraordinary. As early as 1934, Post Office engineers reported that passing aircraft could interfere with radio reception. Less than a year later, Robert Watson-Watt demonstrated by a simple experiment in a field outside Daventry that aircraft could be detected by radio. Radar was born. Remarkably, it was only two years after this that Lindemann demonstrated to Churchill that tinfoil strips cut to a certain length and jettisoned from a height would simulate aircraft on the enemy's radar screen and baffle anti-aircraft batteries. Churchill, always a sucker for gadgets, loved the idea, but the scientists in charge 'looked down their noses at the suggestion', according to Lindemann's protégé R. V. Jones, who had first thought of it. Partly they didn't care to see their amazing discovery so quickly outfoxed, but also they worried what would happen if the Germans got hold of this simple device. For the next five years, no research was done on Window – as the scheme came to be known. So in the first raids of the war British bombers flew over German defences like so many flights of sitting duck.

What none of them then knew was that exactly the same

thought process had occurred in Germany. A technician had suggested silver strips to Göring, who immediately saw the danger to the German defences. All papers relating to the idea were impounded and strict orders issued that it should never be mentioned again. Thus both sides had denied themselves the use of anti-radar for fear of what the other side would make of it. Each preferred to protect its own civilians from being bombed rather than its bomber crews from being shot down.

As late as spring 1942, just before the thousand-bomber raid on Cologne, Window was still being held back until its likely effects had been tested. It was at this moment, with bombers and their crews being destroyed at a horrific rate, that on to the scene charged the exotic figure of Flying Officer Derek Jackson. He had already flown sixty sorties as a navigator with 604 Squadron, resulting in eleven combats, five enemy bombers destroyed, with four more damaged. He was also a lecturer in spectroscopy at Oxford, part-owner of the *News of the World*, a rampant bisexual, partly fascist and wholly outrageous in his views. Jackson was put in charge of the trials – or 'Jackson's Air Farce' as they quickly came to be called.

By chucking handfuls of tinfoil out of the cockpit, he quickly discovered how much was needed to blot out the enemy radar, then, conversely, how an improved radar system could learn to detect the aircraft through the chaff. In the process he was himself shot down by an ill-informed Spitfire. By this stage it was agreed that the dangers of German bombers using Window effectively against Britain were much diminished (most German bombers were now flying against Russia), and even the sceptical Bomber Harris came round. It is estimated that Window saved about a hundred British aircraft in its first week of operation. Air Marshal Portal calculated that it might have saved the lives of the crews of 250 bombers had it been introduced four months earlier.

This was by no means the end of Jackson's wartime

achievements. Before D–Day he devised a new type of Window strip to persuade the German radar operators that two 'invasion fleets' were approaching the French coast some distance to the east of the actual Normandy landing. And he found in a captured Junkers 88 a detector, known to the Luftwaffe as Flensburg, which he discovered to his horror was superbly effective in locking on to Monica, the tail-warning radar issued to Bomber Command. As well as alerting British bombers to impending attack from the rear, Monica also allowed the enemy fighter to zero in. Jackson carried out a mass trial himself, flying the Junkers in pursuit of a gaggle of seventy-one Lancaster bombers and homing in without difficulty on each of them. That was the end of Monica. Harris had her removed and more pilots lived a little longer.

There was a glorious impatience about Jackson at war which, combined with a meticulous capacity for research, enabled him to get his own way. I like to think of him whirling around the English skies, homing on to Lancaster after Lancaster, chattering away over the intercom, often in German as he liked to in the air, proving to his satisfaction that these people were suicidal idiots to fasten these pieces of kit to their rear ends. In the officers' mess he was a loud and flamboyant figure, waddling in with his splay-footed gait, still carrying his parachute, to make the next move in the chess game he had started before being scrambled. When the news of his Distinguished Flying Cross for 'devotion to duty' was announced in the evening news bulletin, Jackson was heard bellowing from the bar in his strange, gravelly voice: 'Devotion to duty? What about bwavewy?'

His rumbustious arrogance was intolerable, unstoppable and, in war at least, indispensable. He was bred to it. His father, Sir Charles Jackson, was a Monmouthshire architect-developer, lawyer and politician who, among other things, built up a large collection of silver which virtually *is* the National Museum of Wales's collection and bought shares in a then obscure Sunday newspaper called the

News of the World, of which he became chairman. He did not put this fact in his *Who's Who* entry. As sales rose from 40,000 to 4.4 million in 1941, the 25 per cent shareholding Derek and his identical twin brother, Vivian, inherited in the paper – the *Flesh and the Devil*, as it was known before a rougher age called it the *News of the Screws* – became so hugely valuable that when Attlee put the supertax rate up to 19s 6d in the pound, Derek fled the UK never to return. In Ireland, where he took refuge first, the *News of the World* was banned, and to keep an eye on his investment he had it sent to him under plain wrapper.

He and Vivian had little contact with their elderly, distant parents. Their only deep emotional engagement was with each other. Both of them went for anything that moved, of either sex. 'I ride under both rules,' Derek said, referring to the different codes for flat racing and jumping. The twins argued – and agreed – about everything. Vivian too was a brilliant physicist. Wherever they went, from schooldays on, they bought the finest spectroscopes and interferometers, sometimes equipping entire laboratories when university funds were short. Vivian was killed in a sleighing accident in the winter of 1936, and Derek was never quite the same again, never able to achieve real intimacy with anyone, except dogs and horses. His long-term collaborator at the Clarendon Laboratory, the German refugee physicist H. G. Kuhn, summed him up perfectly: 'Jackson's strong feeling of independence had been enhanced during his upbringing by the sense of power that money gives, and even in his development as a physicist he was largely self-taught: he had never done any research under or with anyone and probably had hardly ever been contradicted by anyone of his age.' Yet Kuhn found him courteous and considerate and never discovered any inclination to fascism in him.

In *As I Was Going to St Ives*, his deliciously slim life of Jackson, Simon Courtauld tells the story of a remarkable human being – well, remarkable being. Even Diana Mosley, Jackson's best friend, had to concede that he wasn't quite human, and it takes one to know one. Courtauld provides as lucid an account of his work as the layman could hope for, and it would be hard to improve on his laconic, inconspicuously ironic treatment of Jackson's seven marriages (six and a half to be strictly accurate), which are responsible for the book's silly title. To call his carry-on goat-like would be grossly unfair to goats, who seem celibate, faithful and even-tempered by comparison. He married Augustus John's daughter Poppet first, then Pamela Mitford, then the femme fatale Janetta Woolley, one of whose previous husbands was Robert Kee. On the day Janetta gave birth to Rose, his only child by any of his wives, he ran off with her half-sister Angela. When he dumped Angela three years later, he did so over lunch in the same restaurant in which he had persuaded her to leave her husband. Maybe goats are more sensitive, too.

When he began his affair with Janetta, he told her that the last person he had slept with was Francis Bacon – this, Courtauld hazards, on the night he gave Bacon and Anne Dunn dinner at Claridge's before they all went to bed together. He also gave them £100 each, a lot of money in 1950. Only a few months after Princess Ratibor became his fifth wife, he complained to her cousin, the actor Peter Eyre, that she could be ratty and was frequently boring. Then he made a pass at Eyre. He took on tougher opposition with Number Six, the ferocious minx Barbara Skelton, part-original of the lethal Pamela Flitton in *A Dance to the Music of Time*. She had already scored with a whole bestiary of sacred monsters. Jackson would boast that 'after King Farouk, Cyril Connolly and George Weidenfeld, I was the pretty one.' Skelton, like many of his wives and lovers and Jackson himself (his brother Vivian too), was besotted with animals. She was particularly in love with her coati, a raccoon-like creature which she used as a weapon in her fights with Jackson in the Ritz, thrusting its wicked snout into his face, urging it to bite chunks out of his lip. When Janetta said the animal should be put down, she retorted, as animal fanatics do, that people who talk of putting animals down ought to be put down themselves.

Jackson loved horses as much as he loved dogs, indeed he was known to his friends as Horse. He went on competing in steeplechases until his sixtieth year, riding with short stirrups like a monkey on a stick. He took part in the Grand National three times. My father rode in many chases alongside him, both of them often on horses trained by Captain Bay Powell. He admired Derek's dash rather than his elegance, in and out of the saddle.

For us children dragged along in his wake, Derek was not so easy. Like Rose and his transient stepchildren, I found him an unnerving presence. He would set out to be genial and interested, perhaps thrust a fiver in your hand – he was always generous with his cash, not least to his ex-wives, though perhaps not as generous as the divorce courts today would have forced him to be – but his glittering eye, his hurried, overbearing manner of speech, his South Walian swagger betrayed such a volcanic impatience that it was impossible for you to be any more comfortable in his company than he was in yours. He had a wearisome itch to get a rise out of everyone, to upset or unnerve or frighten, especially while driving his Bentley or Mercedes, racing up to level crossings as the gates were closing, putting his foot down on narrow Irish roads until the needle crept up to ninety, and Janetta could not help crying out: 'No, Derek, please, not so fast.'

He did not want children of his own – too much competition. The same could be said about his loathing of God, 'that grey-bearded monster'. His dislike of organized religion was so strong that he could not even bear to take an apartment which had a view of Notre Dame. He detested Bach and Mozart because they wrote 'church music', but adored Wagner. All this arose partly from his desire to shock. He asked Oswald Mosley, in the presence of two devout Spanish Catholics: 'Do you think Christ was a bugger?' He adored Mosley, perhaps even more so after Mosley had been disgraced and they were both living in exile in Paris. Jackson would always greet him with a kiss on both cheeks, followed by a sharp pinch on the bottom, a feat not easily achieved, since Mosley was about a foot taller; and one not much welcomed by the Leader, who was accustomed to do the bottom-pinching himself.

Courtauld pitilessly records all the fascist spoutings with which Jackson liked to annoy people, his habit, even after the war, of singing the 'Horst Wessel Lied' in Austrian hostelries and referring to Hitler as The Great Man. He records too, without overmuch comment, the view of Jackson's friends that this was 50 per cent teasing. That may be more or less true without constituting a valid excuse. In his milieu, such things could be said only in a teasing way. What strikes one, on the contrary, is that Jackson had a pretty complete fascist mindset, with the possible exception of anti-Semitism, which didn't interest him.

He was possessed by a fear and loathing of socialism. He was contemptuous of the lower orders who read the *News of the World* and paid for his racehorses and his wives, and he liked to bellow out Gilbert and Sullivan's 'Bow, bow, ye lower middle classes, bow, bow, ye tradesmen, bow, ye masses'. His visceral love of Germany was trumped only by his fierce patriotism. Typically fascist too were his intoxication with speed and danger and his dislike of the milksop *Sklavenmoral* of Christianity. At the same time, as fascists often are, he was superstitious, would not walk under ladders or work on a Friday if it happened to be the 13th. The worst event of his life – Vivian's death in the snow – had been foretold by a fortune-teller in a nightclub.

Nor was the greatest obsession of his life, nuclear physics, incompatible with the fascist cast of mind. Since scientists are more inclined to veer to the extreme left, lured by the scientific pretensions of Marxism, it is often forgotten that fascists too worshipped science as something true and hard and modern. In a hazy light, therefore, one might identify Derek Jackson with the Übermensch, or on a lower plane with Zouch, the Superman who takes up fox-hunting in Anthony Powell's *From a View to a Death*.

No journalist would be able to resist describing Jackson as 'a colourful personality'. Yet in a curious way he seemed almost colourless, evanescent. It is an inspired touch of Courtauld's to choose as his epigraph the anecdote of Derek at a nuclear-physics conference in Rome in the 1970s strolling with a young English delegate who tells him that there's an extraordinary man at the conference, a brilliant physicist who had an outstanding war in the RAF and rode three times in the Grand National, and was fabulously wealthy and had been married six times. Jackson: 'I think I ought to tell you, before you go any further, that I'm the man in question.' 'Oh, really?' the young man says. 'I'm sorry, but we haven't been introduced.' 'I'm Derek Jackson.' Young man (after a pause): 'No, that wasn't the name.'

What remains fascinating is the contrast between Jackson's brusque impatience and infidelity when in the beau monde and his dedicated, courteous, endlessly patient behaviour in the laboratory. His first seminal paper for the Royal Society, on 'hyperfine structure in the arc spectrum of caesium and nuclear rotation', was published in 1928 when he was twenty-two. Fifty years later, according to Heini Kuhn, he was still poring over spectral lines on his old microscope, 'measuring their spacings as accurately as – or even more accurately than – anyone else could have done'. The photoelectric scanner (like the MRI scanner, the indirect result of his researches) would have supplied him with digitized results in half the time, but Jackson would not have enjoyed it so much: 'The continuing challenge of skill and judgment would have gone.'

I cannot help thinking of Darwin in his last years on his hands and knees measuring the worms whose habits he had first studied thirty years earlier, insisting on the same old instruments and refusing to buy state-of-the-art kit. Darwin was a devoted paterfamilias who strove to avoid giving offence to the Christian religion. Jackson could hardly have been more different, except in his dedication to his art. After a tour of German radar installations in the Baltic at the end of the war, he infuriated an air marshal when asked to describe a piece of equipment by saying 'it was so pretty that I wanted to stroke it.' Nothing else in the world would he have stroked with such genuine love.

GERMAINE GREER: STILL STRAPPED IN THE CUIRASS

'She's back and she's angry' – thus the *Daily Telegraph* puffed its extracts from Germaine Greer's new book. Can one imagine houseroom being given in such a quarter to a serious enemy of comfortable society – Marx or Foucault, say? This kind of mock-alarming reception is normally reserved to drum up custom for an aging boxer or tennis star whose legs have gone but who can still gouge an ear or terrorize an umpire. Despite her best efforts, Professor Greer has always been held in some affection by those whose certainties she purported to undermine. In my experience, middle-aged tycoons are particularly responsive to her charms, much in the same way that Masters of Foxhounds often have a penchant for the ballet. For a British audience, being Australian helps in this respect. We find it difficult to take umbrage at the foulest language if hurled at us in a North Queensland accent, let alone shrilled in Germaine's pleasant Melburnian mezzo. Greer also lays about her so vigorously, belabouring weak sisters and feminist backsliders with as much vim as she belabours brutal and cloddish men, so that no one group of her victims can feel unfairly singled out.

The Whole Woman is no exception to her usual practice, and it follows naturally at another decade-and-a-half interval from her earlier works, *The Female Eunuch* (1970) and *Sex and Destiny* (1984), to form a remarkable trilogy. Those who aspire to chart an alteration, even a repentance in her, are, I think, picking and choosing from her work, taking discourse A from one book and contrasting it with discourse B from another, when in fact A and B are to be found, perhaps in varying dosages, in most of what she writes. No pentita she, except in her willingness to denounce her former comrades. If we are honest, what many of us remember best about *The Female Eunuch* is that soft cuirass on the dust jacket, representing the burden of femininity strapped on woman by oppressive man. This prosthetic device has a brilliant ambiguity: who exactly designed it? Can you put it on yourself? What are we to imagine lying under it? Another woman-shaped body with all its attendant inconveniences and miseries? Or some untrammelled physique, simultaneously angelic and feisty, which is equipped to enjoy life at its richest – children, sex, art, sun-dried tomatoes – without any of the old inconveniences?

Sometimes Greer embraces the warm, smelly, blood-soaked physical destiny of being a woman. Sometimes she dreams of women escaping from their fleshly burdens and living in sisterly bliss with their children. In *The Female Eunuch*, for example, she imagines communes where children are free to choose their parents, while grown-ups stroll from one weightless love to the next. All her major books (*Sex and Destiny* much less so, being the least showy, least remembered and, I think, best of the three) are peppered with these inconstancies. But that is part of their appeal, their vivacity. And inconsistency is not the kind of accusation likely to slow the author down. As Walt Whitman pointed out, that's the only way to sing the *Song of Myself*: 'Do I contradict myself? / Very well then I contradict myself / (I am large, I contain multitudes)'.

The Whole Woman is made up of four sections – Body, Mind, Love, Power – each divided into half-a-dozen 'chapterkins'

averaging ten pages each and devoted to specific topics, such as
'breasts', 'shopping', 'sorrow', 'wives' and 'emasculation'. It has
not, I think, been much noticed that *The Female Eunuch* follows
exactly the same pattern, uses several of the same headings and,
alas, quite a few of the same arguments. Still, every page she
writes is never less than readable and sometimes fizzes with sar-
donic aperçus, but taken as a whole this method doesn't work too
well. The array of topics is so overwhelming and the chapters are
so short and packed with statistics and chunks from teen zines,
interspersed with boxed quotes from feminists, most of whom are
a good deal wilder or sillier than Dr Greer, that the total effect is
filling but curiously unsatisfying, like a meal in a Chinese restau-
rant. Arguments are pursued with great ferocity, then undercut
or dropped.

This choppiness also prevents any coherent historical analysis
of what has happened to women, let alone to men, over the past
thirty years. There is a curious reluctance to mention the most
obvious landmarks since 1969 – the advent of women priests,
the appearance of women prime ministers all over the place
(Margaret Thatcher is mentioned only as the victim of a 'sexist'
putsch – after eleven years in power, surely a rather slow-burning
sort of sexism). In some cases, Greer actively refuses to take note
of change in the real world, continuing to assert, for example,
that newspapers are all run by older men, when in fact Rosie
Boycott, among other things, has edited the *Independent*, the *Inde-
pendent on Sunday* and the *Daily Express*, and tabloids have been
edited by women, not to mention the phalanx of younger female
deputy editors on the broadsheets. The truth is that achieving too
much reform is bad for business. For rage and indignation must
be maintained at boiling point. Greer has a reputation to keep
up. The victims' club accepts only life members. It is hard not to
feel that she is a victim herself, a victim of success, and that her
supple mind has been prostituted to the need to keep her audience
whooping.

More damaging still, we are left with the impression that the 'women's movement' or the 'feminist revolution' started more or less from scratch in 1969. There is no mention of Simone de Beauvoir, let alone of the suffragettes or Marie Stopes. This short perspective is no accident, since to refer back to that earlier movement would be to recall a struggle which really did have implacable declared enemies. The eerie thing about the post-sixties feminism is that it has had few proper opponents willing to show themselves. The gates of each decayed Bastille turned on their rusty hinges – the colleges of Oxford and Cambridge, the Stock Exchange, the Jockey Club – to reveal only a handful of frightened middle-aged men falling over themselves to show their new colleagues around.

The only serious fight that could be picked – and Greer is nothing if not a scrapper – was within the sisterhood, with men as bemused bystanders. This ideological equivalent of female mud wrestling (an analogy Greer herself uses in *The Whole Woman*) was not exactly new. Its terms of engagement had changed little since the days of the New Woman and Mrs Humphry Ward. In the red corner, there was the insistent and uncompromising quest for equality between the sexes always and everywhere. In the blue corner, there was the claim that women were deeper, more creative, closer to the mysteries of life, in harmony with the moon and the tides, singled out not by a curse but by a wise wound, white witches, goddesses. These two driving principles, one of absolute sameness, the other of profound difference, do not have to be driven very far before they come into conflict. Nor is either of them entirely unfamiliar or even uncongenial to some of the male bystanders: gender equality has been part of the egalitarian ideal from 1789 onwards, and it has been a central theme among authors from Goethe to Graves, men who would no more have dreamed of joining the women's movement than of taking up ice hockey, that only *das ewig weibliche* can revivify the poor dried-up male and reconnect men to the roots of being.

Greer herself wobbles a bit here. Now and then, she rehearses the standard line that there is a natural condition of 'femaleness' which has been overlaid by a false and oppressive social construct of 'femininity' (the same for men, of course, except that both the natural condition and the social construct seem to be pernicious). But as the book goes on, femaleness seems to envelop almost everything, leaving only flirting and a taste for frilly underwear as the affectations of femininity. Women, it seems, by nature love more passionately, bear pain more uncomplainingly, work harder, are averse to violence, are endlessly forgiving. Towards the end, even conventional feminist assertions about the ill effects of gendered upbringing – boys are demand-fed, potty-trained later – give way to a resigned admission that 'no matter how gender-free their upbringing, children will invent gender for themselves'.

Greer frequently sneers at the sort of 'feminists everyone can like' who are content to work for mere equality. Women, she says, should not waste their lives trying to imitate men and clawing their way into those oppressive male hierarchies, such as Parliament or the armed forces. Yet, of course, a good deal of what she demands depends on just those dowdy campaigners for equality in pay, in political representation, in access to the professions and so on. If they expect any gratitude from Dr Greer, they can forget it. Some of these campaigners happen to be men. If they expect any recognition of this fact, they can forget that too. She can write acutely and touchingly, and does so here now and then, about motherhood and children, for example, or in her chapterkin on the necessary place of sorrow in life. But even there she feels duty-bound to go over the top: every woman has to learn that men will never admit her to true comradeship, we are living 'in a poisoned world that becomes crueller and more unjust every day', in which 'there is no longer any free space where individuals might develop alternative cultural and social systems'.

Turn over to the next chapterkins, of course, and you will find little parenthetical admissions that, on the contrary, women's lives are better, if more challenging now, 'the forces of darkness having been by and large routed', that women are carving out free spaces for themselves and that quite a lot of machinery to remedy discrimination against women is now in operation – although naturally she has to complain that it is warped and inadequate. But these qualifying asides are brief, and the diatribe quickly picks up steam again.

The chapterkin on daughters is almost entirely taken up with the subject of father–daughter incest. 'These behaviours', we are told, 'are less aberrant than normal. They may be outlandish, but they are manifestations of the governing principle that runs the everyday.' The only fathers who have not yet got around to doing a bit of manifesting are, it seems, those who have already deserted the nest to avoid their obligations – or those who are too busy beating up their wives. The chapter on fathers is entirely composed of horror stories about violence and delinquency. Not that staying home to help raise the kids will earn you any remission of guilt. You will merely be perpetuating the oppression of women and adding to the laundry bills. Perhaps Greer's fiercest condemnation – fiercer even than her fury against cosmetic surgeons and the 'fertility moguls' – is reserved for housework in general and the washing machine in particular. Far from these domestic appliances being a boon to the 'housewife' – 'an expression that should be considered as shocking as "yard nigger"' – they have made cleaning more time-consuming than ever. Yes, and switching on the heating is so much more exhausting than chopping firewood.

The Whole Woman shares with other great dogmatic texts – Marx, Freud, Foucault – the quality of being irrefutable. Any instances that might on the surface seem to weaken or contradict the teachings of liberation feminism can be shown in reality to reinforce them. You might think, for example, that because female genital mutilation is now condemned as a violation of human rights by every international organization, while male genital mutilation is ignored, women for once were better off. Not a bit of it. The campaign against female circumcision merely shows Western man's determination to impose control on women in the Third

World. Again, the obsessive determination to improve screening for cervical cancer, while prostate cancer is neglected, is not a sign that we care more about women's health but rather one more example of the determination of men to control the sexuality of women. Nor should you imagine that male doctors are attempting to bring joy to childless women by inventing new fertility treatments. On the contrary, 'fertility treatment causes far more suffering than it does joy', and the 'fertility magnates' are simply exploiting women for their own gain and glory.

I would not advise any male suffering from our sex's deplorable excess of testosterone to retort that women continue to live on average five years longer than men, that five times as many young men as women commit suicide, that men are twice as likely to be unemployed and find it twice as hard to get another job, that men are infinitely more likely to suffer industrial accidents and diseases which may destroy their lives. None of these apparent disadvantages begins to compare with the misery – Greer's favourite word – daily endured by women, and in any case men deserve it. Men can't win and shouldn't. Who needs them anyway? Greer entertains a suspicion that 'if heterosexuality is not in future to be buttressed by law and religion and family pressure, it will collapse'. Not that Greer cares that much for gays; to her they look just as violent as and rather more promiscuous than other men. She is not even very enthusiastic about lesbians, and she is positively contemptuous of transsexuals' blundering efforts to deny their biological nature.

But there remains, of course, one small problem in a world where men are properly marginalized and left to stew in the pub and the locker room. How are children to be brought up? Even after we have consigned to history's dustbin 'the ghastly figure of the Bride', there remains the awkward fact that, in her words, 'A woman without a partner and with children is usually a woman in trouble.' Greer, in a significant shift, concedes that 'In *The Female Eunuch* I argued that motherhood should not be treated as a substitute career; now I would argue that motherhood should be regarded as a genuine career option.' And now that they have this licence to breed professionally, women should be paid enough to raise a child in decent circumstances.

But who is to pay them? Who is to be the 'partner'? Not, of course, a man, though every social statistic screams that a child brought up by two parents does better in life. Not the extended sisterhood of traditional society, the loss of which she mourns now as in 1969. Sisters may provide a network of comfort and support, but they cannot be expected to win the bread. Naturally the answer is the age-old one of all utopians: the state must be the new father. The state doesn't snore or get drunk, the state doesn't beat you up or waste its weekend gawping at muddied oafs or torturing fish, the state doesn't call out 'nice tits' as you walk past and it never says 'how like a woman'. And if it seems a touch paradoxical that a movement that yearns for total liberation from oppression and commitment should end up by shackling itself to the railings of Whitehall, that would not be the first time this has happened. Egotism has a habit of drifting into statism. That is why egotism is not enough, as I am sure Nurse Cavell would have said if she had survived to see the women's movement in full flow.   Everything that Greer argues – and in places she argues so magnificently, with such wit and zap – leads, it seems to me, to precisely the opposite of the conclusion that she sets out to draw.

Ghastly as men are – in fact, precisely because they are so ghastly – the only hope of even half-civilizing them, and their male children, must lie in some social institution, some pattern of shared obligations, which looks remarkably like old-fashioned marriage, looser, more equal, purged of its grosser patriarchal aspects but nonetheless recognizably marriage. Many marriages are unhappy and most marriages have their unhappy patches, but Greer's insistence that, at the deepest level, women today are no happier than they were thirty years ago does not suggest that she has found a better option.

EARLY MODERNS

Historians today attach a lot of importance to what they call the Early Modern Period. For such a supposedly significant period, the suggested dates wobble alarmingly: did it start in 1300, or about 1560, and when did it end – with the Restoration in 1660 or the Great Reform Bill in 1832? In any case, this seems to me a twisted, self-regarding way of looking at the past, not for its own sake and on its own terms, but as a clumsy prelude to modernity, by which of course we mean Us.

I use the phrase here with a quite different purpose: to cover writers who lived through a brief and fairly precise historical moment, from 1890 to 1930. And I do so, not to mark out the march of progress but rather to identify a period of great apprehension and ambiguity, in which fear throbbed as hard as hope.

There was plenty of hope all right. As the *Guardian*'s man in Moscow, Arthur Ransome, observing the Russian Revolution at the closest possible quarters, was filled with joy to have shared in this 'wonderful experience' and to have had the privilege of knowing Lenin, who was 'like a lighthouse shining through fog'. John Maynard Keynes prophesied that the future would see 'the euthanasia of the rentier' and that under the new state capitalism (he envisaged something rather like China today) all the economic problems would be solved and human beings would scarcely need to work at all, at most three hours a day. 'The spontaneous, joyful attitude now confined to artists and free spirits' would be 'diffused throughout society as a whole'. The world would become one glorious giant Bloomsbury.

There were more modest, and as it turned out, more realistic hopes voiced too: E. M. Forster's quiet insistence that human beings should treat each other with a certain minimum decency; Virginia Woolf's hopes for the equality of women, so robustly, yet good-humouredly argued in those essays which I think are the best part of her.

But there was fear out there too, a dread all the more unnerving and disabling because it was often impalpable: that the world was on the edge of irreversible, uncontrollable change, and not change for the better; that, after a century of peace in Europe, we were on the brink of a terrible war (this fear had been expressed as far back as the 1870s); that the British Empire was liable to collapse, or, perhaps worse still, to a fatal moral degeneration (for all his cocky character, never was there a more worried imperialist than Rudyard Kipling); that the last enchantments, the last whispers of the divine were fading from a coarse, materialist universe, desperate intimations expressed in different ways by Arthur Machen, M. R. James and George Gissing.

It is this intense sensitivity to the fragility of the world around them, this agonized and accelerating fear that the old certainties were crumbling, that marks out the Early Moderns. I can't think of another period quite like it, except perhaps the years of the English Civil War.

RUDYARD KIPLING:
THE SENSITIVE BOUNDER

He was a noisy boy from the start. At the age of two, he was taken out for walks in order not to disturb his ailing grandfather and he would march down the main street of Bewdley shouting, 'Ruddy is coming!' Or sometimes, 'An angry Ruddy is coming!' Despite these precautions, his grandfather died and Kipling's aunts and uncles believed that Ruddy's tantrums had hastened and embittered his end. When he left the United Services College at Westward Ho! and returned to India, he quickly gained a reputation in the Punjab Club for boorish and bumptious behaviour. A visiting colonel wanted to thrash him for making disparaging remarks about the Indian Civil Service; two lawyers were so annoyed by his persistent interruptions that they kicked him down the club's front steps. He didn't mind who he was rude to or about, from the Viceroy and the C-in-C to the smartest ladies of Simla and South Kensington. When Mrs Macmillan, wife of the publisher, told him that India was now fit to govern itself, he told her that she was suffering from hysteria because 'you haven't got enough to divert your mind'. Literary curmudgeons of our day – Sir V. S. Naipaul, Sir Kingsley Amis – seem models of tact and discretion by comparison. Every brigadier and boxwallah from Bombay to Calcutta would have agreed with Max Beerbohm that 'the schoolboy, the bounder and the brute – these three types have surely never found a more brilliant expression of themselves than in Rudyard Kipling.'

Few of Beerbohm's drawings have skewered their victim more memorably than the one captioned 'Mr Rudyard Kipling takes a bloomin' day aht, on the blasted 'eath, along with Britannia, 'is gurl'. Britannia has swapped her helmet for Ruddy's bowler, while the beetle-browed Nobel laureate in a vulgar check suit is tootling through his moustache on a penny trumpet. Yet for all his cruel cartoons and parodies, Max felt compelled to admit, sotto voce, that Kipling was 'a very great genius', though one who was not living up to the possibilities of his genius. Henry James instantly identified Kipling as 'the most complete man of genius' he had ever known. But he too couldn't stand the public poetry, 'all steam and patriotism'. And he implored Kipling to chuck public affairs, which are an ignoble scene, and stick to your canvas and your paintbox. There is the truth. The rest is humbug. Ask the Lama.

Why couldn't Kipling follow the Tibetan Buddhist Lama into a life of contemplation in the Himalayas, as Kim does at the end of that remarkable novel (or whatever you want to call it, because it isn't like any other novel ever written)?

At times, you feel that in *Kipling Sahib* Charles Allen too shares this impatience with his noisy, ink-spattered hero. Why didn't Kipling follow the intuitive, Indian side of his head? Why did he moulder down in that gloomy house in Sussex with a wife nobody liked, churning out patriotic verse for a public that had become disenchanted with such stuff? Allen has written copiously on India, Kipling and the Raj in various combinations, but of all his books this account of Kipling's Indian years is the one he felt destined to write. Like Kipling, he himself is a child of the Raj, or rather an orphan of it, cast out of Paradise at an early age and seemingly abandoned by his parents in an alien land among unknown people. The young Kipling worked for Allen's great-grandfather's

newspaper, the *Civil and Military Gazette*, in Lahore, in which
many of Kipling's first and finest stories appeared. In the dining
room of the Allen grandparents' home in East Sussex, there hung
two of the ten plaster plaques made by John Lockwood Kipling to
illustrate the first edition of *Kim*, those odd muddy images which,
like everything to do with Kipling, have a tang which is quite
unlike anything to do with anyone else. Who else ever thought
of asking his father to illustrate his novel with photographs of
plaster plaques?

With delicious detail and an unfailing command of his mate-
rial, Allen recounts these brief, intense years which make up the
total of Kipling's experience of India – the five years of infancy at
Bombay (even those broken by the trip to England for the birth
of his sister, Trix), then the 'seven years hard', as he called them,
up to the age of twenty-four sweating on local newspapers in
Lahore and Allahabad, then a couple of years later when he was
already famous, a brief final visit to Lahore. He said goodbye to
his ayah, and never saw India again. By the time he finished *Kim*,
he had exhausted his reservoirs of experience. As Allen says, he
was pretty much written out at thirty-five. 'The craftsmanship
stayed with him for the rest of his life.' As T. S. Eliot wrote,
'There is hardly any poem in which Kipling fails to do what he
has set out to do.' But Allen is surely right in discerning that the
spark of genius that gave his writing its sharp, dangerous crackle
was almost gone, along with the desire to jolt that had made the
best of his early work so electrifying to his Victorian readership.

In fact, Allen seems now and then a little doubtful about the
value even of that early work. It is not simply the imperial atti-
tudes that seem out of date; for him the freshness of Kipling's
literary techniques has faded too: 'The shock-value of "Danny
Deever", "Tommy" and the best of the *Barrack-Room Ballads* has
faded over the years – and the rest have not aged well. "Man-
dalay" sounds almost maudlin. Kipling's cockneyfication seems
contrived.'

This isn't how I feel at all. I still shiver when the ballad of 'Danny Deever' turns nasty. And I am still stirred by the old Moulmein Pagoda lookin' lazy at the sea. All those dropped hs and gs are indeed a contrivance, but a magnificent in-your-face contrivance, a rubbing-it-in way of making palpable the soldiers and engineers who built the Empire and who for Kipling are not only as good as Gunga Din (and vice versa) but as good as the Colonel's Lady. What other writer has had Kipling's ingrained democratic curiosity? In those seven years as a young reporter in India, he was everywhere, annoying the officers' mess, pumping the sergeants and privates for their experiences on the North West Frontier, prowling the alleys and brothels and opium dens of Lahore all through the night. He was always scrounging for copy, picking up the jargon of engineers and jockeys and bureaucrats, so that they began to think he must have spent time in their trade instead of just being an inky magpie. At the same time, he was an intensely literary writer who mastered every metre from the music-hall ballad to the sestina. He might not have gone to university, but at Westward Ho! he read everything from Dryden and Donne to Pushkin and Oscar Wilde.

As for the early short stories, there is nothing like them in English – you would need to go to Maupassant or Lermontov to find any competition. But even the foreign masters don't change mood with such an audacious flip as Kipling does. At one moment you are reading a light anecdote full of the persiflage that was later to be done so delightfully by Saki and Wodehouse, and then suddenly the characters are plunged into bewilderment and disaster. Within a short space – most of the stories in *Plain Tales from the Hills* and *Wee Willie Winkie* are only 2000–3000 words long, to fit a 'turnover' in the *Civil and Military Gazette* – their whole lives are weighed and, well, not always found wanting. Kipling can be charitable as well as pitiless. In 'False Dawn', the characters set out for a moonlight riding picnic by an old tomb in the desperate heat. Saumarez, an arrogant civil servant, resolves to propose to the elder Miss Copleigh in the romantic atmosphere, but a terrible duststorm gets up and in the confusion he proposes to the wrong sister. That is all there is to it, a story Kipling probably picked up in some out-of-the-way station. Yet 'False Dawn' leaves you sweating and the throat parched as if the sand had blown up off the page.

Kim itself switches mood and theme to and fro as casually as *Don Quixote*, which Kipling took as his model. At one moment it is a spy story, at another a spiritual adventure or a travelogue or the story of an abandoned child. Some people have found it hard to get on with, as I did when I first tried it in my teens. I returned to it about ten years ago and was transported. To this day it is the English novel that Indian writers most often mention with gratitude and affection.

That intensity, that miraculous compression which marks his best work did not come cheap. Under his rowdy front, he had always been abnormally sensitive and inclined to melancholy, and even as an adult was fearful of the dark and hated to be alone at night. Like all the great books for children (like the great books for adults too) the Jungle books are full of the smell of fear:

> Ere Mor the Peacock flutters, ere the Monkey People cry,
> Ere Chil the Kite sweeps down a furlong sheer,
> Through the Jungle very softly flits a shadow and a sigh –
> He is Fear, O Little Hunter, he is Fear.

When Kipling was decanted upon strange foster parents in Southsea, the 'House of Desolation' as he called it, he began to have hallucinations and contracted neurotic habits, hitting out at trees as if they were threatening him and running across the room to check that the walls were real. When he went to stay with his Baldwin cousins after five years of maltreatment by 'the Woman', as he called her, his cousin Stanley, the future prime minister, said that he was 'half blind and crazed to the point of suffering delusions'. Now and then biographers have tried to minimize the ordeal he and his sister Trix suffered when abandoned by their parents to the harsh mercies of Mrs Holloway. It has been suggested, for example, that Kipling might have borrowed from *David Copperfield* the story of being paraded through the streets of Southsea with a placard on his back saying LIAR, but Trix confirms the story, and in any case Mrs Holloway might herself have borrowed the idea.

It does not seem so odd to Allen that Alice and Lockwood Kipling should have abandoned their children to two total strangers for more than five years. The same thing happened to Allen himself and thousands of other children of the Raj. Yet I think he rather skates over the behaviour of Alice, the prime mover. She had, after all, plenty of sisters in England whose homes could have offered Ruddy a warmer lodging, especially the Burne-Joneses and the Baldwins, of whom he was so fond. All Allen can report is that there were 'complications' which led her to answer the Holloways' newspaper advertisement. Perhaps she was ashamed of having to ask for her sisters' charity. It has to be said that Alice sounds an unappealing character, more interested in making a good impression on the Viceroy with her caustic wit.

The remarks of hers about Ruddy which Allen quotes sound patronizing rather than supportive. To the headmaster at Westward Ho!: 'The lad has a great deal that is feminine in his nature and a little sympathy – from any quarter – will reconcile him to his changed life more than anything.' She felt compelled to apologize to the departing Viceroy, Lord Dufferin, for Ruddy's poem 'One Viceroy Resigns', which purported to be His Excellency's late-night reverie: 'I and my husband have been grieved to note from time to time offences which no cleverness, not even genius can excuse. His youth and inexperience in the world in which he does not live are I feel sure the explanation.'

As for his abilities as a storyteller, Alice told her son, 'you know you couldn't make a plot to save your life'. All in all, Alice strikes me as a social-climbing bitch. And despite his protestations of devotion to 'the Family Square', I think it is of his mother that Kipling is thinking when he writes in the last paragraph of his story 'Baa Baa, Black Sheep', which describes his and Trix's life in the House of Desolation: 'When young lips have drunk deep of the bitter waters of Hate, Suspicion and Despair, all the Love in the world will not wholly take away that knowledge.'

By contrast, Carrie Kipling has had a bad press, which I don't think she deserves. Only Adam Nicolson's little book about her, *The Hated Wife*, makes some amends and shows how she carried Kipling through and what a lot she had to put up with. Most biographers have preferred to ignore Carrie as far as possible and instead sought to ferret out a homosexual or at least homoerotic streak in Kipling, especially in his relationship with Carrie's brother Wolcott Balestier: the principal evidence being the brutal speed of Ruddy and Carrie's marriage after Wolcott's death, and the fact that he changed 'Dear Lad' to 'Dear Lass' in his poem 'The Long Trail'. The latter strikes me as no more than the artist's economy of effort shown by Elton John in substituting 'England's Rose' for 'Norma Jean'. The wedding was indeed a weird and brisk affair. According to Edmund Gosse, one of the four men who attended the ceremony at All Souls, Langham Place (Alice and Trix were both down with the flu), it was as if Ruddy had been hurried into matrimony, like a rabbit into its hole. 'At 2.8 the cortège entered the church and at 2.20 left it. Both bride-groom and bride are possessed by a very devil of secrecy.' Henry James, who was giving the bride away, described her as 'a hard devoted little person whom I don't in the least understand his marrying' – and nor one feels can Charles Allen.

Yet the first time Alice set eyes on Carrie, she exclaimed, 'That woman is going to marry our Ruddy'. She might, I suppose, have meant 'because she is a hard little American who wants to marry a world-famous young author'. But I think rather that she could see that Ruddy, a fragile character who had always been solitary and was now in a frantic state, wilfully withdrawing deeper into himself, needed someone who could take him in hand and look after him, someone older not just by the two years of the calendar but in terms of being grown-up and capable, the sort of older woman that he had always gone for as a companion, even while he was whoring in Lahore. Allen describes him as 'locked in an increasingly bleak marriage' even before the death of his beloved elder daughter Josephine from whooping cough, not to mention the death of his son Johnnie in the Great War. But I very much doubt whether any other woman would have made him happier. He was bleak by nature. And his misfortunes only intensified the way he was. He became obsessively secretive too, he and Carrie holding periodic bonfires of all his papers. His autobiography, *Something of Myself*, could, as Charles Allen remarks, more accurately have been entitled 'As Little About Myself As I Can Get Away With'.

Yet his self-obliteration, his wilful absence as a person, only enhanced his eerie sharpness of perception. It was partly because he had been away from India for eleven years that he could see how fragile, how absurd, yet how amazing the whole edifice of the Raj was and what a permanent lowering shadow had been left by the Mutiny twenty-five years earlier. No longer did the British in the subcontinent speak of themselves as 'Indians' but as 'Anglo-Indians', and for many of the whites the 'natives' were now 'niggers'. The racial divide had become an abyss. He wrote 'home' to his cousin Margaret Burne-Jones: 'Underneath our excellent administrative system; under the piles of reports and statistics; the thousands of troops, the doctors, and the civilians of the Indian Civil Service runs wholly untouched and unaffected the life of the people of the land – a life as full of impossibilities and wonders as the Arabian Nights.'

The gorgeous apparatus of the Raj might be blown away in a moment and the roles of master and servant reversed, as they are in the story called 'The Strange Ride of Morrowbie Jukes', a literal-minded civil engineer who finds himself in the Village of the

Dead, which turns out to be a republic where he has to obey the rule of the Brahmins. 'The Man Who Would Be King', perhaps the most famous, certainly the most filmed of all Kipling's stories, is a hideous parable of the rise and fall of British rule, where a couple of deadbeat rogues, Peachey Carnehan and Daniel Dravot, first terrorize the distant native kingdom of Kafiristan with the power of their guns and use Masonic ritual (to which Kipling was devoted) to inspire awe, then start building bridges and holding councils, before the inevitable mutiny and hideous bloody end.

Kipling was an imperialist, yes, but he was the most apprehensive and morally demanding imperialist who ever lived. And it would be a sad thing if the political correctness of today separated Kipling from his mass readership. How horrified he would be to think that he had become more admired by highbrows than the general public, for there was nothing he abominated more than the society of intellectuals and being forced to:

> Consort with long-haired things
> In velvet collar-rolls,
> Who talked about the aims of Art
> And 'theories' and 'goals'.

For Rudyard Kipling went beyond the art that conceals art to the art that conceals the artist. And he concealed himself too well for his own good.

GEORGE GISSING:
THE DOWNFALL OF A PESSIMIST

In some moods, I would rather read George Gissing than any other nineteenth-century English novelist. In the 1890s he was ranked with Hardy and Meredith, at a time when they had finished writing novels and he was only just getting into his tortured stride. Orwell called *The Odd Women* 'one of the best novels in English'. But somehow Gissing has fallen off the shelves, not out of print but of public regard, fatally obscured by a reputation for gloom and pessimism. Gissing – the very word is like a South London street on a wet Monday. He himself rather revelled in that reputation. When he discovered that the next tenant in his old lodgings in Brixton had killed himself, he noted in his diary: 'The atmosphere I left behind me, some would say, killed the poor man.'

Yet reading any of his best novels – *New Grub Street, Born in Exile, In the Year of Jubilee* – is in fact an exhilarating experience, like splashing through icy puddles with the rain in your face. They move at a breakneck pace, partly because he wrote them at unbelievable speed, making other famously facile writers like Trollope and Simenon look positively constipated. He finished *The Odd Women* – 336 pages in the Virago edition – in fifty days. His mind was always bubbling with new plotlines, which generated any number of false starts. In the year after finishing *Born in Exile*, he began and then abandoned at least nine other novels. It comes as a shock, though it shouldn't, that someone who wrote so much about defeated people – struggling writers, devitalized shop assistants, unloved spinsters – could himself master anything he tried his hand at. The son of a Suffolk pharmacist with literary tastes who migrated north to Wakefield, George Gissing passed out top in the whole country in English and Latin when he sat his London BA at Owens College, Manchester, a feat never achieved before. He also taught himself Greek, French, German, Italian and Spanish. He chucked out Christianity, read Darwin, Schopenhauer and Nietzsche, walked fifty miles in a day, was a competent illustrator and knew more about flora and fauna than Thomas Hardy. He was a handsome man too, with a great mane of swept-back hair, grey-blue eyes and a profile as fine as Rupert Brooke's. For all his grouchiness, he didn't have an enemy in the world – until he got married. E. W. Hornung met him in Rome towards the end of his life and said: 'Gissing is really a sweet fellow, he has charm and sympathy, humour too and a louder laugh than Oscar's. That man is not wilfully a pessimist. But he is lonely – there has been a great sorrow and ill-health too.'

So what went wrong? Well, that is the question pipe-sucking professors used to put, and though professors may no longer suck pipes, at least on college property, that is the question Paul Delany can't stop asking. This is a highly enjoyable life of Gissing, lucidly written and carefully researched. Unfortunately, it is also so horribly bland, so wretchedly wrong-headed from start to finish, in the most important aspect of that life that it made me want to seek out the nearest ninth-storey window to hurl it from. However, let us remember our anger-management training and strive to condemn a little less and understand a little more.

The facts of Gissing's first downfall are well-known. They remain startling. At the back of the estimable Owens College, which later turned out Nobel prizewinners in droves, were the slums along the River Irwell. And in the handily situated brothel in Water Street, Gissing met Nell Harrison and fell in love with her, or with the idea of reclaiming her from her fallen state, or both. He stole books and clothes from his fellow students to raise money for her boozing and her VD treatment. He bought her a sewing machine too. Then he stole 5s 6d and was caught and sentenced to a month's jail with hard labour, which meant the treadmill: climbing the equivalent of 10,000 feet a day. After his release, far from making a big deal of his month inside, he never spoke of it and did his best to keep it dark for the rest of his life. The governors of the college remained keen to help their star pupil, and raised about £50 to speed him on his way to America where he could forget Nell and be himself forgotten.

No such thing. Gissing returned, having gained nothing from his year in the US 'except to have studied with tolerable thoroughness the most hateful form of society yet developed'. American readers should not take too much offence at this. Gissing was a great hater of wherever he happened to be. After his stay in Exeter, he told Nell that, 'I should fancy no town in England has a more unintellectual population. And the country people are ignorance embodied.' After an evening at the Authors' Club, he recorded that 'to mingle with these folk is to be once and for ever convinced of the degradation that our time has brought upon literature'. Brighton was 'simply a lump of wealthy London put back to back with a lump of Whitechapel and stuck down on a most uninteresting piece of coast, a more hideous and vulgar sea-side town the mind of man has not conceived'.

Anyway, far from giving up Nell, he poured more money down her throat, and since they could not share lodgings while unmarried, and despite his hatred of the Church, he married her in St James's, Hampstead Road.

Through all this process – a decidedly gruelling one, to put it mildly – Professor Delany has been tut-tutting and pursing his lips and shaking his head. 'Many Owens students made an occasional visit to a brothel, with no harm to their future careers,' he sighs in his broadminded way. Gissing, though, 'brought doom on himself by deciding to save Nell from her way of life', for 'if she was just an ordinary girl of the streets, Gissing had been a great fool.' Even writing to her from the States 'showed that he had learnt nothing from being sent to prison'. Nothing like the treadmill to prevent prostitutes from finding husbands.

Why on earth could he not settle down with a nice middle-class girl and write nice middle-class novels for the circulating libraries? 'He might have suffered much less from loneliness and sexual deprivation if he had chosen women whose status was closer to his own,' Delany tells us in his worldly-wise way. 'All Gissing needed to do,' he explains, sounding more and more like one of those ads on the back page which promise you the infallible recipe for turning out bestsellers, 'was study his market and then meet the demand for material.'

Nell and Gissing eventually separate and she dies in ghastly poverty at the age of thirty, although he never stops sending her what little money he has (at one point he is supporting no fewer than fifteen members of his family from his scant earnings – Delany calls him 'a soft touch'). The cause of death was probably the syphilis for which she had been receiving treatment, although the death certificate used the frequent euphemism of 'acute laryngitis'.

Gissing then endures a solitude so all-consuming that he speaks to nobody but his landlady for weeks. In a frenzy of loneliness, he rushes out into the Marylebone Road and picks up the first girl he sees. This is Edith Underwood, a stonemason's daughter, who after a long courtship, platonic according to Gissing, becomes his second wife. There is no evidence that she was on the streets in any other sense, although Delany likes to fancy that she might have been, or alternatively that Gissing thought she was and was disappointed to find that she was more respectable than he bargained for. By now Delany seems to have come to dislike Gissing quite strongly, almost as strongly as Gissing came to dislike Edith. The second marriage was as disastrous as the first. Edith gave George hell and vice versa. They separated and she spent the last fifteen years of her life in a mental asylum.

Delany is now growing impatient with Gissing's lack of upward mobility and has begun complaining that 'his inability to convert the reputations of his books into social success was a chronic handicap in building his literary career'. If he hadn't insisted on his 'perverse choices', 'there was no external reason why he should not have found a loving young woman who could have helped him up the ladder.' Yes, and bought a lovely home in South Ken and joined the Authors' Club, or even the Garrick.

Gissing might be bitter, solitary and self-destructive, and he might be vulnerable to romantic illusions, but what Delany seems uncomfortable with, or bewildered by, is that he was also fiercely intelligent. He was always quick to see the shape of the future. He could see, for example, that Wilhelm II coming to the throne 'might in all probability lead to wars of incalculable duration'. In Berlin in 1898, he found 'rampant militarism everywhere about'. The Italy which he loved was 'being very quickly ruined, owing to the crazy effort to be a first-class power'. He did not share the optimistic hopes about democracy, which he saw, on the contrary, as 'full of menace to all the finer hopes of civilisation', and likely to be much worse when combined with the revival of monarchic power based on militarism. 'There has but to arise some Lord of Slaughter and the nations will be tearing at each other's throats.'

Having thus nailed down the Kaiser, Mussolini and Hitler, Gissing was no more hopeful about the prospects of improvement at the individual level. A century before the age of celebrities and hedgefunders, he diagnosed the new elites as 'incapable of romantic passion, children of a time which subdues everything to interest, which fosters vanity and chills the heart'.

At the same time, he was not blind to what he himself was like. He traced the unhappy story of his life to 'my own strongly excitable temperament, operated upon by hideous experience of low life.' A change of circumstances would not, however, perk him up: 'It will never benefit me to take change of air. I am a hermit wherever I go; I merely carry a desert with me'. Delany tells us that Gissing was 'trapped in a particularly English kind of shabby-genteel poverty'. What's so particularly English about it? Think of Balzac's clerks, or Gogol's. And he was trapped only in the sense that a potholer gets trapped, as an occupational hazard. Gissing plunged into the lower depths because he felt that there was no other way to write truthfully or, just as important, to live honestly. He had, after all, explored the upper reaches of genteel literary society too, staying with his patrons, Mrs Gaussen in the Cotswolds with her Pre-Raphaelite connections and the positivist Frederic Harrison in Bayswater, and was soon as ill at ease there as with Nell Harrison in Kings Cross: 'Reflecting upon those more cultured grades which I have also known, I was shocked by the gap between the two classes – not in the mere commonplace matter of material comfort, but in the power of comprehending each other's rule of life.'

Just as he had insisted on returning to Nell and marrying her, so later he deliberately chose to move to Brixton to join the lower-middle class which had escaped the misery of the slums into lives which he saw as pinched, phoney and vulgar.

Other writers such as Orwell have briefly descended into the social underclass, but not many of them have chosen to live south of the river. Between A. C. Swinburne (who was dreaming of the Aegean rather than Putney) and J. G. Ballard, offhand I can think only of Thomas Hardy in Tooting Bec and V. S. Naipaul in Stockwell, and they were just passing through, not engaged on a mission as Gissing was.

In all his wanderings he was consistently distressed by the hard-hearted society which he thought the prevailing social Darwinism had generated: 'If we tread upon the feeblest competitor and have the misfortune to crush the life out of him, we are merely illustrating the law of natural selection.' He still hated the gloomy dogma of the Church he had been reared in, but he feared that the end of Christianity inevitably meant a great flowering of egotism. We could not hope for happiness in this world or anywhere else. The least bad course was 'to cultivate our perception of man's weakness. Let this excite our tenderness.'

Gissing worshipped classical civilization and came closest to happiness when he was clambering over some ancient ruins in an unspoilt wilderness with a view of the Mediterranean. Delany does not seem to grasp, though, that in his outlook Gissing was anything but classical. Greek moderation and Roman self-control were alien to him. He was in fact a Christian post-Christian, for whom suffering-with was the supreme imperative. When we read about the lives of the five women who were murdered in Ipswich in 2006, should we be so quick to condemn Gissing's project to rescue Nell?

It is natural enough to compare him with Orwell, who died at the same age, forty-six, and who was such an enthusiast for Gissing's work. But even the appreciation that Orwell wrote in 1948 shows the difference. There he advances Gissing's novels as a reason 'for thinking that the present age is a good deal better than the last one'. The poverty and squalor that Gissing describes so relentlessly had become, if not unimaginable, at least rare in post-war Britain. Gissing himself would not have been so easily satisfied. He would have detected all sorts of deeper cultural and spiritual ailments which Mr Attlee had not yet cured. He was, as he said himself, not a realist but an idealist, and an unappeasable one.

None of which prevented him from being a domestic disaster area. Nell and Edith are not the only unhappy writers' wives to have suffered from living with a man who writes ten hours a day and hates social life. But Mrs Hardy, Mrs Milton and Mrs Shake-speare did not, I guess, at the same time have to endure being told that they were coarse and vulgar and in need of a complete social and intellectual makeover.

We see Gissing at his most unpleasant when he refuses to allow Edith to answer letters from a middle-class friend, claiming that 'she has long since given up hope of learning to write, so I will answer for her' – when in fact perfectly coherent letters from Edith survive to this day. He was almost as horrible to their two sons. Walter, the elder, was 'deplorably ugly', as well as being 'ill-tempered, untruthful, precociously insolent, surprisingly selfish'. He never saw the boys or Edith for the last five years of his life, which he spent at Pau with Gabrielle Fleury, a French literary groupie who acted as his third wife, though Edith was still alive. They settled in the Pyrenees in the mistaken belief that the climate was good for his lungs. In fact, what he was dying of was syphilis, probably contracted from Nell all those years ago in Water Street. In the Pyrenees, he yearned for the lanes round Guildford.

VIRGINIA WOOLF:
GO WITH THE FLOW

What if a writer is more interesting than the stuff he or she writes? Worse still, what if she isn't (let's leave the men out of this) but the reading public mistakenly thinks she is?

Virginia Woolf was alert to this problem, if that's what it is, because she was alert to most things she was reading. In reading Byron, she said, it was always 'difficult to be certain whether we are looking at a man or his writings'. While analysing *Aurora Leigh* for the *Yale Review*, she noted that the Brownings' love story attracted more attention than their poetry – and then she got hooked herself: 'I lay in the garden and read the Browning love letters, and the figure of their dog made me laugh and I couldn't resist making him a Life.' Hence *Flush*, which naturally turned out to be a runaway success with a nation of dog-lovers. Woof, Woolf.

But this will not do if we are to cement Virginia Woolf into the modern pantheon. If she really is 'the greatest of all British women writers', as it says on the dust jacket of Julia Briggs's book, then we must concentrate our minds on the dedicated artist and iron-willed feminist and not let our attention stray to the gossipy, bitchy, serpentine, snobbish, occasionally raucous, intermittently anti-Semitic, quintessential Bloomsberry. If Woolf is to be canonized as the patron saint of gender studies, then we may countenance her affair with Vita Sackville-West (though perhaps raising an eyebrow at its more skittish upper-class moments), but we must airbrush anything which suggests that now and then she took a more favourable view of marriage and conventional life. For example, when Leonard stopped her from going to Paris to comfort her grief-stricken sister whose son Julian had just been killed in Spain: 'Then I was overcome with happiness. Then we walked round the square love making – after 25 years we can't bear to be separate. It is an enormous pleasure, being wanted: a wife.' You would need a stony heart too not to be touched by her reflection a decade later on their decision not to have a child (mostly Leonard's and taken on very dodgy medical advice): 'A little more self-control on my part, and we might have had a boy of 12, a girl of 10. This always makes me wretched in the early hours.'

Julia Briggs is too conscientious and fair-minded a biographer not to let us see these sides too, but for the most part she sticks to her mission, which is to show us Virginia Woolf not only in a room of her own but on her own in it. Although evidently a highly sociable person, Briggs tells us, 'it was what she did when she was alone, walking or sitting at her desk, for which we now remember her'. An odd formulation this, one which would go without saying for almost any memorable writer whether male or female, from Pascal to P. G. Wodehouse, from Jane Austen to George Eliot, but which somehow does need to be asserted in the case of Virginia Woolf, as though there would otherwise be something shaky or blurred in the case for her greatness, as though even after taking Mrs Woolf out of Bloomsbury we were still worrying whether it would be possible to take the Bloomsbury out of Mrs Woolf.

This is a Virginia with little or no Lytton or Carrington or Duncan or Maynard or Saxon. The Stephens and the Stracheys hardly get a look-in. We start with Virginia, at the age of twenty-one, just after the death of her father, walking along the down by the edge of the sea at Manorbier, Pembrokeshire, wanting to write 'a book – a book – but what book?' There right at the beginning of her career we may sniff a clue to both the splendours and the poverty of Woolf's writing. Other people start out wanting to write a book about Venice or the discovery of sex or the trade-union movement. Virginia Stephen just wants to write a book.

Professor Briggs's method is to take us through the books she did write, devoting roughly a chapter to each: how they were composed, the wearisome series of drafts they went through, their critical reception and their sales. We are told what Leonard thought of each one, what Morgan thought, what Tom Eliot thought. At the end of each chapter, the dust jacket by Vanessa Bell is reproduced – the principal appearance by the sister who in most portraits of Virginia plays such a key role.

This resolutely literary approach to Virginia's life has both an enhancing and an unsettling effect. Julia Briggs brings out Woolf's sterling qualities: her courage in dealing with her recurrent overwhelming depressions, her determination to do her very best and not to let her work slip down towards mediocrity as she defined it, her soldiering on in both life and letters.

But Briggs cannot altogether exclude the other, more frivolous and wilful Virginia, whose sudden bursting-in gives us quite a shock, since we have been given so little warning of her existence: the Virginia who says 'I do not like the Jewish voice, I do not like the Jewish laugh'; the Virginia who, walking along the towpath, shudders as she has to pass a long line of 'imbeciles' – 'It was perfectly horrible. They should certainly be killed'; the Virginia who wearies of her serious feminist friends going on about the massacre of the Armenians – 'I laughed to myself over the quantities of Armenians. How can one mind whether they number 4,000 or 4,000,000?'; the Virginia who cannot see what her sister sees in Clive Bell, 'that funny little creature twitching his pink skin', before herself making up to the funny little creature, now her brother-in-law, and being disappointed that he doesn't kiss her. We are spared here the stream of complaints about the vulgarity and stupidity of the lower orders that fill her diaries, although Briggs does mention that when Woolf's annoying but devoted cook, Nellie Boxall, went into hospital for a kidney operation, Virginia instantly advertised for a replacement in *Time and Tide*.

Briggs sometimes excuses her subject's more startling callousnesses as a sign that she is about to go mad again. The treatment here of this subject, admittedly a very difficult one, is not entirely consistent. We are given first to understand that its origin is largely inherited. Virginia's father was a depressive. Her half-sister Laura spent most of her adult life in an institution. Her cousin, J. K. Stephen, the heroic scholar and athlete, went mad and cut his throat. Within the family Virginia herself had been notorious as a child for her uncontrollable rages – 'Goat's mad', the cry would go up.

At other times, though, Briggs toys with Laingian ideas of the dysfunctional family being the cause of supposed insanity (goat = scapegoat), and even with the notion that 'the very practice of her art required her to adopt a position as a critic and outsider, even as "mad", if the society she criticised defined its particular prejudices as "sane"'. This is surely to brush aside Virginia's own agonized accounts of the horrors of her condition and to caricature the robust and plainspoken quality of her critiques of society – usually appreciated as such by those who might not necessarily agree with them.

Nor will it do to blame Leonard Woolf, as her more fanatical admirers like to do. She herself constantly repeated that the 'twist in her head' came from way back. And it was with Leonard's unflagging help that, after her catastrophic breakdown and overdose of Veronal in 1913, she managed to keep on anything resembling an even keel for nearly thirty years until her final breakdown and suicide. It is hard to imagine how any companion of either sex could have done more to make her life seem worth living than Leonard did. And she knew it and said it.

Julia Briggs makes me think better of Virginia Woolf as a person – in her own style gallant, sympathetic, stoical – while leaving, perhaps without meaning to, a trail of fresh clues as to why I find most of her novels in some way unsatisfying, especially those which are widely regarded as landmarks of modernism.

As a diarist, Woolf is unputdownable. Yes, she is sometimes horrible. So are most of the diarists and memoirists we continue to read, from Pepys and Saint-Simon to Chips Channon, Harold Nicolson and Alan Clark. As an essayist, she is magnificently plain and thumping, now and then almost Johnsonian – she loved Samuel Johnson and borrowed from him the title for her collections of reviews – 'I rejoice to concur with the common reader'. Her writings in the women's cause are the best possible advertisement for feminism: vigorous, good-humoured and irresistible. No writer of non-fiction could be less affected or less bowed down by theory.

What a contrast with her approach to fiction, which she embarks on festooned with slogans and banners. The time had come to abandon 'this appalling narrative business of the realist'. Future novelists would leave the description of reality more and more out of their stories, taking a knowledge of it for granted. She told Katherine Mansfield, whom she alternately loved and loathed, despised and envied, 'What I'm at is to change the consciousness and so to break up the awful stodge' – the materialist, earth-bound fiction of the dreadful Arnold Bennett and the unspeakable H. G. Wells. 'We believe that we can say more about people's minds and feelings. Well then, it becomes less necessary to dwell upon their bodies.'

This dematerializing not only represented the future of art for her, it also accorded with her own instinctive preference. Even when young, she had now and then expressed distaste for the flesh, most notoriously only seven weeks after getting married when she wrote to Molly McCarthy, 'Why do you think people make such a fuss about marriage and copulation? I find the climax immensely exaggerated.' She was not yet fifty when she remarked that she hated 'the slow heaviness of physical life and [I] almost dislike people's bodies, I think, as I grow older.'

What she valued in fiction was the flow. Style, she told Vita, was simply a matter of rhythm and should flow like a wave; 'as it breaks and tumbles in the mind, it makes words to fit it'. She was always pleased with herself when she had written a long passage on the run, whatever the nervous cost to her afterwards: 'I shall never forget the day I wrote "The Mark on the Wall" – all in a flash, as in flying.' In finishing the second draft of *The Waves*, she boasted of 'having reeled across the last ten pages with some moments of such intensity and intoxication that I seemed only to stumble after my own voice'.

But is flow enough? If the flow is making up its own words as it crashes and splashes across the page, may it not come perilously close to gush? In the last ten pages of *The Waves*, it is not Virginia's voice but Bernard's that is supposed to be washing over us. But he speaks/thinks in this weird, attitudinizing, implausible fashion which is like no human being ever born but like someone inventing a character for themselves in an interminable Bloomsbury after-dinner game. The other five characters speak in just the same way, thus hopelessly blurring the intended distinctions between them, Susan the earth mother, Jinny the man-mad and so on. Julia Briggs is by no means blind to this blurring, recognizing that in *Mrs Dalloway*, for example, the experiences of the neurotic Septimus Warren Smith seem surprisingly similar to those of the other characters who are better adjusted to the world around them. But she does not pause to enquire whether this swimmy, samey quality may not have a deadening effect on the work as a whole. Indeed, for an avowedly literary biography the book is remarkably abstinent in its critical evaluation, which in a way is refreshing but cannot help leaving unproven Woolf's claims to greatness as a novelist.

Since character and narrative are deliberately broken down and homogenized into a continuous poetic flow, the reader is bound,

in the absence of the normal diversions, to become attentive to
the uneven quality of that flow, at times sparkling and dancing
but at other times, far too frequently, whipping itself into a foamy,
scummy sort of texture. The opening page of *The Waves* – the
description of dawn breaking over the sea – contains half-a-dozen
extended similes: a wrinkled cloth, the breath of a person sleeping,
sediment in an old wine bottle, a woman raising a lamp, flames
leaping from a bonfire. By itself, each is rather stale and unprofit-
able. Together they produce a messy smudge.

There is, I think, a paradox about modernism which Woolf
seems unaware of: the more you make soup of the old bones of
plot and character, the more materialistic, the more naturalistic
even you have to be, not less. Compare the last ten pages of *Ulysses*
with the last ten pages of *The Waves*, Molly's soliloquy with Ber-
nard's. Compare Bloom's day with Mrs Dalloway's. Both writers
are trying to think themselves into a very different sort of person's
head. But while the tumbling stream of thoughts in *Ulysses* is so
coarse, so abundant, so immediate as to overwhelm disbelief, in
Mrs Dalloway you never quite manage to forget that this is Mrs
Woolf ventriloquizing a woman she would have run a mile from
at a cocktail party.

Woolf initially dismissed *Ulysses* as 'an illiterate, underbred
book, the book of a self-taught man, and we all know how dis-
tressing they are'. She could not understand why Great Tom Eliot
thought it on a par with *War and Peace*. Although she thought of
herself as in some sense in competition with Joyce, and noted on his
death (just before her own) that he was about a fortnight younger
than she was, she always found his 'indecency' and 'sordidity'
too off-putting to learn much from. Ditto with D. H. Lawrence.
They were incredibly proud in Bloomsbury of being able to say
semen and shit and bugger in mixed company, but when it came
to creative writing they retreated into a gentility that would have
appeased E. M. Forster's aunts.

The counterexample of *Orlando*, so wicked, so light-footed, so ingenious, showed how much she could have done with the novel form, but she was caught in this pseudo-poetic slipstream which at its worst has no more purchase on the imagination than those Omega workshop tables and screens painted in their tremulous whorls and stripes which infest the shrines of lower Bloomsbury. Far from it helping her reputation to detach her novels from her diaries, essays and letters, the closer they stick together, the better their chances of survival. In the same way, I think it is better to stick the whole Virginia back together and remember a woman brimming with wit, malice, common sense, imagination and caprice rather than to worship a plaster saint for a godless age.

ARTHUR RANSOME:
LENIN IN THE LAKE DISTRICT

'Ransome, when he turned up, proved to be an amiable and attractive man, with a luxuriant blond soup-strainer moustache, a rubicund complexion, a large mouth from which more often than not a pipe protruded, and a hearty disposition.' Malcolm Muggeridge immediately took to Arthur Ransome when he first met him in Cairo in 1929. Most people did. The philosopher R. G. Collingwood, a close friend from their shared childhood in the Lake District, gave Ransome his entire life savings to pay his legal costs when he was sued by the incurably litigious Lord Alfred Douglas. Edward Thomas was devoted to him. John Masefield drank claret with him at teatime as they sang sea shanties together in Ransome's mother's kitchen.

And Ransome took to most people; he was not choosy. In fact, he was inclined to instant and lasting hero worship from which nothing could shift him, for he also had a stubborn conviction of his own rightness. His innocent egotism was underpinned by the belief that he was an excellent fellow who could do no wrong. These were dangerous qualities which in combination drew him into a career so bizarre that now, as during his long lifetime (1884–1967), it takes your breath away.

For years, Ransome's place as the pipe-sucking deity of children's literature seemed unassailable. The latest adventures of John, Susan, Titty and Roger could safely be placed in the hands of the most impressionable child, and placed they were by wholesome parents every Christmas holidays between 1930 and 1943: *Swallows and Amazons*, *Coot Club*, *We Didn't Mean to Go to Sea*, every one a bestseller to be avoided with horror and loathing by any young person with the slightest vestige of humour or subversion. It is not just that the Fearsome Foursome live in a world of nannies and apple-cheeked farmers' wives filling their milk-cans and calling them Miss Susan and Miss Titty (not an appellation which most farmers' wives today could manage without corpsing). That, after all, is standard for children's fiction of the period. It is their unspeakable goodness, their unflagging enthusiasm for outdoor pursuits, their intolerable expertise in handling boats and their never, ever being cross or bored. When Susan has a spare moment, she improves it by scouring the dishes again or by sewing buttons back on her younger brother's shirt. Her elder brother, John, meanwhile practises tying some of the knots in *The Seaman's Handybook*. In Arthur Ransome's Lake District (and his Norfolk Broads), there are no wasps or midges, it hardly ever rains and no boat capsizes. One longs for them all to be deported to the island in *Lord of the Flies*, if not actually to share the fate of Simon and Piggy. In fact, of course, they sail home to a scrumptious tea with Mother. It's hard to imagine that a grown man whose life's ambition it was to be a great writer could have brought himself to turn out 300 pages of this stuff, let alone 3000.

Yet there was also a very different Arthur Ransome, a ruthless and tireless propagandist for the Bolsheviks and their Revolution, a double agent courted simultaneously by Lenin and Lord Curzon, a man whose total lack of qualm or scruple baffled the spymasters of East and West alike. This other Ransome was, I think, first brought to public attention by David Caute in *The Fellow Travellers* (1973), then by Hugh Brogan in his 1984 biography, more recently in papers declassified by MI5 in 2005 and now by Roland Chambers in this new biography.

It should be said at once that the bulk of the evidence was never secret, being set out in Ransome's own articles for the *Daily News* and the *Manchester Guardian* (his early stuff was often reprinted in the *New York Times* as well), and in his pro-Soviet pamphlets, *On Behalf of Russia* (1918), *Six Weeks in Russia* (1919) and *The Crisis in Russia* (1921), and only half covered up in his autobiography, which was in any case published posthumously in 1976. It is Ransome who leads off Caute's parade of useful idiots on the first page of his first chapter.

Chambers tells essentially the same story as Brogan, though his emphasis is different. The bulk of his pages concentrate on Ransome's adventures in Russia and the Baltic, with his career as a children's writer tacked on, rather perfunctorily, at the end. He declares candidly that when, at the age of forty-five, Ransome began writing the books for which he is now remembered, 'the most interesting episode of his life, from a biographer's point of view, was already over.' Brogan presents a more rounded picture, and his touch is surer. Chambers is shaky on the minutiae, getting in a tangle, for example, about the names and titles of Foreign Office staff, lurching between Lord Cecil and Sir Robert Cecil for Lord Robert Cecil, Sir Esmie instead of Esme Howard and Sir Cavendish Bentinck for Victor Cavendish-Bentinck. More seriously, Muggeridge is described as 'an enthusiastic apologist for Stalin', when in reality he had not been in Russia three months before he was writing to tell Beatrice Webb, his wife's aunt, of his 'overwhelming conviction that the government and all it stands for ... is evil and a denial of everything I care for in life'. Chambers also has an occasional weakness for the cliché: 'In 1914, Serbia stood in relation to the great powers of Europe very much like a match next to a barrel packed with gunpowder.' If the book had source notes and a better index, it would be easier to be clear who said what and when. All the same, Chambers tells the story with verve and a stylish deadpan manner when recounting Ransome's more amazing excursions and effusions. It is a story not to be missed.

Ransome went to Russia in the first place to get away from his wife, Ivy. He hated Ivy with an unrelenting venom, later describing her as 'an incarnate devil and nothing else'. Not everyone agreed. Ivy deeply admired her husband and helped him with his work, as well as keeping the household going while he disappeared to go on long walks or visit his friends. Of the two of them, Edward Thomas's wife, Helen, greatly preferred Ivy and thought that Arthur was turning into an intolerable Superman. Arthur refused to see their only child, Tabitha, throughout her adolescence and never met her children at all, except when Tabitha tricked him into coming to see her in Somerset and introduced him to his granddaughter Hazel, by then aged eighteen. Ransome was enraged by this stratagem and stormed off to Taunton station, refusing Tabitha's offer of a lift. He did have a substitute family in the shape of the real-life Susan, Titty, etc., the children of Collingwood's sister Dora, but in old age he turned against them too. There were decided limits to his family affections.

But his political affections were unbounded. He had a front-row seat at the February Revolution, watching the siege of Litovsky Castle from his office desk. He was never short of courage, visited the Eastern Front three times and came under fire while surveying the battlefield from a Russian biplane. Like many other foreign observers, he welcomed the fall of the tsar: 'It is impossible for people who have not lived here to know with what joy we write of the new Russian Government.' Kerensky was his first Russian hero: 'Then, as on a dozen other occasions, Mr Kerensky saved the situation.'

Ransome was at the Finland Station to see Lenin's return; and soon he had a new hero. Lenin was Russia's Oliver Cromwell, a modest, simple man; every line on his face was 'a line of laughter'.

Two years later, Ransome reflected in *Six Weeks in Russia*: 'Walking home from the Kremlin, I tried to think of any other man of his calibre who had had a similar joyous temperament ... I think the reason must be that he is the first great leader who utterly discounts the value of his own personality. He is quite without personal ambition.'

During the October Revolution, Ransome was back in England, fishing and making a half-hearted effort to patch things up with Ivy. He returned to Russia in time to see the Bolsheviks dissolve the elected Constituent Assembly, a spectacle which moved him to write: 'I tell you I walk these abominable, unswept, mountainously dirt-clogged, snow-clogged streets in exultation. It is like walking on Wetherlam or Dew Crags, with the future of mankind spreading before one like the foothills of the Lake Country.' As soon as Lenin looked like winning, Ransome abandoned Kerensky and parliamentary democracy without a backwards glance.

The suppression of the assembly was not simply a regrettable necessity, it was a glorious moment in history. As he listened to the exposition of his other new hero, Trotsky, 'I felt I would willingly give the rest of my life if it could be divided into minutes and given to men in England and France so that those of little faith who say that the Russian Revolution is discredited could share for one minute each that wonderful experience.'

When Fanny Kaplan shot Lenin in August 1918, Ransome hurried to compose an obituary, describing how the common peasants worshipped Lenin as a saint. In the event, the obit was not needed.

When Lenin did die in 1924, after suffering his third stroke, Ransome also composed the obit that appeared in the *Guardian*. Lenin had been 'like a lighthouse shining through a fog'. It had never occurred to him that the Revolution rested in his hands alone, or that he had for one moment approved unnecessary killing in his name.

Of course, other enthusiasts were to say similar things, then and later (Lincoln Steffens, the Webbs, H. G. Wells, Walter Duranty of the *New York Times*, Bernard Shaw), but it was Ransome who first coined those glowing phrases that lingered in the Western mind for so long. He was thus a valuable commodity, as his great friend Karl Radek, the presiding genius of the Comintern, was quick to realize. To the mercurial British agent in Moscow, Robert Bruce Lockhart, Ransome might be only an incorrigible sentimentalist, 'a Don Quixote with a walrus moustache', but that was just what the Bolsheviks needed: a propagandist who was not one of them but was obviously good-hearted and sincere. Ransome's pamphlet *On Behalf of Russia* was written in close collaboration with Radek and was circulated by Russian agents among Allied troops. And when Lenin objected that *Six Weeks in Russia* failed to follow the party line, Radek pointed out that it was the 'first thing written that had shown the Bolsheviks as human beings'.

Ransome was beautifully ignorant of the sacred texts of Marxism-Leninism. What he had instead was a narrative gift and an eye for local colour. He was one of the pioneers of the celebrity interview. How seductively he describes Trotsky's simple furniture in his office in the Smolny Institute, marked only by a piece of paper pinned to the door with the words 'People's Commissary for Foreign Affairs'. From the great man's striking head, with its high forehead and lively eyes, Ransome deduces in a flash that this is a man who will do nothing that will not best serve the revolutionary cause that is in his heart.

A statuesque secretary, Evgenia Shelepina, over six feet tall in her high heels, is taking notes at this first of many interviews. Later, Ransome and Evgenia, looking for someone to stamp his telegram, find the censor nodding off over a pot of potatoes on a Primus which is sending up clouds of black smoke. Evgenia and her sister Iroida invite Ransome to stay and drink tea. The whole scene is so delightfully innocent and Russian.

Ransome soon abandons his dark, chilly room at the Elite Hotel and moves into a merchant's palace, which he shares with the Radeks and the Shelepin girls. He describes with open glee the abject terror of the millionaire who is being evicted. The amusing incident is recorded in his notebook under the title 'Requisitioning a Flat'. Eventually, Evgenia is smuggled out of Russia to become Ransome's second wife and spend the rest of her life making tea in the Lake District. Also smuggled out with the happy couple are thirty-five diamonds and three strings of pearls to be sold to fund Comintern activity in the West. Ransome denies knowledge of these items of luggage, but he is an old hand at the game. On an earlier exit, he has smuggled out 3 million roubles in cash for the Swedish Comintern. Iroida stays in Russia. She joins the Cheka and in 1926 is promoted to deputy director of the Moscow region forced labour camp. She continues at this exacting post in a busy part of the Gulag until the early 1930s.

We must not think that Ransome, as a foreign correspondent, was somehow shielded from the grim realities. On the contrary, his matchless contacts gave him access to the worst horrors. Besides, he was an energetic reporter who always wanted to see for himself. He saw, for example, in company with Yakov Peters, No. 2 at the Cheka, the ghastly aftermath of the Cheka's massacre of the anarchists. Bruce Lockhart went on another tour with Peters's boss, Feliks Dzerzhinsky, and wrote a horrified account of the blood and squalor. But Ransome (who as a boy in Leeds had been taught ice-skating by the exiled Prince Kropotkin) entirely approved of Dzerzhinsky's actions: 'The Soviet has finally shown itself capable of uprooting a movement which all previous governments have not dared to touch.' Though keen on all the Bolshevik leaders, Ransome had an especially soft spot for Dzerzhinsky: 'He has been much in prison [under the tsar], where he was remarkable for the urgent desire to take upon himself the unpleasant labour of other criminals, such as cleaning cells and emptying slops.'

More generally, Ransome told his readers, the situation in Russia was nowhere near as bad as it had been painted. He had anecdotes to prove that reports of the Terror in the countryside had been grossly exaggerated. Mass terror was anyway impossible in

Russia, 'because there can be no such thing unless the mass feels inclined to terrorise, which they do not.' The dictatorship of the proletariat meant that every working man could cast his vote. As for free speech, 'I have never met a Russian who could be prevented from saying whatever he liked whenever he liked, by any threats or dangers whatsoever.'

Ransome was useful not merely as a propagandist. For a time, he seemed to the Bolshevik leadership their best, if not their only contact with the West. When Lenin was in despair that the peace talks at Brest-Litovsk might be about to break down and leave Russia still trapped in a war that would destroy the Bolsheviks, Ransome was one of the two Westerners he telegrammed, imploring them to seek the support of their ambassadors. The other was Colonel Raymond Robins, head of the American Red Cross, best remembered for his view that Trotsky was 'a four-kind son of a bitch, but the greatest Jew since Jesus Christ'. At one point, Lenin granted Ransome three interviews in three weeks. When Bruce Lockhart told him of the Allied plans for military intervention in Russia, Ransome went straight to Lenin, in effect to warn him.

The amazing thing is that, for the latter half of his time in the East, Ransome was also an accredited British agent, hired originally on the suggestion of the foreign secretary, Arthur Balfour, who had been impressed by Ransome's article about his first meeting with Trotsky. The Foreign Office was just as desperate for any contact with the Bolsheviks as the Bolsheviks were desperate for any clue to the West's intentions. After a time, Ransome's activities began to arouse some misgivings, and he had several menacing interviews with Rex Leeper at the Foreign Office and the head of Special Branch, Sir Basil Thomson, who succumbed to his charm. Even those officials who were scornful of his character and suspicious of his motives mostly agreed that he should be allowed to go back to Russia. And the new foreign secretary, Lord Curzon, agreed too. Thus there could be no question of having Ransome shot for treason, as urged by Colonel Knox, the British military attaché in Russia, or even prosecuted, for he had been hired with the approval of two foreign secretaries and in the full knowledge of all his views and activities, including the smuggling.

The fatal attraction of having a man on the inside overwhelmed common prudence. In the Foreign Office, only Leeper, later to found the British Council (not the Arts Council, as Chambers has it), seemed aware of the damage that Ransome had done and could continue to do as a soft propagandist. And even the sceptical Leeper comforted himself by arguing that 'Mr Ransome is not an agent of the Bolsheviks. He had not enough sense to see through them.' The British chargé in Russia, Sir Francis Lindley, exploded: 'You don't seem to realise that these people are our enemies.' The harm he might do seemed somehow mitigated, if not excused, because he was so obviously thick.

Chambers seems equally baffled. At the end of the book, he can't make up his mind whether his subject was a double agent, or a peace broker, or merely one of Lenin's useful idiots. But surely the answer is that he was all three. The illusion is to imagine that in order to be effective an agent must be (a) secret and (b) intelligent; and that a double agent must be twice as secret and twice as intelligent. Ransome was both dense and transparent; everyone always knew what he was up to and assumed that because he was so stupid his activities could be turned to their own advantage. At times, he reminds me forcibly of William Boot in *Scoop*, the innocent countryside writer who is pitched into bewildering and horrible events in a very strange country. Ransome's early works, after all, included *Pond and Stream* and *Highways and Byways in Fairyland*, quite a match for Boot's 'Lush Places'.

But few people reckoned with Ransome's remarkable energy and ingenuity where his own self-preservation was concerned. He could charm his way out of any tight corner. He also reminds me at times of P. G. Wodehouse's antihero, Stanley Featherstonehaugh

Ukridge, with his pince-nez made of ginger-beer wire, his untidy clothes and his utter lack of scruple. Like Ukridge, Ransome's schemes invariably went wrong but he always bobs back up again.

An essential part of his survival kit was his total lack of self-questioning, either about his double role or about his shifting allegiances within Russian politics, at first an enthusiast for democracy and the Constituent Assembly, then an ardent apologist for Lenin and the Red Terror. Nor did he ever admit to any disappointment that the Revolution had not lived up to the original high hopes. Even after Lenin's death, he seems to have suffered few doubts about later events, as one by one his old friends – Zinoviev, Bukharin, Radek and eventually Trotsky – were shot or beaten to death. On his last visit to Russia in 1928, he covered Stalin's first purges and found them regrettable but necessary, grumbling only that the members of the Central Committee were now a bit too rough for his liking.

Looking back, he claimed to have associated with the Bolsheviks in much the same way as he had once associated with artists in Paris: 'not as a rival painter but as a mere writer who was very much interested in what they were doing'. He was at least an artist in whitewash. Were the last forty years of his life a prolonged lying-low, in which he could hope to forget the terrible events he had witnessed and suppressed – and hope that other people would forget too? Or were they simply a return to the Boot Magna he should never have left? Perhaps a bit of both. Certainly, his rehab was a slow business. He remained on the Home Office blacklist of suspected Bolshevik activists until 1937. He had to wait another twenty years for his CBE.

E. M. FORSTER:
SHY, REMORSELESS SHADE

Inever liked E. M. Forster much. He was too preachy and prissy, too snobbish about the suburbs, too contemptuous of the lower classes. I know this is not how a review is meant to begin. You may legitimately kick off by admitting that you have a soft spot for your subject, even perhaps that you used to be friends. But reveal a long-standing dislike in your first paragraph, and the reader may reasonably wonder why the editor did not give the book to someone else.

My only excuse for this confession is that I am not alone. For a novelist, essayist and critic of such acknowledged eminence, Forster has had a surprising number of enemies. There was something about him that got people's goat, and still does. Some people disliked him, some people disliked his books, some people disliked both. After listening to Forster's Clark Lectures at Cambridge in 1927, F. R. Leavis denounced his 'curious lack of grasp' and his 'spinsterly touch'. Ten years earlier, Katherine Mansfield made much the same point more vividly: 'E. M. Forster never gets further than warming the teapot. Feel this teapot. Is it not beautifully warm? Yes, but there ain't going to be no tea.' Readers and acquaintances alike have found him chilly, maiden-aunty and, Natasha Spender's word for him, censorious.

Our greatest living critic, Sir Frank Kermode, has devoted his
own Clark Lectures eighty years later to explaining (to himself, I
think, as well as to the rest of us) exactly why he doesn't really like
Forster either. He doesn't put it quite in this way, because he is a
man of open mind and generous sympathies. But he does keep on
returning to what is wrong with his famous predecessor. 'Forster',
he says, 'irritates readers who nevertheless feel obliged, in the end,
to do him honour.' Kermode agrees with these readers, and insists
at the outset of this fascinating little book that he 'will pay the debt
of honour without ceding my right to some bouts of irritation.' Sir
Frank has just turned ninety, and it is as though he cannot bear to
put away his pen until he has E. M. F. bang to rights.

He only met Forster for ten minutes and had what sounds like
a rather stilted conversation with him. But he had rooms in King's
College, Cambridge, for almost as long as Forster had, and so
met plenty of people who, either as undergraduates or dons, had
had tea with the great man and even gone on holiday with him.
'Some claimed to have liked him extremely, and some did not.'
There have been warmer personal endorsements.

In the first half of the book – the lectures themselves –
Kermode examines Forster's novels and promises to be 'only
occasionally censorious'. As if this wasn't enough, in the second
half he embarks on what he calls a causerie in which he further
attempts to understand this talent 'so considerable and yet so
straitly limited'. Here 'Forster is reduced in size, placed in a wider
context and occasionally scolded for not being altogether the kind
of author I should have preferred him to be.' I am sure that, in
other circumstances, Kermode would come down hard on any
critic who complains that the author has failed to write the sort
of book he wanted him to. But it seems Forster is so uniquely
annoying that he is not protected by the normal rules of critical
sympathy.

Not that Edward Morgan Forster was incapable of standing up
for himself. On the contrary, that weedy figure with the droopy

moustache (so like the moustache given to Leonard Bast, the vulgar bank clerk in *Howards End*), who lived with his mother until her death when he was sixty-six years old, had the self-assurance normally attributed to oxen and Old Testament prophets. Christopher Isherwood called him 'immensely, superhumanly strong. He's strong because he doesn't try to be a stiff-lipped stoic like the rest of us and so he'll never crack.'

In his literary judgments Forster certainly gave every bit as good as he got. His critique of Henry James, the sort of writer he might have been expected to admire, was savage and direct: 'Most of human life has to disappear before James can do us a novel.' He objected both that 'James's novels are gutted of the common stuff that fills characters in other books, and ourselves', and that there was no food for the soul in them either, no philosophy and no religion, except an occasional touch of superstition; no juice, no smell, no sex and no God either. Not exactly a spinsterly indictment. Yet Kermode frets for page after page that Forster the dedicated artist should have failed to revere the Master and finds it 'extraordinary' that in the famous literary quarrel between James and H. G. Wells he should have taken the side of Wells, the coarse literary tradesman.

There is something very odd going on here. Forty years after his death, Forster remains an indelible presence. He occupies most of a page in the new *Oxford Dictionary of Quotations*. Five of his six published novels have been turned into rather successful films, justifying his claim which has annoyed so many modernists that 'yes – oh dear yes – the novel tells a story.' And we still cannot get his famous maxims out of our heads: 'Only connect!', 'Personal relations are the important thing for ever and ever, and not this outer life of telegrams and anger', 'If I had to choose between betraying my country and betraying my friend, I hope I should have the guts to betray my country'. He nags at us still. But in some queer way we cannot stand him and persistently try to write him down, if not off.

When I say a queer way, I do not mean to suggest that it is Forster's homosexual subversion which continues to agitate our conventional sensibilities. Plenty of gay writers have soon found general acceptance and esteem, from James Baldwin and Gore Vidal to Edmund White and Alan Hollinghurst. Forster presents some unique aggravation which has nothing to do with his famous declaration in middle age that 'I want to love a young man of the lower classes, to be loved by him and even hurt by him. That is my ticket.' We are not annoyed by Forster because he fell in love with a married policeman. It is Forster's attitude to class, not his attitude to sex, that makes him so offensive, certainly to modern readers. Kermode speaks for many in convicting him of being a comfortably off, out-of-date Edwardian who had little sympathy with, or understanding of, the poor (Forster's mother was an heiress of Thornton's Bank, and he was an only child who never lacked for cash). The narrator in *Howards End* famously remarks that 'we are not concerned with the very poor. They are unthinkable and only to be approached by the statistician or the poet.'

Kermode's indictment fastens on the unbearable character of Leonard Bast. He argues that 'to a surprising extent one's attitude to *Howards End* depends on one's response to Bast' – and in particular to his excruciating dialogue with his even coarser mistress, Jacky, who turns out to have also been the mistress of the prosperous and otherwise invulnerable Mr Wilcox. Why does even the narrator gang up on Bast and make him so unmitigatedly ghastly? Why, Kermode asks, does Forster fail to investigate the genuine upward mobility – spiritual and intellectual no less than material – which was already happening among the Edwardian working classes and which has been so brilliantly brought back to life by Jonathan Rose in his book *The Intellectual Life of the British Working Classes*?

Well, that is exactly what I thought when I first read *Howards End* fifty years ago. Leonard and Jacky seemed to be portrayed in a repellently patronizing and unconvincing fashion and to bring the whole book crashing to the ground. And I thought much the same about Forster's treatment of the charming but unreliable Indians in *A Passage to India* and of the charming but unreliable Italians in *Where Angels Fear to Tread*.

But wait a minute. Isn't all this meant to be excruciating – Leonard's barging in on the exquisite cultivation of the Schlegel household in boorish pursuit of his lost umbrella, his peevish, empty spats with Jacky, the revelation of her rackety past? Forster seems to be thrusting us deeper into it, rather than standing back with the reader at a safe distance. Isn't the stale monotone of the Leonard–Jacky dialogue intended as a stylized cadenza, not unlike, for example, the interminable talk about breakfast between Meg and Petey in *The Birthday Party*? When he catches you on the raw, it is because he means to.

May it not be that Forster is a more adventurous, trickier writer than we first thought? Notice how all his ideas about the world float in and out of his characters, so that sometimes it's Margaret Schlegel who is saying or thinking 'Only connect' and sometimes it's the narrator talking – and the phrase finishes up, or rather starts us off, as the epigraph to the whole book, which doesn't usually happen to the thoughts of a character in a novel. Far from being a spinsterish Olympian, Forster is a rare, immersing kind of operator who shares in the reveries, the disappointments and, alas, even the prejudices of his characters – and makes us share them too. We all plunge in together into the Hindu festival at the end of *A Passage to India* and come out breathless, soaking and smeared with every kind of spice and sweet. It is a scene unimaginable in Henry James, because of its sloshy carnality, and unimaginable in D. H. Lawrence, because of its gaiety.

Apart from steeliness, Isherwood detected in Forster a unique kind of 'silliness', not fatuousness but silliness in its original sense of saintly simplicity. Virginia Woolf thought that 'there is something too simple about him – for a writer perhaps, mystic, silly but with a child's insight.' In other words, she thought that a writer needed a kind of critical hardness. Isherwood, though, believed that 'his silliness is beautiful because it expresses love and is the reverse side of his minding about things', and insisted that 'we need E. M.'s silliness more than ever. It gives courage.'

For me at any rate, Kermode's inquisition leaves the accused enhanced rather than reduced in size. At the end of it, what we come to see is how original Forster was. He has a serious gaiety, especially in *A Passage to India*, which is hard to find in most English novelists but which has something of the great Russians whom he admired.

How funny he can be, how deft in conveying the banter of friends and families, almost as good at persiflage as his near contemporaries, Saki and Wodehouse. His humour can be sly and cutting, or amiable and generous. Even in the grand stuff, you can always hear a trickle of irony somewhere like a hidden underground stream. Kermode recognizes, of course, that the aside about not being concerned with the very poor was a big tease, but I suspect that now and then some of the ironies do escape him. Literary criticism is a solemn business, after all, and it is hard to stay alert to the possibility that the author may simply be enjoying himself.

Notice how wonderfully fair Forster usually is. While we plunge in alongside the Schlegels, the philistine, money-making Wilcoxes are given room to breathe too. In *A Passage to India*, we see things from everyone's point of view – Dr Aziz, Fielding, Adela Quested, even her mutton-headed fiancé Ronny. Kermode quotes plodding critics who complain that Forster does not come out clearly enough for the cause of Indian independence, but the justice and the inevitability of that cause radiate from every page.

Kermode suggests, rather nervously, that modern readers may find some of the crises in the novels a little tame – a kiss, a broken engagement – but modern readers are surely not quite so dense. In any case, there is no shortage of violent and shocking incidents – murder, disgrace, a baby's death in an accident – such things often presented baldly with scarcely a word of comment. Forster can be tough as well as silly when he chooses.

None of this may be quite what Sir Frank intended to come out of his beguiling causerie. But I am grateful to him all the same, not just for worrying away at this absorbing elusive subject, but for sending me back to the novels. I now realize that I was hopelessly wrong. I do like E. M. Forster and like him very much. In fact, I like him better than most of his great contemporaries. And I salute his shy, remorseless shade.

ARTHUR MACHEN:
FAERIE STRAINS

Modern eyes do not care to peer too closely into the Celtic twilight. Those misty apple-garths and faerie glens are off limits to the respectable critic. Still more unnerving is any suggestion of magic – black, white or greyish. 'Decadence' of the nineties sort is less unacceptable, preferably when coupled with deathbed conversion to Roman Catholicism, but the academic trade has always found it profoundly inconvenient that W. B. Yeats should have gone on insisting that, if he had not studied magic in The Order of the Golden Dawn, he would not have written half his early verse. As for Arthur Machen, well, the less said of him the better.

Yet Machen keeps on popping up. Perhaps no one cares now that the life of the composer John Ireland was transformed when he picked up Machen's *The House of Souls* off a bookstall on Charing Cross Road. That belongs to the same lumber room of cultural history as Lord Alfred Douglas's belief that *The Immortal Hour* was the best thing since Shakespeare. Bosie told John Betjeman that he had seen the show fifty times. Rutland Boughton's lyricist, Fiona Macleod – alias William Sharp – has suffered a similar obliteration from the literary canon. Indeed, Sharp's only accepted achievement is to have invented for his female alter ego that Christian name which has since been hallooed across a thousand Caledonian nights.

In the same way, if anything is popularly remembered now of Arthur Machen (pronounced Macken), it is that he invented 'the Angels of Mons'. Even this story drips with cruel irony. All his life, Machen struggled cheerfully against recurring poverty and obscurity. He had his ups too: the family legacies which enabled him to write his best work, and later a brief vogue in the 1920s, following the publication in 1918 of the first book about him, *Arthur Machen: A Novelist of Ecstasy and Sin* (the sort of title I recommend for any writer who feels neglected). There was even a uniform edition of his works published. But he quickly fell back into penury and literary oblivion – although he remained productive right up to his death in 1947 at the age of eighty-four.

But when he had his one instant dazzling success with 'The Bowmen', nobody would believe he had made it up himself. This very short story appeared in the *Evening News* of 29 September 1914 – only a month after Smith-Dorrien had brought the Old Contemptibles back from Mons. All sorts of people wrote asking Machen to reveal who had told him about the archers of Agincourt (not angels) coming to the aid of the desperate British troops. Sermons were preached, variants of the story elaborated, dead Prussians were alleged to have been found on the battlefields with arrow wounds on their bodies. Somebody's cousin who had served on Smith-Dorrien's staff knew for a fact, and so on. And poor Machen, who always had trouble in achieving fictional verisimilitude or narrative impact, never got the credit, or indeed the royalties, since the copyright belonged to the *Evening News* – which later fired him when the paper published Machen's obituary of Bosie, in which Machen described him as 'degenerate', which he may have been, but dead he was not.

This handsome volume of what, to be strictly accurate, ought to be described as The Selected Machen makes grand amends. But even here, I fear, we are left with an imperfect picture of the man and his work. The facts of Machen's life are not in dispute. He was born Arthur Jones, the son of an impoverished clergyman, at Caerleon-on-Usk, which was not only fabled in Arthurian legend but had earlier been Isca, the fort of the 2nd Augustan legion, and was later a centre of Welsh Christianity. Caerleon – Caermaen in *The Hill of Dreams* and other Machen works – was, not surprisingly, a sacred place for him. He went to Hereford Cathedral School as Arthur Jones-Machen, his father having added his wealthier Scottish wife's surname, perhaps in the hope of a legacy. Arthur later dropped the 'Jones'. There was, however, no money to send him to university, and by the age of seventeen he was in lodgings in Wandsworth, studying to be a surgeon, with no success. He spent the next decade in the grimmest parts of New Grub Street, tutoring, translating, cataloguing occult books.

Of the nineties, he later claimed to be 'not even a small part, but no part at all', although he did say that Oscar Wilde had told him he could not stand the taste of absinthe. But in fact Machen's first successful, indeed notorious work, *The Great God Pan*, was published the year before the Wilde trial by John Lane with a Beardsley frontispiece of an epicene Pan, looking rather more like Brigitte Bardot than Mick Jagger. It is an amateurish but irresistible tale, somewhere between Lord Dunsany and fin-de-siècle science fiction. A scientist performs a brain operation on a beautiful girl to enable her to see the Great God Pan: 'We are standing on the brink of a strange world, Raymond, if what you say is true. I suppose the knife is absolutely necessary?' 'Yes; a slight lesion in the grey matter, that is all; a trifling rearrangement of certain cells, a microscopical alteration that would escape the attention of ninety-nine brain specialists out of a hundred.'

The girl wakes up a hopeless, grinning idiot. But nine months later ... well, nameless, unspeakable horrors ensue.

Unfortunately, Mr Palmer does not include *The Great God Pan*. Indeed, he writes off Machen's nineties stuff as 'weirdo classics' and speaks only of him 'dabbling in the occult' after his first wife's death. The selection is dominated by *Far Off Things*, the first volume of Machen's charming, evocative but scarcely informative autobiography, and *The Hill of Dreams*, which is the nearest Machen came to a serious literary achievement. The selection concludes with a mélange of Machen's newspaper sketches of the byways of Old London, Chestertonian stuff, full of rumbling paradoxes and trencherman's reminiscences. The whole effect is to build up an image of Machen as 'one of Fleet Street's greatest characters', a jovial storyteller, never happier than in an inglenook by a blazing fire with a tankard in his hand, or rolling down the Strand in his great Inverness cape to some music hall, apparently looking like Dr Johnson (from the photographs here, he looks more like Mr Asquith in his squiffier moments).

The starveling young Welshman, alone in his dismal lodgings in Notting Hill or prowling round the British Museum reading room in search of kabbalistic lore, does not get much of a look-in. Mr Palmer's Machen does not sound like the sort of chap who could write *The House of Souls* (also not included here) – a book so compelling that Aleister Crowley, the Wickedest Man in the World, wrote in his copy: 'This book is the property of G. H. Fra Perdurabo Abbot of Dam-Car' – the Beast's equivalent, I suppose, of 'If this book should chance to roam'.

Father Brocard Sewell in his little memoir of Machen adopted the same dismissive tone towards Machen's occultism: 'Apart from some of his early works, written when his mind was unsettled and when, along with Yeats and others, he was attracted by the occult-ism of the "Order of the Golden Dawn", Machen's "outlook" was as consistently Catholic as was that of the earlier Chesterton.'

But however short his membership of 'the GD' – as insiders called it – Machen's obsession with the occult lasted a good twenty years and started long before his first wife's illness. To identify Machen as an *anima naturaliter catholica* does not begin to tell the whole truth about him.

Machen did indeed hate Protestantism – especially of the hearty public-school variety, which he satirized so fiercely in *The Secret Glory*, a favourite work of the young Betjeman. Machen described the Reformation as 'the most hideous blasphemy, the gravest woe, the most monstrous horror which has fallen upon the hopeless race of mortals since the foundation of the world'. What he yearned for, though, was not so much the Roman as the old Welsh Church – primitive, elemental, a faith of the whaleback hills and hidden woods of his native land. The hero of *The Hill of Dreams*, who has passionate, erotic visions while stretched out on the turf of the Roman hillfort at Caermaen, is a world away from Puck of Pook's Hill – or indeed from Chesterton's disciplined use of the supernatural. From the first words – 'There was a glow in the sky as if great furnace doors were opened', all hell and heaven are let loose:

> He himself was in truth the realisation of the vision of Caermaen that night, a city with mouldering walls beset by the ghostly legion. Life and the world and the laws of the sunlight had passed away, and the resurrection and kingdom of the dead began. The Celt assailed him, beckoning from the weird wood he called the world, and his far-off ancestors, the 'little people', crept out of their caves, muttering charms and incantations in hissing inhuman speech; he was beleaguered by desires that had slept in his race for ages.

These trances and visions are contrasted with the mean snobberies of the modern town and, worse still, with the horrors of London:

> the brick and stucco deserts where no trees were ... Nothing fine, nothing rare, nothing exquisite it seemed, could exist in the weltering suburban sea ... It appeared to him that vulgarity and greasiness and squalor had come with a flood, that not

only the good but also the evil in man's heart had been made common and ugly ... the very vices of these people smelt of cabbage water and a pothouse vomit.

No right-wing moralist could outdo the repulsiveness of Machen's description of Saturday night and Sunday morning in a working-class district – the drinking, the whoring, the hangovers, the vandalism, the Sunday newspapers. It is this loathing of modern urban life and this unappeasable longing for the imagined pre-industrial, pre-Reformation world of passion, beauty and unspoilt nature which are the true Machen, not the affable Fleet Street character composing whimsical 'turnovers' on 'Merrie Islington' and 'the Fogs of Yesteryear'. Mr Palmer's selection is, of necessity, too brief to exhibit in full that potent turn-of-the-century amalgam of Celtic nationalism, purple-stained Pan worship, Catholic religiosity and, by no means least, the plunging rather than dabbling in the occult.

Like Catholic apologists, the nationalist movements are diligent in cleaning up their bit of the act. The Scottish nationalists do not like to recall that the first president of the Scottish National Movement, Lewis Spence, claimed to be able to hear 'faerie singing, wordless, and of wonderful harmony', but only, I think, in the early mornings. For that matter, Fabians do not much care to be reminded how closely they once mingled with Mrs Besant and the theosophists.

Nor is it as if the faerie fanciers were unaware of their motives. Fiona Macleod, in her essay 'Celtic', acknowledged that the nationalist tradition was not solely a matter of geographical affection and loyalty:

it is also true that in love we love vaguely another land, a rainbow-land, and that our most desired country is not the real Ireland, the real Scotland, the real Brittany, but the vague land of Youth, the shadowy Land of Heart's Desire. And it is also true that deep in the songs we love above all other songs is a lamentation for what is gone away from the world, rather than merely from us as a people . . .

Machen's work is a fascinating compendium of these lamentations – sometimes poignant and evocative, especially in his descriptions of landscape and townscape, sometimes creepy and nauseating, sometimes merely awkward and embarrassing. And one can trace lines of descent from Machen in all sorts of directions – through Crowley and the GD to Crowley's young Californian disciple, L. Ron Hubbard, who was to evolve that pseudo-scientific cult of the higher knowledge which he called 'Scientology'; through the hippies and the alternative culture to the revival of interest in prehistoric magic and the numinosity of standing stones and ley lines; through artists like Sutherland and Ceri Richards, to the Neo-Romantic art of thorn thicket and hollow lanes, and so on, in an infinite diversity of religious and nationalist enthusiasms, all variously in revolt against the modern world. I should have thought that Heathcote Williams's vision of a gentle, erotic, whale-rich Albion was a truer descendant of Machen than the 'protestantized' Catholic Church of the 1980s.

Mr Palmer rightly adds to the list the influence of Machen avowed by Michael Powell (also a son of the Welsh foothills), in his strange supernatural films of the 1940s, and the transformation of Machen themes – the Wild Wood, the Roman Road – into the milder romance of *The Wind in the Willows* and of many another children's book. Indeed, at times it seems as if the peoples of these islands are all engaged in one great sprawling, conspiratorial enterprise of quasi-mystical pastoral nostalgia, into which Continental and American modernists only occasionally manage to intrude, before being roughly thrown out again. If so, Arthur Machen must be ranked among the prime conspirators, and he deserves another volume including *The Great God Pan, The House of Souls* and *The Secret Glory.*

It is easy enough to anatomize his technical imperfections; the lack of artistic ruthlessness, the lapses into sentimentality, the fuzzy outlines and the stock themes. Much the same criticisms could be made of 'A Paradise Lost' – that remarkable show of 'the Neo-Romantic imagination' at the Barbican in 1987. For me, the whole exhibition was almost painfully moving, since the world it evoked was the world of my childhood – of the Shell Guides, and John and Paul Nash, and John Piper and John Minton. English – or Celtic – nostalgia is evasive, but there is an evasiveness in international modernism too. The acceptance of brutality and alienation as the dominant themes of art is in its own way just as facile as the invention of a lost paradise of gentle and true affections. Some of the things Machen struggled to achieve still look worth struggling for.

FRED PERRY:
WINNER TAKES ALL

As Fred Perry came back into the dressing room after becoming the first Englishman to win Wimbledon in twenty-five years, he heard a club official murmur to his opponent, Jack Crawford: 'The better man lost.' Crawford, a popular, easy-going Australian and the outgoing champion, was given a bottle of champagne. Perry claimed that he was left empty-handed. The All England Club members' tie, automatically awarded to the new champion, was left unceremoniously draped over the back of a chair, as though nobody on the committee could actually bear to present it.

When Perry turned professional in 1936 after retaining the title for the next two years, his membership was immediately withdrawn, with almost audible relief exhaled from blazered breasts. This was, it is true, an automatic consequence of the venomous war between the amateur officials and the professional promoters that continued to rage in the world of tennis for over thirty years. 'Swapping glory for gold' was only slightly less bad than abandoning British citizenship and becoming an American three years later, which Perry also did.

The American officials were just as fanatical. Their greatest champion of the period, Ellsworth Vines, having turned pro, was strong-armed out of Forest Hills when he arrived to do a radio commentary. But there was something about Perry that provoked especial animosity from the half-colonels and commanders who ran British tennis then. It was mostly a question of snobbery and class hatred, twin contagions which had their epicentre in SW19. Perry was not forgiven for having gone to Ealing County School rather than Rugby or Repton, or for his father having been a Labour MP. Sam Perry was the most upright and honourable man imaginable. He started work in a Cheshire cotton mill at the age of ten on a shilling a week, devoted his life to the co-operative movement and declined a peerage. Yet even this patriotic and moderate-minded public servant had to put up with Young Conservatives in dinner jackets yelling at his election meetings, 'Which flag do you stand for, Perry, the red flag or the Union Flag?'

Fred was a far more abrasive, driven and unscrupulous character than his father. What he was also not forgiven for was his deter-mination to win whatever it took. This included not only intense physical preparation scarcely known among his fellow players, but also a willingness to twist the truth and, not least, outrageous gamesmanship. He would try anything to demoralize his oppo-nents from the moment they came on court, and then he would grind them into the dust after they were beaten. After defeating Crawford, he turned a cartwheel and hurdled the net to show how little the match had taken out of him, the first example of this triumphalist gambit since copied by the jockey Frankie Dettori and every centre forward who can manage it without doing in his knee. When his opponent played an ungettable shot, Perry would say 'Very clevah' in a sarcastic tone. Quite early in the knock-up, he would call out to his opponent 'Any time you're ready', indicat-ing that he needed scarcely a minute's practice. Jean Borotra, the Bounding Basque, then a little past his prime but still a formidable opponent and gamesmaster extraordinaire, liked to make great play of swapping between a number of berets that he brought on court before strolling over to talk to the pretty girls in the crowd. Playing him on his home clay at Roland Garros, Perry followed him to the umpire's chair where he himself put on a silly big peaked cap, then chased a smash from Borotra over the barrier to finish in the lap of a gorgeous model who had been brought along for the purpose. He jeered at umpires as rudely as any Connors or McEnroe. When he fell down, he rolled over on his back as exaggeratedly as any Chelsea striker diving for a penalty. Although normally immaculate, he irritated the finicky Baron Gottfried von Cramm in their Wimbledon final by leaving the lining of his trouser pocket hanging out – and won the most one-sided final ever. Nothing, though, quite equalled his bribing the court marker in El Paso to move the service line three inches nearer the net, so that the big-serving Ellsworth Vines thundered down a series of faults.

But Perry kept on winning. He was the first man in the modern era to retain his Wimbledon title, the first man to win all four Grand Slam tournaments. He and Bunny Austin (also stripped of his All England membership, for joining the Moral Re-Armament movement and becoming a conscientious objector) held the Davis Cup for four years, with Perry never losing a match. If he had not turned pro, his tally of titles would surely have equalled that of Rod Laver and Pete Sampras and Roger Federer.

Just as remarkable was Perry's already having won the world table-tennis championships in Budapest at the age of nineteen, in front of an incredulous crowd who had never seen a Hungarian beaten. Perry had taught himself the game and had never won any tournament before. Admittedly, the world championship was still fairly rudimentary. It had started only three years earlier in Memorial Hall off Fleet Street and had initially been billed as the European championships, but eight Indian students turned up and asked to take part. Some of the competitors did not bother to change out of their suits and shoes.

When Perry took up lawn tennis, again he taught himself, with the result that he played the game pretty much like ping pong, with a backhand like a butcher chopping liver and a forehand which came over the ball almost on the half-volley and smothered it with top spin. Peter Ustinov, a lifelong Perry fan, remarked that 'he took the ball so early that it seemed almost as unfair as bodyline bowling to those who regarded tennis as a kind of prescribed choreography in which the strictest orthodoxy was de rigueur'. Jack Kramer, champion of a later generation, believed that Perry's forehand was such a pernicious stroke that it 'screwed up men's tennis in England for generations to come'. When I played a few games forty years later with two ex-Davis Cup players who had played with and against Perry, I was startled by the jerky, abbreviated swings with which they despatched the ball to the most unlikely corners of the court. I assumed then that this was their technique for coping with old age, but perhaps it was Perry's influence which turned the 1930s into the era of clipped swings just as it was the era of clipped accents.

The Last Champion was no doubt conceived not only to celebrate the centenary of Perry's birth but in the hope that this year (2009) at last there might be another British player with the grit, speed and ingenuity to win Wimbledon. It is striking that Andy Murray has, like Perry, come a long way without so far winning the public's heart. The book is worth reading, in any case, not just for the portrait of the unstoppable Fred but for the easy-flowing manner in which Jon Henderson, the doyen of tennis correspondents, evokes the glamour of the sporting 1930s, a much-needed counterpoint to the low, dishonest side of the decade. Perry was perhaps the first modern sportsman to take full advantage of his celebrity, making a splash in nightclubs from Paris to Hollywood and marrying into showbusiness four times, in between stepping out with Marlene Dietrich, Loretta Young, Bette Davis and even Jean Harlow, who suggested they give dinner a miss.

Henderson is good on the smoking too. Bunny Austin was so nervous when Perry was playing a crucial Davis Cup match against the French that he chain-smoked throughout, while his wife, the actress Phyllis Konstam, found herself puffing at two cigarettes at once. When Perry won the first of his three US titles, his opponent, again Jack Crawford, wandered over to chat to his wife during the break players then took after the third set, and they relaxed with a cigarette. Perry himself preferred his pipe, which became almost as much his trademark as it was for Stanley Baldwin and Harold Wilson. When he went into sportswear, he suggested that the pipe should be his emblem, following Lacoste's crocodile, which Henderson says was the first brand icon on a garment. Perry reluctantly accepted the LTA's laurel wreath instead. That too became an instant hit. I recall the pride with which I wore my first Fred Perry shirt and being put out when the art master said 'What's that seaweed round your nipple?'

It seems somehow appropriate that, fifty years later, the Fred Perry logo (now owned by a Japanese firm), like the Burberry check, should have become a must-have for hoodies and skinheads, an indispensable emblem of classless class. Perry was not the only sportsman of his day to foreshadow the transition to ruthlessness. Don Bradman, Douglas Jardine and Gordon Richards also believed in winning at all costs. But Fred lacked the dourness of modern professionals. He had an innocent gaiety, and ultimately he didn't give much of a damn. What he believed was that you should be able to go anywhere and do anything. Which he more or less did. In his way, Fred, like his father, turned out to be an example to us all.

M. R. JAMES:
THE SEXLESS GHOST

He always comes on his own, this bachelor of antiquarian tastes. Sometimes he is a book dealer, more often an academic. He is a dry, crotchety character, not particularly sympathetic. He is usually on holiday, in East Anglia or an old town in France or Denmark. He is staying in an inn or a hotel, an uncongenial sort of place far from his familiar institutional comforts. In fact, he is way out of his comfort zone. And then it begins ... the tapping at the window or the rustling or the tangling of the bedsheets.

We know what we are in for, just as surely as we do when we open an Agatha Christie or an Elmore Leonard. The formula is simple, repeated with variations in most of M. R. James's thirty-three ghost stories, and still guaranteed to give pleasure today just as it did to those fuddled dons and sleepy schoolboys who first heard James read them by the light of a single candle in the provost's lodgings at King's College, Cambridge, or, in his last years, as provost of Eton.

It may seem heartless or unsporting to deconstruct these little tales, for the author made no very exalted claim for them. 'If any of them succeed in causing their readers to feel pleasantly uncomfortable when walking along a solitary road at nightfall, or sitting over a dying fire in the small hours, my purpose in writing them will have been attained.' The excuse must be that James himself was eager to unpack the formula in the prefaces and occasional articles he wrote on the subject. He was happy to share his own ideas on how a ghost story should be laid out if it was to be effective. 'The setting should be fairly familiar and the majority of the characters and their talk such as you may meet or hear any day.' But 'a slight haze of distance is desirable.' Unlike the detective story, the ghost story should not be too up-to-date. 'Thirty years ago' or 'Not long before the war' were proper openings. Close enough in time, therefore, for the reader to think: 'If I'm not very careful, something of this kind may happen to me.' The ghost ought to be a contemporary of the person who sees it, just as Hamlet's father and Jacob Marley were.

The important thing was atmosphere. The setting had to be carefully prepared and evoked. James does this particularly well with the coastal landscape of Suffolk around Aldeburgh – Peter Grimes country. Then it is time for the 'nicely managed crescendo'. And then it is time for bed. No doubt it is partly because of the proximity of bed (it is from his own bedroom that he has emerged with his spidery manuscript and the single candle) and the arrival in the morning of the ominously named 'bedder' that the provost is insistent on one thing: there must be no sex. James tells us more than once that sex is a 'fatal mistake' in ghost stories. It spoils the whole business. 'Sex is tiresome enough in the novels ... as the backbone of a ghost story, I have no patience with it.'

Yet, as Darryl Jones, a specialist in horror fiction at Trinity College, Dublin, points out in his first-rate introduction to this compendium of all James's ghost stories, the phantoms themselves repeatedly break the rules he has laid down for them. What happens, after all, in the typical James story? The bachelor don or antiquary discovers a lost manuscript or artefact – a whistle or an inscription on stained glass – which unleashes supernatural forces that shake his comfortable assumptions about reality. What we can't help noticing is that these supernatural forces tend to be female. In the build-up, by contrast, scarcely a woman appears, except as a comic rustic or tiresome servant in the inn. But the ghosts themselves are so often women, spurned or murdered or guilt-ridden: Mrs Mothersole in 'The Ash Tree', Ann Clark in 'Martin's Close', Theodosia Bryan in 'A Neighbour's Landmark' and the terrible figure in 'a shapeless sort of blackened sun-bonnet' in 'Wailing Well'. We don't need to have read any of the Freud which James would have run several miles from to interpret what Mr Dunning in 'Casting the Runes' finds when he puts his hand into the well-known nook under his pillow: 'What he touched was, according to his account, a mouth, with teeth, and with hair about it, and, he declares, not the mouth of a human being.'

Jones detects a *vagina dentata*, and it is hard to dodge the sexual vibrations here or in the other slimy, clutching, intensely hairy phantasms which finger and stroke the beleaguered single man. The spectral bedsheet in 'Oh, Whistle and I'll Come to You, My Lad' attempts to thrust its 'intensely horrible face of crumpled linen' close into the face of Professor Parkins as he cries for help. The gender of the bedsheet is unclear, but the fear of domesticity and the fear of sex, tangled and intertwined like the bedsheet, are unmistakable. And even when the ghosts and their victims are both male, the erotic overtones still hum. How horrified James would have been to find 'Lost Hearts' or 'The Residence at Whitminster' included in an anthology of gay ghost stories, but both would certainly deserve their place, especially the latter.

How much was James aware of the vibrations? How far did he intend them? 'Reticence,' he said, 'may be an elderly doctrine to preach, yet from the artistic point of view I am sure it is a sound one.' But the reticence he practised went far deeper than the stories he tossed off in the intervals of his vast scholarly endeavours. It went all the way down. His friends thought him as sexless as an angel.

Montague Rhodes James (1862–1936) lived the unexamined life in spades, in the way that only an unmarried don of his generation could. The son of an Anglican vicar of evangelical inclinations, he won a scholarship to Eton, then another to Henry VI's sister foundation, King's College, Cambridge, at that time still largely an Etonian preserve. He spent the next thirty-six years at King's, as successively undergraduate, dean, tutor and provost, as well as being director of the Fitzwilliam Museum for fifteen years. He catalogued the manuscripts in all the college libraries as well as several other great collections and became the world's leading scholar on Apocryphal literature. He then returned to Eton for the last eighteen years of his life as provost. He had thus spent his entire adult existence in 'Henry's holy shade', untroubled by marriage, poverty or anything much else.

Even among his fellow dons his insulation was thought remarkable. His best friend, A. C. Benson, declared that Monty's 'mind is the mind of a nice child – he hates and fears all problems, all speculation, all originality or novelty of view. His spirit is both timid and unadventurous.' James's knowledge, he conceded, was 'extraordinarily accurate and minute' but mainly concerned with unimportant matters. 'No one alive knows so much or so little worth knowing.' His mind had nothing constructive in it. 'He seems to me to be an almost perfect instance of high talent: a perfect second-rate man.' Benson himself was tormented by his homosexuality as well as by frustrated or delayed ambitions and he was subject to terrible mental collapses. While Master of Magdalene, he spent more than two years in a nursing home (amazing to think that such a tortured soul wrote the words of 'Land of Hope and Glory'). He could not forgive Monty's insouciance or his unthinking resistance to change.

Among the people and things that James hated and refused to countenance at King's or Eton were: T. H. Huxley ('a coarse 19th-century stinks man'), Henry Sidgwick and his philosophy, the German higher criticism, anthropology and comparative mythography, Aldous Huxley, James Joyce, Bertrand Russell, J. B. S. Haldane and John Maynard Keynes (for being a renegade Eton-and-King's man who thought the college needed shaking up). Lytton Strachey returned James's contempt: 'It's odd that the provost of Eton should still be aged 16. A life without a jolt.'

The only modern innovations that I can discover James adopting were the rear-driven safety cycle and the Dunlop pneumatic tyre, which between them enabled him and his friends to cover huge distances on their Continental excursions to forgotten cathedrals and unknown libraries. Even his old school tutor H. E. Luxmoore was shocked by the frivolity of James and his circle. After spending Christmas at King's one year, he complained: 'O how the time goes in talk, talk, talk and overmuch eating.'

> Last night Monty James read us a new story of most blood-curdling character, after which those played animal grab who did not mind having their clothes torn to pieces and their hands nailscored. The cleverness and gaiety of them all is wonderful and yet if it goes on like this in term time – and it does – where is the strenuous life, and the search for truth and for knowledge that one looks for at College? Chaff and extravagant fancy and mimicry and camaraderie and groups that gather and dissolve first in this room and then in that, like the midges that dance their rings in the sunshine, ought to be only the fringe of life and I doubt if here it does not cover the whole, or nearly so.

James himself did not resist this impeachment. In his sixties, he ruminated: 'Do you know, I have written an immense deal of stuff and find myself almost incurably frivolous.'

That may be why his phantoms do not, on the whole, *haunt*. They lie doggo in their holes and only when roused make a single surprise appearance. They are cabaret turns, not implacable disturbers of the peace. The morning after, normality returns. Only in James's very last published story, 'A Vignette', is the first-person narrator repeatedly haunted by the horrifying white face that appears at the hole in the gate of the fir plantation. Indeed, I haven't noticed the word 'haunted' used much anywhere else in the stories. James declared himself dissatisfied with 'A Vignette' as 'short and ill written'. On the contrary, I find it one of his few genuinely disturbing tales. Partly because the scene is based on his childhood home at Livermere, Suffolk, partly because it has a first-person narrator and partly just because it has no plot, there is a genuine worrying quality to it, an ambiguity for which the word 'haunting' fits.

The *OED* derives 'haunt' from the French '*hanter*', which it says is 'of uncertain origin'. But Dauzat's *Dictionnaire Etymologique* has no such doubts, declaring firmly that it comes from the same root as '*habiter*'. So haunting is a matter of inhabiting; habitual residence is of its essence. The ghostly connection comes later: for the French, '*maison hantée*' is a nineteenth-century Anglicism. In English, the ghostly connection is at least as old as Shakespeare. Richard II tells us that some kings are 'haunted by the ghosts they have deposed.' Ghosts then were regular revenants, resident nuisances. In James, they are vestigial; they may not outlast the memory of those who knew them in life. The grandmother in 'An Evening's Entertainment' tells her grandson that 'maybe things like that do die out in the course of time.' At the end of 'A Vignette', the narrator asks the almost elegiac question: 'Are there here and there sequestered places which some curious creatures still frequent, whom once on a time anybody could see and speak to as they went about on their daily occasions, whereas now only at rare intervals in a series of years does one cross their paths and become aware of them?'

If ghosts are on the way out, does the same apply to other supernatural things, perhaps even to the Christian faith which so sustained James and the rituals of which were the heart and soul of his daily existence? That is not a question which James would have asked himself or permitted his audience to ask. His whole life can be seen as a series of defensive operations: to protect King's against the stinks men, to protect the Christian Church against critique and to protect himself against reality. At times, he reproached himself with indolence. But he was never indolent when he was defending his own certainties.

Towards the end of his life, in 1929, James wrote a survey of ghost stories for the *Bookman*, beginning with Lope de Vega in the seventeenth century and culminating with Dickens and, his favourite, Sheridan Le Fanu. The article ends in a characteristically self-deprecating but also unusually abrupt way: 'There need not be any peroration to a series of rather disjointed reflections. I will only ask the reader to believe that, though I have not hitherto mentioned it, I have read *The Turn of the Screw.*' Deafening is the only word for the silence. Why will he say no more? What does James think of his namesake's ghost story, published in serial form in *Collier's Weekly* in 1898, just at the time when he was writing his first 'Antiquary' stories? Does he admire its deliberately unresolved ambiguities? Does he hate its sensuous implications of ill-defined evil? Or both or neither? Is Henry's exhaustive psychological analysis precisely what Monty will not permit himself, even if he were capable of it? Like Bertie Wooster, M. R. James seems not entirely at home with the psychology of the individual; for that sort of stuff, he relies on Jeeves. On his only recorded meeting with the other James, he thought that Henry looked 'like a respectable butler'.

Curiously, both writers claim to be free of responsibility for their creations. Monty declares that 'I have not been possessed by the austere sense of the responsibility of authorship which is demanded of the writer of fiction in this generation.' Henry speaks in his own preface of 'this perfectly independent and irresponsible little fiction'. But they mean quite different things. Monty wants to reassure us that his tales are harmless trifles which a housemaster may safely read to his pupils after they have finished their prep. Henry, by contrast, is warning us that he cannot be responsible for where his little story may end up; it is likely to take us into some dark places from which we may not emerge unscathed.

Many megabytes have been expended on trying to resolve whether Peter Quint and Miss Jessel are 'real' or whether they are the creations of the new governess's highly strung brain. It seems probable, to put it no higher, that the author means to keep us in suspense on this as on many other questions. But what is certain is that the ghosts in *The Turn of the Screw* are pervasive and persistent presences, and that the damage they do is cumulative. That is what haunting means. Real ghosts, like real art, are always irresponsible. They do not go away when they are told to. That is why they are best kept out of the provost's lodge.

WILFRED OWEN:
THE LAST TELEGRAM

When Wilfred Owen discovered that Shelley used to visit the sick and poor of the Thames Valley, he was overjoyed: 'I *knew* the lives of men who produced such marvellous verse could not be otherwise than lovely.' This is not the usual view. There are too many cases of great poets who were selfish, cold and cadging, indifferent to the welfare of their nearest and dearest, Percy Bysshe Shelley himself not excluded. But Wilfred Owen was a lovely man.

His life was short as Keats's. They both died at the age of twenty-five, but their lives feel shorter still, because these slight, little, bright-eyed men both came across as so incurably youthful. Owen had a special affinity for children of all ages, and he thought that any true poet ought to be childish. 'Now what's your Poet but a child of nine?' was his playful answer to Wordsworth's question about the nature of a poet.

But, like Keats whom he worshipped, Owen also had a sharp intelligence and a searing wit, which makes the reader jump out of any sentimental reverie. His verse is intensely realistic and direct. And so are his letters. Guy Cuthbertson says in his new biography that Owen's letters achieve 'Matthew Arnold's aim for literature that it should see the object in itself as it really is'. There is no English poet, except Keats again, whose letters I would rather have by my bedside.

It is a pity then that Cuthbertson does not quote as copiously from them as did the poet Jon Stallworthy in his wonderful 1974 biography. Instead, Cuthbertson tends to wander off into digressions on other writers and artists who don't really seem to have much to do with Owen. In the space of two pages, he gives us little riffs on Joyce in Berlin, Toulouse-Lautrec in Bordeaux and Isherwood in Berlin. Elsewhere we are told about the painter Augustus John's concussion, W. H. Auden's ideal college for bards and a character called Mr Owen in the novel by Agatha Christie which used to be called *Ten Little Niggers* but now isn't. I'd prefer more of Wilfred and less of this motley supporting cast.

Wilfred Owen was born in 1893, the son of a stationmaster on the Welsh borders. Cuthbertson seems keen to prove that Owen was not really Welsh at all, although his name and his short stature suggest otherwise. Besides, at Oswestry, Shrewsbury and Liverpool where he was brought up and educated at unremarkable schools, he was surrounded by Welshmen, often Welsh-speaking ones, who had spilled over the borders. I don't think it's too fanciful to see something Welsh, too, about his flaring-up and forgiving nature, and the easy way he made friends when he wanted to, although his temperament was shy and naturally aloof.

Owen was certainly resentful about the start in life he was dealt. Cuthbertson rightly points out that few writers want to be lower-middle class – especially if they feel, as the Owens did, that they had come down in the world. It was 'a terrible regret' for Wilfred that he did not go to Oxford instead of a dim college which was scarcely yet a university. But even his complaints of his modest origins were partly playful, as was his father Tom's occasional claim that he was really a baronet in disguise. Wilfred had an unquenchable gaiety which made people seek his company. He said himself, 'You would not know me for the poet of sorrows.'

Was he gay in the modern sense, and how relevant was this to his life as a poet? Gay-ish, and not very, Cuthbertson suggests, and convincingly so. The impression he gave to his friends was virginal, even sexless. There is no doubt that the most important thing in his life, apart from poetry, was his mother Susan, to whom he wrote unceasingly: 'I stand (yes and sit, lie, kneel and walk too) in need of some tangible caress from you ... my affections are physical as well as abstract, intensely so.' She certainly mothered, if not smothered her favourite son. Well into his teens, she was still peeling his apples for him. Yet Owen did not feel short of experience. He said before he joined the army in 1915: 'I know I have lived more than my twenty-one years, many more; and so have a start of most men's lives.'

He had not volunteered with alacrity. In fact, he was tempted to dawdle on at Bordeaux where he was teaching English. Rather than being keen to make the supreme sacrifice, 'I feel my own life all the more precious and more dear in the presence of the deflowering of Europe.'

But join up he did, and he turned himself into a popular and efficient officer with the same brisk despatch that he had mastered the techniques of verse and added a few of his own, notably those slithery half-rhymes which give his elegies such a haunting quality (leaves/lives, ferns/fauns, cauldron/children). From the start, he had none of the illusions that are romantically attributed to war poets:

I suppose I can endure cold, and fatigue, and the face-to-face death as well as another, but extra for me is the universal pervasion of *Ugliness*. Hideous landscapes, vile noises, foul language and nothing but foul ... everything unnatural, broken, blasted; the distortion of the dead, whose unburiable bodies sit outside the dug-outs all day, all night, the most execrable sights on earth. In poetry we call them glorious.

It is impossible to read a life of Owen, as it is a life of Keats, without coming close to tears. And Cuthbertson's heart is in the right place. But he seems strangely eager to hurry over those tragic last two years as if they were too much for him. There were three momentous episodes in Owen's war service in France: when he was smashed up at St Quentin in April 1917 and shortly afterwards invalided home with shellshock; then on his return to France in September 1918 when he won the Military Cross in a blistering hand-to-hand attack; and finally on 4 November that year, when he was killed crossing the Ors Canal under relentless shell and machine-gun fire. Up to the very last, Owen describes all this with his unforgettable candour and vivacity, while the military archives make clear in detail just how suicidal the missions were. Unfortunately, each time Cuthbertson telescopes what happened into a couple of sentences. Here's a snatch of what we are missing:

All one day we could not move from a small trench, though hour by hour the wounded were groaning just outside. Three stretcher-bearers who got up were hit, one after one. I had to order no one to show himself after that, but remembering my own duty, and remembering also my forefathers the agile Welshmen of the mountains I scrambled out myself & felt an exhilaration in baffling the Machine Guns by quick bounds from cover to cover. After the shells we had been through, and the gas, the bullets were like the gentle rain from heaven.

The news of his death reached his parents at noon on the day the Armistice was declared. The bells were still ringing in the local church when the little chimes at the Owens' front door announced the fatal telegram.

What passing-bells for these who die as cattle?
Only the monstrous anger of the guns.
Only the stuttering rifles' rapid rattle
Can patter out their hasty orisons.

But Wilfred Owen's orisons are still ringing in our heads.

JOHN MAYNARD KEYNES: COPULATION AND MACROECONOMICS

To catch Keynes on the hoof, the gallop is the pace to go at. All his life Keynes reached rapid conclusions and revised them just as rapidly. Nor was he ashamed of what others called his inconsistency. The perfectly consistent fellow was 'the man who has his umbrella up whether it rains or not.' It's not quite clear to whom he allegedly retorted: 'When the facts change, I change my mind. What do you do, sir?' But it is clear that no scholarly scruple slowed him down. 'Words ought to be a little wild, for they are assaults of thoughts upon the unthinking.'

Nervous readers may worry that of the seven lives Richard Davenport-Hines attributes to Keynes in his sparky headlong biography – 'Apostle', 'Lover', 'Connoisseur' and so on – he finds no room for 'Economist'. This puckish tactic is, I fancy, designed to give us a jolt. Keynes had only eight weeks' training in economics (though from the great Alfred Marshall), he never sat an exam in the subject and he embarked on his theoretical work only after years of experience in managing real-world crises. He thought economics a queer sort of science, if science at all, and one which needed taking down a peg: 'If economists could manage to get themselves thought of as humble, competent people, on a level with dentists, that would be splendid.' The irony is that his own dazzling career was instrumental in raising the profession's status to that of modern rainmaker and all-purpose wizard. In any case, if you are looking for technical stuff, the economic equivalent of data on drills and implants, you won't find it here. Davenport-Hines swims past Keynes's masterwork, *The General Theory of Employment, Interest and Money*, with barely a sideways glance.

For the fiendishly complex arguments between Keynes and his critics, you will need to go to the middle one of Robert Skidelsky's three volumes. And marvellous though that book is, even then you may end up a little bemused. At times, after reading Skidelsky, you get the feeling that almost everyone is a Keynesian at heart (public works and printing money are not exactly novel remedies for unemployment). At other times, you feel that nobody is, not even Keynes himself, for the Master has already moved on from his first thoughts.

What Davenport-Hines makes vividly clear is that Keynes's indisputable greatness was as a public servant. For thirty years, from the outbreak of the Great War to his death in 1946, he was at the elbow of power, indefatigable, ingenious and dazzlingly quick, in Virginia Woolf's words, 'like quicksilver on a sloping board – a little inhuman but very kindly, as inhuman people are'. For a prime minister or governor of a central bank who wanted advice on how to stop a panic half an hour before the markets opened, Maynard was your man. As a junior Treasury staffer in the liquidity crisis of July–August 1914, he guided Lloyd George to reduce bank rate, guarantee outstanding bills and pump money into the capital markets – the sort of thing which we now call quantitative easing and which then enabled the Allies to pay for the war. He more or less repeated the advice in the Great Crash of 1929. There is never much new about great financial crises, and not much mystery about how to solve them either.

Keynes's detractors, envious of the influence he had gained with so little apparent effort, denounced him as showy and unsound, even a little sinister. John Buchan cast him as the shifty stockbroker, Joseph Barralty, in *The Island of Sheep*. D. H. Lawrence was typically more visceral: 'Why is there this horrible sense of frowstiness, so repulsive, as if it came from deep inward dirt – a sort of sewer – deep in men like K?' When Keynes's tract against the Versailles Treaty, *The Economic Consequences of the Peace*, had its worldwide success, H. G. Wells described him as 'a man who believes himself to have been brilliant, but was really only opportune.' It was, after all, already a popular view at the time that the Allies were storing up trouble for the world by imposing such harsh terms on the Germans. The great physicist J. J. Thomson, declared that what Keynes said in that book 'was only what every sensible person knew already. He merely got easy publicity by mentioning things that he could have known only by being in the public service, such as Clemenceau's wearing mittens.'

Like many economists who achieve fame outside their profession, Keynes possessed enormous charm, both in person and in print, just as Walter Bagehot and John Kenneth Galbraith did. Every page of his contains a fetching wisecrack or a vivid character sketch. And he was a relentless persuader. Looking back on his Cambridge days, he wrote of the Apostles who moulded him: 'Victory was to those who could speak with the greatest appearance of clear, undoubting conviction and could best use the accents of infallibility.'

He could charm the trousers off a guardsman as easily as he charmed money for the ballet out of the Treasury. When he showed off the statistics of his sexual conquests to his fellow Apostles, he became known as 'Maynard, the iron copulating machine'. Unlike his first biographer, Roy Harrod, who was constrained by the law, and Skidelsky, constrained I think by delicacy, Davenport-Hines gives us the sex life, hot and strong, blow by blow. It is worth noting that Keynes also used the language of flirtation and seduction to describe his negotiations with bankers and politicians.

Some critics have attempted to elide his sexual practice and his economic theory. Both were, after all, promiscuous, a series of one-night stands. Was Keynes not famous for saying that 'in the long run we are all dead'? For all the density of his theoretical writings, was he ultimately anything more than the maestro of the quick fix?

Certainly it is easy to point to the things he got wrong: his belief in the 1930s that there was not going to be another world war or another world slump, his forecast of 'the euthanasia of the rentier', his fervent belief that by the twenty-first century we would have overcome the problems of scarcity and would all be free to pursue the lives of civilized pleasure then available only to the fortunate few of Bloomsbury. He not only lacked any religious sense, his sunny nature blinded him to the tragic possibilities of life and made him slow to grasp the menace of the Nazis.

On the other hand, his forceful advice to governments of all parties for so many years did, literally, do a power of good. At the end of the Second World War, already desperately ill with then incurable heart disease, he drove himself to the grave by crossing and recrossing the Atlantic to nail down the American loans which saved millions in Europe from starvation. It was a hero's end to a hero's career.

Davenport-Hines does not give much space to reflecting on Keynes's legacy either to economics or to politics. The implication, though, is that he taught us what to do about slumps, but that he did not live long enough to teach us what to do about inflationary booms. Yet even his notorious opponents, Hayek and Friedman, had enough respect for the suppleness of Keynes's intellect to be confident that he would have saved us from the pseudo-Keynesians.

His most dubious legacy is the enhanced prestige that economists have come to enjoy, despite their repeated failure to predict the next crisis, so acutely pointed out by HM the Queen. Keynes famously claimed that 'practical men, who believe themselves to be quite exempt from any intellectual influence, are usually the slaves of some defunct economist'. Recent experience would tend to suggest that something like the reverse is often the case. These days you find economists spinning theories in support of the conventional wisdom of businessmen, for example, the Efficient Market Hypothesis which declares that the market always prices things correctly. This hypothesis took a purler in 2008–09, as did the notion of 'the Great Moderation', which convinced Ben Bernanke and Gordon Brown that there would be no more boom and bust.

It could be argued too that Keynes's inexhaustible ingenuity has helped to imbue governments with an unjustified confidence in their own ability to 'steer the economy' and to find overnight solutions to deep-seated problems. Perhaps it is not Keynesian economic theory that has done the damage but the Keynesian political style.

DIVINE DISCONTENTS

Before he was hanged by the British, the Neapolitan admiral Francesco Caracciolo achieved immortality with his wisecrack that 'England has sixty different religions but only one sauce'. Neither the foodie explosion nor the waning of faith has dented the truth of his remark. The English do have a remarkable capacity for devising their own sects. What is remarkable is not simply the number of them but their endless variety: from the implacable plainness of the Quakers to the baroque ritualism of the Anglo-Catholics, from the tearful exuberance of the early Methodists to the modern Happy Clappies, not to mention Anglican plainchant and the glories of the Book of Common Prayer. In intensity too, these churches range from the ferocious discipline of the Plymouth Brethren to the virtual absence of dogma in the more spaced-out regions of the Church of England. The varieties of English atheism too are noteworthy, from the severe demands of the National Secular Society (as insistent as those of the old Lord's Day Observance Society) to the laid-back indifference of large swathes of the British public.

The most interesting religious leaders of the past century and a half do seem to define their faith in terms of a certain idea of what England could or should be. Religious conservatives are, I think, mistaken when they accuse liberals of simply adjusting their Christianity to the conventional wisdom of the day. That, for example, is the complaint which old-fashioned Catholics made against Basil Hume's leadership. Yet this saintly ex-abbot achieved, deliberately or not, something which had evaded all his predecessors: he transformed the Roman Church in Britain from a perceived foreign implant into a faith which sat at ease in the country. Similarly, the Red Dean's blindness to Soviet tyranny was risible and deplorable, but his attempt to reconcile the Church's social teaching with Christ's surely had something to be said for it. So did Charles Bradlaugh's crusade to demonstrate that an atheist could be a proud and noble person and not just a sour naysayer.

Perhaps the most fascinating of all English religious inventions was that of Methodism and the other variants of nonconformity. Their leaders were not so different from other religious innovators, magnetic, intolerable and intolerant. But their congregations devised not only a new style of worship for the mushrooming industrial settlements of Wales, the West Country and the North but almost a new civilization and an extraordinary refreshing of life. In fact, every reforming movement in England since the beginnings of the Reformation, from the Lollards through to the Puritans and the Quakers and on to the Baptists and Methodists, brought with it, along with the regrettable sectarian squabbles and ostracisms, a giddy surge of joy which was experienced most powerfully by the poor and the lower-middling sort. Transported to North America and more recently on to South America, this has turned out to be the most vibrant current in religion today. The exuberance of nonconformist worship baffled and shocked the Anglicans of the time, just as it was to baffle and infuriate modern socialist historians like E. P. Thompson. Yet there was a glorious zest about it. In its decline in Britain if not elsewhere, we have lost something irreplaceable.

BASIL HUME:
THE ENGLISH CARDINAL

The only time I met Basil Hume was at a wedding rehearsal in a South Kensington flat. I was the best man, and the newly elected Abbot of Ampleforth was putting us through our paces. He had been housemaster to the bride's brothers at the school attached to the Abbey, and they had been star pupils, one a great rugger player and the other a scholarly altar boy. As Basil finished pushing us this way and that in the sitting room of Alexandra Court, surroundings rather too fully furnished for fleshing out the moves in a nuptial Mass, I became aware of an overwhelming aura emanating from the gaunt Benedictine, at that moment, I think, discussing the prospects of next year's Ampleforth First XV. Even in my unregenerate state I recognized the unmistakable odour of sanctity, but not that alone. There was also present an equally unmistakable schoolmasterly aroma, but perhaps more potent than either of these – or so it seemed in the midst of this voluble Scots-Peruvian family – was the cool dew of Englishness that he exuded.

Hume was always unashamedly what he was, never pretended to be less or to be other. He confessed quite readily that the eight years he spent as housemaster of St Bede's were the happiest of his life. When he met the BBC war correspondent Kate Adie in Rome, and complimented her on her hat, and she said lamely that she never normally wore hats but when in Rome ... he interrupted her: 'Oh no my dear, you must never feel that. Always remember that you are English, it's a very proud thing to be'. Yet like many super-Englishmen, he was himself scarcely of English descent. His mother, Mimi, was a French girl who had fled from Lille with her family to escape the advancing German army and fell in love, at the age of eighteen, with a 35-year-old Border Scot, Dr William Hume, who was billeted next door to them in the Pas de Calais while working in the British military hospital at Boulogne. They were married in the Pyrenees, because Mimi's father was serving as military attaché at the Spanish Court. After producing two daughters, Mimi prayed that her next child should be a boy, and at her confessor's suggestion promised that, if her wish were granted, she would do her best to see that he became a priest – all a common enough story in a Catholic royalist family, but not exactly in the English tradition. By the age of sixteen, George, as he was christened, was already flirting with the Dominicans. And in September 1941, just turned eighteen, he became a novice at Ampleforth, taking the monastic name of Basil.

Thus from the time he entered the school in 1933 to the moment he resigned as abbot to become Archbishop of Westminster in 1976, Ampleforth was the only world he knew, apart from a brief curacy in the local village and his years studying at Oxford and in Belgium. No more cloistered preparation for the leadership of Britain's Roman Catholics could be imagined. He had not been a bishop, he had not travelled much, he had minimal experience of parish work. Yet in the eyes of the world he was a triumphant success, conveying to Catholics, Protestants and non-believers alike an image of the Christian vocation unrivalled in England in the twentieth century. Above all, he managed almost instinctively to complete the integration of the Catholic Church into English life. It is easy now to forget how bleak and rigid the separation between the Churches used to be. Sir William Hume, as he became, never darkened the door of a Catholic church after the baptism of his elder daughter, preferring the golf course for his Sunday communion. The first Anglican service Basil ever attended was his father's funeral in 1960. Anthony Howard, the son of a Church of England clergyman, cannot recall a Roman Catholic priest ever crossing the threshold of any vicarage or rectory his family lived in. And to an earlier generation, it would have seemed extraordinary, too, that an outsider such as Howard, who describes himself as 'a wistful agnostic' and who is best known as a political columnist and former editor of the *New Statesman*, should have been invited by Hume's literary executors to write Hume's life.

But it was a perceptive decision, for what made Hume such a memorable primate was not his theological originality (of which he claimed to have none) or even his pastoral energies, though these were creditable enough. What imprinted him on the map was his graceful negotiation of the relations between faith and country. And even if the secret of Hume's charm remains elusive, Howard is an alert and knowledgable guide to the political and ecclesiastical background to this crucial dimension of Hume's twenty-three years at Westminster. Encounters between local loyalties and the supranational claims of the universal Church are always pregnant with the possibilities of misunderstanding, suspicion and open conflict; but nowhere more so than in England, even when the twilight of faith might seem reason enough for the Churches to huddle together for warmth. Even Hume's near-perfect pitch let him down once, when he incautiously talked in an interview with the *Tablet* of his hopes for 'the conversion of England' after what he saw as a precipitate decision by the Church of England to ordain women. This let loose some triumphal effusions from overexcited Catholic commentators and even one or two counterblasts from intemperate Protestants (including me). Hume rushed to explain that he had been misinterpreted and the row was soon forgotten, as both the hopes and the fears proved to be exaggerated.

Howard chronicles Hume's long reign with clarity and concision, disentangling the story of the cardinal's sustained and successful campaign to establish that the Guildford Four and the Maguire Seven had been the victims of miscarriages of justice, and of his patient efforts to allow Mgr Bruce Kent to continue leading CND. Howard is particularly good on the machinations which brought a shy schoolmaster-monk to Westminster, to the great surprise of the general public but not of insiders. For it was an outrageously Establishment coup. The campaign for Hume was started off by articles in the *Sunday Times* and the *Economist*, the latter by the magazine's editor, Andrew Knight, an old Ampleforth pupil. The Duke of Norfolk and other assorted patrician recusants put their muscle behind Basil, some of their palms no doubt having felt the smack of his ferula, a curious whalebone instrument of punishment at St Bede's. When the Apostolic Delegate, Bruno Heim, was trying urgently to get in touch with Hume to tell him the news of his elevation, he could call on his next-door neighbour who happened to be not only Hume's brother-in-law, but also secretary to the cabinet. Most extraordinary of all, Mgr Heim liked to claim in later years that the appointment was clinched when he called on the Archbishop of Canterbury, who told him that the Abbot of Ampleforth was the only man for the job – a meeting, as Howard says, inconceivable at any other time since the Reformation.

Thus Hume was both the product and the symbol of a great rapprochement. He was surfing a wave, but nobody could have surfed it better. Yet this was not how he himself looked back on his time. He always felt that he was overestimated, and lamented that he had failed to pass on a healthy and happy Church to his successor. As in other Churches in Britain and in Catholic communities elsewhere in Europe, attendance at Mass fell rapidly and the number of vocations dwindled to vanishing point. Only the ordination of women, which was such a setback to hopes of ecumenical progress, helped to bolster the Anglican priesthood. Hume himself had no strong objection to women priests: 'I personally, if the authorities of my Church agreed to the ordination of women, would have no problem with that. But I am a man under authority'. He did chafe under that authority, however loyally he upheld it. He was particularly disheartened by the Pope's rejection of the Liverpool National Pastoral Congress, the brainchild of Archbishop Derek Worlock, to conservative Catholics the object of unrelenting suspicion and loathing. *The Easter People*, as its report was entitled, expressed in public for the first time the views of 2000 Catholic clergy and laity, views which turned out to be startlingly open and tolerant on most of the vexed issues of the day, from birth control to the reception of non-Catholics at Mass. Hume personally presented a copy to John Paul II at Castel Gandolfo, only to see the Holy Father wave it away impatiently without reading it. Hume's tussles with the future Pope Benedict XVI on the subject of homosexuality were no more productive. Here I think Howard's treatment is a little bland, giving the impression that Hume was speaking for a united English Catholic community against an implacable Roman Curia. The truth is that there was a war on inside English Catholicism too, and Howard underplays the hostility of conservative Catholics, especially in the media, who made up in ferocity what they lacked in numbers.

But what impressed people about Hume was not his public pronouncements on matters of doctrine or discipline, which tended to be both rare and guarded. What caught and held the attention was his unfeigned humility, his willingness to admit he was wrong, and his limitless capacity to forgive. He even made a firm friend of his contemporary, later a senior courtier, who had in 1941 accused him of cowardice for becoming a monk rather than joining up, and at the end of hostilities wrote to him saying, 'You can come out now – it's quite safe'. Nor could Hume be dismissed as an Establishment sycophant. Long after Margaret Thatcher had left Number 10, when he was driving past Downing Street he would chant 'Maggie Out! Maggie Out!' Above all, he conveyed a sense of human fragility, an unguarded vulnerability, which both made people feel that he was like them and so could speak to them, and also reminded them of what they took to be the original spirit of the Church.

This appearance of fragility was deceptive. Basil Hume was more robust than he looked or than he felt himself to be. In his early years as a monk he had experienced what is known as 'aridity', a sense of God's absence. He willingly admitted that he would like to have been married and, when asked whether he often thought about it, he answered 'Yes, every day'. Yet in the long run his vocation seems to have been as strong as his wiry physique, and his will fully adequate to the demands made on it. Howard sums up by saying that Cardinal Hume's two great achievements were 'to identify English Catholicism with English culture' and 'to symbolise Christian values in an increasingly sceptical society'. This is true enough, but it is perhaps a little tamely phrased. For the frisson that Basil Hume generated was more unnerving than Anthony Howard conveys. He was the witness, not only or not so much to the truth of the religion he happened to be born into, as to a possibility of life that seemed no longer available, and his voice was like the whistle of a train that stopped running years ago but which you can sometimes hear at night on the far side of the valley.

THE RED DEAN

In his prime, Dr Hewlett Johnson was one of the most famous men in the world. Almost from the moment he was made Dean of Canterbury in 1931, he became instantly recognizable everywhere as the Red Dean. His faith in the Communist Party, and in Stalin in particular, was unshakable. Purges and famines, executions and persecutions passed him by. Though he never saw the need actually to join the Party, he remained a tankie to the last, until he was finally winkled out of the deanery in 1963, when he was pushing ninety.

The only occasion in his whole life when he admitted to experiencing doubt was in the early 1890s, when he was an engineering student at Owens College, the forerunner of Manchester University. He had retained the biblical certainties of childhood, and was knocked sideways by a lecture given by Professor Dawkins, the eminent Darwinian: 'I turned from the lecture room with a passive face and a calm voice. But within there was tumult and utter darkness. The evolution theory was true – of this I was convinced. And it made the story of Genesis and the Bible false.'

We have barely recovered from this delicious coincidence of surname – the Dawkins in question was the geologist and palaeontologist Sir William Boyd Dawkins, not a direct ancestor, if ancestor at all, of the present carrier of the Darwin meme – before Johnson has recovered from his spiritual despond. In a twinkling he has reconciled God and Darwin. Thereafter his magnificent self-confidence never flags, his melodious voice booms on, wowing sympathetic audiences all over the world. In 1946, already into his seventies, he gave a prizefighter's salute to a crowd of 30,000 inside and outside Madison Square Garden, eclipsing Paul Robeson and Dean Acheson. An awestruck young Alistair Cooke reported in the *Guardian* that 'he looks like a divinity and he looks like the portrait on every dollar bill.' The resemblance to George Washington is undeniable, although there is a creepy hint of Alastair Sim too.

Never one to underestimate his own impact, he reported to his second wife, Nowell, that a colleague had said he was 'one of three English public men who could command the greatest audiences everywhere.' 'I know it is true,' he added, while dutifully sharing the credit between the Almighty and the Communist cause. He recorded in his autobiography that when he and the Marxist scientist J. D. Bernal were in an exuberant crowd at the World Peace Conference in Rome in 1959, Bernal turned to him and said: 'Did you hear that, dean? They are shouting: "An honest priest, he should be our Pope."' It's a thought that might well have crossed the dean's own mind, feeling as strongly as he did about the imperfections of the Catholic Church, certainly as compared with the unimpeachable performance of the Communist Party of the Soviet Union, and the CPs of China and Cuba too.

His self-assurance was anchored in a happy family, where untroubled faith went hand in hand with an untroubled income from Johnson's Wire Works of Manchester. The firm was founded in 1791 and continues to this day as AstenJohnson, exporting papermaking machinery to fifty-six countries. Hewlett, born in 1874, felt quite at home with the paternalism which could flourish within a firm that remained in the hands of a single family, though he deplored 'the harder and less human atmosphere' which came with technological change. He didn't disdain the Johnson's dividends he received, or the settlement from his first wife's father which came to him on her death.

During the General Strike, his sympathies were of course with the miners, though one of his uncles, Alfred Hewlett, was chairman of the Mining Owners' Federation and another, William Hewlett, was chairman of the Wigan Coal Company. I am not sure whether the Hewlett brothers were included in Lord Birkenhead's celebrated comment that 'it would be possible to say without exaggeration that the miners' leaders were the stupidest men in England if we had not had frequent occasion to meet the owners.'

In 1952, when many capitalists were still strapped after the war, Johnson owned four flats and three garages in Canterbury, two properties in the nearby village of Charing, two more in South-east London and a holiday home in North Wales, where Nowell and their two daughters had taken refuge during the war. He also possessed a nicely spread portfolio, which included holdings not only in Johnson's Wire Works but in Lonrho, not yet unmasked as the unacceptable face of capitalism. The prize money of £10,000 (perhaps £200,000 in today's money) from the Stalin Peace Prize which he had won the year before was icing on a substantial cake.

John Butler is a Canterbury man and an emeritus professor at the University of Kent, best known for his book *The Quest for Becket's Bones*. The dean now and then compared his own struggles for truth with those of St Thomas, though the dean's bones and indeed the rest of him are easier to track. But it was politics rather than saintliness which got him the deanery, through the rare coincidence of a Labour prime minister in the shape of Ramsay MacDonald and a leftish archbishop of York, William Temple. This is an excellent biography, crisp, sometimes cutting, but never less than fair and always as sympathetic as humanly possible to its subject even in his most maddening moments. Aided by access to the dean's archive, Butler brings out all Johnson's good humour and generosity of spirit. In everything bar his politics, he was a rather traditional Anglican dean, broad in his theology, simple in his faith. He enjoyed food and wine and family life, gave his money away to anyone down on their luck, believed that his cathedral should be a place of light and beauty, filled it with flowers and revived the choir school. Left to himself, he would have introduced incense too. He was also the first prelate since Archbishop Baldwin in the twelfth century to argue that Canterbury should have its own university.

He was a brave and restless man, exulting in travel, adventure and his own celebrity. When the Germans repeatedly bombed Canterbury, he strode about the debris with relish, writing to Nowell that 'I would not have missed this for anything ... The Cathedral looks *glorious* without its windows.' One is reminded of Churchill saying to Margot Asquith in the darkest days of the Great War that 'I would not be out of this glorious, delicious war for anything the world could give me.' On VE Day, the dean was in Moscow with Stalin. Two weeks later, he was among the first British observers to enter Auschwitz. He wrote about what he saw with a superb angry eloquence.

But there is no doubt that Johnson was gullible. Butler does not mention the period in the 1930s when he strode up and down the country preaching that Major Douglas and Social Credit were destined to 'win the world', until he discovered that Douglas had come out for Franco. Like many egomaniacs, he was extremely interested in his own health, and always ready to swallow the latest dietary fad. He was convinced that a Romanian doctor called Anna Aslan had discovered a drug, Gerovital H3, which could reverse aging and restore hearing loss. The drug turned out to be nothing more mysterious than procaine hydrochloride, now better known as Novocain, the local anaesthetic used by dentists. But Johnson continued to swear by it until his death.

After he had swallowed something once, he never stopped taking the medicine. David Caute begins *The Fellow-Travellers: Intellectual Friends of Communism* (1973) with the story of Hewlett and Nowell escaping from the World Peace Council and clambering aboard a local bus going they knew not where and Hewlett saying to the driver: 'Tickets to the end of the line, please.' And he toed that line all the way. Victor Gollancz, who published Johnson's bestseller *The Socialist Sixth of the World* in 1939, tried to make Johnson add something critical about the Nazi–Soviet Pact, which had just been signed, but he merely blamed Finland and defended the pact as a regrettable but necessary expedient. After the war, he gave evidence in support of French communist journalists when they were sued by Victor Kravchenko for alleging that he had invented his stories of Christian churches being persecuted in the Soviet Union. In the same year, 1949, he sided with the Hungarian secret police when they arrested Cardinal Mindszenty on trumped-up charges of treason. Later on, he remained deaf to Khrushchev's speech to the 20th Congress and defended the Soviet invasion of Hungary.

Of all the rapturous moments he enjoyed in the company of the great, I would pick out his stay at the Habana Riviera hotel in the year after the Cuban Missile Crisis, when he was nearly ninety. At a glittering reception (there is a touch of Sylvie Krin about the dean's memoirs – the receptions are always 'glittering', just as the women are always wearing 'splendid gowns'), he met not only Castro but the 'strong, vital, buoyant' Che Guevara and 'a lady with a sad, beautiful face', whom he and Nowell recognized as the implacable Dolores Ibárruri, better known as La Pasionaria. He was among his own people, big people.

His admiration for communism was inseparable from his worship of power. Not for nothing was *The Socialist Sixth* retitled *The Soviet Power* for the American market. Nettled by squabbles in the cathedral chapter, he put down the archdeacon by announcing that he was off to Russia because 'I felt that I ought to use all my spare time for something bigger.' During the war he consoled Nowell that, if there were an invasion and the Germans were brutal to him, it would be because 'we stand for something big and Eternal; and it is upon that which is Eternal and upon the Source of all that is big that we can confidently rely'. Stalin, God and the Dean – that appeared to be the command structure of the Big Battalions, but not necessarily in that order.

For someone of Johnson's temperament, to be made a dean was both ideal and fatal. It is no accident that all the most vicious feuds in Anglican life should centre on the deanery, as Trollope spotted and as was made manifest more recently in the row over the Occupy encampment at St Paul's. A cathedral dean, once appointed, is virtually irremovable by either Church or State, as Archbishop Fisher made clear to the House of Lords when back-woods peers staged a debate in the hope of getting rid of Johnson. Archbishop Lang had tried and failed; now Fisher, that flinty disciplinarian, offered Johnson the same deal: curb your public utterances or resign. Hewlett gaily rejected both options and sailed on, loathed by his canons, abhorred by the headmaster of the King's School, Canterbury, John Shirley, who was as guilt-ridden as Johnson was nonchalant, and eventually by the pupils too, 300 of whom signed a petition after Hungary, saying, 'We hope that this appeal to your strong humanitarian sense will shatter your mis-conceived faith in the Soviet Union.' Some hope. The dean might be 'blind, unreasonable and stupid', as Fisher claimed, but nothing except extreme old age could shift him from his little kingdom. And nothing could shut him up.

What infuriated his critics, from Gollancz on the left to Fisher on the right, was that there was no evidence that Johnson had made any but the most superficial study of the issues that he spouted on with such mellifluous certainty, from famines in the 1930s to germ warfare in Korea. He believed everything his minders in Russia and China told him. It is hard to guess how much Marx or Lenin he had actually read.

Some reviewers found *The Socialist Sixth* so incredible that they wondered whether Johnson had actually written it himself. They were nearer the truth than they knew. Butler uses the archive to demonstrate that large parts of that book and of *The Upsurge of China* (1961) were copied, word for word, out of propaganda supplied by state organizations such as the Society of Cultural Relations with the USSR. The same is true of the memorial address he delivered to the British-Soviet Friendship Society after Stalin's death, later published as a sixpenny pamphlet, *Joseph Stalin*, 'by the Very Rev. Hewlett Johnson, Dean of Canterbury'. He had no pride of authorship and was as happy as any other Party hack to do anything for the cause. He didn't have much interest in public debate: he orated, he didn't argue. Tricky questioners were palmed off with a copy of *The Socialist Sixth*. His autobiography was entitled *Searching for Light*, but there was a good deal of humbug in the title, as there is in most titles couched in the participial optative. He had found the light first go, and what the light seemed mostly to illuminate was the persona of Dr Hewlett Johnson.

Butler expresses some puzzlement that both Stalin and Mao were so willing to grant the dean private but well-publicized audiences. Is this so mysterious? The dean was the prototype of the useful celebrity who could authenticate the benign intentions of the regime and, in particular, rebut accusations that it was persecuting the Church. He was an unguent for internal as well as external application. The patriarch of Smolensk told him that *The Socialist Sixth* had been of such value to the Church in Russia that he had given a copy to every priest in his diocese. The dean was all the more valuable because his office was so easily confused with the archbishop's, which further enraged both Lang and Fisher.

In his last years, when he had become something of a joke, his usefulness to the Soviet bloc diminished, and his prominence probably served only to blight the prospects for Christian socialism in Britain. Twenty years after his death, the members of the Archbishop of Canterbury's Commission on Urban Priority Areas were bewildered to find their report *Faith in the City* rubbished as 'Marx in the City' – a caricature of its mild and thoughtful critique. Johnson had never seemed interested in any varieties of socialism. For him, it was communism and only communism that had recovered 'the essential form of the real belief in God which organised Christianity has so largely lost'. 'While we're waiting for God, Russia is *doing* it.' There was no more to be said.

It was futile for the canons of Canterbury to write to *The Times* in March 1940 dissociating themselves from the dean's political utterances but insisting that they too believed it was the duty of all Christians to further social and economic reform. For Johnson, Stalin's way was the only way. Instead of carrying on the milder tradition of F. D. Maurice and Charles Kingsley, of R. H. Tawney and Dick Sheppard (briefly his predecessor as dean), he obliterated the memory of it, just as Lenin and Stalin had obliterated the social democrats.

Besides, far from wishing to smooth over any little local difficulties, Hewlett exulted in them, though he pretended not to. He had every reason to oust the egregious Canon John Crum, who described him as 'a slimy liar' and boasted in a meeting of the chapter that 'I always try all the time to pour ridicule and contempt over the dean.' When the canon was finally forced out, Hewlett wrote to his wife: 'CRUM IS GOING! How sad that I should have to rejoice but I do.' More Heepishly, he wrote to Archbishop Temple: 'My earnest prayer is that this good man's sacrifice may be used by God to purge me if possible from faults which He alone sees.' No question of anyone else being able to see any such faults.

Did he ever pause for a moment towards the end of his long life and wonder whether he might have been wrong about anything? Did he ever have another moment of doubt such as he had suffered in Professor Dawkins's lecture room? In his summing-up, Butler charitably offers the possibility that 'perhaps the realisation finally dawned on him that he had reached a point at which he could no

longer rethink his position without destroying himself and there-
fore had no option but to go on.' Even that much self-knowledge
sounds implausible. Hewlett Johnson was never much given to
rethinking. Like many charismatics, he lived in an eternal pres-
ent, a land of gestures without consequences, never looking back,
always on the lookout for the next big thing. He would not have
weakened at the last.

CHARLES BRADLAUGH:
THE ADMIRABLE ATHEIST

He was 'unquestionably a great and good man'. Who could forget 'his gigantic stature, his warm temperament, his good health and good humour, his bull-necked obstinacy, his generous and open temper? ... He had many enemies and fought them all with generosity ... In the last glimpse of the enormous "Iconoclast", he is a priest defending an altar.'

This was the verdict of G. K. Chesterton on the death of Charles Bradlaugh (1833–91), atheist and republican, publicist for contraception – and, in short, for pretty much everything Chesterton hated. This genial tribute from the champion of Orthodoxy with a capital O to the self-styled 'Iconoclast' (Bradlaugh's pen name) was not simply another piece of glittering paradox, one more instance of Chesterton's determination to startle the reader at all costs. On the contrary, that was the way most people saw Bradlaugh. From the moment he burst on to the scene as a teenage preacher to his last days thundering at the Bar of the House of Commons, he struck everyone as enormous: physically so, six feet two, broad-browed, broad-shouldered (in later years elephantine and ponderous of gait) and gifted with a resonant voice which could reach audiences in their thousands without any visible effort;

but also eloquent, serious, immensely moral and decent. He was the Gloria Steinem of atheism, an inexhaustible public personality who lent star quality to an unpopular and alarming cause. He defied in his own person the caricature so crudely chalked by Lord Randolph Churchill that the supporters of atheism 'were for the most part . . . the residuum, the rabble and the scum of the population; the bulk of them persons to whom all restraint – religious, moral or legal – is odious and intolerable.'

Nobody could possibly say any such thing of Bradlaugh. For one thing, he was a lifelong teetotaller. After he had been sacked as a Sunday-school teacher for pointing out the discrepancies in the Thirty-Nine Articles and the Gospels, he took the Queen's shilling and was enrolled in the 7th Dragoon Guards, where he was nicknamed Leaves because he preferred tea to alcohol and spent much of the time turning the pages of a book. All his life he was desperately concerned about appearances. He fired the poet James Thomson from the paper he edited for drunkenness ('The City of Dreadful Night' first appeared in Bradlaugh's *National Reformer*). And though he was more or less in love with his long-time collaborator Annie Besant (and she desperately so with him), there could be no question of their living together so long as her ghastly husband, the Rev. Frank Besant, was still alive.

Born poor, Bradlaugh never lost his sympathy for the poor classes he came from. His father was a solicitor's clerk, his mother a nurse, and he left school at the age of eleven to work as a wharf clerk in a coal merchant's. Never embittered, never corrupted, he stayed poor. As a teenage soldier in Ireland, he had seen the horrors of the evictions after the Famine. When he became an MP, he was dismayed by how little interest his fellow MPs took in the sufferings and struggles of the Indian people. He was soon known as 'the Member for India'.

But his compassion didn't temper his critique of Christianity. In the first issue of his first periodical, the short-lived *Investigator*, he set out his editorial aims bluntly enough to satisfy any

Hitchens or Dawkins: 'We believe all the religions of the world are founded on error, in the ignorance of natural causes and material conditions, and we deem it our duty to expose their falsity. Our policy is therefore aggressive.' And it was.

It was also unremittingly constructive. Derision and demolition were only necessary preliminaries. Bradlaugh was never more mid-Victorian than in his determination to build an alternative secular society. It was his predecessor George Jacob Holyoake who coined the term 'secularism' – 'the province of the real, the known, the useful and the affirmative' – in the year of the Great Exhibition, and it was not the least of the achievements of the age. But it was Bradlaugh who, still only twenty-four, became president of the London Secular Society, elbowing aside the more hesitant Holyoake. For the rest of his life, he was the leader of English free thought. Though not always unchallenged, he saw off every challenger in briskly contested elections for any post that was going.

Bradlaugh believed in the Unchurch Militant. He despised the Beatitudes. 'Poverty of spirit is no virtue,' he wrote. 'Honesty of spirit, manliness of spirit, bold, uncompromising, determined resistance of wrong, and assertion of right, should be taught in lieu of that poverty of spirit which allows the proud and haughty in spirit to trample upon and oppress the highest human rights.' Here he is at one with Nietzsche, his near contemporary, for whom the worship of weakness was the worst thing about the Christian religion. Indeed, Bradlaugh forms one more link in the great chain that joins Lucretius' praise of Epicurus for breaking the shackles of superstition and teaching man to stand up, through Bertrand Russell in *Why I Am Not a Christian*, to Dawkins's call for 'atheist pride' and Hitchens's abhorrence of the 'guilty pleasures of subjection and abjection'. Those who preferred to stay on their knees were literally benighted, crouching in the dark, victims of the ultimate False Alarm. 'Get off your knees' has been the humanists' trumpet call down the ages, and no one has trumpeted it more thrillingly than Bradlaugh.

He was not so much a philosopher or a writer as a public man, most at home on the platform, in the witness box or hammering on the doors of the House of Commons. Bryan Niblett is a barrister, computer scientist and judicial arbitrator, and he is nicely attuned to his subject. This excellent biography, the first for nearly forty years, makes us understand why Bradlaugh deserves more than a footnote in political and legal history. His contemporaries understood this well enough. Half-a-dozen biographies were published in his lifetime and several more after his death. His funeral procession to Brookwood Cemetery required three special trains and was attended by many young men who were to be heard much of in the next century, notably Gandhi and Lloyd George. Lord Queensberry was also present, to bear witness to his loathing of 'Christian tomfoolery'. So was Walter Sickert, who painted the enormous portrait of Bradlaugh that now hangs in Manchester Art Gallery.

To the last, Bradlaugh remained a pioneer of customs we now take for granted, his daughter Hypatia arranging for him to be buried in one of the London Necropolis Company's earth-to-earth coffins made of papier-mâché. Bradlaugh had called her Hypatia after the fourth-century bluestocking who was said to have been the last librarian of Alexandria and who was martyred by a fanatical Christian sect, her body mutilated with pottery shards. He was never less than consistent.

To later generations, though, Bradlaugh's impact has faded. His long struggle to be admitted to his seat as MP for Northampton without swearing the oath has come to seem a dusty curiosity, a picturesque hiccup in our seamless progress towards a secular world. It didn't appear that way at the time. Niblett's lucid and painstaking account of the saga forms the centrepiece of his book, and is not to be missed. In retrospect, Bradlaugh's seemingly unpatterned clashes with the authorities look more like a neat row of milestones on the road from the pre-modern polity to the one we now live in. Every battle he threw himself into turned into a test case. He was often rebuffed at first. Yet in the long term he mostly prevailed, and his prevailing unblocked a remarkable sequence of changes in attitudes, practices and institutions.

As a journalist, he was in trouble from the start. WHSmith, by the 1850s a presence at every large railway station, refused to stock the *National Reformer*, out of a hostility towards subversive publications which the firm has sturdily maintained throughout the succeeding 150 years. In 1868, the Attorney General attempted to squash the *Reformer* on the grounds that it had not gone through the hoops demanded by the Newspaper and Stamp Duties Act of 1819 – one of the notorious Six Acts enacted during Lord Liverpool's repressions after Peterloo. The paper in time-honoured tradition carried the banner: PROSECUTED BY HER MAJESTY'S ATTORNEY GENERAL. The jury found against Bradlaugh, but within three months the government passed the Newspapers, Printers and Reading Rooms Repeal Act 1869, which repealed the 1819 Act, and eight more statutes that fettered free speech in one way or another. This was the final extinction of a tradition, dating back to the Middle Ages, that publication was not a right but a privilege to be licensed by the authorities.

Sometimes Bradlaugh deliberately invited prosecution. When in 1877 he and Annie Besant reissued a pamphlet on contraception, entitled *The Fruits of Philosophy: or The Private Companion of Young Married People*, he sent copies to the chief clerk of magistrates at Guildhall and to the police, advising them that the book was on sale at Stonecutter Street. The jury found that the pamphlet was obscene and a short jail sentence was imposed, but the Appeal Court found the prosecution defective, and Bradlaugh and Annie were set free. By then, the pamphlet (which had been selling quietly ever since it was first published in Britain in 1833) had sold over 100,000 copies: the topic of family planning could never be effectively suppressed again.

For Annie, the personal consequences of the prosecution were grim. In a rage, the Rev. Frank Besant filed an action to recover custody of their daughter Mabel. Sir George Jessel, Master of the Rolls and the first Jew to be appointed a judge, said that Annie's writings in support of atheism 'must quite cut her off, practically, not merely from the sympathy of, but from social intercourse with, the great majority of her sex'. He did not believe, he said, that 'a single clergyman's wife in England would approve of such conduct, or associate with Mrs Besant'. As for *The Fruits of Philosophy*:

> The pamphlet itself, even if it had been couched in the chastest and most refined language, would be grossly immoral; and it would be subversive of all human civilised society if the female population of our country were once imbued with the idea that they might safely indulge in unchaste intercourse without fear of any of the consequences such intercourse entails upon them.

After this effusion, surpassing even Mervyn Griffith-Jones's remarks in leading the prosecution of *Lady Chatterley's Lover* eighty years later, it was not surprising that Jessel ordered custody of Mabel to be given to Besant. Annie then launched an appeal for a judicial separation, which Jessel refused. This judgment effectively barred her in perpetuity from petitioning for divorce. She was stuck with Besant until he died, which wasn't until 1917. Her dream of marrying Bradlaugh was shattered. The only consolation was that Mabel and her brother Digby both opted to live with their mother when they grew up.

How much did Bradlaugh mind? Hard to say. He was compassionate but he was also ruthless and single-minded. Any of his collaborators who got in his way were sidelined or pushed out: James Thomson; Edward Aveling, Marx's son-in-law; Annie herself when she took up socialism and then theosophy, equally detestable aberrations in Bradlaugh's eyes. Like Annie, he had no sense of humour and not much imagination. His own wife, Susannah, declined into chronic alcoholism and retired to live with Bradlaugh's parents in a Sussex cottage. She died there aged forty-five, sending 'great love to dear Papa'. Niblett records all this without much comment, but it is hard not to see Susannah as having been bundled out when she became an embarrassment to the cause. Bradlaugh liked fishing – he held the record for the largest carp caught with rod and line – and dogs. He doted on Annie's St Bernard, Lion, which looked remarkably like him. Yet in private life there was something unappealing about him, an unyielding, flinty quality.

Which no doubt he needed to persist in his extraordinary struggle to take his seat in the House of Commons. He was elected for Northampton in 1880 at the fourth attempt, on a 90 per cent turnout. His fellow candidate for the town, Henry Labouchère, who was as cynical and free-living as Bradlaugh was earnest and straitlaced, remarked on hearing the news: 'Oh! They've swallowed Bradlaugh after all, have they?' But after a repellent display of prejudice and self-contradiction on the part of the House, Bradlaugh was not allowed to affirm. Although the Parliamentary Oaths Act of 1866 had given this right to 'Quakers, and every other Person for the time being permitted to make a solemn Affirmation or Declaration instead of taking an oath', the Tories maintained that such 'permitted Persons' did not include avowed atheists. At the same time, a second select committee found that Bradlaugh was not a fit person to swear the oath of allegiance either, since he didn't believe in it. Again and again, Bradlaugh pleaded at the Bar of the House, again and again he was chucked out, and again the voters of Northampton returned him at by-election and general election alike.

Bradlaugh sued the sergeant-at-arms, Captain Gossett, and lost. But in his judgment in the case of *Bradlaugh v. Gossett*, the lord chief justice, Lord Coleridge, ruled that 'what is said or done within the walls of Parliament cannot be inquired into in a court of law. The jurisdiction of the Houses over their own members, their right to impose discipline within their walls, is absolute.' This judgment remains the classic authority on the powers of Parliament over its members.

And so on it went. Finally, years after being first elected, Bradlaugh was at last allowed to take his seat thanks to a cool and masterly coup by the speaker, Arthur Wellesley Peel, Sir Robert's youngest son. No sooner had Peel been re-elected speaker on 12 January 1885 than he got up and said: 'I have come clearly and without hesitation to the conclusion that it would neither be my duty to prohibit the honourable gentleman from coming nor to permit a motion to be made standing between him and his taking of the oath.' The leader of the House, Sir Michael Hicks-Beach, rose to object. The speaker silenced him, reminding him that Hicks-Beach had himself not yet taken the oath. And that was the end of it.

What is so remarkable is that Bradlaugh took the oath, which is precisely what he had sought not to do at the outset. Even more remarkably, he took it twice, because the crowd around the speaker's chair was so great that the clerk was not sure he had done it the first time. So twice he swore allegiance to the Queen whom he wanted to see the back of, in the name of a God in whom he did not believe. Twice he kissed the Bible. And he shook hands with the speaker and everyone agreed that it was all a good show. Three years later, Mr Bradlaugh MP introduced a Private Members' Bill consisting of two short clauses, permitting anyone who objected to being sworn to affirm instead. The bill sailed through, and even Lord Randolph and the Archbishop of Canterbury voted for it, for all the world as though they had never thought anything else. There's progress for you.

For a deeper insight into what was happening, it is worth going back to the debates on the Affirmation Bill that Gladstone's government (not the GOM himself, who was recuperating in Cannes at the time) had formulated in February 1883. In the event, the Tories defeated the bill by three votes, 292–289, but Gladstone very nearly swung it with his amazing speech. When he first became an MP, he had had an almost theocratic vision of politics. In 1838, he had violently objected to the renewal of the modest government grant to the Catholic seminary of St Patrick's Maynooth, and through the 1840s zigzagged to and fro on the issue. In *The State in Its Relations with the Church*, he had passionately argued that the state had a duty to uphold the national Church and so by extension to deny recognition to any other Church, let alone to atheists. Now, fifty years later, he told the House that they must 'leave no distinctions between man and man on the ground of religious differences'. And he quoted, in Latin, six lines from Lucretius' *De rerum natura*, which he described as 'noble and majestic' and translated as meaning: 'Divinity exists in remote inaccessible recesses of which we know nothing; but with us it has no dealing, with us it has no relation.' Niblett tells us that members were visibly moved, by the learning of the prime minister as much as by the meaning of the words.

But there was more to it than that. Here was the embodiment of Victorian Christianity quoting, as a clinching authority, the words of the most famous materialist of the ancient world. The gods took no interest in our affairs; they were unmoved by our merits or demerits; we were on our own. One can hear the hinge of history creaking, with Bradlaugh rattling at the doorknob.

What may seem in retrospect so surprising is how popular he remained throughout his struggles, among a far wider public than his fellow atheists and republicans. When he was ill with Bright's disease towards the end of his life, several churches offered up prayers for him, setting off false rumours that he was no longer an atheist. He was popular in part because he was a fine fellow, but also because he didn't add socialism to his atheism and republicanism. He was no threat to property. He remained a thoroughgoing Gladstonian Liberal all his life, claiming that 'socialists are the most unwise and illogical people you can happen to meet.' He asserted that property owners in England were in the enormous majority. 'All savings in the Savings Bank, the Co-operative Store, the

Building Society, the Friendly Society and the Assurance Society are property, and I will show you that there are millions of working men in that condition.'

Even his republicanism was of a kind familiar to us, witty, sardonic, but ultimately harmless: 'I do not pretend to have pleaded for republicanism. I have only pleaded against the White Horse of Hanover . . . I loathe these small German breast-bestarred wanderers, whose only merit is their loving hatred of one another. In their own land they vegetate and wither unnoticed; here we pay them highly to marry and perpetuate a pauper prince race.' Like many modern republicans, he didn't call for the Queen to be thrown out; he merely wanted to avoid the Prince of Wales succeeding. In this sense he posed no immediate or serious threat to the status quo. There can have been few men who brought about more change and gave less offence.

As he lay dying, the resolution of June 1880, denying him the right either to take the oath or to affirm, was expunged from the journals of the House, very nearly nem. con. In supporting the motion, Gladstone reiterated the point he had made at the start of the whole miserably protracted business: that in trying to exclude a properly elected MP, the House was overreaching its jurisdiction. 'In an assembly possessed of almost immeasurable powers and with no possibility of appeal, excess of jurisdiction is the greatest fault the House can possibly commit. It is one of the highest functions of this House to limit its own functions and jurisdiction.' This problem of self-limitation remains as pressing as ever; it steams from every manure heap and quacks from every duckhouse. What hay Bradlaugh would have made with it all.

MR GLADSTONE'S RELIGION

W hat is Gladstone trying to tell us? Through the matted
undergrowth of his prose, with its vatic pronouncements,
its interminable subordinate clauses, its ponderous hesitations and
protestations, its sudden whimsical excursions and conjectures,
something – not a message exactly but not a philosophy either,
perhaps the only word would be a mind – is struggling to declare
itself. A mind, moreover, that insists on its continuing vivacity,
and claims our attention not merely as a brilliant relic of its own
time but as an unstilled voice in the conversation of ours. We may
explore and even admire the minds of Gladstone's mentors and
contemporaries: Peel's earnest reforming zeal, Palmerston's gung-
ho gunboat liberalism, Disraeli's sugar castles of Empire – though
each is splendid in its way, they do not speak to us directly. But
Gladstone haunts us still; he is the greatest of the undead.

Over the past ten years and more, I have become aware – a little
reluctantly because he never used to be one of my heroes – that
we are faced in Britain with an agenda that Gladstone would have
recognized as his own: the devolution of power to the four nations
of the United Kingdom, the revival of the little platoons and the
protecting of local government from the pretensions of Whitehall,
the shrinking of the overblown state ('retrenchment and reform',
to use the resonant phrase so often attributed to Gladstone but

actually coined by John Bright), and then the most ticklish question of all, how to undo the disadvantages of the poor without denting their self-confidence and damaging their independence. In the wider world, our present agenda has an even more Gladstonian ring: the defence of human rights, the protection of small, faraway oppressed nations, the defeat of piracy and terrorism, the restoration of the European balance. Is there a single theme that Blair has articulated which Gladstone did not articulate before him, and with greater resonance? More than once in the past couple of years, politicians have been unable to resist quoting Gladstone's reminder that 'the sanctity of life in the hill villages of Afghanistan, among the winter snows, is as inviolable in the eyes of Almighty God as can be your own.'

The Gladstonian agenda does not apply solely to government, or even to a single party. Over the past two decades, each of the three main parties has experienced a Gladstonian moment: first, Labour came to understand that individual self-development was not compatible with state socialism and that only free trading could maximize prosperity. Then the Conservatives came to the conclusion that there was such a thing as society after all; or rather they remembered that they had always thought so and wondered why they'd ever found themselves spouting such crude Manchester liberalism. Finally, the Liberal Democrats rediscovered retrenchment and reform and began to shuffle away from the vapid tax-and-spend policies they had drifted into. Their new spokesmen, whose thoughts were captured in the so-called *Orange Book* – Vincent Cable, David Laws and Mark Oaten – were the first prominent Liberals since Jo Grimond who could seriously claim to be heirs of the Grand Old Man.

Political commentators point out that parties make such shifts because otherwise they have little hope of getting elected. Gladstone himself, whose eye for the main chance remained undimmed, would not have thought that an unhealthy motive. But there were deeper motives at work, too. In all three parties there was a dawning awareness that the dogmas they had come to adopt did not fit the case: they failed either to relate to the circumstances of modern British society or to echo the underlying philosophy that was supposed to drive the party. Gladstone would have recognized these intimations: he felt them at recurring moments both in his long political career and in his personal religious and philosophical life.

Why then are we not more eager to attend to Gladstone's revisions and recantations as the forerunners of our own? Why is David Bebbington's *The Mind of Gladstone* such a lonely enterprise? First, because of the sheer difficulty of reading Gladstone. His contemporaries often found his writings 'diffuse and laboured', a criticism that with his habitual self-chastisement he took to heart by underlining it. 'Sometimes,' the *Athenaeum* remarked in 1879, 'we have a sentence so long and involved that nothing but a passionate intensity of meaning and a profuse vocabulary could have avoided a disastrous collapse.' T. H. Huxley, perhaps the most ferocious and unwavering of all Gladstone's opponents, accused him, with some justice, of rhetorical artifice. Many other critics, such as Mrs Humphry Ward, denounced him for lacking any sense of evidence and for being ready to make sweeping deductions from narrow premises.

Gladstone was well aware of his defects as a writer. As early as his thirties, he confessed to his brother-in-law that he wrote 'not by a genuine elasticity of spirit but by a plodding movement'. He knew his shortcomings as a scholar, too, and resolved in his diary that he would in future be 'avoiding scholarship on account of inability'. He noted of a damning review by E. A. Freeman of his *Studies on Homer and the Homeric Age* that it 'ought to humble me'.

But it didn't. On the contrary, he went on and on, and then some. His early *Church Principles Considered in Their Results*, which he described as 'a work of very sanguine Anglicanism', was 528 pages long. Much taken by Farini's *Stato Romano*, largely for its denunciation of the Jesuits, he translated it into four volumes of about 400 pages each — and then reviewed it himself, anonymously, in the *Edinburgh Review*. *Studies on Homer*, by no means his only writings on Homer, ran to three volumes of 576, 533 and 616 pages respectively. Then there were his sermons, mostly delivered to his family and servants, which fill a further three volumes. As prime minister, he became worried that he might be thought to devote too much time to these pursuits and hastened to write a letter to the *Spectator* denying the allegation that he began every day with 'his old friend Homer'.

The verdicts that these massive works provoked were often scorching. Sir George Cornewall Lewis, Gladstone's successor as chancellor of the exchequer and a formidable classical scholar, said that he was 'fundamentally wrong' about Homer. Tennyson thought his opinions on Homeric religion 'hobbyhorsical'. Huxley denounced Gladstone's ventures into palaeontology as 'the intrusion of an utter ignoramus into scientific questions'. True, Huxley was also increasingly enraged by Gladstone's appeal to the masses and by his failure to provide more state funding for science (plus ça change), but on this occasion he was on strong ground, since Gladstone's attempt to defend the historical veracity of the account of creation in Genesis had carelessly argued that birds came before land creatures.

This amateurishness, combined with the intolerable length of Gladstone's writings, has provided posterity with an excuse for not reading them and justified his biographers in dismissing them in a page or two as 'somewhat crackbrained', to quote Richard Shannon. Shannon's two-volume life offers a fuller account of Gladstone's intellectual development than other modern biographies, yet even he allots as much space to Macaulay's mesmerizingly destructive review of *The State in Its Relations with the Church* as he does to the contents of the book itself.

There is, besides, the natural tendency of political biographers to concentrate on the political struggle. Roy Jenkins's life gives us an entrancing account of the life of Victorian politicians: when they went to bed and got up, what they drank, what trains they took (Jenkins was a Bradshaw buff). But about what went on in Gladstone's head Jenkins leaves us not much the wiser. Here was a marvellous character, a great man, no doubt of that. But what precisely was he on about? Gladstone's contemporaries were just as puzzled. The knockdown vigour with which he put forward his opinions was equalled only by the alacrity with which he abandoned them. Gladstone said of his great mentor that 'there is a manifest and peculiar adaptation in Peel's mind to the age in which he lives and to its exigencies and to the position he holds as a public man.' But Peel's 'adaptations' were nothing compared with Gladstone's.

'The rising hope of those stern unbending Tories' (the opening phrase of Macaulay's lacerating review) began political life by passionately opposing the Great Reform Bill in the Oxford Union. The man who in old age was to be both revered and mocked as the People's William started out with the firm conviction that 'the majority will be in the wrong.' And the startling steps by which he found himself among the Liberals were interpreted by many of his associates not as a journey of honest discovery but as timeserving in the most literal sense.

Is there then anything more coherent, more deserving of our attention, than the zigzags of a charismatic, volcanic politician whose make-up was a queer mixture of genuine piety and ill-disguised humbug? Are Gladstone's U-turns and doublings-back prompted by anything more profound than a politician's need to respond to the great challenges of the middle and later nineteenth century: Irish nationalism, the rise of the industrial working class, the decay of faith and the unstoppable march of Darwinism ('the darling of our age', Gladstone called the doctrine, while at the same time claiming that 'there is nothing in his account of the production of man which ought in the slightest degree to shake the faith of the Christian' – God had simply farmed out the business of creation to natural selection, a matter of devolution rather than evolution)? Was Gladstone engaged in anything more intellectually formidable than a lifelong rearguard action?

Bebbington, in his patient, clear-sighted way, demonstrates both that Gladstone's thought does possess a coherent purpose and that this purpose is what makes him so alive and relevant. *The Mind of Gladstone* has at least three virtues that its subject's works seldom exhibit: it is unfailingly lucid, it is not a word too long and it never strays into overarguing its case. Bebbington takes Gladstone's mind seriously. He is not blind to the self-seeking aspects of his conduct or the embarrassing weaknesses of his outpourings, but his working assumption is that we shall never understand him properly unless we follow him all the way down. It is not enough simply to mark his classical and religious studies according to how far they measure up to the scholarship of his day or ours. Gladstone did like to be thought well of by contemporary scholars in the fields into which he so blithely trespassed, and he badgered them for sources that might help to prop up his dicier speculations. But his ultimate aim was not so much to provide scientific explanations as to recreate imaginative realms from which political, social and religious lessons might be drawn.

Unless we appreciate how passionately these enquiries absorbed Gladstone, his political actions will often appear mysterious, not to say dotty. Take the first great crisis of his political life, and his first U-turn, the Maynooth affair. It had been a routine matter ever since the Act of Union for Parliament to renew each year the modest government grant to the Catholic seminary of St Patrick's, Maynooth, a few miles from Dublin. Why should Gladstone so violently object to the 1838 renewal? Why did he change his mind and vote for renewal in 1842? Why, above all, having caved in, did he then resign on the matter in 1845? Worldly men were baffled at the time, and worldly biographers today are still scratching their heads.

The violence of Gladstone's opposition in 1838 arose largely from his being enmeshed in the final stages of *The State in Its*

Relations with the Church, which stipulated in passionate terms that in the interests of national harmony the state had a duty to uphold the national Church and so by extension to deny support to any other Church. In relation to Ireland, this meant concentrating support on the Church of Ireland – an absurd proposition since the overwhelming majority were unbudgably Roman Catholic. Macaulay had no difficulty in making mincemeat of Gladstone, teasing him for his half-measures: 'Why not roast Dissenters at slow fires?'

The would-be theocrat soon abandoned the implications of his position, regretfully dismissing them as impractical in an imperfect world. But by following him through the steps of the argument, Bebbington shows us what he was trying to get at. We start life, Gladstone argued as a young man (and this was the basic position he never abandoned), born into a state as well as into a family: 'Each man came into the world and practical life of the world under a heavy debt, in extent such as he could not estimate and in kind such as he could not pay ... Hence each successive man has *found* a government and his first duty has been to submit to it.'

'It is historically untrue,' Gladstone asserts, 'that existing governments emanated from popular will.' The idea of a social contract is a pernicious fiction. He might in the course of time become something that could be labelled a Liberal, but he never became a Lockean, still less a Rawlsian. All his life he remained a dedicated follower of Aristotle and a believer that the most important fact about man was that he was a social animal. Gladstone was an Aristotelian Christian. Civil association was God's will. Genesis had declared that it was 'not good that man should be alone'. The *polis* was the highest form of *koinonia*, of that common life which demanded a surrender of the individual will. And the spirit of community had to be nurtured by reverence.

Bebbington shows very clearly how this dwelling on the key quality of reverence led Gladstone astray into the extremist programme of *The State in Its Relations with the Church*. But the underlying question remains, even if now more often couched in secular terms, and it is still being tossed around, as Bebbington points out, by communitarians and others on both sides of the Atlantic, notably Amitai Etzioni, Charles Taylor and Alasdair MacIntyre. Utilitarianism is not enough. If solidarity is to be a real presence in our lives rather than a hollow slogan, then there must be some shared focus of – I can't think of a better word than reverence.

Speeches by David Blunkett and Gordon Brown during the Labour years signalled a sea change in the party's attitude. It no longer appeared to be Labour's aim to foster a multicultural society in which no particular set of beliefs and customs might aspire to dominate. On the contrary, in our public practices, such as the ceremonies for welcoming new British citizens, we are to celebrate an overarching monoculture, comprising all its traditional elements, including – glory be – an oath of allegiance to the Queen. It is only within such a framework of reverence that minority religions and traditions can flourish. Stripped of its confessional bias, Gladstone's argument is closely attuned to the revisions of New Labour.

Gladstone wasn't insensitive to the difficulties of reconciling reverence with tolerance. Long before he became a Liberal, he was decidedly liberal in his attitudes to other sects and faiths. He annoyed the Tractarian ultras by sticking up for Dissenters, then annoyed them again by speaking in favour of Jewish emancipation, then stuck up for them when they in turn were being hounded. 'The ultimate issue,' he declared in 1848, only a few years after Maynooth, 'is social justice, or proportionate dealing as between man and man.'

This expansion of tolerance accompanied – and was fuelled by – the decisive shifts in his religious allegiance, from the narrow evangelicalism of his youth to an Anglo-Catholicism as broad as it was high. This included above all a theological shift from his early concentration on the Atonement to a deep and lasting love of the doctrine of the Incarnation: that is, from a doctrine that empha-sized the fallen state of man to one that celebrated the dignity that Christ had brought by assuming human flesh.

There was an exuberant fleshliness about the religion of the mature Gladstone, a quality so strange and rich that it unnerves us as much as it unnerved his contemporaries. The night-walks with prostitutes began when he was at Oxford. They were a recurring source of temptation, to which his diaries make it fairly clear that he succumbed in one way or another. But these long conversations into the small hours betokened also his recognition of the equal worth of every human being, a worth which wasn't diminished if the girl failed to reform. You get the feeling, in fact, that reform was only a secondary goal: the communion was the thing.

The same carnality is a crucial quality in Gladstone's writings on Homer. In scholarly terms, his claims to have discovered the origins of the Christian narrative in the fables of Mount Olympus may have been 'nonsense', to quote Jowett. Anthropologists joined with orthodox clergymen in an unusual alliance against Glad-stone's thesis and his picturesque illustrations of it. It was absurd to suggest that the doctrine of the Trinity had any connection with Poseidon's trident. And to claim that Homer's Latona prefigured the Virgin was to advance one of those theories which, as Matthew Arnold caustically remarked, was attended by the inconvenience 'that there really exist no data for determining them'. Gladstone climbed down a bit, in his usual furtive, roundabout style, and admitted that much early religious practice could be explained as simple nature worship. But he persisted in his efforts to inject the religion of Homer into the British bloodstream as a corrective to the otherworldly tendencies of Christianity. Homeric religion was 'filled with human geniality and warmth', greatly preferable to what he termed 'the Christianity of isolation'. Its anthropomorphic quality was what 'associated it so closely with the whole detail of life'. Rather than finding the character of Zeus an embarrassment, Gladstone described the father of the gods as 'the masterpiece of the Homeric mythology', a figure whose frailties made him as sympathetic as Falstaff.

For Gladstone, the Incarnation was not a formal charade (rather like those festivals of misrule at some schools when the masters take on the role of the boys); it was a full-blooded entering into the human state. And with this revaluation of human dignity comes a revaluation of liberty. In 1878, he admitted: 'I did not learn when I was at Oxford that which I have learned since – namely, to set a due value on the imperishable and inestimable principles of human liberty.' Far from insisting on unquestioning submission as he had in youth, he now thought it 'the business of every oppressed people to rise upon every reasonable opportunity against the oppressor'. Moreover, the working people were the best judges of their destiny: the masses were more likely to be right than the classes, by which he meant those vested interests which came together only for selfish purposes.

He was no communist or socialist: 'It is the individual mind and conscience, it is the individual character, on which human happiness or misery depends.' Self-reliance was indispensable to a sturdy *polis*: 'The best thing the government can do for the people is to help them to help themselves.' So much, as Bebbington remarks, for the nanny state. This is Thatcherite rhetoric, but it is also the common political language of the twenty-first century. As an old man in 1892, Gladstone commented that although retrenchment was currently out of fashion, it would be enforced again whenever the people demanded it – which was the case nearly a century later.

Gladstone's political ideas were too manifold and multiocular to be confined within a single political creed. If part of his philosophy finds echoes in present-day communitarianism, another part finds echoes in Michael Oakeshott's ideas of the self-fashioning human agent; and another part again in Isaiah Berlin's argument that diverse and incommensurable goals are endemic to the human condition. It is ironic that neither of these two latter-day sages, infinitely amiable as they were in many other ways, could bear to hear a good word said of the other. Yet both their doctrines have much in common with the thinking of the mature Gladstone.

The reconciliation of solidarity and self-reliance remains the most difficult of political undertakings. As yet, the British political class, while perceiving its necessity, has fashioned only the preliminary rhetoric for it. By contrast, its actions in government throughout the twentieth century tended towards a more or less benign managerialism, mediated partly through the welfare state and partly through the state corporations such as the BBC and the publicly owned industries. Opportunities for the masses to make their own lives have been sparse and cramped. And there hasn't been much perceptible convergence between what Gladstone called the masses and the classes.

Equality of opportunity is supposed to bridge the gap. But is equality of opportunity a sufficient social creed, even if it were being abundantly realized, which it isn't? No politician today would dream of imitating Gladstone's words to a gathering of artisans in Greenwich in 1875: 'Be not eager to raise your children out of the working class but be desirous that they should remain in that class and elevate the work of it.' But is that so very far from what William Morris had in mind? If, by contrast, we place all our hopes on social mobility, some of us are bound to be disappointed.

Gladstone annoyed almost everyone in one way or another. Liberals like Acton could not abide his insistence on the supreme importance of national allegiance. Conservatives were suspicious of his claims to trust the judgment of working men. Socialists did not care for his unabashed inegalitarianism. Capitalists were made uneasy by his assertion that material prosperity threatened the morale not of the poor, but of the prosperous classes. Progressives did not like his description of the late-Victorian period as 'the age of sham', symbolized by the arrival on the market of a butter substitute called 'oleo-margarine' – to the unhealthy influence of which he skittishly attributed the irrational revolt among the educated elite against the obvious virtues of Home Rule.

What was intolerable above all was the old man's oracular certainty, the insistence of that harsh voice with its flat Lancashire *a*. Labouchère did not object, as he indelibly put it, to Gladstone always having the ace of trumps up his sleeve but only to his pretence that God had put it there. And the worst of these divinely inspired revelations was that they never stopped.

Can we imagine 5000 working men turning out today in pouring rain to listen to Gladstone for two or three hours, as they did again and again in the Midlothian campaign? Curiously enough, I think we can. For it was the same restless refusal to be satisfied which showed the people that he had not forgotten them.

THE RISE AND FALL AND
RISE OF METHODISM

S ometimes intellectuals develop such an aversion to a subject that
they can scarcely be persuaded to pay it even passing attention.
For several decades in the last century, the free market became so
repugnant to the intelligentsia that only professional economists –
and by no means all of them – could bear to study its workings in
any depth, let alone with any sympathy. Even less fashionable, and
for far longer, has been the history of the Nonconformist Churches
and of Methodism in particular. Apart from confessional historians,
an anxious and partial fraternity, the general run of social histori-
ans tackled Methodism only as a source for the rise of the Labour
movement, to test the truth of Harold Wilson's remark that the
British Labour Party owed more to Methodism than to Marx.

That, for example, was the impetus behind the notorious chap-
ter, 'The Transforming Power of the Cross', in E. P. Thompson's
The Making of the English Working Class (1963). Thompson, himself
from a Methodist background, loathed Methodism. John Wesley,
he claimed, had 'dispensed with the best and selected unhesitatingly
the worse (*sic*) element of Puritanism'. As a result, Methodism in its
early years became 'a ritualised form of psychic masturbation', and
'the blackening chapels stood in the industrial districts like great

traps for the human psyche'. Yet at the same time the movement's mysterious energizing qualities did impel Methodist working men and even preachers to take a leading part in working-class politics. In Thompson's eyes, the appalling enthusiasm of the love feast and the camp meeting was thus transformed into the legitimate agitation of the protest march and the party rally.

Personal revulsion against a narrow or gloomy Methodist upbringing could reach violent extremes. In *Up from Methodism* (1926), a sort of American *Father and Son*, Herbert Asbury, the great-great-nephew of Francis Asbury, the most indefatigable of all the Methodist pioneers in America, railed against the platitudes and mummeries of all faiths, but particularly that in which he had been raised. He vowed that if he ever had a son who showed any signs of becoming a preacher he would 'whale hell out of him'.

Opponents in the older Churches often pretended to ignore the Methodists and underplayed their impact. Mark Pattison, Rector of Lincoln, Wesley's Oxford college, in his eighty-page essay 'Tendencies of Religious Thought in England 1688–1750', failed to mention Wesley once. When a leading local Methodist preacher said he was astonished that Oxford should so neglect a religious movement then (in the 1880s) numbering some 25 million members worldwide, Pattison interrupted: 'Surely you mean 25,000'. Today, Methodism in the English-speaking world has declined in step with other Free Church traditions. But the number of adherents to Pentecostalism, which is unmistakably a lineal descendant of Methodism, has passed 250 million. If the present rate of growth in Africa, Asia and South America continues, by mid-century there may be a billion Pentecostals – as many as there would then be Hindus. Yet, as David Martin has argued, 'because Pentecostalism is personal and cultural it does not need to deal in the violence intrinsic to political action, which is why it is virtually unnoticed by the Western media, and comes as a surprise to the Western academy'. It may seem odd that the affluent arbiters of secular and religious opinion should be hard on a religion which is so much the option of the poor, especially of the black female poor.

But then that was the fate of Methodism in its heyday, and for the same reason: that although it recruited so widely among the working classes, whom the established Churches had such difficulty in reaching, it recruited them as Christian soldiers, and not as the shock troops of the Left. Which is why the evolution of Methodism and its critical reception remain of such relevance to us. David Hempton, of Boston University, a Methodist foundation, has written several first-rate studies of connections between Methodism and political and popular culture. His new book is a sharply focused account of Methodism in and for itself. Always readable and with a crisp turn of phrase, he provides an admirable introduction to this extraordinary subject, and also leads us on to ponder in what circumstances any religion can hope to survive the onrush of secular modernity, and for how long.

Hempton begins by reminding us of the unexpectedly complex roots of Methodism. John Wesley was, after all, not only an Anglican priest, like his father and grandfather, but also a fair theologian and classical scholar. The peculiar doctrine he evolved and then enforced with his famous angry will was drawn from a bewildering array of elements: first, from Count Nikolaus von Zinzendorf and the Moravian Pietists he met on his voyage out to Georgia on his first pastoral excursion, but also from patristic sources, such as Gregory of Nyssa; from Fenelon; from Jeremy Taylor (though with reservations); from Hooker; and Thomas à Kempis. What Wesley fashioned out of all this was highly individual. He dispensed with the quietism of the Moravians. In his view, 'the ideal Christian life was one of ceaseless, cheerful activism'. He repudiated the gloomy predestination of Calvinism. Most controversial of all, he devised and vigorously defended a doctrine of entire sanctification, or Christian perfection. When Jesus said, 'Be ye therefore perfect' he meant what he said. To be sure, this doctrine was qualified by a theology of 'responsible grace', but it was this assent to perfectibility that marked out the Methodists and dowered them with their cheerfulness. This combination unleashed a restless, energetic faith that was both introspective and optimistic, egalitarian, missionary, often provoked by a dramatic conversion experience and dependent on a direct, unmediated relationship with God – the kind of religion which we have come to think of as typically American, in fact, and which Europeans find so unsettling in the Weltanschauung of George W. Bush, born an Episcopalian and born again as a Methodist.

Such a faith, as Hempton shows, could spread with amazing rapidity across wild or unsettled terrain, as it did across America as the frontier moved west. Among immigrants or in new industrial settlements, Methodists could quickly come to dominate, as they did in the Cornish tin mines and the valleys of South Wales. They found it much harder to break into established religious cultures, especially in Roman Catholic countries or among peoples who were resistant to Anglo-American agriculture and commerce, such as the Native Americans. Methodists had to push on. As Bishop Francis Burns wrote from Liberia in 1859, 'this staying here within hearing of the ocean's waves will be the death of us! Christianity, in order to preserve its vitality among any people, requires expansion, and we must spread or die'. In fact they did both, as most white missionaries succumbed to disease within a few years of arriving in Africa. The burden of preaching was carried on very successfully by Africans and deepened by the numerous schools and colleges that the Methodists set up. The trouble was that the itinerant preachers – hardy, solitary, living for nothing except the joy of preaching the good news – inevitably gave way to married ministers, settled congregations and ambitious building programmes. The hallelujahs were drowned by arguments about the accounts. The grander the churches they put up to demonstrate that the Methodists really had arrived, the faster faded the freshness and spontaneity that had been their original appeal, and the more irrevocably the direction of the

Church fell into the hands of the merchants and shopkeepers who were paying for it.

As George Eliot lamented in *Adam Bede*, the popular image of Methodism was no longer of a crowd of labouring men and women out of doors drinking in a faith that lifted their weary spirits and suffused their souls with the sense of a loving Presence. In her own day, 'Methodism may mean nothing more than low-pitched gables up dingy streets, sleek grocers, sponging preachers and hypocritical jargon'. And did not Methodism, like all the other faiths jostling for converts in the religious marketplace, carry within it the seeds of its own downfall? Once allegiance to a Christian body became a matter of consumer choice, its authority became less certain. 'As an agent of pluralism,' Hempton remarks, 'Methodism ultimately paid the price of pluralism.' Harvey Cox, in *The Secular City* (1965), famously argued that secularization was an irreversible current which, by bringing tolerance in its wake, fatally undermined every Church's claim to a monopoly on truth.

Yet Hempton points out that thirty years later, after venturing out from Harvard Square to visit some black and Hispanic Pentecostal congregations in Boston, the same Cox detected in all the laughing, dancing and speaking in tongues that he witnessed there 'the harbinger of one of the great surprises of the twentieth century, the massive and unanticipated resurgence of religion in a century many had thought would witness its withering away'. The inevitability of secularization no longer looked so secure. This reversal of the current might of course represent no more than a series of eddies and backwaters. People who had been torn away from customary modes of life, and were only just clinging on in a world they found alien and alarming, might be seeking consolation in new forms of religion, just as those displaced by the Industrial Revolution had found anchorage in the direct and simple teaching of the early Methodists. But that need for consolation might be temporary. Once settled in suburbia, these new forms, too, might dwindle into tepid conformity.

But are modernity and Methodism so inherently ill-suited? There are, after all, still 9 million Methodists in the United States. The cheerful, work-oriented egalitarian ethos of Methodism seems pretty well adapted to the values required of Corporation Man. There is a stripped-down quality to Methodism, and a lack of hostility to the present. As Irving Kristol has pointed out, such an absence of lamentation for a lost past is also what differentiates neo-conservatives from traditional conservatives. Nor is this refusal to disown the contemporary world a recent deviation from the original spirit of Methodism. Hempton has an interesting passage on Wesley's relation to the Enlightenment. Nobody who believed as passionately as Wesley did in God's immediate supervising providence could be described as belonging to the mainstream of Enlightenment thought. On the other hand, Wesley was also very much a man of his own times, in philosophy a Lockean empiricist, a boyish enthusiast for scientific experiment, a keen believer in human progress and human rights, and an unwavering hater of slavery and persecution. David Hempton's account in his *Methodism: Empire of the Spirit* is reminiscent of Ernest Gellner's analysis of modern Islam in *Plough, Sword and Book* (1988). Far from Islam's being an awkward medieval hangover in societies that are still ill at ease with modernity, Gellner argues that the 'Protestant' features of the Muslim faith make it surprisingly compatible with modern life. The stress on sobriety and orderly conduct, the equidistance of all believers from the deity, the lack of clerical hierarchy and the relative absence of superstitious encrustations all seem to Gellner 'highly congruent with an urban bourgeois lifestyle and with commercialism'.

Much of this would surely apply to Methodism as well. Methodism's sharp decline in Britain may have had less to do with its intrinsic unsuitability for a consumer society than with the reluctance of Wesley and his English successors ever quite to renounce the Anglican pretensions in which they had been reared, so that Methodism came to seem less like a passionate alternative to the

Church of England than a dingier version of it. The secular world prefers to focus on the fundamentalists in both religions, for the good reason that they are the ones threatening to blow us all up or trying to teach our children that Darwin was wrong. Their weird practices and outlandish superstitions are so clearly irrational that they need cause us no intellectual discomfort, though they may cost a fortune in security measures. It is a more unsettling thought that both Christianity and Islam might at the same time be also evolving mutations that actually fit the world as it is.

IN SEARCH OF ENGLAND

It's a quick-change landscape. Every twenty or thirty miles, everything's new: the buildings change from chalk and flint to red and blue-nosed brick, from creamy limestone to hot-hued ironstone. The woods change too, from box trees on blown downland to beechwoods in steep hangers, from alders and willows leaning aslant the river banks to the thick old oaks of the Weald and the Forest of Dean. And the voices mutate also, from buttery Devon through burry Hampshire to corncrake Norfolk, from Brummie whine with its melancholy fall up to that Geordie gurgle with its hint of hidden amusement. Despite the efforts of officialdom to parcel them out of existence into mere postcodes, the English counties (many of them older than the nation state itself) continue to resonate in our ears and still command our loyalties. In the early heyday of the BBC it was argued that the mass media would flatten out local accents. No such thing. A burr or a brogue is the passport to media success. Regional character is hammed up rather than eroded. It is the modern age which has invented Essex Man and intensified the competition for the Greatest Living Yorkshireman.

Writers are local spirits too. Sometimes you wonder whether the landscapes really existed before they invented them: Hardy's

Wessex, Crabbe's Norfolk, Tennyson's Lincolnshire, Belloc's Sussex, Bunting's Northumberland, Wordsworth's Lake District, Coleridge's Quantocks, Shakespeare's Forest of Arden. This isn't just a rural thing. Every London patch has its laureate: Keats's Hampstead, Stevie Smith's Palmers Green, Anita Brookner's Marylebone, Anthony Powell's Fitzrovia, the Bloomsbury of the Group, Patrick Hamilton's Earls Court, the Bromley of H. G. Wells, the Shepperton of J. G. Ballard.

This inexhaustible diversity provokes in us an appetite for further and better particulars. To a certain sort of English person, topography is as irresistible as pornography, better really because fuller of surprises. The old Shell Guides masterminded by John Piper and John Betjeman, *England's Thousand Best Houses* and *Churches* of Simon Jenkins, above all Nikolaus Pevsner's gloriously unrolling series of the Buildings of England – these for us are anthologies of a poetry which is peculiarly our own.

Growing up on the undulations of Salisbury Plain, as gentle as they are bare, I have always been intensely aware of how worked and scored the English landscape is: the ancient burial tumps and barrows, the Iron Age camps and Roman forts on the hilltops, the grassy terraces that mark the deserted British villages of the Dark Ages, the chalk pits and limestone quarries, the windswept new fir plantations, the old coppiced copses of oak and hazel, the abandoned military camps of the Second World War, the fresh tank trails across the downs. Man has been everywhere here and left his mark, not to speak of his bones. For me, these bones live.

PEVSNER IN BERKSHIRE

In most people's minds, poignancy and Nikolaus Pevsner do not go together. John Betjeman did his damnedest to make us think of his lifelong rival as dry-eyed and thin-lipped, the archetypal Prussian pedant. Yet it is hard to imagine a sadder start to any book than the foreword to the first edition of Pevsner's *Berkshire*:

> Berkshire is the first English county I had to travel and describe after my wife had died. She had driven me through nearly all the preceding counties, had done all the day-to-day planning, and more and more also visited the buildings. Four eyes see more than two, and her eyes were quicker than mine. I fear this volume will have suffered from that private circumstance. The journey could not have the zest, the fun, the cursing in common which all belonged to so well tried a partnership.

Some readers have endorsed this touching self-criticism and found the book as a whole a little spiritless and some of the entries too peremptory. I would prefer to point out the terrific pace at which Pevsner was proceeding with The Buildings of England. By the time *Berkshire* came out in 1966, he had dealt with thirty counties in fifteen years, with another sixteen to come over the following eight years, before the series was completed in 1974. He had assistants and informants, of course, apart from Karola Pevsner, but his was the judging eye and the driving force – well, in fact non-driving force. The magnificence of this one-man achievement must excuse the occasional over-laconic or dismissive entry with its dread interposed semi-colon: 'Nave perp; dull' and the hasty, unanswered question: 'Can this be eighteenth-century?'

The new edition occupies more than twice the 355 smaller pages of its 1960s predecessor. It is gloriously comprehensive, both in its coverage and in its architectural explications, as the new Pevsners always are. The Yale University Press deserves all the plaudits it has already received for perpetuating the series and bringing it as close to perfection as is possible in an imperfect world. The photographs, by Angelo Hornak, match the sharpness and vivacity of the text. And while a great number of the entries have been rewritten as well as expanded, enough of the curiosity and acerbity of the Master survive, just as a robust Norman arcade may continue to underpin later embellishments.

Pevsner's legacy to this particular volume was to provide his successors with a justification for keeping to the historical boundaries of Berkshire, before the graceless surgery of Ted Heath and Peter Walker tipped the top third of the county across the Thames into Oxfordshire. The old county had endured since King Alfred's heyday, being first mentioned by name in a document of AD 860 in pretty much the shape it was to retain for the next 1100 years.

We need to explore the full Berks if we are to gather a proper sense of the amazing variety to be found in what is only a moderate-sized county (but can one think of any English county of which this is not true?). As the guide points out, you can drive across it today on the M4 in less than an hour without breaking the speed limit – more like forty-five minutes, I would say. Yet in this saggy-sock-shaped stretch of country there are half-a-dozen Berkshires, each with its own quiddities and materials. Here the splendid essay on 'Geology and Building Stones' by Philip Powell is pivotal and a considerable improvement on Terence Miller's slighter effort in 1966.

In the north-west, a limestone ridge divides the Upper Thames from the Vale of the White Horse. As a result, some streets in Faringdon, now a quiet and bypassed little town, look as if they belonged in a Cotswold show village, although the Cotswolds would be hard put to outdo the unpretending beauty of Faringdon House, built for Henry Pye, generally regarded as our worst poet laureate, or match the high camp of its later owner, the composer Lord Berners (Nancy Mitford's Lord Merlin), who painted the pigeons in his dovecote pink and blue, entertained Diaghilev and Stravinsky and built a Gothic tower 110 feet high on a nearby eminence, perhaps the last great folly built in England. His companion and later heir, Robert Heber-Percy, known as 'the Mad Boy', is commemorated, suitably, by a sculpture of Dionysus in the garden.

Only half-a-dozen miles south of Faringdon the chalk country begins under the lazy eye of the White Horse of Uffington, with its sinuous curve across the down, one of the most mysterious monuments in Europe, now ascribed to the Iron Age and at once intensely primitive and stunningly modern. On the other side of the hill sits Ashdown House, the first Earl of Craven's hunting box, described by old Pevsner as 'the perfect doll's house' and compared by new Pevsner to Mansart's Château de Balleroy outside Bayeux. But there is something altogether more magical about Ashdown, the absurdly tall faerie pavilion of glistening white chalk plumped so high on the downs, something impermanent, a Tardis for hunting earls.

Coming down off the chalk, we come into the gravels of the Kennet Valley and mainstream Berkshire, a smaller-scale, more domestic landscape of flint and brick cottages and Nonconformist chapels and old cloth mills and biscuit factories, and new high-tech and IT business parks. Then in the south-east of the county, the gravels shade off into the Bagshot Beds, a sandy wasteland of pine and heather which remained almost uninhabited except for the gypsies, known locally as the Tadley Squires, until the coming of the railways transformed it into the heartland of Stockbroker Tudor and Prep School Queen Anne.

Finally, if we trace our way along the south bank of the Thames, which forms the county's old northern boundary all the way back to Buscot, we find outbreaks of the Edwardian Regatta style: white wooden balconies, tile-hung façades and fanciful belvederes, crouching under steep hills with beech hangers clinging to them.

The small towns of Berkshire stayed small until the later twentieth century. Reading and its suburbs have grown from a population of 120,000 in the 1960s to more than 200,000, Bracknell from next to nothing to more than 50,000, while Newbury has become one of those edge cities which promise high-paid jobs without the hassle of commuting. It is noticeable, I am afraid, that the prettier and thus richer small towns like Abingdon and Windsor have taken more trouble in supervising the scale and architectural tact of the new developments than the mushroom townships in the east of the county.

Berkshire has no ancient cathedral and few great houses. Englefield, the nearest thing to a prodigy house, fails to scrape into Mark Girouard's *Elizabethan Architecture*, perhaps because so much of it was Jacobeanized by the Victorians. In the eighteenth century, City merchants and magnates built some delightful Palladian villas along the southern slopes of the Kennet Valley, but only Basildon Park, in the woods to the west of Reading, makes it into the top division, and that was built for a Yorkshire-born Bengal nabob, Sir Francis Sykes, by another Yorkshireman, John Carr.

What stick in the memory rather are the modest town houses with their creamy pediments and pillared doorways, and above all the brick they are built in, of every colour – orange, and salmon, and rose, and scarlet and blue and grey and purple – and patterned in every imaginable way, in string courses and diapers and zigzags and crosses and saltires and oblongs and rondels. In their *Murray's*

Berkshire Architectural Guide (1949), John Betjeman and John Piper assert that bricks have been better and longer used in Berkshire than in any other county except Kent, and East Anglia: 'the bricks and tiles of Berkshire are seen at their best in crisp winter sunlight, when they seem to glow like fires and, as the sun goes down, to hold the light more warmly than the sunset.'

The guides that Betjeman and Piper did for John Murray are as full of atmosphere and enthusiasm as the Shell Guides over which they also presided. In Berkshire especially they were on home terrain. Piper lived just the other side of the Thames, near Henley, and Betjeman lived at various times in four different houses within striking distance of Wantage. He was a churchwarden of the matchless Early English church at Uffington, and he is commemorated in the tiny downland church of Farnborough by an exuberant Piper window of butterflies, fruit and fishes. So their blood was up when they wrote in their introduction: 'We still believe in the virtue of making clear our reactions to buildings and to towns and villages. We believe that houses and churches do, and should, inspire love and hate, and that it is worth while recording the reactions of two observers, instead of making a cold catalogue.'

Although Pevsner's first county volume was not published until two years later, it is clear enough at whom all this is aimed. The feud had got under way in the 1930s, when Pevsner described the attention being paid to Victorian buildings and design as 'still, with a very few exceptions, of the whimsical variety'. In his second London volume, published in 1952, he denounced 'the excesses of praise lavished on Comper's church furnishings by those who confound aesthetic with religious emotion' – Ninian Comper being Betjeman's favourite living architect. Pevsner's disdain matched Betjeman's prickly paranoia. It is not surprising that there should have been not a single mention of the Murray's guide in Pevsner's.

More than half a century later, a posthumous peace seems to

have broken out. The new Pevsner quotes Betjeman and Piper copiously, for example, their verdict on Bracknell as 'the dullest-looking town in Berkshire'; or of Crowthorne, 'its straight tarmac roads between wellingtonias, deodars and rhododendrons'; or of St Luke's Garford, as 'a brown study in village Perpendicular'. Indeed, comparing all three guidebooks, you begin to wonder what the row was all about; so many of the entries run along the same lines, reach the same conclusions and let rip the same likings and loathings.

Nor can Pevsner be stereotyped as an unreasoning teutonic Modernist. Christopher Hussey in a three-parter in *Country Life* lavishly admired Charters, Sunningdale, the giant white pile built for the electrical millionaire Frank Parkinson by George Adie, better known as the architect of the Stockwell bus depot, but Pevsner dismisses it as 'a typical case of the C20 style adopted willy-nilly, just in order to be up to date. White and cubic it is, but the great hall in the centre has a front to the S with the giant pillars of the Fascist brand and the French windows to its l. and r. are of Georgian proportions'. New Pevsner is rather more charitable to Adie's efforts to bring the *machine à vivre* approach to Sunningdale.

And Pevsners, old and new, are just as energetic as Betjeman and Piper in making the glories of Berkshire sound irresistible: the County Hall of Abingdon, for example, as soaring and majestic as the chapel at Versailles of much the same date, is here acclaimed as 'the grandest in England'. The winding walk from the County Hall down East St Helen Street to the Thames is rightly presented to us as one of the most enticing in any English town: the houses on both sides in the warmest rosy brick or rendered in primrose and sea-grey and dating from the fifteenth to the eighteenth century, and at the end the spire of St Helen's surrounded by three amazing almshouses, again spanning the fifteenth and eighteenth centuries, the furthest seemingly about to topple into the river behind it, with the arches of Abingdon's fifteenth-century bridge reflected in the water: 'no other churchyard anywhere has anything like it'. Nor, says old Pevsner, is there an ensemble anywhere in England like the fourteenth-century paintings of kings and prophets on the ceiling of the north chapel of St Helen's. New Pevsner tells us that the interior of the church is 'unforgettable' and that its four arcades set asymmetrically produce 'a curious sliding effect as one moves about'. So it is, and so they do.

I quote these snatches to show that enthusiasm as well as expertise radiates from every page of the new enriched and enlarged Pevsner. The tour de force comes in its brilliant and intricate account of Windsor Castle, the greatest inhabited castle in England, or anywhere, for all I know. While Betjeman and Piper lazily offload this task by recommending 'the excellent Official Guide to Windsor Castle (price 1/-)', Pevsner painstakingly but with great clarity peels back the layers of successive buildings and rebuildings to show us exactly where the Middle Ages end and Wyatville begins – not least in raising the Round Tower by 33 feet, which is why it can be seen for miles. Conversely, even the most patently nineteenth-century bits of the castle are a palimpsest, offering glimpses of Plantagenet and Tudor beginnings, even in the Albert Memorial Chapel, at the east end of St George's Chapel. Originally intended by Henry VII as a lady chapel and shrine for Henry VI, it is now a Victorian Valhalla. 'The first look into this chapel is one of amazement,' says old Pevsner. 'The room is now dominated by Sir Alfred Gilbert's masterpiece', the monument to the Duke of Clarence, the eldest son of the Prince of Wales, who outlived him to become Edward VII. Pevsner can scarcely contain his admiration for the prince's approval of Gilbert's 'exceedingly daring, radically novel monument. The iconographical daring is as great as the aesthetic originality'. Or 'Gosh', as Betjeman might have said to camera. This is perhaps the supreme effusion of delight in the whole of Pevsner's *Berkshire*. And it is inspired by seeing the most uninhibitedly, outrageously late-Victorian work of art you can imagine. I only wish that Mrs Pevsner had lived to see it, too.

OLIVER RACKHAM:
MAGUS OF THE WOODS

'What a place it must have been, that virgin woodland wilderness of all England, ever encroached on by innumerable peasant clearings, but still harbouring God's plenty of all manner of beautiful birds and beasts, and still rioting in a vast wealth of trees and flowers,' sighed G. M. Trevelyan in his *Shortened History of England*. Such romantic pictures of England at the Conquest have delighted historians for generations – highwaymen lurking in the Wildwood, monarchs with a passion for the chase galloping beneath the immemorial oaks, great forests stretching for hundreds of miles across the country, of which only pitiful fragments now remain – Epping, Wychwood, the Weald.

These are some of our most potent images of an untamed, irrecoverable past. Ecology has made nostalgia respectable. Alas, scholarly ecology also has a habit of destroying nostalgia's most precious artefacts. Dr Oliver Rackham of Corpus Christi, Cambridge, has been at it for some years now, in a majestic series of books on ancient woodland. In an earlier work, he described Hatfield Forest, Essex (not to be confused with Hatfield, Herts, the Cecil place), as a unique medieval survival, 'the only place where one can step back into the Middle Ages to see, with only a small effort of the imagination, what a forest looked like in use'.

Nestling in that corner of Essex where the M11 meets the ever-growing Stansted airport, Hatfield Forest now bears the dreaded blue footprint on the Ordnance Survey map, marking it out as an accredited leisure resource. Yet it is still the most complete example of a medieval forest that we have, and on a quiet winter's afternoon (you can just hear the traffic, but only just), it is an enchanting, almost deserted place. No, 'enchanting' is not quite right. That suggests strangeness. Better to say it is a natural place.

Drawn on by this come-hither, the unwary reader may settle himself in for a pleasant ramble through a thousand acres of rural Essex and a thousand years of its history. He is in for a shock, or rather a series of shocks, for there is scarcely a page on which Dr Rackham does not deliver, with a sly ecologist's smile, a sharp poke at conventional expectations (usually my own expectations too).

The truth is, it seems, that medieval England was not especially wooded. Most of the primeval forest had been cleared centuries before. And the bits that were wooded were not particularly to be found in Royal Forests, which were established by the Normans to protect deer rather than trees and, on average, contained no more woodland than non-forests. Making an area a Forest probably had less immediate effect on land use than declaring it a National Park today. The Forest authorities neither enclosed woodland, nor made much effort to stop any grubbing up of trees. Again, there was no great dense woodland stretching from Essex to the Chilterns. The Forest of Hatfield was much the same size as it is today and contained much the same mixtures of woodland and open plains dotted with pollarded trees, rabbit warrens and gravel pits. The countryside round about, for as far back as written records go, has always been an intricate, small-scale landscape of hedged fields, winding lanes, ponds and scattered farmsteads. William the Conqueror may have 'loved the tall stags as if he were their father', but, apart from that and the manner of William II's death, there is no abundant evidence of English royalty's love of blood sports until centuries later. The deer were there for food for the royal table and were mostly hunted professionally.

Ancient woods were intensely *used*. The typical wood was divided into quarters by rides and coppiced, cut down to the ground and then allowed to bush out again (the 'spring' – a word only later applied to the season of the year), on a cycle of anywhere between eight and eighteen years to provide the underwood, with its myriad uses – hurdles, hop-poles, fences, thatching spars, above all, firewood. Amid the underwood, some trees were left to grow tall to provide timber for building houses and ships. Pigs rooted for acorns. Deer browsed on the leaves. Cattle, sheep, geese and goats grazed on the plains.

Trees when pollarded or coppiced grow faster (between 3 and 10 feet in the first season) and live much longer. The famous Doodle Oak at Hatfield which survived into this century (what may be a sucker from it is growing today) was planted well before the Conquest. Many of the giant oak 'stools' of the ever-broadening stumps of coppiced trees go back at least to the days of Robert the Bruce (an early lord of Hatfield Forest).

Rabbits, far from being a pest, were delicate beasts newly imported from Sicily and had sweet little 'pillow mounds' dug for them – like miniature burrows – to help them survive on the unfriendly Essex boulder clay. A ring of pillow mounds is clearly visible in the warren at Hatfield.

The melancholy, sinister type of ancient forest is *neglected* woodland, Arthur rather than Oliver Rackham country. A coppiced wood with its springing quarters, each at a different stage of regrowth, is a light and cheerful spot – no place for the neighbourhood sex maniac. Although there were indeed highwaymen lurking, the medieval authorities made anti-highwaymen 'trenches' – 200-feet-wide clearings – along woodland roadsides.

Anglo-Saxon man was fully in control of his landscape and was enmeshed in a web of rights and arrangements, on most of which cash values were precisely computed. His relationship with the lord of the manor often reminds one more of a modern repairing lease from the Westminster Estate than of the romantic and oppressive feudal loyalties described by continental historians.

The evidence from the forest tends to confirm Alan Macfarlane's thesis that medieval Essex people behaved less like archetypal peasants and more like Essex people today, buying and selling everything, including land, for cash and not for barter, hiring labourers and hiring themselves out, bequeathing their property as they pleased. Much of the business of the Forest courts involved exasperated landlords trying to extract a reasonable grazing rent under the guise of fines.

One more of the old props of Marxist history looks a little shakier. 'Feudalism', however defined, begins to seem somewhat less important than it used to. The Norman Conquest may have brought new landlords, but did it really bring a new world? Thirty years ago, in *The Making of the English Landscape*, W. G. Hoskins first familiarized us with the principle that, in these matters, 'everything is older than we think.' Rackham seems to be pushing the process yet one stage further back.

And behind the myth of the Saxon Wildwood, there is another myth at risk, older and deeper perhaps – the myth of man as a natural nomad, and of his settling down as being a fairly recent and, on the whole, mistaken development, which has gradually destroyed the spontaneity and happiness of his earlier life as a wanderer. Even in dear old Trevelyan, one catches echoes of the songlines: 'In Tudor times the popular songs of the day give the impression that the whole people has gone a-maying. Did not some such response to nature's loveliness move dimly in the hearts of the Saxon pioneers, when primrose, or bluebell, or willow-herb rushed out over the sward of the clearing they had made in the tall trees?'

Well, perhaps – if they could spare the time to look up from liming and dunging the soil, digging gravel pits for road-metal, pollarding and coppicing the trees and preparing interminable law-suits about pannage, avesage, hedgebote, stakebote, estovers and all the other valuable rights and obligations of medieval forestry. They were, it seems, thatchers in every sense. In any case, the clearings had been made earlier and on a vast scale, in fact, as soon as man had developed the flint axe. Neolithic man in England began woodland management too, coppicing and pollarding, as well as pasturing his beasts there. Round our parts, anyway, the itch to settle down and get weaving with secateurs and chainsaw appears appallingly primordial.

The only records of carefree woodland revels are relatively modern: the disgraceful scenes in the nineteenth century when 'the idle and disorderly Men and Women of bad character' from Bishop's Stortford came out 'under pretence of gathering Nuts ... to take beer and spirits and drink in the forest which affords them an opportunity for all sorts of Debauchery.' Between the wars, there were motorbikes scrambling in the coppices.

It seems to be not medieval but modern man who has destroyed a great part of the woodland that was standing at the Conquest. The setting up of the Forestry Commission after the First World War and the development of agro-business after the Second were the two obvious calamities, but the general trend towards enclo-sure, the grubbing up of hedges, and the felling and replanting of woods has been gathering pace for over a century now. Pollarding came to be regarded as ugly, and coppicing as archaic.

The story of Hatfield Forest has a hero – Edward North Buxton, not the last of that numerous East Anglian clan to do great ser-vice to conservation. On his deathbed in 1924, Buxton bought the forest and, resolved to 'ensure that the Forestry Commission never sets a single foot on a single inch', gave it to the National Trust. Unfortunately, he did not live long enough to explain to the Trust how to look after it. And they made all the then fashionable mistakes, tidying the place up, selling and clearing 'dying' trees, planting exotic trees, many of which really did die, 'improving' the grassland. Now, like the rest of us, they know better. Nothing is more subject to the whirligig of fashion than land management.

This is a wonderful book, a brilliant miniaturization of the author's great *History of the Countryside*, by turns acerbic, lyrical and unflaggingly informative. Rackham's hymn to coppicing should persuade anyone who is lucky enough to own any woodland to join those growers who have resumed the practice, often together with tall trees in a mixed wood. The economics of coppicing as opposed to 'high forestry' are disputed. How far do the earlier returns compensate for the much lower value of the wood? But the returns to the countryside are not in doubt:

> The massed flowering of the primroses or oxlips, in the second spring after felling, is one of the grandest sights of English woodland, and in the years when coppicing was unfashionable was all too seldom seen.
>
> Small birds crowd their territories into the dense thickets of young underwood. The nightingale, which prefers five to eight years' growth, disappeared from the Forest in the mid-1960s but came back when coppicing was resumed. Coppiced areas encouraged many insects: for example, hoverflies which feed on the nectars of summer-flowering plants, and fritillary butterflies whose caterpillars require abundant violets.

Although Dr Rackham ends his review of prospects for sensible management of the forest by saying that 'human nature does not encourage me to be optimistic', he is not by nature a misery. The worst of the acid rain, he thinks, is over; pollarding and coppicing have been resumed; the deer are prospering; the improved grassland is slowly returning to nature; even the picnickers may assist the rare plants by disturbing the rough ground; the motorbikes have long been banned; the cowslips are back, also the pyramidal orchid; even the elms are suckering defiantly and may yet 're-create an astonishing variety of elms to delight and instruct

another generation.' Elm disease, after all, recurs through his-
tory and elms 'like dandelions and hawkweeds, have largely given
up sex as a means of reproduction' and these days prefer to clone
rather than mate. As for the Great Storm of 1987, the Forest was
on the edge of it and only slightly touched but, in any case, ancient
coppices are not much worried by storms. Forest fires? 'Nobody
ever succeeded in burning down a native wood.' Why shouldn't
Hatfield provide a blueprint for the 'urban forests' which the gov-
ernment has established in the former industrial Midlands and the
bleaker bits of central Scotland? Could not the 'last forest' be the
model for the new New Forests?

Wandering back to the car in the twilight through a grove of
hornbeam pollards (to the twentieth-century forester as strange a
sight as date palms), I caught sight of the ice-blue lights of Stansted
airport only half a mile away and for the first time remembered
exactly where I was. No municipal park of cherry and lime could
confer such solitude.

THE LAST OF BETJEMAN

A t the age of thirteen, William Norton, the son of a police
sergeant and a Post Office worker, wrote to John Betje-
man warning him of the impending destruction of Lewisham's
Victorian Gothic town hall. In no time Betjeman put Wil-
liam on to the recently founded Victorian Society, urged him
to organize a petition, wrote him several long letters alerting
him to other fine churches in Lewisham and Catford and then
turned up at the town hall to be photographed with the boy.
Despite all this, Lewisham town hall was demolished. It was
still 1961, after all. England still slept. Betjeman at the same
time was vainly battling to save the Euston Arch and the great
glass rotunda of the Coal Exchange. Who else would have
turned aside from those gruelling national campaigns to help an
obscure schoolboy in one of London's dimmest quarters to try
and save a grimy town hall by George Elkington (no, I hadn't
heard of him either – his town hall in Bermondsey has been
demolished too)?

It is in these years, Betjeman's fifties and sixties, that he is
transformed from a popular versifier and telly poppet into some-
thing approaching a magus. He turns up everywhere with the
battered felt hat thrust down over the Roman emperor's skull,
the lopsided, green-toothed chuckle instantly enchanting the ill

at ease and seducing the frosty – his catchphrase 'Ooh I am enjoy-
ing this', uttered with every semblance of sincerity in the most
trying circumstances. After hours of an interminable coach trip to
Bucharest, Betjeman was heard to pipe up, 'Oh, I am enjoying the
boredom.'

This is the third and final volume in Bevis Hillier's huge life of
the most popular of all poets laureate, and it is a triumph. The job
could, I suppose, have been done in a single volume and has been,
as Hillier generously points out in his preface, by Derek Stanford
in 1961 and by Patrick Taylor-Martin in 1983. Impatient readers
may wonder why they need quite so full an account of the early life
of Barry Humphries or the history of the quarrying business once
owned by the family of John Nankivell, the topographical artist
who doorstepped the poet at the Mead, his home on the outskirts
of Wantage, and became a friend. We could also have done with
less exhaustive accounts of Betjeman's dinners with camp clergy-
men and the making of his television films, landmarks in the genre
though they were (film producers reminisce about old campaigns
more relentlessly than old soldiers).

But Hillier's long-distance rambles are always enlivened by his
deep but unshowy knowledge of the things Betjeman loved – arts
and crafts, architecture and poetry. A more compact version would
not, I think, have quite conveyed the impact that Betjeman made
all over Britain and Ireland and at every level of class and brow.
Thirty years after his death, the alteration in our sensibility that
he helped to bring about can still be seen and felt. If we are more
tender and attentive to the country we have inherited and less con-
temptuous of the obscure and unregarded, then he had quite a bit
to do with it.

It is not just the buildings that he opened our eyes to and helped
to save, though, God knows, there are plenty of those: Norman
Shaw's Bedford Park – 'the most significant suburb built in the
last century, probably the most significant in the Western world'
(Betjeman never minded overegging the prospectus in an urgent

cause) – the great barn at Avebury, the old Foreign Office, the choir screen in Hereford Cathedral, St Pancras, the purlieus of the Clifton Suspension Bridge, the Marx Memorial Library and so on *ad gloriam infinitam*. There were also the campaigns to restore the human scale that he began fifty years ago and which are still churning on with varying degrees of success – against supermarkets, against motorways and tower blocks and intensive agriculture:

> We spray the fields and scatter
> The poison on the ground
> So that no wicked wild flowers
> Upon our farm be found.

Most people who count themselves civilized now pay some lip service to these causes, and it is easy to forget how numerous and high-placed their enemies used to be. Worse even than the planners and developers in Betjeman's book were the traitors within, such as Sir John Summerson, who damned the Euston Arch with his faint praise and did his best to damn Bedford Park too, or Sir Edward Playfair, former permanent secretary at the Ministry of Defence and later chairman of the National Gallery, who wrote to *The Times* urging that St Pancras station be pulled down and declaring that 'not enough is said about the virtues of demolition'.

Not least among those rotting in Betjeman's well-populated hell were the clergymen who referred to their churches as 'plant', like the demolition-minded rector of that temple of the Arts and Crafts, Holy Trinity, Sloane Street:

> You your church's vastiness deplore:
> 'Should we not sell and give it to the poor?'
> Recall, despite your practical suggestion,
> Which the disciple was who asked that question.

Betjeman had always possessed what his not uncritical friend Anthony Powell called 'a whim of iron'. In professional matters he knew what he wanted. When demanding black endpapers with bells on them for *Summoned by Bells*, he said, 'I don't insist. I only know I am right.'

At the same time he never ceased to be nagged by self-doubt and a sense of harassment amounting to paranoia. In the early fifties, just as he was coming to the years of fame that were to lead, it seemed ineluctably, to the laureateship, he wrote to James Lees-Milne, 'I travel third and am cut by people who count and looked down upon by the new refugee "scholars" who have killed all we like by their "research".' In his ongoing feud with Nikolaus Pevsner, it was JB who was mostly the aggressor against someone who, however dry as dust and disparaging he might be, was on the same side in most of the big scraps. And just as he resented academic architectural historians out of an unjustified sense of inferiority, so he resented the Leavisites and other litcritters who wrote him off as a penner of sentimental jingles:

> When all the way from Cambridge comes a wind
> To blow the lamps out every time they're lit
> I know that I must light mine up again.

The better poets of his time all recognized and sometimes loved his work – Auden, Dylan Thomas, Roy Fuller, R. S. Thomas, Larkin. But professional critics continued to reproach him for his lack of formal innovation. Only a younger generation of poet-critics such as James Fenton and Craig Raine had the wit to see what he was up to. In Raine's words, 'You can scarcely understand Betjeman's poetry until you have grasped that he writes "badly" in order to write well.' This was not merely, I think, a matter of his subverting (to use a trade term he would not have cared for) traditional verse forms. There were always subtleties and surprises in his use of everyday motifs – slang, advertising slogans, brand names.

These were, so to speak, first dipped in irony and then shown from another angle to remind us that these things were part of our own experience in all its heartbreaking seriousness. 'Nostalgia,' Betjeman claimed, 'is a word my critics always use about my verse. I describe what people have been through.'

Everyone thinks they can do a Betjeman parody, and Hillier quotes plenty. Whether composed by fans, friends or enemies, they are almost invariably dire and instantly distinguishable from the real thing. Larkin, always excellent on Betjeman, warns us not to discard the funny poems in order to invent a uniformly serious poet: 'Quite often there are things that you can only say as jokes.'

Yet you will still look in vain for Betjeman's name in most encyclopedias of poetry and poetics. This is not because his preference for rhyme and metre is out of fashion (it is not), but rather because his whole view of poetry is antipathetic to the modernist project which insists on distance, disruption and estrangement, on the shattering of the heart's affections, whereas Betjeman, like Blake, stood for their holiness and wholeness. In fact, he reminds me more and more of Blake, both in his anger at the cruelties of the world and his determination to render that world in what Blake called 'minute Particulars'. Two tubby Londoners in search of lost innocence, looking for a time when

> The fields from Islington to Marylebone
> To Primrose Hill and Saint John's Wood
> Were builded over with pillars of gold
> And there Jerusalem's pillars stood.

Behind the never-failing jokes and the ever-growing veneration, this is a sad book, which has to chronicle Betjeman's physical decline through the slow-showing onset of Parkinson's, later punctuated by a series of strokes. He becomes prey to fits of weeping, panic attacks and deep pools of guilt about his abandonment of his wife Penelope for Lady Elizabeth Cavendish who selflessly cared for him through his last years. He held the two of them in a state of tension, never willing to let go of Penelope entirely – though at one period they only met for gloomy lunches at the RAC – but at the same time never quite publicly acknowledging Elizabeth. Was this, like Dickens, because he thought his respectable public wouldn't like it? Or was there a deeper reason?

In his second volume, Bevis Hillier quoted a curious passage from Alan Pryce-Jones's disappointing memoir, confusingly also called *The Bonus of Laughter*, though it was Betjeman who coined the phrase. Pryce-Jones claimed that, at the funeral of John's father Ernest, a second Mrs Betjemann (it was John who dropped the final n) turned up complete with second family, of whom until that moment nothing had been known. A fascinating detail, to put it mildly. But Hillier tells us no more. Was it true? And if Ernest was another Ackerley père, then were John's feelings of guilt deepened by the realization that he was treating Penelope just as Ernest had treated his mother?

Certainly he prettified the views he had originally held of his parents. Hillier records a searing passage that was in the original text of *Summoned by Bells* but later suppressed:

> These hideous people, were they really his?
> That sagging woman with her 'Craven A'?
> That beefy business man with steely eyes –
> 'Sir James was telling me the other day' –
> The studied ease with which he said 'Sir James',
> The half-pay colonels whom he called his friends,
> Their jolly voices and class-conscious air,
> The war-time captains who were more his sort:
> 'How well he thought of men who made their way' ...
> And in some gas-lit bedroom did they mate?
> And was I the undesired result?

Betjeman's attitude towards his son Paul strikes a chilly note too, in which it is hard not to diagnose jealousy, Paul being good-looking and charming without having to work at it. In the two volumes of John's letters published by his daughter Candida, there is only one letter to the adult Paul, known as the Powlie (significantly a neuter noun); he complains to Penelope that Paul is selfish and 'still hung up in his sub-conscious'. Paul's decision to become a Mormon, live in America and be a jazz musician suggests a strong desire to get as far away from his father as possible. Paul also collected snakes. Thirty years ago I was billeted on the Mead for a party and put to share a bedroom with Paul and his snake tanks. Both Paul and the snakes were delightful, it was the absent John who cast the pall.

Well, pied pipers are not much good at family life, and Penelope, though just as amusing and original in her own style, could be insufferably bossy and disinclined to share the limelight. But even John's greatest friends had to concede that he sometimes showed the heartlessness of a child. Indeed, John himself conceded that he was a case of arrested development – 'arrested, I should say, at about the age of 13'. He had the child's sudden uncalculated generosity; he would give you the picture you were looking at together or the book he happened to have in his hand. And he could express, with a child's lack of self-consciousness, all the terrors he felt. Which was also why he could instantly click with children of all sorts and ages – like the thirteen-year-old William Norton.

Perhaps that was also why he could enter so completely into the moment and draw you in too. I remember an evening he took a party to Deptford town hall to see the stars of the old music hall, by then in their seventies if not their eighties – Hetty King the male impersonator, Wee Georgie Wood, Randolph Sutton singing 'On Mother Kelly's Doorstep'. As with other Betjeman outings, nostalgia was decidedly not the word for it. The ancient comics and hoofers were so ebullient, so very much all there, pounding the dusty boards and making the rafters ring, that the whole thing was a live celebration not a commemoration.

This wonderful biography is bursting with such moments. Here's one, no more than a footnote to page 471. During a visit to the Isle of Man, one of his favourite haunts, on Hallowe'en some Cubs outside were singing the Celtic song 'Jenny the Witch', while JB was studying some pictures by Archibald Knox, the Manx Art Nouveau artist and jeweller. He invited the Cubs in and they sang, in the Manx tongue for all I know, 'Jenny the Witch flew over the house, To fetch a stick to lather the mouse', while the old laureate went on squinting at Archie Knox's watercolours – neither of them so nouveau any more – and when the Cubs had finished, he murmured in that inimitable Tennysonian moan, 'We are as near heaven tonight, in this house, as any of us will ever be.' Sentimental? All right, but who cares?

RONALD BLYTHE:
GLORY IN THE RUTS

Ronald Blythe has not budged much. In eighty-nine years, he has moved only a few miles down the Stour Valley, and he has never left his home on the Essex-Suffolk border for more than a month on end. Nor did his ancestors, a long line of Suffolk shepherds who took their surname from the River Blyth, which dawdles past the great windows of Holy Trinity, Blythburgh, into the estuary at Southwold. Rootedness on this scale may seem odd to us who like to feel footloose, but it comes naturally to our great country writers: Thomas Hardy and William Barnes in Dorset, Richard Jefferies in Wilts, and John Clare in Northants (though William Cobbett did get about a bit). They stand out from other writers, too, by coming from the labouring classes as often as not, the sons of stonemasons and farmers, and in youth often labourers themselves. They have now and then been joined at the plough by the sons of the professional classes, such as John Stewart Collis and Adrian Bell, but the native sons of the soil are somehow different.

By staying put, they develop a uniquely painful sensitivity to change. Their most poignant effects come from observing the way that history cuts so brutally across the recurring seasons.

Blythe's masterpiece, *Akenfield: Portrait of an English Village* (1969) records a dying agricultural past of which he himself just caught the tail end. Yet the book is anything but an unqualified lament. It has the iron ring of a spade on Suffolk flint. So unsparing is the description of an agricultural labourer's life and of the unthinking callousness of farmer and squire, that a Norfolk landowner is said to have tossed the book out of the window in disgust before the train reached Colchester. Blythe, like his hero John Clare (he is president of the John Clare Society), sees 'glory in the ruts'. But he describes every bone-shaking, clay-cloying, mud-splattering step of the cart track. *At the Yeoman's House* is an elegy, but an elegy in a harsh key, for Bottengoms, the very old farmhouse Blythe has lived in ever since he inherited it from the painter John Nash, whom he nursed when he was dying (from the nursing came another of Blythe's most admired books, *The View in Winter: Reflections on Old Age* (1979)).

For centuries, Bottengoms was a farm with 70 ill-favoured acres, from which the yeoman, defined by Cobbett as 'above a farmer and lower than a gentleman', scratched a precarious living. Gradually the acres fell away into other hands. In the 1920s, what was left was sold for £1820, in 1936 for £1200 and in 1944 Captain John Nash, official war artist, snapped it up for only £700. Now there is only the tumbledown brick farmhouse, together with Eric Ravilious's even more tumbledown greenhouse donated by his widow and giving new meaning to the term 'lean-to'. Indoors, the sole change since the Nashes' day seems to be that the local stream no longer flows in an open brick channel across the kitchen floor. Outside there is the horsepond:

> this was where the work horses drank century after century,
> sinking belly-high in the blissful coolness in July, throwing up
> their huge heads in the shade, and the water running ceaselessly,
> clouding then clearing. For ever and ever. I have waded naked
> in it to weed it and rake its outlets, and it became a liquid silk

Sir Kingsley Amis

Alan Bennett

Dame Muriel Spark

John le Carré

John Osborne

Professor Derek Jackson

Germaine Greer

Denis Healey

Harold Macmillan with
President Kennedy

Sir Robert Peel

Margot and Herbert Henry Asquith

Sir Oswald Mosley

Charles Dickens

Samuel Taylor Coleridge

John Keats

Sir Nikolaus Pevsner

Sir John Betjeman

Cardinal Basil Hume

Dr Hewlett Johnson
(The Red Dean)

Rudyard Kipling

Virginia Woolf

Fred Perry

Wilfred Owen

on my skin. Dead ash had to be dragged from it, soddenly preserved boughs looking like spars from the Mary Rose. In the spring its surface is a mat of marsh marigold, caltha palustris, and in late summer a diadem of dragonflies. But there are weeks when it can descend into sullenness like a Thomas Hardy place for suicide.

But now the horses are all gone, along with the cows, chickens and goats, and all those women gleaning in the fields and the eight-year-old children harvesting the flints for pennies, as Blythe himself was one of the last to do when he was that age.

As he says, you have to be pretty old now to have witnessed the depth of agricultural toil, to know what it was like to give all your bodily strength to the same few acres, year in, year out. Blythe confides that even when he was writing *Akenfield*, he found it impossible to believe that all of it was going for good. His latest book has 'a requiescat quality', the phrase he uses to describe *Men and the Fields*, the collaboration between Adrian Bell and John Nash just before the war, which was an earlier homage to the landscape created by the yeomen who had stubbornly farmed the valley that Bottengoms is sunk at the bottom of.

At the time Nash was illustrating the book, he was mourning the death of his only child in a motor accident. So even the inheritance of Bottengoms has its tragic aspect. Blythe never underplays the hardness of the past. But he never over-sneers at the present either. The incomers wondering whether their Chelsea tractors will make it down the track do receive the odd sideswipe, but he is quick to point out that there are probably more trees in Suffolk now than when Elizabeth I made her royal progress to visit Sir William Waldegrave's enormous new mansion at Wormingford.

This is a production of old age, gentle but not soft, both tough-minded and charitable. Blythe is a lay reader in the Church of England and nearly became a priest, like William Barnes and

George Crabbe and Gilbert White before him. Yet I find his unillusioned, lyrical tone curiously similar to those ruralists who were lifelong atheists, Thomas Hardy and Richard Jefferies. It is as though the unblinking countryman's eye has no room for religion, one way or the other.

One of the incidental pleasures of *At the Yeoman's House* is Blythe's delight in euphonious lists. He breaks off to give some of the names on the sixteenth-century marriage register in the local church: 'Alexander Sturdyfall and Annis Bird, Thomas Coo and Anes Hollburrowes, Leonarde Hartlife and Joane Lurkine'. He can hear their long-dead feet making 'brick music' on the kitchen floor at Bottengoms. And so can we.

THE SUBURB AND THE VILLAGE

The late J. G. Ballard was famous for living in suburbia, Shepperton to be precise. He thought it odd that anyone should think this odd. The suburbs were, in his view, the logical subject for any writer seeking to track shifts in culture, for the important post-war cultural trends had started there. The 'burbs were where it was at; they were socially as well as geographically edgy, to use the sort of language he wouldn't have used.

It is hard to think of a more unfashionable claim. To the intelligentsia, the suburbs were and always have been the place where nothing happens, or nothing good. While the fates of the city and the countryside vex every bien-pensant breast, nobody pays much attention to the people who live in between, except to finger them as the Enemy. Lewis Mumford, in his heyday as the urban guru, declared that the flight to the suburbs 'carries no hope or promise of life at a higher level'. D. H. Lawrence wrote in *Kangaroo* of the 'utterly uninteresting' suburbs of Sydney (where he had been for all of a fortnight): those myriads of bungalows offered 'no inner life, no high command, no interest in anything, finally'. From Byron to Graham Greene and Cyril Connolly, the 'leafy middle-class suburbs' have been denounced as smug, small-minded and spiritually derelict.

Architects and planners made common cause with novelists

and poets to deplore the relentless advance of the little boxes and the little people who lived in them. Clough Williams-Ellis and his wife Amabel Strachey launched two famous polemics between the wars: *England and the Octopus* (1928) – the octopus being ribbon development – and *Britain and the Beast* (1937) – the beast being the bungalow. The latter was a volume of essays written by, among others, Maynard Keynes, Cyril Joad, G. M. Trevelyan and Patrick Abercrombie, the great planner and preserver, and endorsed by a blaze of luminaries – Lloyd George, George Lansbury and Julian Huxley. Every sword in Bloomsbury leapt from its scabbard to fight against the development of Peacehaven on the cliffs above Brighton. And they did indeed make sure that such a thing never happened again, for the Town and Country Acts of 1947 introduced state control of land use on a scale that even William the Conqueror might have thought excessive.

Even today when four out of five of us live in the suburbs, they are little studied, let alone defended in print. The publisher's blurb introduces *The Freedoms of Suburbia*, Paul Barker's enchanting and persuasive pictorial essay, with a nervous defiance as if the book were proposing free heroin for toddlers. This is not a systematic history like F. M. L. Thompson's *The Rise of Suburbia*. Barker, a former editor of *New Society* and a prolific writer on architecture and planning, proceeds *ambulando*. These are Suburban Rides, which in a gentler style echo Cobbett's suspicion of people who take pleasure in bossing other people about. By this seemingly oblique method, Barker manages to convince the reader of several propositions which might have made little impact if presented in a more formal academic fashion.

The book is sumptuously illustrated, giving us on every page a marvellous range of semis, bungalows, villas, prefabs, shacks, chalets and mobile homes in every imaginable style – classical, Tudor, Queen Anne, Gothic, Arts and Crafts, even Modernist. Nine out of ten of these dwellings sprang from a collaboration between the speculative builder and the client, without the sniff of an architect. From about 1830 on, after John Nash built the *cottages ornés* in Park Village East, the architectural profession largely withdrew from the suburbs to await orders from grander clients, such as the Grosvenor Estate and the London County Council. Thereafter architects built town halls and lunatic asylums and company headquarters. They did not accept and were rarely offered commissions for 'Dunroamin' or 'Mon Repos', not least because most of them believed such abominations should have been strangled at birth. Build up, not out, they chorus. High-rise equals civilized, a theme recently reprised in Richard Rogers's paper 'Towards an Urban Renaissance', which, as Barker points out, is a plea for London to become more like Lord Rogers's native Florence.

Barker, by contrast, speaks up for Non-Plan against Plan, for Jane Jacobs against Lewis Mumford, for higgledy-piggledy plotlands against streets in the sky, for the human and the individual against the machine à vivre. But he does so temperately and with a generous eye. He reminds us that architects and planners can build desirable suburbs: Norman Shaw's Bedford Park, Raymond Unwin's Hampstead Garden Suburb and Letchworth Garden City. So can benevolent employers and landowners: the Cadburys at Bournville, Lord Leverhulme at Port Sunlight, the Anstruther-Gough-Calthorpes in Edgbaston.

Above all, there is Milton Keynes. Here in the flattish bit of Bucks, the planners have created a remarkable city which has now grown almost to the size of Nottingham and whose inhabitants still love it and call it MK, on the analogy of LA. One of MK's charms is that it contains a variety of building styles: from Bovis's reed-thatched black-and-white executive homes at the top end to cheap Modernist bungalows designed by the Norman Foster partnership in its early days. The town's enormous grid, studded with roundabouts, is also enlivened by the occasional ancient village centre which has long been swallowed up: Woolston and Wolverton, Woughton on the Green and Shenley Church End.

Those villages have been suburbanized, just as Thomas More's Chelsea and Pope's Twickenham and Keats's Hampstead were turned from delectable villages into London suburbs, as highly prized in their new role as in their old. Suburban change is remorseless and unpredictable. Islington was once the home of London's dairies, and the playing fields where Thomas Lord turned out as a bowler for White Conduit Cricket Club; then it was developed as a 'walking suburb' for city clerks, then it slipped downhill into bedsitshire and has spent the past fifty years climbing back to gentility. When Eric Hobsbawm, a newly demobbed sergeant, moved into a flat in Gloucester Crescent, Camden Town, just after the war, he thought of it as 'the western outpost of the vast zone of London's bombed and yet ungentrified East End'. To think of this epitome of metro chic, the home of Mark Boxer's Stringalongs, as part of the East End takes some stretching now, as much as regarding present-day fashionable Hoxton as an extension of the West End.

Far from being sunk in unenquiring apathy, the suburbs are in constant flux. Barker points out that H. G. Wells would scarcely have recognized a single building in the high street of his native Bromley. The old shopping parades of the 1930s have been eclipsed by the out-of-town hypermarkets. Colin Ward, the doyen of anarchist anti-planners, regards the unfinished, transitional nature of the suburbs as one of its great attractions for a child. There were secret places for solitude in the fields and copses that had ceased to be farmland and were not yet residential. This edge-of-things feeling is beautifully caught in *Spies*, Michael Frayn's child's-eye novel.

When asked to choose their preferred type of home, Britons always put the bungalow top, with the Manhattan-style loft and the tower block nowhere. The Bengali peasant hut, the banggolo, triumphs over the officially approved ziggurat. Anthony D. King, in his social history of the ultimate low-rise residence, declares that 'in the first half of the twentieth century, the bungalow was the most revolutionary building type established in Britain'. It was the people's choice, not designed, directed or even approved by the artistic establishment. Nor will it do to sneer at the suburbs as smug enclaves for the middle classes. There are working-class suburbs at Dagenham and Barking, as there are at the scruffier edges of most conurbations. There are plutocratic suburbs at St George's Hill and Wentworth and Winchmore Hill. Every morning a fleet of white vans swarms into the capital from the suburbs of Kent and Essex and Herts to minister to the plumbing, plastering and electrical needs of the bankers of Notting Hill and Chelsea. The suburbs themselves become workplaces, as back offices migrate to cheaper premises on the M25, and Croydon becomes Edge City. Beyond the Green Belt, towns like Newbury become 'exurbs', the most desired places of all to live in, just as Lakeside and Bluewater are the most popular places to shop in. These malls are not to be put down as tawdry American imports, since they derive ultimately from the glassed-in *galeries* and *gallerie* of Continental Europe – Thomas Jefferson was so impressed by the Palais-Royal that he wanted to copy it back home in Virginia.

Barker begins his book by watching a tower block in Hackney being blown up. He ends it by reflecting that scarcely any semis have ever been demolished, except when they stood in the way of road-building schemes. The sourest critics eventually succumb. John Betjeman, after all, began as a modernist, but by 1940 had repented to become the laureate of the suburbs. Even Slough forgave him in the end. But the orthodoxy was strong. Stationed in the Middle East during the war, J. M. Richards wrote a homage to the suburbs, *The Castles on the Ground*, but on his return to the *Architectural Review* he toed the Modernist line.

The planning laws in their present rigid state give rise to the only serious corruption in British politics: they enable landowners to capture enormous unearned profits; even in a time of prosperity, they cause crippling housing shortages. Above all, in an age when thousands of acres are no longer needed for agriculture, they prevent ordinary people from living where they would most

like to live (and from fostering biodiversity in their back gardens).
As the Treasury report on land supply pointed out in 2003, current
policy is bringing about 'an ever widening economic and social
divide'.

Paul Barker does not press these lines of argument too far. He
stresses that he is not proposing to 'concrete over' the English
countryside; he is as keen as anyone to protect the Lake District
and the Yorkshire Dales. He argues only that '"positive" plan-
ning is best done with the lightest of hands'. He urges too a gentle
bias towards preserving the streets as they are, for they are a city's
memory bank. But none of these things should be achieved at the
cost of preventing people living the life they wish to live. Plan-
ning either slows change down to a glacial pace, or it is swift and
destructive, as we can see from the post-war history of Liverpool,
Birmingham, Bradford and Hull, to name but a few great provin-
cial cities that have had their hearts ripped out. Better to yield to
the mild incursions of the suburbs, and to the preferences of the
people.

Barker declares that 'we ought by now to know that the worst
mistakes in planning come from trying to force other people to
live in the way they wouldn't choose to and often the way we
wouldn't want to live ourselves'. Why not go one step further and
contemplate the possibility that the solutions to the rural problems
ventilated by the Countryside March may sometimes lie in allow-
ing people to do things they presently aren't allowed to do? That
indispensable anarchist Colin Ward, for example, advocates reviv-
ing the Plotlands. From the 1870s until 1939, speculators, unable
to sell land into a depressed market, even at throwaway prices, hit
upon the idea of dividing the worst land into small plots and selling
them to city dwellers to do whatever they fancied with them –
start a smallholding or chicken farm, build a holiday home or a
retirement bungalow. All along the North and South Downs and
the Kent and Essex marshes, and along many northern coasts and
estuaries, these untidy pockets of chalets, allotments and prefabs

appeared, until the 1947 Town and Country Planning Act killed off the practice. But if you designated a couple of fields outside every village to be sold off to locals as the new Plotlands, the rural housing shortage would soon dwindle.

As would the problem of rural employment, if every village set aside a few acres of poor land to be leased out for workshops. The upper-class English may flee to Tuscany, but the working-class Italians flee to the Veneto where the ramshackle back lanes allow them to set up workshops without fuss and at knockdown prices – 'the Third Italy', as described in Paul Hirst's essay on informal rural development. All over the Continent, you find these industrial districts, centred on some smallish town, where a host of little firms collaborate on particular products like furniture or knitwear. That, after all, is the way British manufacturing first developed two or three centuries ago, not least in the valleys round Stroud, where Laurie Lee drank cirder with Rosie. Such districts win no prizes for tidiness. The well-bred mind recoils from the sight of a Palladio villa surrounded by noisy small factories.

Yet without some considered and selective relaxation of planning controls, any hopes of bringing work back to the countryside must remain wind and waffle. I saw no banner on the Countryside March demanding any such relaxation. Nimby and Nimrod still hunt together. In taking over a house, Roger Scruton rightly points out, the National Trust finally extinguishes the life that was lived in it. The house's restoration is an act of taxidermy – no doubt a necessary act, as Robert Grant argues in his essay 'History, Tradition and Modernity', yet one which betokens in Grant's words, 'the loss, not so much of a past, but of a confident, unselfconscious, tradition-saturated present'. But the 1947 Planning Act does much the same to a pretty village or an urban conservation area. Deprived of all possibility of change in themselves and set in an equally frozen landscape, they too are embalmed.

And here, sadly, we come to the final dichotomy laid bare by this excellent volume of essays. For Town and Country are not at odds. Far from it, they are joined together in an embalmers' league against the ambitions of Suburbia. Just as incomers quickly develop nostrils sensitive to the slightest pong from the local pig farm, so I developed quite abnormal sensitivity while reading *Town and Country* to the faintest condescension to the suburbs. Sometimes, the sniff was barely audible, as in references to 'new' people who don't quite understand country ways. At other times, as in Roger Scruton's otherwise cogent closing essay, hatred of 'those suburbs dropped from nowhere' bursts out with full ammoniac pungency: 'The commuter suburbs violate the landscape partly because they violate the sense of rural time. Even if they remain there for ever, people feel, it will be with a stagnant impermanence . . . they will be dilapidated without ever becoming weathered.' But just when did this violation begin? When Hampstead became a suburb two centuries ago, or Streatham, or Croydon? At what point did the weathering stop?

Walking through suburbs like East Molesey or Enfield, I am struck by an utterly contrary feeling: that these are places of deep settlement, not liable to be eviscerated at intervals like most English cities or knocked about by agricultural depression or technological change as the English village has been at intervals since the Middle Ages. Suburbs generate clubs and societies and cricket teams, just as Scruton's local village of Crudwell does. True, their populations do not stay put over the generations, but then historians now realize that the population in English villages was much more mobile than we used to think.

In detective stories, villages are always sleepy, just as suburbs are always leafy. The English village is lodged in our minds as the great good place where nothing changes, a refuge from the rat race and a retirement dream. But Clive Aslet, in his brisk, evocative, occasionally waspish prose, sets out to show us in 500 page-long snapshots how fragile, accidental and often tragic has been the history of the villages he has chosen. What happens to them is so often not the result of natural growth or decline but of some economic bonanza or hammer blow or some landlord's benevolence or greed. Even those features of the rural scene which we think of as natural and time-honoured may well be the result of human activity, and often activity of the sort we now think undesirable, like the peat-digging which created the Norfolk Broads or the hedges which were grown to enclose land that had formerly been held in common.

So many villages have disappeared, two or three thousand of them since the Norman Conquest (Aslet is uncertain of the figure). Some, like Hallsands in Devon or Covehithe in Suffolk, have been washed away by the sea. Others have been taken over for military ranges, such as Tyneham, Dorset, and Imber, Wiltshire. But far the largest number have been simply swept away and sometimes burnt to the ground by landowners who preferred sheep to villagers – or would rather look out on a romantic vista designed by Capability Brown than on a huddle of smoky hovels. The Clearances in the Highlands at the beginning of the nineteenth century are the most notorious, but the same terrible fate could strike any village deemed unprofitable by its owner at any time from the Dissolution of the Monasteries or even earlier. The inhabitants of Wharram Percy in North Yorkshire had been evicted by 1403. Only a few humps and hollows in the grass remain.

Many villages which look so picturesque today began as untidy and squalid mining camps, like Burwash in the Sussex Weald, which was a centre of the Elizabethan iron-making industry three centuries before Rudyard Kipling came to live there and celebrate its magic in *Puck of Pook's Hill*. All over Britain, settlements mushroomed to house workers digging out every kind of mineral – tin, lead, copper, manganese, even gold – as well as the coal and iron on which the Industrial Revolution was based. Strontium was discovered at Strontian, on the shores of Loch Sunart; titanium, first called Manaccanite, at Manaccan, by the Helford River in Cornwall.

But when the seam was worked out, these boom villages lost their reason for existing. Tin and copper had been mined at Cornwall's largest mine, the 'Great Work' at Godolphin, since long before the Romans came and the Godolphin family waxed plutocratic on the proceeds, but when the mine closed in the mid-nineteenth century, so did the village.

Some mine-owners were more philanthropists than profiteers and built handsome model villages using the best architects of their day. So did other industrialists: the Quaker chocolate kings, Cadbury, at Bournville, Rowntree at New Earswick just outside York; Lord Leverhulme at Port Sunlight and Thornton Hough in Cheshire; the store tycoon William Whiteley at his Whiteley Village in Surrey (his benevolence did not protect him from being shot dead by the deranged son of one of his shopgirls who believed he was Whiteley's illegitimate son). These model villages mostly survive, now shorn of their founders' bans on alcohol and fun, and are much prized by their new tenants for their quaint and cosy atmosphere.

Life in the old villages was never a honeysuckle idyll. As the poet George Herbert, rector of the parish of Bemerton, near Salisbury, remarked, 'Country people live hardly.' The truest accounts of rural life in the old days, such as Flora Thompson's *Lark Rise to Candleford,* John Stewart Collis's *The Worm Forgives the Plough,* and Ronald Blythe's *Akenfield,* all remind us mercilessly of the back-breaking toil that had to be endured in all weathers as well as the perpetual insecurity of being dependent on the harvest and the squire's goodwill.

Although Aslet covers the whole of Great Britain, he half-admits that it is the English village which provides the heart of his subject: 'North of the Border, rural settlements are not always villages, as they would be understood in southern England. Much of the country did not acquire villages before the eighteenth century, when

they were built by landowners wanting to improve their estates
or to promote fishing.' In Wales, too, the countryside was dotted
with scattered farmsteads; only in the bits of Wales first settled by
the Normans – South Pembrokeshire, the Vale of Glamorgan –
do you find the English-type clustered village with its church and
manor and farmhouses around a village green.

Over the past fifty years, though externally it may look just
as lovely and unspoilt, the English village itself has changed
dramatically. Chitterne, the remote village on Salisbury Plain
where I was brought up, had declined from 800 souls in the mid-
nineteenth century to 250 in my childhood. Yet it still possessed
a primary school, a horse-racing stable, two firms of builders, a
blacksmith, a garage, two shops, a Baptist chapel and no fewer
than six dairy farms. All gone now. Only the parish church and
one of two pubs survive. Like many other such places, Chitterne
is now a dormitory for commuters and retired couples, no longer
a more or less self-sufficient workplace. Under its lovely skin of
brick and flint it is a new kind of suburb.

And what exactly are the suburbs being derided for? For being
too quiet, too leafy, too orderly – but these are the virtues which
we attribute to old-fashioned village life and which we greatly
admire. And what is to be done with the awful truth that, as
Paul Barker points out, 'suburbia gives most of the people what
they want from a house, most of the time'? That also goes for
the institutions associated with suburbia. Those dark satanic
malls are the people's choice. And the true people's architecture
is the semi-detached, the Voysey inheritance. As for the sup-
posed moral inferiority of the suburbs, here I stand with Sherlock
Holmes in the belief that 'the lowest and vilest alleys in London
do not present a more dreadful record of sin than does the smil-
ing and beautiful countryside'. Fred West was a country boy
come to town. It is hard to imagine him settling in Esher. Deep
down, what both urbanists and ruralists dislike about suburbia
is its self-chosenness, its refusal to accept an imposed pattern of

community. This self-chosenness is often reviled as 'anomic' or smug or selfish. Yet it would be hard to demonstrate that suburbanites respond less generously to serious moral challenges. They too have their war memorials. What sticks in the ideologue's throat is really their refusal to be planned by someone else, whether by Le Corbusier or Lord Loamshire. Tim Mars, laureate and former resident of Milton Keynes, describes beautifully how the original scheme for the New Town, known as 'Pooleyville' after Fred Pooley, Buckinghamshire's county architect, was to be a gleaming Modernist array of cluster blocks complete with monorail. In came the American sociologist Melvin Webber, who wanted to build an unapologetically suburban Little-Los-Angeles-in-Bucks. And despite the fact that the eventual chief architect of Milton Keynes also saw the project in urban terms, his fellow urbanists regarded the end result as a failure as a city. But when the actual residents were quizzed, they didn't regard Milton Keynes as a failure at all. In fact, they liked it precisely because it was a series of villages.

MARK GIROUARD AND
THE ENGLISH TOWN

Waking up in a strange English town is a pleasure I find hard to explain to most Englishmen. Even the smell of burnt coffee from the dining room and the hum of the Hoover in the shuttered bar quicken the anticipation. In fact, the Trust House Forte experience is a necessary prelude to stepping out into the market square and looking for the cathedral tower behind the scaffolding, the sooty mass of the old town hall (closed, except Wednesdays), the Georgian terrace dolled up in Civic Trust pastel shades, the Corn Exchange, now reserved for bingo and the amateur dramatics society. Was much corn ever exchanged there? The merchants usually preferred the pub. Even the havoc wrought by the ring road and the multistorey car park cannot put off a hard-core urbanist, a perversion not often confessed to in this nation of rural romantics. By contrast, I find a faint melancholy stealing over me on joining the queue to pay £4 for a guided tour of Sir Leicester Dedlock's seat at Chesney Wold (Teas and Gift Shop in the Stables).

It is a delight to recognize in Dr Girouard a fellow deviant. In this neat and beautiful volume, the author of *The Victorian Country House* and *Life in the English Country House* takes to the streets and, so to speak, comes out. He speaks with unrestrained nostalgia of driving down, when an officer cadet at Eaton Hall, off the treeless and terrifying moors into Huddersfield:

> What a city! For a mile or so we drove along a street of palaces – palaces which were admittedly as bleak and unadorned as the neighbouring Pennines, but still amazing in the height and power of their mighty stone facades, piled up storey after storey, and row after row of windows. I had never been to Florence, but this, it seemed to me, must be what Florence was like.

It is fifty years ago that I went to Huddersfield and I still remember that same uncovenanted thrill. Newcastle, the Newcastle of Dobson and Grainger, not of T. Dan Smith, was almost as good. And as for Trowbridge – such a silly name – as a child I had imagined it a wilderness of municipal offices reeking of Usher's Ales and then, aged sixteen, I went there and gaped out of the bus window at the splendour of the clothiers' mansions in the 'southern Manchester' – one of those fanciful nicknames one cannot imagine actually using, like calling High Wycombe 'the Venice of Buckinghamshire'. Dr Girouard evokes a fistful of other such shared enthusiasms: for the great India Mill tower at Darwen, its dark-purple brick soaring out of the stone milltown, for the marvellous pastoral vistas still to be had from the high crescents of Bath, for the grandness of Bolton: its airy and bright Market Hall of 1851, described by the vicar as 'a market house which Europe herself might admire and emulate', its town hall an imperial extravaganza on a Castle Howard scale, its piazza a homelier version of the Place de la Concorde.

Does he miss anything out? Well, if one is being fussy, there is not a great deal about the pargeting-infested little towns of Essex or about the Cinque Ports, now Mapped and Lucianized to the point of suffocation but still full of pretty buildings. Does he quite do justice to Harrogate, Yorkshire's rolling epitome of rus in urbe? And the account of the pleasure palaces of the late nineteenth century fades away to leave no mention of the cinemas and sports stadia which are, after all, the dominant features of most poor districts. Nor does he have much to say about clubs – gentlemen's, political or working-men's – which took over so many of the functions of the assembly rooms and the coffee houses and taverns.

But these are quibbles which should not divert us from considering the unusual and ultimately sad story that Dr Girouard has to tell – unusual, I mean, by the standards of many European countries, where social and political history would be largely the history of the pride and fall of great cities. England does appear to be different. We seldom seem to have cherished our towns in quite the same way. There is an accidental, almost distrait air about both their growth and their decline.

One by one, the medieval guilds did manage to squeeze their charters out of the monarch. The resulting corporation was controlled by the freemen who often elected the town's two MPs and were principally occupied in defending their own privileges. Until the Municipal Corporations Act of 1835 brought in representative democracy, the old corporations showed only fitful symptoms of a civic conscience. The Improvement Trusts of the eighteenth century which did such brilliant work in the heart of places like Taunton (now mostly ripped out again), Newcastle, Liverpool, Bath, Yarmouth and Frome had to be ratified by individual Acts of Parliament. Although they tended to spring from the initiative of public-spirited city residents, they had nothing to do with ideas of local democracy. They corresponded more, I suppose, to the present-day Urban Development Corporations.

Until Victorian times, English urban government was

haphazard, marginal and, as they say nowadays, underfunded. That is just what makes its buildings so lively, the guildhalls and assembly rooms and market crosses all so modest, light and delicate, especially when compared to the monumental edifices being deposited on the adjoining countryside by the new magnates.

Dr Girouard points out that this restraint was not because of the smaller size of towns before the Industrial Revolution. 'Towns no larger than the bigger 18th-century towns were to build much more grandly in the 19th century.' As long as local government remained unrepresentative, it could levy rates only in a small way for limited purposes such as paving, lamp lighting and street sweeping. The introduction of councillors elected by ratepayers made possible the great municipal imperialism of the later nineteenth century. Alderman Foodbotham, much though he might have loathed the idea, was the child of representative democracy.

The architects followed the money. Carr of York lived mainly off building country houses. A century later, architects like Barry would live off public buildings: town halls, banks, warehouses, museums, law courts. Waterhouse's Eaton Hall may have cost the Duke of Westminster £600,000, but his Manchester Town Hall cost a cool million, and that was the shape of the future. Colossal sums were spent on street widening, drainage and gas and water supply by all the great towns and cities of the Midlands and the North. Despite the Chamberlains' reputation as the pioneers of 'gas and water socialism', Birmingham was by no means in the lead.

Yet the irony is that, even before these Herculean feats of civic improvement had reached their mid-Victorian peak, the city ideal had begun to fade. As royal personages processed around the country opening enormous town halls, usually amid torrential downpours, the middle classes had already begun to decamp. The triumph of the English urban spirit, such a laggard and hesitant thing to emerge, coincided with the beginnings of its decline.

Who was the first commuter? Dr Girouard suggests the Thorntons of Clapham in the late eighteenth century, or possibly William Roscoe the banker and philanthropist who moved out of his house in central Liverpool to the pleasant suburb of Islington at about the same time. It was probably a process so gradual that even the pioneer exurbanites themselves were scarcely aware of having altered the pattern of their lives for good, perhaps regarding the letting of their town house as a purely temporary measure.

Holman Hunt's father used to live in his Cheapside warehouse for cotton and velvet thread before moving out to the suburbs with his family. The Ruskins started off in Brunswick Square within striking distance of John James Ruskin's City wine business, taking summer lodgings in Hampstead or Dulwich before finally moving out to a semi-detached house in Herne Hill with a large garden and a carriage sweep. A generation later, William Rothenstein had happy childhood memories of playing with the workmen in his father's warehouse in Bradford's Little Germany, but already the family lived in a smarter part of town. As a child, John Betjeman used to prowl round his father's works – 'Fourth generation yes, this is the boy' – in the Pentonville Road (recently the premises of the Medici Society and being gutted at the moment):

> And once I found a dusty drawing-room,
> Completely furnished, where long years ago
> My great-grandfather lived above his work
> Before he moved to sylvan Highbury.

'A town without a prosperous, powerful, resident middle class is a town in trouble' is the menacing burden of Dr Girouard's epilogue, 'and so is a town in which the middle class think the country is better.' Rural romanticism may have produced the imitable delights of Bedford Park and Hampstead Garden Suburb and the garden cities which have between them helped to shape suburbia all over the world. But it has also had a draining, demoralizing impact on the English city, one which has not been remedied yet and which never seems to have afflicted Continental cities so badly.

Why did the middle classes leave? Well, 'on winter days in London, the smoke of fossil coal forms an atmosphere perceivable for many miles, like a great round cloud attached to the earth.' That was Louis Simond, a French-born American visiting the city in 1810. By the time of the Regency, then, the smog was already as bad as it is in Istanbul or Katowice today. Coal was the prevailing fuel and had been so for a century or more. And until Count Rumford's invention of the Rumford stove in 1796, with its narrow chimney throat and more effective draught, much of the heat disappeared up the chimney taking with it clouds of unburnt coal dust which hung over the city. Then there was the filth in the streets, and the traffic jams, and the real danger of a street sign falling on your head or of falling down an uncovered manhole. And the noise. A German visitor arriving in London at midnight in 1770 found that 'the noise in the street was as great as in other places at midday'.

Above all, there were the area steps, or rather the lack of them until about 1770. Cruickshank and Burton, in their admirable exposé of the practicalities of Georgian life, point out that this meant that all night soil had to be removed via the front door by the nightmen tramping through the middle of the house with their wooden tubs. Sweet dreams were hard to come by. The only alternative was to connect the cesspit to the main drain; strictly against the rules and, even if tried, liable to end in blockage and disaster. By the later Georgian period, the genteel household would certainly own a water closet or two, but the irreducible problem of solid waste disposal remained. It is charming to notice in the sketches of the early town-garden designers the 'Conveniency' or 'needful edifice' or 'temple of Cloacina' nestling in the corner of the plot, only half-hidden by some arbour of fig or vine.

Neil Burton shows that the garden-design business was well under way by the mid-eighteenth century. Thomas Fairchild's *The City Gardener* of 1722 lists plants that will do in London and also places where they can be seen flourishing: 'there are now two large mulberry trees growing in a little yard about 16 ft square at Sam's Coffee House in Ludgate.' One might take just as much pride in a town garden as in a country one. The sparky Mrs Delany wrote to her sister in 1734 from No. 48 Upper Brook Street: 'You think madam that I have no garden perhaps, but that's a mistake. I have one as big as your parlour in Gloucestershire and in it groweth damask roses, stocks variegated and plain, some purple, some red, pinks, philaria, some dead and some alive, and honey-suckles that never blow.'

There was, it seems, less to be proud of in Georgian building methods. The leasehold system encouraged speed and economy rather than sound construction. In particular, the cost of bricks being far greater than the cost of labour, it was a standing temptation to cut some of the expensive façade bricks in half so that the headers never bonded with the much cheaper place bricks behind and the wall was from the start made up of two separate skins and so liable to bulge and bow in all directions. In Spitalfields, the minister's house in Fournier Street was built by Hawksmoor at the same time as Christ Church according to sound building methods and cost £1461 15s. Round the corner, the jerry-built No. 15 Elder Street, not all that much smaller, probably cost less than £200 to put up.

But when it came to aesthetic matters, no trouble was spared. The correct proportions of the windows were heatedly discussed in journals and set out in pattern books. So were the right combinations and ingredients for the paint, the proportions and ornament of the bannisters, the wainscoting and the fire surrounds. Cruickshank and Burton lead us deep into a minestrone of technicalities, of astragal nosings, quirked cyma reversas, bolection mould lags and bressummers, of crotia and smalt and indico. It is easy to ridicule the classical dogmatism of Georgian architects. How could there be said to exist a single ideal relationship between the size of the windows on the different floors of a terrace house when that ideal changed so often over the course of the century? But what did not change was the obsessive belief in and pursuit of that ideal.

In their different ways, these two enchanting books cannot help making the Georgian city sound like an attractive place to live in, even after every allowance has been made for the poverty and squalor, the banging of the night-soil buckets in the small hours, the gentlemen pissing in chamber pots in the dining room after the ladies had retired, the stifling overcrowding at the routs remarked on by so many foreign visitors like Prince Pückler-Muskau at Brighton in 1827: 'There are now private balls every evening; and in rooms to which a respectable German citizen would not venture to invite 12 people, some hundreds are here packed like negro slaves.'

Provincial cities too had their fairs and their race weeks which drew all classes to them. In high-minded old age, William Wilberforce sighed for the bright days of his youth in Hull: 'It was then as gay a place as could be found out of London. The theatres, balls, great suppers and card parties were the delight of the principal families in the town. No pious parent ever laboured more to improve a beloved child with sentiments of piety than they did to give me a taste for the world and its diversions.'

Enough of that fine city, Larkin's 'lonely northern daughter', survives to give us a feeling of what must have been as evocative a waterside as any in England, Dr Girouard tells us, despite so much destruction during the war and, unforgivably, worse destruction after it. But would even its revamped and wine-barred waterside so beguile a young Wilberforce today? And whatever happened to the English passeggiata? Where are those thousands who used to walk along the Mall, or the Grand Parade in Bath, or the seafront at Sidmouth, or the Quarry at Shrewsbury? Come to that, whatever became of 'polite society', which was originally not an excluding but an including notion? Part of Bath's charm in its early days was that it broke down class barriers, in the upper regions anyway, and enabled duchesses to walk the streets unattended and mingle with trade. Anyone who dressed properly and could afford the subscription could frequent the Assembly Rooms. I suppose the answer is that the whole business has moved to the Costa del Sol where the English now perform their lobster quadrille, if not in such a seemly fashion.

Now in the evening in the market square of an English town, Dr Girouard mournfully observes, 'when the shops have shut and the cars have gone, groups of boys and girls shriek and giggle outside McDonald's or Wimpys. The lights glimmer through the windows of the half-deserted pubs. Otherwise there is no sign of life at all.' Is not all this fractionally out of date? It seems to me that English towns at night, though scarcely buzzing, are not quite as dead as they were. All the same, it has to be admitted that the signs of a major return to the city are still faint and uncertain. The dream of suburban independence, despite decades of modish mockery, remains the dominant one. And if 'inner cities' are still deserted and forbidding places, the middle classes have nobody but themselves to blame.

For it is not the lager louts spilling out of the pubs who have frightened them away. It is the middle classes who have abandoned the city to the yobs. And both have lost something by it. There is a certain emptiness all round, a gap which even neighbours cannot fill.

No, we are not to use the word 'community' to describe what has been lost, especially since what strikes one about the English town in its heyday was its sprightly individualism, its very lack of communal solidarity. 'Townliness' is the best I can do, though it is not much better. But we all know what Dr Girouard is on about.

Meanwhile, there is still Hull in store for me, and Ludlow, and Richmond, North Yorks. Not everything has gone, and what is left is worth a dozen detours yet.

SOME OLD MASTERS

Is there something they had, and we have lost, perhaps even without knowing what it is? Auden famously begins his poem 'Musée des Beaux Arts':

> About suffering they were never wrong,
> The Old Masters: how well they understood
> Its human position; how it takes place
> While someone else is eating or opening a window or just
>   walking dully along;

As Icarus falls out of the sky, the ploughman goes on ploughing, the ship sails on. But of course this doesn't just apply to suffering. The Old Master's eye takes in everything. Only the petit-maître narrows his gaze and sticks to the matter in hand.

To the literal-minded, this juxtaposing of the tragic and the commonplace looks like a cheap trick. Voltaire, along with many others, could not be doing with the porter's speech in *Macbeth,* which he denounced as '*les plaisanteries de polichinelle*'. In the eighteenth century the scene was often omitted or, as in Alexander Pope's edition, relegated to the margin. How could you have a pissed porter wittering on about drink and lechery while the King was being murdered next door? The answer of course is that the porter was just as likely to be pissed on the night of Duncan's death as any other night, and if his speech is squalid, it's nothing to the physical and moral squalor of the murder.

The Old Masters do not blink. When Thomas Hardy went to see sixteen-year-old Martha Brown hanged in Dorchester, he noted what a figure she made against the misty rain and how the tight black silk gown set off her figure as she wheeled half-round and back. At the hanging of Mrs Manning, Charles Dickens too noticed the shape of her dress: 'a fine shape, so elaborately corseted and artfully dressed, that it was quite unchanged in its trim appearance, as it slowly swung from side to side.' Dickens went to another hanging, that of a valet named Courvoisier who had cut his master's throat. By coincidence, Thackeray had been sent to report on Courvoisier's hanging, but he was so sickened that he could not bear to look – which is why Dickens is an Old Master and Thackeray, much though I love his novels, is not.

Samuel Pepys was not an artist at all but a pushy bureaucrat, and so, strictly speaking, does not deserve to be included here, except that his diary is a work of art, precisely because he has that all-inclusive appetite for experience and that unblinking eye. In a single day, he goes from watching the hanging, drawing and quartering of Major-General Harrison at Charing Cross – 'he looking as cheerfully as any man could in that condition' – to eat oysters with some naval cronies at the Sun Tavern, then home to have a red-hot row with Elizabeth Pepys about her untidiness, in his anger kicking – and breaking – the little basket he had bought her in Holland. And he puts everything down.

We think of the Romantic poets as weaving rainbows out of gauzy, delicate stuff, but when you read the letters and notebooks of Keats and Coleridge, you find the same unexpurgated attention, the same hearty curiosity – about the filthy breakfast they serve in Kirkcudbright, or the correct derivation of the word 'cunt', or the idea of a washing machine, the quality of different sorts of opium, the colour of wet slates after rain at Ullswater. In Coleridge, this ravenous appetite for life slides into a sort of pantheism, as in his early poem, 'The Eolian Harp':

> O the one life within us and abroad,
> Which meets all motion and becomes its soul,
> A light in sound, a sound-like power in light,
> Rhythm in all thought, and joyance everywhere—

At the end of the poem, he fancies himself being recalled by his fiancée Sarah Fricker to orthodox Christianity from 'these shapings of the unregenerate mind'. But the truth is that Coleridge, like most Old Masters, evades any such confining commitment. For the Old Masters don't, in any profound sense, do God. They don't like the competition. It is as though there is room for only one Creator at a time.

Hardy is the most explicit atheist, Keats the most overtly hostile to priests and churches, but Dickens too seems to prize Christian pity and kindness rather than Christian faith. He certainly despised the ecstasies of the nonconformists. As for Shakespeare ... The question whether he was or was not a Roman Catholic seems to me not much more important than whether he was left-handed. Not a single one of his thirty-seven (or thereabouts) plays is a religious drama. The bishops and cardinals in them are strictly secular players. The themes of redemption and repentance have little specifically Christian content. If Shakespeare had a god at all, you feel that he would have looked more like Michel de Montaigne than the god of either the Old or the New Testament.

If we are reluctant to recognize how indifferent to organized religion most of our greatest writers have been, we also do not dwell on the interesting fact they mostly came from nowhere much: Shakespeare was the son of a glover, Keats of an ostler, Dickens of a feckless navy clerk, Hardy of a stonemason. In their lifetimes, they were mocked for their low origins and for the lack of higher education: Shakespeare was an 'upstart crow', who 'had small Latin and less Greek'; Keats 'a Cockney rhymester'; Dickens 'Mr Popular Sentiment'; Hardy 'the village atheist'. It hardly needs noting that these sneers came from men who had been to public school and university, as I suspect do most of the nutters who refuse to accept that Will from Stratford could have written the works of Shakespeare. But this was precisely the luck of the Old Masters, that they had no connections to the great world. They were free to make their own.

THOMAS HARDY:
THE TWILIGHT OF AFTERING

When Wessex, his adored wire-haired terrier, died at the age of thirteen, Hardy composed a farewell poem from the dog to his master and mistress:

> Do you look for me at times,
> Wistful ones?

It has to be said that few visitors to Max Gate would have recognized Wessex's voice in these lines. When ringing the Hardys' bell, one was well advised to be watchful rather than wistful. 'The Famous Dog Wessex – Faithful, Unflinching' Hardy had inscribed on his tombstone, but it was mostly other people who did the flinching. There was not much to choose between Wessex's bark and his bite. He was one of those horrible, snappy, aggressive, attention-hungry little dogs who attract such inexplicable devotion from their owners. Yet the dog, like the region he was named after, has been prettified by posterity, and Wessex now slumbers in eternity at the hearthside of the bright-eyed old Master Countryman without an apparent ounce of malice in either of them.

Hardy himself is often eulogized by the Hardy industry as though he were a busy hon. sec. of the local branch of the CPRE. Mr Gordon Beningfield paints Hardy's Wessex in an azure haze as a lost arcadia where never a drop of rain falls nor an hour of manual toil is performed. In his pleasant paintings and drawings of Dorset scenes, there is no sign anywhere of Tess and Marian hacking swedes in the driving rain on the stony uplands of Flintcomb-Ash. The sun always seems to shine on Egdon Heath, and the tombstones in the churchyard are so nicely weathered they look somehow dissociated from mortality.

Ah, no; the years, the years;
Down their carved names the rain-drop ploughs.

Not in Mr Beningfield's Wessex, it doesn't.

Hardy was certainly sad to see the countryside of his youth disappearing, but he would have been appalled by the idea that he was destined to be remembered as a confectioner of quaint pastoral idylls. On the contrary, he regarded himself as a prime exponent of 'the ache of Modernism'. And it is another of Life's Little Ironies that his memory should be suffused by precisely the sort of sentimental glow he spent his life dispelling.

His own character has been tidied up too in the twilight of aftering, as he might have put it. In what is now the standard life of Hardy, Professor Michael Millgate of Toronto, editor of this selection as well as joint editor of the seven-volume collected letters (the selection is surely better value, Hardy was not the frankest or most flowing of letter-writers), is always eager to show Hardy in the least bad light. Even that bizarre deception by which Hardy published his autobiography under his wife's byline is described by Millgate as 'a perfectly sensible down-to-earth undertaking'. Millgate excuses Hardy's concentration upon his links with the more middle-class members of his family as an entirely natural interest in those few who had in some way departed from the otherwise

monotonous pattern of employment and marriage within the
inherited boundaries of place, caste and occupation. Well, snob-
bery is an entirely natural interest, but it is still snobbery. It seems
strange, to put it no higher, that it is Hardy's letters which are
filled with doings and sayings of fashionable ladies but that it
should be Emma, going a bit dotty down at Max Gate, who is
denounced for her pretentiousness.

Perhaps Hardy was not quite such a creepy, secretive character
as Robert Gittings' earlier two-volume biography made him out
to be, but I am not sure that it is any improvement to make him
out as a good-humoured, normal sort of chap who just wanted to
get on with his scribbling. Whatever else Hardy was, he was not
ordinary.

Nor were either of his marriages. Millgate asserts that 'there is
no criticism of Emma in any of Hardy's surviving correspondence
either before or after her death'. I must say that Hardy's replies to
letters of condolence do not wholly support this contention: 'She
was peculiar and difficult in some things, but in others she was
so simple and childlike as to be most winning ... in spite of the
differences between us which it would be affectation to deny and
certain painful delusions she suffered from at times ...'

Wessex the dog surely got a better sendoff.

Dr Pinion in his collection of critical essays speaks repeatedly
of Hardy's 'altruism', by which he seems to mean capacity for
sympathy. Yet one wonders, for example, how much the Rider
Haggards can have appreciated Hardy's letter of commiseration
on the death of their only son at the age of ten: 'To be candid,
I think the death of a child is never really to be regretted, when
one reflects on what he has escaped.' This letter scarcely reads
any better when set beside the very different letter, full of fine
condolences and elevated quotations, which he wrote much
later to Sir Henry and Lady Hoare of Stourhead on the death of
their only son. Can one honestly imagine the two letters being
switched?

Hardy certainly did hate cruelty of all kinds, to animals, to women, to the poor and defenceless. Yet there is a certain distance about his compassion, as though from where he was sitting beside the President of the Immortals it was difficult to share too closely in the feelings of 'a fly on a billiard table of indefinite length' (Tess in the Valley of the Great Dairies) or 'flies crawling over a brown face' (Tess and Marian in the swede fields). He hated war passionately; and yet he tired out Emma walking her over the battlefield of Waterloo in order to work out every move in the battle. He hated hanging and yet could not resist rehearsing the memory of how he had seen sixteen-year-old Martha Brown hanged in Dorchester for the murder of her husband.

Hardy's famous camera-eye technique now and then produces in the reader a sort of voyeur shudder – rather in the way Hitchcock sometimes makes you feel you have been lured to the scene by unscrupulous means and you ought not really to be there. It is this trembling on the verge of lubriciousness which makes his pessimism so vivacious and which thereby both unnerved and allured his contemporaries. In some of his novels, the contriving of visual violation is by far the strongest thing in the book. *A Laodicean*, for example, opens with the scene of a red-brick chapel at dusk: a young architectural enthusiast is peering in to see a tall young woman in a flowing white robe reluctantly descend the steps to the baptismal pool and then turn away shaking her head, refusing immersion, despite the entreaties of the minister. Then later on, we see the same young woman, Paula Power, the daughter of a great railway contractor, from behind the eyes of two cigar-smoking villains who are peering through a peephole in the gymnasium in the castle shrubberies where she is performing her exercises in a pink flannel costume, 'bending, wheeling and undulating in the air like a gold-fish in its globe' as the noonday sunlight pours down through the lantern, 'irradiating her with a warm light that was incarnadined by her pink doublet and hose'. I forget the rest of the book.

These eerie, sensual, near-melodramatic tableaux seem to me to be the distinguishing magic of Hardy's novels rather than the philosophical top-dressing or the pretentious literary allusions which so impress Dr Pinion. I do not, for instance, think it adds anything to the scene in the gymnasium that 'it would have demanded the poetic passion of some joyous Elizabethan lyricist like Lodge, Nashe or Greene, to fitly phrase Paula's presentation of herself at this moment of absolute abandonment to every muscular whim that could take possession of such a supple form'. What matters is what comes next: 'The white manilla ropes clung about the performer like snakes as she took her exercise, and the colour in her face deepened as she went on.'

The finest, most unbearable moments in the novels are composed with great simplicity and no display of learning or metaphoric ingenuity – the discovery of the bodies of Jude's children, Tess waking up at Stonehenge to find the police closing in. Indeed, it is the simplicity of the narration which puts to flight the shadow of melodrama. The memory is right to discard the ponderous parenthesis, 'in Aeschylean phrase', from the sentence about the President of the Immortals having ended his sport with Tess, although Hardy was keen to put it in, so as to share the blame for this grim view of life with a respectable dead Greek dramatist. At times, Hardy's pessimism is hard to resist: 'Well, what we gain by science is, after all, sadness, as the Preacher saith. The more we know of the laws and nature of the Universe, the more ghastly a business we perceive it all to be.'

But he was like many pessimists, as he himself told Edmund Gosse, a cheerful soul: 'The very fact of having touched bottom gives them a substantial cheerfulness in the consciousness that they have nothing to lose.' Behind the scandalous merchant of despair, there was a resilient, flinty little old cove capable of cycling 24 miles over the Dorset hills at the age of seventy and giving as good as he got when anybody criticized his work.

It is his relentless vigour as an artist which seems to me to distinguish him from virtually all British-born writers of his time. And I think things have gone decidedly askew when Dr Pinion tries to present him to us as a solid sort of West Country George Eliot who occasionally wrote poetry as well. Dr Pinion's loyalties are divided; he is a vice-president of the George Eliot Fellowship as well as of the Thomas Hardy Society, and it is, I fear, the drawback of these literary fan clubs that full marks have to be awarded all round. Thus we are told that Hardy's rustics are 'an unfailing source of humour' and that, while George Eliot's evocations of farm life are rich, Hardy's rustic speech is 'more selective, more artfully fashioned, at times comparable to Shakespeare's'. Alas, Hardy had about as much sense of humour as a milk churn, and to say that he is more amusing than George Eliot is like saying that Mr Heath is a greater humorist than Mrs Thatcher. His yokel-speech sounds to me strictly ersatz Mummerset, and Dr Pinion's contention that it must be first-rate because it is directly drawn from life is surely based on a muddled view of what makes dialogue genuine.

It is more bewildering still to find Dr Pinion claiming that Hardy usually conveys 'a deeper, more imaginative and more memorable awareness of character at critical points in the action than a writer such as Henry James, who depends largely on the refinements of psychological analysis.' He indignantly rejects those critics who think that taken as a bunch Hardy's men and women show little individuality and who say they cannot tell which is Giles and which is Gabriel and whether the girl in the corner is Grace or Anne or Fancy or Elfridge. I am afraid I have the same trouble. James's finicky 'refinements of psychological analysis' tend to stick longer in the mind, as do the quirks and tics of characters in Dickens or Surtees. Flicking through Dr Pinion's excellent Hardy dictionary, I find that all but the most prominent characters are little more than names to me.

What we remember in Hardy are surely scenes rather than characters. It is the sight of Bathsheba and Gabriel working through the storm to save the corn which is engraved on the memory rather than what either of them is like as a person. I don't think it will do to eulogize such brilliantly lit scenes as 'psychological pictorialism', as Dr Pinion does. What really matters is the picture itself rather than the simple character outlines which are implied and defined by the picture.

Hardy does seem to lack something of the novelist's concrete differentiating power, that ability to make the reader say, only a sentence or two after the character has appeared, 'Yes, I know him' – not because he is just like a long-dead uncle or someone we met only last week but because we have a confident, instant, vivid sense of the person's reality. By contrast, Hardy has in abundance the poet's concrete universalizing gift. The scene, the plight, the moment – the highlight, in the precise meaning of the term – that is the essence. Character is secondary.

Unwittingly, Dr Pinion himself now and then goes halfway to admitting this, when, for example, he points out that in Hardy a man smoking a cigar is invariably up to no good. If you see a red coal glowing in the arbour at twilight, then evil is afoot. Alec D'Urberville, Wildeve in *The Return of the Native*, Fitzpiers in *The Woodlanders*, Baron von Xanten in *The Romantic Adventures of a Milkmaid* and the rotters in *A Laodicean* are all cigar smokers. Many have black moustachios as well. This crude symbolism may contribute to superb dramatic effects, but it scarcely counts as profound characterization.

It is only by admitting quite candidly how vapid, crude, melodramatic and sentimental the novels can be at their worst, especially the early ones, that we can begin fully to estimate the seriousness of Hardy's determination to break out of his limitations. There is a lot to be said for Ezra Pound's view that Hardy's success as a poet was 'the harvest of having written his novels first', and so having got rid of a good deal of surplus baggage.

Dr Pinion sounds a bit uncomfortable with the modern view that Hardy is a greater poet than novelist. He believes that 'the novel can stir the reader more often and with a cumulative strength quite beyond the range of a short poem'. Well, yes and no. But the real trouble is that Dr Pinion, like many Wessex addicts, does not seem to care that much for the poems at all. He finds Hardy 'crotchety in his arbitrary use of his words, sometimes to the detriment of his poetry'. True, he does quote Hardy's famous letter to an unnamed young poet: 'dissonances and other irregularities can be produced advisedly as art, and worked as to give more charm than strict conformities, to the mind and ear of those trained and steeped in poetry'.

But I do not think he gives anywhere near full weight to Hardy's unrelenting efforts to revive the language of verse by trying every conceivable kind of break, skip, dip, slur, dwelling, swelling, new-minting, old-exhuming, dodge, fancy, quirk, irony, meiosis, graveyard-gaiety, summer-gloom, daydream and nightmare that any single human being could ever have thought of. The spectacular reflowering of his poetry after Emma's death is a unique event in twentieth-century English literature. By comparison, many modern poets who are revered for their innovatory energy can sound a little flat. When all is said and done, is not Eliot sometimes rather prosy, and is not Auden inclined to be a bit glib? Philip Larkin said that he did not 'wish Hardy's *Collected Poems* a single page shorter'. Larkin was not given to gushing.

CHARLES DICKENS:
KINDLY LEAVE THE STAGE

On a hot Wednesday afternoon in August, walking up Piccadilly on my way back from the London Library with a carrier bag full of Dickensiana, I was musing in a drowsy way (like so many of the books in my bag) on Dickens and realism – all those starvelings and cripples and dwarfs, and that business of Krook and the spontaneous combustion, a bit over the top surely. I suddenly became aware that I was walking behind a man in beige shorts and sandals with a hunchbacked dwarf riding piggyback on his shoulders.

Outside Fortnum & Mason, the man gently unclasped the dwarf's hands from round his neck and let him slide to the ground. They stood side by side looking at the rich array of potted meats and crystallized fruit and picnic hampers in the window. The dwarf was unshaven and wearing jeans and a green check shirt. He must have been about thirty. The man was the image of Charles Dickens in his middle years, but about two stone fatter (Dickens was always a sparing eater, although he liked to watch others tuck in): the same Louis Napoleon beard and moustache, the same frizzy wedges of hair, the same bright commanding eye – what Henry James called Dickens's 'merciless *military* eye'.

After they had gazed their fill, he swung the dwarf up on his shoulders again and strode off in the direction of the Ritz. Coming the other way, Lord Crickhowell, the chairman of the National Rivers Authority, his mind until that moment doubtless running on parched reservoirs and hosepipe bans, could not stop his eyes popping out of his head. We had been transported into one of those fanciful late-Victorian magazine illustrations in which Dickens is depicted surrounded by his characters with Smike and Squeers, Pickwick and Micawber buzzing around his head or perched on his armchair.

Dickens himself was always quick to notice when life was limping along to catch up with him. When both the landlord of his lodgings in Brighton and the landlord's daughter were taken away raving to the local asylum, Dickens commented 'quite worthy of me and quite in keeping with my usual proceedings'. He believed that extraordinary things would keep on happening to him, and that he possessed an unrivalled knack for making use of them. At the age of twenty, when applying for a job as a comic impersonator to the stage manager at Covent Garden (at various times, he toyed with the idea of becoming an actor or a barrister or of emigrating to the West Indies), he was already claiming that, 'I had a strong perception of character and oddity, and a natural power of reproducing in my own person what I observed in others.'

In his otherwise damning notice of *Our Mutual Friend*, Henry James approves of the way that 'Dickens reconciles us to what is odd', but this is surely an understatement. Dickens pursues oddity, embraces it, caresses, melodramatizes oddity, transfigures it. Like nobody else since Shakespeare, he somehow goes beyond engaging our sympathies for his twitching, misshapen, gabbling, dropsical or skeletal creatures to give us the irresistible sense of their being made of the same stuff as the rest of us.

I doubt whether any other biographer of Dickens can have shown as exhaustively as Ackroyd does in this massive four-pounder, nigh-on-1200-pager how unrelentingly Dickens refused to disengage from this pursuit of oddity. His love of melodrama, his dislike of highbrow company, his preference for the louche, japing *Punch* crowd – 'he is in a bad set,' Ruskin said, 'yet he is I believe a good man' – on closer inspection look less like symptoms of laziness or intellectual inferiority than a wilful, almost austere determination to stay in touch not merely with his readers but with the gnarled roots of his art.

Ackroyd never lets us forget that Dickens was always in training. He stretched himself physically to the limit, with 20-mile hikes and gruelling tours, first, of trashy melodramas which he insisted on writing, directing and starring in, then later, of the notorious readings of his own works, which did help to kill him, although Ackroyd tries to minimize the damage. In between, he darted about London, popping into rag-and-bone shops, pubs, police courts, cheap lodging houses, schools (he hurtled up to Yorkshire for a couple of days to 'do the research' for Dotheboys Hall), rookeries and morgues.

He loved a good morgue, especially the Paris Morgue with 'the ghastly beds, and the swollen saturated clothes hanging up, and the water dripping, dripping all day long, upon that swollen saturated something in the corner, like a heap of crushed overripe figs'.

To Trollope and the more intellectual writers of the later Victorian period, Dickens was 'Mr Popular Sentiment'. But in the practice of his craft, he was a hard, not to say hard-boiled sort of character. When Mrs Keeley, playing Smike in a dramatization of *Nickleby*, said a line about 'the pretty, harmless robins,' Dickens told the prompter 'Damn the robins. Cut them out.' And he worked up to his grand deathbed scenes with a certain anticipatory relish. 'Paul I shall slaughter at the end of number five,' he wrote to his dogged friend and biographer, John Forster, while he was working on the early numbers of *Dombey and Son*.

Nor was he unconscious of the springs of his own creativity. He says of his childhood ordeals – working in the blacking factory, visiting his improvident father who had been imprisoned for debt in the Marshalsea – that 'all these things have worked together to make me what I am'. The quasi-autobiographical passages in *Copperfield* reinforce our sense that he understood perfectly well how he had come to be as he was.

He knew more or less where his appalling, inexpiable restlessness came from: 'I seem to be always looking at such times for something I have not found in life' – or, as he puts it in the novel, 'I felt a vague unhappy loss or want of something overshadowing me like a cloud.' He told Forster that it was better to go on and fret than to stop and fret, and that, as to repose, for some men there was no such thing in this life.

But here we knock up against the first problem confronting Dickens biographers (a large and ever-growing band). It is impossible to write a dull life of that unstoppable, unsquashable genius, but it is also hard to improve on the 7000-word autobiographical fragment that Dickens himself wrote for Forster and which Forster included more or less verbatim in the first of his three volumes. The fragment breaks off at the moment Dickens leaves Warren's Blacking Factory at the age of fourteen:

From that hour until this at which I write (a quarter of a century later), no word of that part of my childhood which I have now gladly brought to a close has passed my lips to any human being. I have no idea how long it lasted; whether for a year, or much more, or less. From that hour until this, my father and my mother have been stricken dumb upon it. I have never heard the least allusion, however far off and remote, from either of them. I have never, until now I impart it to this paper, in any burst of confidence with any one, my own wife not excepted, raised the curtain I then dropped, thank God.

Until old Hungerford-market was pulled down, until old Hungerford-stairs were destroyed, and the very nature of the ground changed, I never had the courage to go back to the place

where my servitude began. I never saw it. I could not endure
to go near it. For many years, when I came near to Robert
Warren's in the Strand, I crossed over to the opposite side of
the way, to avoid a certain smell of the cement they put upon
the blacking-corks, which reminded me of what I once was. It
was a very long time before I liked to go up Chandos Street.
My old way home by the borough made me cry, after my eldest
child could speak.

Ackroyd does describe in its proper place – twenty-five years
later – the incident which triggered this extraordinary confes-
sion: Forster had told Dickens that his friend Charles Dilke had
once visited the blacking factory with Dickens's father and had
given Dickens half-a-crown and had received in return a very
low bow. Earlier lives, by Fred Kaplan (1988), for example,
throw away this crucial unlocking of memory by tossing it into
the narrative of Dickens's time at the blacking factory. How
much more dramatic to spring it upon the apparently invul-
nerable world-famous novelist. Ackroyd, as a novelist himself,
often shows a more telling sense of detail than his predecessors.
He tells us of the letter Dickens wrote to Miss Burdett-Coutts
about her home for fallen women, on returning from his sister
Fanny's funeral: 'His hand was unsteady and the letter is filled
with blobs.' Kaplan tells us only that 'he could not keep the pen
steady'. Neither of the two standard modern biographies – by
Edgar Johnson and Norman and Jeanne MacKenzie – mentions
the detail at all. More telling still would have been to point out
that it is Dickens himself who says: 'I am afraid I write illeg-
ibly – but I have been at my Sister's funeral today, and my hand
is not as steady as usual.'
    Here and there, alas, Ackroyd shows distressing early signs
of Holroyd's Syndrome (in its later stages, the disease proves
fatal to the work thus afflicted). The underlying cause of this
complaint is an overvaluation of the biographer's trade, and

its symptoms are a recurring tendency to go on about his prob-
lems and to lucubrate repetitiously and at inordinate length on
the psychological complexities of the relationship between the
biographer and his subject. Ackroyd says of *Dombey and Son* that
Dickens 'is almost too much with us; he seems to be doing all the
work, determining the reader's reaction to events, suggesting the
nature of the characters.' The same could sometimes be said of
Mr Ackroyd.

Traditional-minded readers may not care for the little interludes
spattered through the book in which Dickens and Ackroyd engage
in imaginary conversation, sometimes in company with Ackroyd's
earlier subjects, Eliot, Wilde and Chatterton. I do not mind these –
except for the penultimate one, where Ackroyd has a rambling
conversation with himself which is both banal and self-indulgent.
When a biographer starts telling us that he uses files and card boxes
and indexes, we can only say: we do not wish to know that, kindly
leave the stage. Mr Christopher Sinclair-Stevenson, whose first
production this is and otherwise a magnificently produced one too,
really might have plucked at his sleeve.

And should anyone who believes as Ackroyd does that 'family
ties and early childhood are the two most boring elements in any-
one's life' go in for writing biographies, certainly not a biography
of Dickens, who was more obsessed with his own childhood than
almost any other human being? Ackroyd seems to regard Dick-
ens's father and mother as feckless nuisances of little interest and
appears as eager to pack them off to Devon as Dickens himself
was. Yet John Dickens must have been one of the most splendidly
absurd figures ever to have existed, the epitome of every variety of
self-deception and self-inflation and thus the source, to a greater
or lesser extent, for so many of Dickens's immortal male comic
creations: Micawber and William Dorrit, of course, but also Skim-
pole, Chadband, Podsnap and many another. Nothing Dickens
himself thought up could outdo the begging letters of the real-life
Father of the Marshalsea, to Miss Burdett-Coutts, for example:

'Contemporaneous events of this nature place me in a difficulty from which, without some anticipatory pecuniary effort, I cannot extricate myself . . .' He wanted twenty-five quid to finance the move back from Devon to London.

In his zeal to plumb the resonant chambers of a writer's inner life, Ackroyd is also a bit skimpy in his treatment of Dickens's circle – that merry band of tipsy hacks, addicted to puns and punch and facetious toasts and post-prandial leapfrog. It will not really do, for example, to write off what Thomas Hood, an occasional member of the circle, called the Traditional Priest as 'a certain Father Prout, writer of articles and critic'. The Reverend Francis Mahony, that acerbic, alcoholic, unfrocked Jesuit, under the alias of Father Prout, wrote the immortal 'Bells of Shandon', which lulled me to sleep as a child; to have described something of his mixture of sentimentality and disenchantment would have given us a fuller feeling of the world of Dickens's early manhood – a much more rackety, restless place than the mid-Victorian England in which we tend to picture him and in which, as Ackroyd does point out, Dickens seldom sets his novels.

There is, besides, a law of diminishing returns on efforts to sink ever-deeper shafts into an artist's mind. The greater the artist and the deeper you go, the less you may find. All you are likely to achieve is a closer view of his awesome powers of absorption and his huge storage capacity; the glimpse thus obtained is little more privileged than a view of the innards of a top-of-the-range vacuum cleaner. Far richer treasures may lie scattered about on or near the surface. Biography is or ought to be more like open-cast mining.

The more perceptive of Dickens's contemporaries were strongly conscious that he was a marvellous engine rather than a person. Emerson said to American friends who were marvelling at the great man's cheerfulness and high spirits: 'You see him quite wrong, evidently, and would persuade me that he is a genial creature, full of sweetness and amenities and superior to his talents, but I fear he is harnessed to them. He is too consummate an artist to have a thread of nature left. He daunts me!'

Or, as Forster said of his wonderful powers of mimicry: 'He seemed to be always the more himself for being somebody else, for continually putting off his personality.'

I cannot help thinking that, in trying so hard to plunge right down to the core rather than explore the infinite richness of the surface, Ackroyd takes a fundamentally wrong turning. He is looking for something which really is not there, or not there in such abundance as to fill 1100 pages. As a consequence, he often seems to be driven to stretch his chosen material, to squeeze out of it something more exotic and profound than it naturally offers.

This, I fear, is what goes wrong with Ackroyd's treatment of Dickens's separation from his wife and his taking up with the teenage actress Ellen Ternan. Ackroyd conceives the intriguing fancy that Dickens's relations with Ellen were sexless and that the whole romance was a fulfilment of all his visions of innocent child-love. There is no conclusive evidence either way – which is not so surprising considering the lengths that Dickens went to to cover his tracks, in order not to estrange his huge public and so be cut off from the oxygen of adulation on which he was by now hooked.

All things are possible, nowt so queer as folks and so on, but Dickens was a remarkably energetic man of forty-six. He had had ten children by his wife. After he took up with Ellen Ternan, he never flirted with another woman. He was a person of plain and hearty enthusiasms who detested humbug. He set up Ellen and her mother in a series of homes in Slough and Peckham and at Condette, near Boulogne, usually establishing pieds-à-terre for himself nearby. In his other dealings – business, familial, social – Dickens was ruthless, egotistical and impatient. He was as cold and horrible to his wife Catherine as any deserting husband can ever have been (the beastlier he is to her, the more endearing and heroic she sounds). He told a series of disgusting lies about the unhappiness of their earlier life together. In many ways, he was a horrible man – racist, selfish, money-grubbing. But even when he was being a marvellous man, which he also was, he always knew what he wanted out of other people and lost no time in getting it. Is it really conceivable that this whole complex edifice of expense, betrayal and deception was a conspiracy for the purpose of a virginal spooning?

Worse still, now and then, one seems to spot Ackroyd shutting his novelist's eye in order to underplay both the deception and the obsession. For example, when Dickens was commuting to London from the Ternans' cottage at Slough, we are told only that 'he usually caught the train at Windsor Station, perhaps to expose himself less to public comment on the platform'. But according to Kaplan, he used to walk across the back fields from Slough and would date his letters from Eton, explaining casually that he was 'merely walking in the Park here, but write from this place, in consequence of having omitted to do so in town' – which conveys a considerably more devious impression.

After Dickens and Ellen and her mother had been embarrassingly exposed as travelling together by being caught up in the Staplehurst railway accident, Ackroyd tells us that Dickens asked his manservant to deliver a basketful of delicacies to 'Miss Ellen'. Edgar Johnson quotes the instruction in rather more detail: 'Take Miss Ellen tomorrow morning a little basket of fresh fruit, a jar of clotted cream from Tuckers, and a chicken, a pair of pigeons, or some nice little bird. Also on Wednesday morning, take her some other things of the same sort – making a little variety each day' – which sounds not only more solicitous but also somehow fleshier.

The fact that the relationship was not a very happy one does not mean that it was platonic. Nor was Dickens's behaviour necessarily any more complex than that of other successful, strongly driven men who see middle age looming.

'We should not fall into the trap,' Ackroyd warns us, 'of expecting him to behave in a conventional way with Ellen

Ternan.' No, but we should not assume that the workings of great men's imaginations cannot result in conventional physical outcomes either.

In Ackroyd's no-sex thesis, there seems to be an unadmitted desire to make Dickens himself seem odder, more neurotic, less in control of his fantasies. Yet Dickens's own words and behaviour tend to suggest something to the contrary, that he leashed and unleashed his fantasies with a remarkable degree of control and that it was this obsession with being in control rather than the disorder of his emotions that destroyed his life.

This commandingness had huge advantages outside Dickens's writing. In practical matters, especially in political activity, Dickens must be the only great English writer whose public utterances and ventures scarcely ever make one cringe. He was an alert and energetic chairman, a propagandist with a sure aim; *Nicholas Nickleby* did help to get the Yorkshire schools closed down; the advice he gave Miss Burdett-Coutts was usually calm and sensible; his attitude towards beggars, convicts, fallen women and waifs and strays was more of the 'tough-love' variety than the mawkishness which is associated with his name. He detested environmental explanations of crime and knew how quick old lags were to catch on: 'If a notion arose that the wearing of brass buttons led to crime, and they were questioned to elucidate that point, we should have such answers as "I was happy until I wore brass buttons", "Brass buttons did it", "Buttons is the cause of my being here" . . .'

He disliked the humbug of Americans, but he did admire the American government's sense of parental responsibility towards its citizens and contrasted it unfavourably with his own country's. Even more remarkable to modern ears, he thought American prisons were too soft, believing as he did that 'jail should be a place of ignominious punishment and endurance'. But he believed in rewards too and was much taken by the points system that Maconochie, the Australian penal reformer, had introduced for the convicts of Norfolk Island; he introduced marks for Miss

Burdett-Coutts's fallen women and even 'prize tickets' for his own servants. All this fitted in with his own obsessive tidiness and cleanliness, which made him a natural partner for Chadwick's heroic work for public sanitation.

Set against the shrivelled fascistic twitches of Pound and Eliot or the varieties of infantile leftism espoused by writers from Tolstoy to early Auden, Dickens seems even more of a giant in his ability to distinguish and detach the precise, humdrum practicalities of social reform from the wild sweeps and throbs of the writer's imagination. He was, as Orwell said, 'generously angry'. At any rate, his public anger was generous (his private rages could be vindictive and long-lasting).

Yet fame did corrupt him and in a particularly virulent way. He had always been harmlessly vain; he irritated genteel people by his loud clothes and his habit of combing his hair in public more times a day than any public man until Dr David Owen. But as he grew older, the obsession of the Inimitable (as he had only half-mockingly dubbed himself when young) with being in control became more overweening, his touchiness more instantaneous and his refusal to admit that he was ever wrong more ungainsayable. 'What a thing it is to have Power,' he told Catherine, and the more he had of it, the more he wanted.

His ever-growing passion to cram in as many public readings as he could was not simply because he wanted the money, although with his large family, his numerous establishments and his perpetual insecurity, he certainly did. It was a moral degeneration as well as a physical self-torture. The thrill of holding an audience so utterly in his grasp became a drug far more potent than laudanum or tobacco (both of which he was fond of).

Towards the end, he was utterly drained and prostrate after each of his performances and only fully alive, it seemed, during them. When he added Nancy's murder to his repertoire, it was not simply a further strain on his powers; it was the ultimate step in his campaign for total control. He had made his readers laugh and weep with him; now they would be terrified out of their wits by him. He had had enough love; now he wanted fear. Other biographies have shown us what a funny and kind and good man Dickens was, and he was too. This biography – gigantic, flawed, sometimes perverse, often brilliant, now and then as manic as Dickens himself – may be the first to show us how frightening he could be.

SAMUEL TAYLOR COLERIDGE:
A WONDERFUL LEAPER

Coleridge had already walked 40-odd miles through Somerset when he first caught sight of Wordsworth's house, Racedown Lodge, a Georgian box in the valley below him. Instead of going round by the road, he hurdled the gate and burst through a field of corn to greet the startled Dorothy. Neither she nor Wordsworth ever forgot this impetuous vaulting into their lives. One never forgot one's first sight of Coleridge. Hazlitt, a shy seventeen-year-old minister's son, was bowled over by STC's sermon in the Unitarian chapel at Shrewsbury: 'I could not have been more delighted if I had heard the music of the spheres. Poetry and philosophy had met together.' Two days afterwards, at the Hazlitt breakfast table, Coleridge received a letter from his equally dazzled young friend Tom Wedgwood, offering him £150 a year if he would waive the ministry and devote himself to poetry and philosophy: 'Coleridge seemed to make up his mind to close with this proposal in the act of trying on one of his shoes.'

His energy was at the same time appealing and appalling. Until well into his fifties, he would plunge into the sea without warning, just as precipitately as he enlisted in the 15th Light Dragoons under the alias of Silas Tomkyn Comberbache, to be discharged four months later as insane. Words poured in entrancing torrents in his never-lost Devon accent from his great slobbering ever-open mouth (he could not breathe through his nose).

Tipsiness, he said, had the

> unpleasant effect of making me talk very extravagantly; and as when sober, I talk extravagantly enough for any common tipsiness, it becomes a matter of nicety in discrimination to know when I am or am not affected – An idea starts up in my head – and away I follow it through thick and thin, Wood and Marsh, Brake and Briar – with all the apparent interest of a man who was defending one of his old and long-established Principles.

He would loll incontinently on young ladies' laps, gorging himself on clotted cream, before slinking behind some door or bed-curtain to dose himself with brandy or laudanum, dashing out for a quick one to chemist or inn if supplies ran short. His literary appetites were just as incontinent. He was a 'library cormorant', in his own famous phrase, and he scribbled as fast as he read, notebooks being filled deep into the night.

Even his fecund pen, though, could not keep up with his promises of great works. Coleridge was, as the later, disillusioned Hazlitt said, the past master of the Prospectus. He promised Godwin a 500-page printed octavo, analysing 'all possible modes of true, probable and false reasoning, arranged philosophically', the first half of which could be 'ready for the printer, at a fortnight's notice'. He promised his brother-in-law Southey a 'six or eight' volume history of British literature which would also include a running history of 'metaphysics, theology, medicine, alchemy ... surgery, chemistry, etc., etc., navigation, travellers, voyagers, etc., etc.'. During his early enthusiasm for the ideal fraternity he and his friends were going to found in Pennsylvania on the banks of the Susquehanna, he instructed his fellow Pantisocrats to learn the theory and practice of carpentry and agriculture and to free their wives from household drudgery by themselves 'washing with a machine and cleaning the House'.

When he became a full-scale drug addict, not only were his nightmares as frightful as any modern junkie's, but he could be just as tediously importunate, writing to friends with naval connections, such as Sir Joseph Banks and Wordsworth's brother John, demanding quantities of Indian hemp or 'Bang'. Some Coleridge worshippers like to portray him as a saintly figure inveigled into the agonies of addiction by neuralgia and silly doctors. There was another, more hedonistic, side, as shown in his letter to Banks: 'We will have a fair trial of Bang. Do bring down some of the Hyoscyamine Pills and I will give a fair Trial of Opium Hensbane, and Nepenthe. Bye the bye, I always considered Homer's account of the Nepenthe as a Banging lie.' Or to Sir Humphry Davy of the wonderful prospect from Greta Hall: 'My dear fellow, I would that I could wrap up the view from my House in a pillow of Opium, and send it to you.'

It would be impossible to write a dull life of this torrential character. And Holmes's two-decker (he has already written an earlier brief life of STC) is a delightful helter-skelter through the first half of Coleridge's life, up to his departure for Malta at the age of thirty-one, his best poetry already written, his marriage already tattered, his self-confidence as a poet shattered by Wordsworth's rejection of 'Christabel': 'as to Poetry I have altogether abandoned it, being convinced that I never had the essentials of poetic Genius, and that I mistook a strong desire for original power.' Holmes wants us, above all, to meet this extraordinary man, 'to set Coleridge talking', to 'unearth his "human story", his living footsteps through the world'. In particular, he wants us to see STC striding over the lakeland fells, over the length and breadth of Wales, over Quantock and Mendip, and up into the Harz mountains of Germany during his intoxicating months at Göttingen. 'I have taken Coleridge into the open air', Holmes tells us, rather in the tones of a therapist who is confident his patient will be quite all right when he gets away from his unhealthy indoor life.

This approach has the great virtue of showing Coleridge at his best – the generous, full-bodied force of nature, with his eyes and his wits so flashingly about him. He was so quick, his sketches so exact. After rain on Ullswater, for example: 'a large Slice of calm silver – above this a bright ruffledness, or atomic sportiveness motes in the sun? – Vortices of flies? – how shall I express the Banks waters all fused Silver, that How too its slates rainwet silver in the sun, & its shadows running down in the water like a column.'

Or making a bonfire on the island on Grasmere lake:

the wood, & mountains, & lake all trembling, & as it were idealized thro' the subtle smoke which rose up from the clear red embers of the fir-apples which we had collected. Afterwards, we made a glorious Bonfire on the Margin, by some alder bushes, whose twigs heaved & sobbed in the uprushing column of smoke – & the Image of the Bonfire, & of us that danced round it – ruddy laughing faces in the twilight.

In this luminous air, that glorious period which produced 'The Rime of the Ancient Mariner', 'Kubla Khan' and 'Frost at Midnight' looks less like a flash in the pan than a tragically brief glimpse of the real Coleridge, his imagination concentrated upon its proper task, undistracted by circumstances (the self-imposed distractions were usually the worst). When Coleridge is on song like this, with his biographer panting along behind, we cannot help wishing that it could all go on for ever. Mr Holmes does tell us that other biographers have been less inclined to take STC's word for it and have found a darker side in him right from the start. Coleridge has been variously described as a humbug, a plagiarist, a liar and a cruel and feckless husband. Holmes merely records the existence of such alternative verdicts without examining them too closely: he himself is setting out to recapture Coleridge's fascination as a man and as a writer. 'If he does not leap out of these pages brilliant, animated, endlessly provoking and invade your imagination (as he has done mine) then I have failed to do him justice.'

But will this approach quite do? We all know Coleridge is a wonderful leaper. It is what he leaps over that is the trouble. We are not judging the national high-jump championships. The accusations made against Coleridge are not merely academic nitpickings, and they cannot be laughed off as the sort of prosaic questions that the Person from Porlock would have asked.

Coleridge's oldest friends warned over and over again that his testimony on any subject was extraordinarily unreliable. Lamb, who had been a Bluecoat boy with him, wrote that as long as he had known Coleridge, so long had he 'known him in the daily and hourly habit of quizzing the world by lies'. Wordsworth said that 'Coleridge is a subject which no Biographer ought to touch beyond what he himself was eye witness of.'

The indictment set out by Norman Fruman, in *Coleridge, The Damaged Archangel* (Lamb's description), is almost heartbreaking it is so overwhelming. For Coleridge's malpractice adds up to rather more than occasional cribbing and fibbing. It is, I suppose, a measure of the breadth if not the depth of his reading that no single scholar could be sure of measuring how much he stole. When Coleridge copies out large chunks of Schelling, Kant and Schlegel, not merely does he fail to acknowledge his sources, he often mangles their intentions beyond recall. His famous critical distinctions, such as the one between Fancy and Imagination, were, Fruman asserts, for the most part not original but commonplace jargon in the Eng. lit. debates of his day.

When compared, say, with the driving steadiness of Wordsworth's great preface to the second edition of *Lyrical Ballads*, Coleridge's ruminations often seem rambling and unfocused, suggestive, yes, but somehow fruitlessly suggestive. Holmes appears to imply that, at any rate in this first volume, we need not bother our tiny English minds with the outpourings of German idealist philosophers. But how far Coleridge's prose writings are the product of his own marvellous sensitivity and acuity and how far they are ill-digested borrowings from imperfectly understood philosophers writing in a language he was still learning is surely a question which our insular self-confidence should not entirely excuse us from tackling – especially since Coleridge is one of the patron saints of the Eng. lit. schools of today.

Worse still, the unacknowledged borrowings in the poetry make deeper and deeper inroads into what Fruman calls 'the shrinking canon' of Coleridge's work. For example, while arguing for Coleridge's later poetry as some of his most moving and revealing, Mr Holmes claims that 'it is impossible to understand him without reference to such works as "A Tombless Epitaph" (1811) which re-explores the symbolic caverns of his youth'. Yet Fruman points out that not only is 'A Tombless Epitaph' based on a poem by the sixteenth-century Italian poet Chiabrera (which Coleridge did acknowledge) but also it bears a remarkable similarity to Wordsworth's earlier translation of the same poem (which he did not).

Most autobiographers – even or perhaps especially those who do not shrink from showing us their own warts – allow themselves a good deal of licence with the truth. It does not really matter whether STC could, as he claims, read a chapter of the Bible by the age of three. Mr Holmes admits to being puzzled by some of the inconsistencies. Sometimes Coleridge describes himself as a spoilt mother's darling, sometimes as being 'hardly used from infancy to Boyhood and from Boyhood to Youth most, MOST cruelly'. Sometimes he claims to have been miserable at Christ's Hospital, sometimes he sounds quite a cheerful or at any rate resigned schoolboy. Both things can be true at once, but at the very least we should be on the lookout and should be wary, for example, of taking at face value Coleridge's picture of his own wife as a commonplace shrew. Another view is forcefully presented in Molly Lefebure's life of Sara, *The Bondage of Love*.

Holmes does not dodge Coleridge's shortcomings entirely, but he lets him down a little lightly. When Coleridge asserts in a letter to Sara that 'in sex, acquirements, and in the quantity and quality of natural endowments whether of feeling, or of Intellect, you are inferior', Holmes merely comments that 'his lack of marital tact had become quite formidable'. Now of course geniuses often make rotten husbands and tend to believe in and act on the principle – enunciated in the same letter – that 'I can neither retain my Happiness nor my Faculties, unless I move, live and love in perfect Freedom'; in other words, Number One must come first all the time. All the same, there is something peculiarly creepy about Coleridge's persistent but unconsummated pursuit of the other Sara, Mrs Wordsworth's sister, Sara Hutchinson, nicknamed Asra. When Sara was about to have yet another baby, he even tried to persuade her to invite Asra to attend her lying-in, so that she could get to know her better.

Coleridge's in-and-out running is no more unusual among poets (or non-poets, come to that) than his self-pity – 'No-one on earth has ever LOVED me'. And if he were to be taken simply as a poet who had a few years of greatness, during his association with Wordsworth, and wrote four or five of the most wonderful poems in the language, then Porlock prodnoses ought to be silent. But his greatness as a poet, like his greatness as a human being, is inextricably entangled with his greatness as a philosopher, critic and sage (one reputation, so to speak, supports the other) and the charges against him do have to be met.

Richard Holmes says he hopes 'this book will read like the most traditional form of popular narrative biography'. Well, so it does, and a fresh, high-stepping representative of that stable too. But STC has been entered in an altogether more demanding race and he deserves a more vigorous if less enjoyable examination.

JOHN KEATS:
WHAT'S BECOME OF JUNKETS?

'What porridge had John Keats?' Browning offers this as the crass sort of question that stupid people ask. But in fact the first person to answer it would have been John Keats himself. He loved to talk about food, good and bad. He writes to his dying brother Tom from Kirkcudbright that 'we dined yesterday on dirty bacon, dirtier eggs and dirtiest potatoes with a slice of salmon'. As Keats and his Hampstead friend Charles Brown tramped round Loch Fyne, he complained that all they had to live off were eggs, oatcake and whisky: 'I lean rather languishingly on a rock, and long for some famous beauty to get down from her Palfrey in passing; approach me with her saddle bags – and give me a dozen or two capital roast beef sandwiches.'

He bathed in the loch, at Cairndow, 'quite pat and fresh', until a gadfly bit him. The inn at Cairndow is still there. So is the Burford Bridge Inn under Box Hill where he finished *Endymion*. You can still follow the path through Winchester which he describes taking while thinking of the 'Ode to Autumn'.

No other dead poet is, I think, quite as intensely present to us still, somehow in the flesh. In his review of Keats's first published volume, Leigh Hunt fastened on the essential thing about him, that he had 'a strong sense of what really exists and occurs'. In this beguiling new biography, Nicholas Roe, the foremost Keatsian around, seeks to wipe away any lingering image of a sickly moony dreamer and to show us the 'edgy, streetwise' livewire who rejoiced in the material world for all of the short time he was in it.

He was only five feet and three-quarters of an inch, but he always filled the room. When he recited poetry – his own or anybody's – he 'hoisted himself up and looked burly and dominant'. Hunt remembered his appearance when they first met: very broad-shouldered for his size, with a face that was 'delicately alive', something pugnacious about the mouth, and large, dark, glowing eyes. Which is just how he looks in Joseph Severn's picture of him listening to the nightingales, painted a quarter of a century after his death. Nobody forgot Keats or what it was like to be with him.

To his friends, Keats sometimes signed himself 'Junkets', and when his restless spirit sent him off on a new excursion, the disappointed cry would go up, 'What's become of Junkets?' At a noisy supper party given by the man who supplied the scalpels he used as a medical student, he and his friends argued about the correct derivation of the word 'cunt'. That evening he won ten shillings and sixpence from cutting cards for half-guineas, high stakes for struggling City clerks. Such episodes of 'delicious diligent indolence' (characteristic of all the Keatses, according to their fussy trustee Mr Abbey) remind one of Bertie Wooster spending a restful afternoon at the Drones, throwing cards into a top hat with some of the better element.

Yet his energies were prodigious, physically and mentally. In Scotland, he and Brown walked 20 or 30 miles a day. He had translated the whole of the *Aeneid* by the time he was fifteen. His collected poems, mostly written over only five years, between the 'Imitation of Spenser' in 1814 and the 'Ode to Autumn' in 1819, fill 437 pages of the old Oxford edition. He could compose with remarkable rapidity. A cricket chirped in the hearth of Leigh

Hunt's home in the Vale of Health, and Hunt challenged him to write a sonnet about it inside fifteen minutes. Keats met the challenge with the sonnet that begins 'The poetry of earth is never dead'.

There have been many fine biographies of Keats since the war, notably by Aileen Ward, Robert Gittings and Andrew Motion. But none, I think, conveys quite so well as this one the sense of Keats as a poet of the London suburbs. Roe reconstructs beautifully the milieu from which he and his friends all came, on the northern edge of the City where they had their day jobs and dreamed of fame.

Keats himself was probably born at the Swan and Hoop at Moorgate, the inn which his father Thomas had taken over from his prosperous father-in-law, John Jennings, and turned into Keats's livery stables. Thomas Keats had been brought up in the workhouse at Lower Bockhampton, Hardy country, and had come to town and married the boss's daughter Frances. Their three young sons were sent up to Clarke's Academy at Enfield, a school for Dissenters which had a far wider and more up-to-date curriculum than Harrow, where Frances had thought of sending them.

Roe describes it, with justice, as 'the most extraordinary school in the country'. The idea that Keats, because of his modest background, was 'under-educated' could not be further from the truth. But his happy start in life came to an abrupt end when in April 1804 Thomas Keats fell from his horse to the pavement outside Bunhill Fields and smashed his skull only a few yards from home.

From this fatal accident, all Keats's troubles flowed. The substantial legacy from his grandfather was tied up in Chancery where it remained for years (his sister Fanny was still trying to extricate herself from the muddle in the 1880s). Only two months later, Frances remarried, to a no-good called William Rawlings, whom she deserted almost as swiftly (Roe deduces, fairly enough, that she was having an affair with Rawlings before she was widowed).

Frances was already addicted to opium and brandy, and the children were shuffled off to their grandmother's in Edmonton and never lived with their mother again until she came up to Edmonton to die.

John nursed her, prepared her meals, read her novels and sat up with her at night, listening to the rattle of her breathing. Though she had more or less deserted them, his devotion was total, as it was to be to his brother Tom when he was dying of consumption. Looking back on his life, Keats was to reflect that he had 'never known any unalloy'd happiness for many days together: the death or sickness of some one has always spoilt my hours.'

Roe takes trouble too to show how diligent Keats was in pursuing his medical training, first as apprentice to a disagreeable Edmonton surgeon, then at Guy's Hospital. When Keats complained that Newton had destroyed the magic of the rainbow, he was doing so not as a fretful dilettante but as someone with as rigorous a scientific training as was then available.

Nor was he in the least soppy about nature. Thirty years before Tennyson's outburst against 'Nature red in tooth and claw', Keats lamented the process of 'eternal fierce destruction'. Beneath the beautiful surface of the sea, 'the greater on the less feeds evermore', and in Highgate Woods while he was gathering periwinkles and wild strawberries, the hawk was pouncing on the smaller birds, and the robin was 'ravening a worm.'

Roe does not spend much time on Keats's views of politics and religion, merely labelling them as unorthodox. Certainly he never ceased to revere the republican heroes of the Civil War or to be hostile to the 'pious frauds' of the Established Church. In his 'Sonnet Written in Disgust of Vulgar Superstition', Keats says how much he hates the gloomy church bells which would have made him feel a damp—

A chill as from a tomb, did I not know
That they are dying like an outburnt lamp.

Yet his description of life as 'a vale of soul-making' and his insistence 'how necessary a world of Pains and Troubles is to school an intelligence and make it a soul' would certainly appeal to Christians then and now. When he was dying, Severn read aloud to him from *Don Quixote* and the novels of Maria Edgeworth, but Keats asked instead for Plato, *The Pilgrim's Progress* and Jeremy Taylor's *Holy Living and Holy Dying*, not the likely choices of a committed atheist such as Shelley.

In his eagerness to show us the streetwise Keats, Roe sometimes slides past the more serious resonances. Especially destructive is, I think, Roe's itch to return to two themes which are to be found in other accounts of Keats's life but which do seem to be overplayed here. These are a) that Keats was dosed to the gills with laudanum when he wrote his last great odes, and b) that from 1816 onwards he was taking mercury, no longer to cure his gonorrhoea but to fend off his emerging syphilis. This may well tickle up a few headlines (indeed it already has), but the evidence is shaky. Dr Sawrey could well have gone on prescribing mercury as a precaution against a return of the clap or as a remedy against the ulcerated throat, a first symptom of the tuberculosis taking hold. There really isn't much licence for Roe to assert that 'some aspects of his distorted behaviour and perceptions towards the end of his life may be attributed to an awareness of this "secret core of disease" rather than to tuberculosis.' Even in full health, Keats was, well, mercurial, and TB is classically depicted, e.g. by Thomas Mann, as inclined to bring on manic behaviour. The argument about the laudanum is reductive too. Yes, of course Keats took laudanum. When he was nursing Tom, they both did when they couldn't sleep. So did thousands of other people throughout the nineteenth century, as a painkiller or just to get high. But does this really make the 'Ode to a Nightingale' into 'one of the greatest re-creations of a drug-inspired dream-vision in English literature'?

The poet tells us explicitly that neither the 'dull opiate emptied

to the lees' nor the beaker of blushful Hippocrene is assisting the
flight of his fancy. To insist that the laudanum was a necessary
stimulant is to insult that intelligence, which other great critics
such as T. S. Eliot have regarded as the keenest of any poet. John
Keats had enough trouble in his lifetime with his first publish-
ers, who said that they regretted ever taking on his verses and
that 'we have in many cases offered to take the book back rather
than be annoyed with the ridicule which has, time after time,
been showered upon it'. He could not help being wounded too
by the gibes of *Blackwood's Magazine*, where the venomous John
Lockhart under the pseudonym of 'Z' declared that his poems
were 'drivelling idiocy' and that this 'wavering apprentice' was no
better than a farm servant or footman with ideas above his station.
This kind of snobbish abuse persisted long after Keats's death. In
patting him on the head for the 'luxuriance' of his verse, W. B.
Yeats described him in 1915 as 'poor, ailing and ignorant ... the
coarse-bred son of a livery stable keeper'.

Besides being accused of being underbred and undersized,
Keats now has to put up with being accused of being under the
influence. Reductive too, I think, is Roe's insistence that any
description of death and suffering in Keats's verse must be drawn
directly from the poet's own family life, as though he couldn't
make it up for himself. Yet all has to be forgiven when we come
to Roe's description of Keats's last days, which it is impossible
to read without coming close to tears. His last letters to Fanny
Brawne remain as heartbreaking as ever. When they were first
published, Fanny was denounced as a heartless flirt by the poet's
more hysterical admirers. It was only when her own letters to
Keats's sister Fanny were published that readers slowly came to
understand how warm and touching and loyal she was.

There is none of this after-history in Roe's book. He ends
rather abruptly, almost as though he is too moved to carry on,
with Keats being buried in the English cemetery in Rome
under the epitaph he had requested of Severn: 'Here lies one

whose name is writ in water.' Which is, I think, a pity. We need
to know how life moved on, how Fanny mourned him for years,
then married and had two children; how Severn lived on in
Rome until 1879, becoming a local celebrity not for his painting
but for being the only friend who had stayed with Keats to the
end.

And we need too to survey the later history of Keats's reputa-
tion, to see how the sad romance of his life made him a hero to
the Victorians, and how he fell out of favour among a generation
which preferred battery acid to honeydew. The reaction against
luxuriance has continued. A distinguished poet said to me not so
long ago: 'I can't see how anyone could think Keats is any good.'
Rereading Keats, though, I am still inclined to echo the judgment
of that acute and implacable critic Samuel Beckett: 'I like him the
best of them all, because he doesn't beat his fists on the table. I like
that awful sweetness and soft damp green richness, and weariness:
"Take into the air my quiet breath".'

There is something irresistible too in the way Keats suddenly
breaks out of the mossy glooms and speaks to us with a high clarity
which makes me shiver, for example in *Endymion*:

> But this is human life: the war, the deeds,
> The disappointment, the anxiety,
> Imagination's struggles, far and nigh,
> All human; bearing in themselves this good,
> That they are still the air, the subtle food,
> To make us feel existence, and to show
> How quiet death is.

And there is always an instinctive tenderness in his poetry, and
in his letters too, which you won't find much in chilly Wordsworth
or sardonic Byron. I cannot stop thinking of the few lines he
scribbled down right at the end, just after he had become secretly
engaged to Fanny:

This living hand, now warm and capable
Of earnest grasping, would, if it were cold
And in the icy silence of the tomb,
So haunt thy days and chill thy dreaming nights
That thou wouldst wish thine own heart dry of blood
So in my veins red life might stream again,
And thou be conscience-calm'd – see here it is –
I hold it towards you.

SAMUEL PEPYS:
FROM THE SCAFFOLD
TO MR POOTER

It is a famous passage, but it needs to be quoted in full, for reasons I shall come back to:

To my Lord's in the morning, where I met with Captain Cuttance. But my Lord not being up, I went out to Charing-cross to see Major-Generall Harrison hanged, drawn, and quartered – which was done there – he looking as cheerfully as any man could do in that condition. He was presently cut down and his head and his heart shown to the people, at which there was great shouts of joy. It is said that he said that he was sure to come shortly at the right hand of Christ to judge them that now have judged him. And that his wife doth expect his coming again.

Thus it was my chance to see the King beheaded at Whitehall and to see the first blood shed in revenge for the blood of the King at Charing-cross. From thence to my Lord's and took Captain Cuttance and Mr. Sheply to the Sun taverne and did give them some oysters. After that I went by water home. Where I was angry with my wife for her things lying about, and in my passion kicked the little fine Baskett which I bought her in Holland and broke it, which troubled me after I had done it.

Within all the afternoon, setting up shelfes in my study. At night to bed.

From the scaffold to Mr Pooter in a day. Within a single diary entry, Pepys moves with glorious unconcern from high and bloody events to the domestic soap. No one has ever done it like he did, and he only managed it for nine years before his fear for his eyesight made him abandon the diary (or possibly his grief for his wife's death robbed him of the zest to carry on). And almost always, as he darts from high to low and back again, you notice a sceptical turn. He distances himself from the old Credulities, here the belief of the Fifth Monarchy Men that the Major-General was due to pop up at the Saviour's right hand on the Last Day. He is impatient with the religious quarrels that tore his country apart throughout his life. He is interested in household improvements, gadgets, new medical techniques, the traffic problems in the City. We cannot help thinking that he is one of us.

Certainly Claire Tomalin in her delightfully readable new life of Pepys (who could write a life of him that didn't bowl along?) wants to claim him: he was 'mapping a recognisably modern world'; his account of the revolt of the City apprentices against the Parliamentary army is 'the first eyewitness account of an urban riot' – 'one we have seen on our television screens so that every point is familiar'.

From Pepys's scattered descriptions we get the first account ever written of how young men with meagre jobs, sharp wits and an appetite for experience live and work in a modern city.

There have been other marvellous lives of Pepys, Sir Arthur Bryant's three volumes in the 1930s and Richard Ollard in 1974, but none has so exactly caught Pepys's enthusiastic yet uncertain embrace of the new world, which was itself such an unstable amalgam of fading superstition and rational enquiry. She confects, for example, a luscious account of how Pepys was cut for the stone. The patient is larded with egg white and rose vinegar and given a cold syrup of lemon juice, radishes and marshmallow, after a thin silver instrument, the itinerarium, has been inserted up the penis into the bladder to help position the stone, before the 3-inch insertion is made just behind the scrotum. No anaesthetic, of course, and the patient is fainting with pain, but within its limitations the treatment of letting the wound drain and leaving it to heal is medically sound, and, though the stone was as big as a tennis ball, according to Pepys's friend Evelyn who saw it later, Pepys recovers and declares his intention of celebrating the anniversary of the operation with a dinner every year for the rest of his life. He is grateful like country people today who cross themselves when the aircraft takes off and clap when it lands safely. We are indeed on the watershed here.

And in the same way Pepys's whole life was spent on the political watershed too, between arbitrary God-given rule and the beginnings of modern parliamentary government. What gives the diary so much of its edge is that Pepys was, as Tomalin says, 'trapped on the wrong side', most of his career serving two kings, Charles II and James II, who wanted to build up their personal power and castrate Parliament. She is less inclined than her predecessors to accept Pepys's career as a given, and she brings out the constant embarrassment and alarm occasioned by his republican past and his contempt for his Stuart masters. He was, after all, remembered as 'a great roundhead at school', who had cheered the execution of Charles I. He certainly worked with enthusiasm for the Commonwealth and always considered 'Oliver' a superior master to Charles II, with his mistresses and his racehorses and his hatred of 'the very sight and thought of business', Pepys himself being one of history's great workaholics. 'My business is a delight to me,' he wrote, and it 'has taken me off from all my former delights' – something of an exaggeration, but then that too is not unmodern, seeing how many tycoons today boast of working

100-hour weeks and then turn out to have several mistresses and a yacht or two.

By the end of his life he was talking of 'we Tories', and he refused to serve under William III, but even in the early days of the Restoration he belonged to a republican club, the Rota. And he was decidedly shocked by the disgusting behaviour of other turncoats like Sir George Downing (of Downing Street fame) who, after having helped the Dutch drive Charles out of Holland, now rounded up old Parliamentarian comrades who had fled abroad and had them shipped back to London and the scaffold. Pepys's own patron and kinsman, Sandwich, simply lay low in Huntingdonshire during the transition, putting it about that he was 'confined to my chamber by a distemper', behaviour reminiscent of another Huntingdonshire eminence, John Major, who happened to be having his wisdom teeth out during the fall of Margaret Thatcher.

Claire Tomalin is also more clear-eyed than Pepys's male biographers about his conduct both in the office and at home. The little man, after all, had a large helping of all the seven deadly sins, except sloth. When he was appointed to the Navy Board, he simply knocked on the door of the house in Seething Lane that he fancied, spent a couple of nights as the guest of the inoffensive Major Willoughby and then told Willoughby to get out – behaviour more characteristic of Robert Mugabe than Sir Robert Armstrong. When he heard that Matthew Wren had been wounded in the Battle of Sole Bay, he instantly wrote to his patron Sir William Coventry asking for Wren's job. When Coventry himself was on the skids, Pepys refused to be seen walking with him in St James's Park.

Nor indeed were his famous dalliances all so innocent. He forced Mrs Bagwell to have sex with him by promising to arrange promotion for her husband, a ship's carpenter. In fact, when Bagwell is at sea fighting the Dutch, Pepys's first instinct is to pop down for a session with Mrs Bagwell. But when she is past forty, he writes to her husband telling him to keep her away from the Navy Office. He fondles Pegg Penn's breasts and thighs, though he finds her unattractive and suspects she has the pox, in order to get his own back on her father, Sir William Penn. And he is notoriously bad-tempered as well as congenitally unfaithful to his wife Elizabeth, whom I am fonder of than Mrs Tomalin seems to be.

For, though she is anything but blind to her subject's weaknesses, in the last resort, like most biographers, she finds it easy to forgive them: 'His energy burns off blame. For a woman, it is the nearest to experiencing what it is like to be a man; it is surprisingly hard to disapprove of him.' My own reactions, I must confess, are often more like those of Randolph Churchill reading the Old Testament for the first time, as observed by Evelyn Waugh: 'God, isn't God a shit?'

If Pepys is indeed the prototype of modern man, that is not an entirely comforting thought. Mrs Tomalin thinks other diaries of the period dull by comparison, and so to the modern reader they are. Yet in reading, say, the diary of the Rev. Ralph Josselin, an Essex clergyman to whom nothing much happened except the usual ills of life, I feel the presence of a human, well, I am sorry to use the word, but soul is really the only one that will do. For all his love of music and women, Pepys does have something about him of the automata that so much fascinated him: his Tiggerish energy, his equal readiness to lie and to confess, his voracious acquisition of high-placed friends, his boasting of his fine works of art, his readiness to pounce on any woman in any circumstances. Why, who does this remind us of? I am afraid it is Jeffrey Archer. True, Pepys is a better writer and went to prison three times as against Lord Archer's once to date, but there is a not-thereness that they share.

Why do I feel this so much more strongly after reading Tomalin than her predecessors? I think it is precisely because her approach is so markedly different in several respects. First, the male biographers are interested primarily in Pepys as 'the saviour of the Navy' (to use the title of Arthur Bryant's third volume) and in the diary as an unmatched historical record, while she is interested in Pepys's *vie intérieure* and in the diary's unique pioneering record of a self at work and play. Her previous full-length biographies have rescued women from the margins of oblivion – Dickens's mistress Ellen Ternan being actually characterized as 'the Invisible Woman'. And here too she beautifully resurrects lesser characters like Pepys's old maids, Jane and the luckless Deb, whose being surprised by Elizabeth in flagrante with Pepys triggered the biggest almighty row husband and wife ever had, which is saying something.

This biography's golden asset is that it brings alive all the other characters in the diary and explains their relationship to Pepys and to each other in a richness of detail that even the wonderful index and companion to the eleven-volume Latham and Matthews edition do not quite achieve. Tomalin thus provides the perfect preparation for reading the diary itself.

But Pepys himself never was invisible. He lives not only through his extraordinary contributions towards a modern navy that was properly trained, supplied and officered but also through his addictive unputdownable writings.

And here, by what is clearly a conscious decision, Tomalin denies us our fix. While telling us over and over what a masterpiece the diary is, she doesn't actually quote from it all that much, and seldom at length. She paraphrases, she chops up, she reorders, but she doesn't give us Pepys's own words and so loses the entrancing effect of the way he runs on.

For example, she records almost every fact in the passage I quoted at the head of this review, but all except ten words – 'as cheerfully as any man could do in that condition' – are Tomalin's, not Pepys's. Somehow this technique drains Pepys of some of his magic and leaves his conduct, when so plainly recounted by another hand, more open to our censure. And now and then the lack of direct quotation leads to omission of the most brilliant detail in the middle of a passage – for example, when the Dutch come up the Medway and Pepys in a total panic sends Elizabeth off to the country with his gold, Bryant and Ollard both mention that Pepys can't think what to do with his much bulkier store of silver and thinks in a wild moment of hiding it down the privy, but Tomalin does not.

Again Bryant and Ollard both describe exactly how the King saves Pepys's bacon when he is accused of trafficking in seamen's wage tickets. In Pepys's own words: 'The King with a smile and shake of his head told the Commissioners that he thought it a vain thing to believe that one having so great trust ... should descend to so poor a thing as the doing anything that was unfit for him in a matter of 0.10s.'

There is none of this in Tomalin.

But she really comes into her own in describing Pepys's last years, not covered by Bryant. It is a touching picture she paints of his retirement in Clapham under the wing of his sometime protégé Will Hewer and his favourite nephew John Jackson and his not quite second wife Mary Skinner, out of the great world but still in touch with his old friends like Evelyn, to whom he wrote, 'Pray remember what o'clock it is with you and me' and Evelyn replied that 'an easy comfortable passage is that which remains for us to beg of God, and for the rest to sit loose to things below'.

Even in his latter years, Pepys had not lost his boyish enthusiasm, nor forgotten how to write. On his voyage to Tangier he goes out rowing by himself and records in his notes: 'I know nothing that can give a better notion of infinity and eternity than the being upon the sea in a little vessel without anything in sight but yourself within the whole hemisphere.'

No, not quite Jeffrey Archer after all.

SHAKESPEARE AT STRATFORD: THE DIVINE PORK BUTCHER

For some reason, snootiness I expect, I had never been to Stratford-upon-Avon before. On a chilly day at the end of March, with only a scattering of Japanese pilgrims about, the place is a revelation. How upon the Avon it is, the church so close to the river that a gale could blow its great east window into the water. When you stand at the altar rails, there slap in front of you is Shakespeare's tomb and, ranged alongside, the tombs of his wife, daughter Susanna and son-in-law. And up above you to the left, there is the coloured bust of him, the one that the critic Dover Wilson complained makes him look like a self-satisfied pork butcher; if so, a pork butcher who has just come back from a fortnight in Marbella, because the eighteenth-century overpainting has gone an ineradicable brown. Despite this, he looks pretty much the same, except fuller in the face, as he does in the Droeshout frontispiece to the First Folio: the same domy brow, thyroid eyes and John Major upper lip. The opposite page in the Folio has the little doggerel verse by Ben Jonson, Shakespeare's longstanding rival and drinking partner, which certifies Droeshout's version as a fair likeness, just as his family must have okayed the bust which was erected only a couple of years after his death.

Yet still people pretend there is a mystery about what Shakespeare looked like. There was even an exhibition, 'Searching for Shakespeare', devoted to the subject at the National Portrait Gallery in 2006, featuring all the alternative more romantic versions of the face, chaps with earrings and hollow cheeks and soupy expressions, none of them bearing much resemblance to the divine pork butcher, like those hopeless lookunalikes at a police identity parade. Even A. D. Nuttall's *Shakespeare the Thinker*, which sets out to clear away the cobwebs, uses for its dust jacket the *Flower Portrait* which was exposed two years ago as a nineteenth-century pastiche – the chrome yellow was the giveaway.

Nobody could be more solidly anchored in his home town than William Shakespeare, christened and buried a few hundred yards from the house where he was born, his sister Joan and her descendants living in that same house for the next 200 years, just as Anne's brother, Bartholomew Hathaway, and his descendants lived in their 'cottage', in reality a substantial timbered farmhouse, for the next 300 years. As you stand outside and look across the cottage garden to the fields and oaks of the Forest of Arden, where his mother Mary Arden came from (her family's farm still standing too), you cannot help being moved, and also puzzled. Where's the mystery?

In fact, scholars are now beginning to admit that we know more about Shakespeare than about most people at the time who were not noble or royal. There was, after all, nothing obscure about his reputation in his lifetime. The wall tablet under the bust says in Latin 'The earth covers, the people mourn and Olympus holds a Virgil in art, a Socrates in intellect and a Nestor in wisdom'. So not just a provincial wordsmith who kept London bums on seats. He was regarded in his own time not merely as the Lloyd Webber of the West Midlands but as a profound thinker. The young John Milton, one of the most learned poets who ever lived, wrote of Shakespeare's 'Delphic lines' which 'make us marble, with too much conceiving'. We remember Ben Jonson saying that his old friend 'had small Latin and less Greeke', but this was just a joshing prelude to comparing him to Aeschylus, Sophocles and Euripides.

Yet the mystifiers remain convinced that a glover's son who had not been to university could not have produced such stuff, that the historical Shakespeare was not up to being 'Shakespeare'. This is mostly snobbery, but also ignorance, for example about the demanding standards of grammar schools like Stratford's, staffed mostly by university men. The plays show that in fact Shakespeare had read more Latin than classicists in universities today.

I remain baffled by the obsessive labours not only of those who waste their lives trying to prove that Oxford or Bacon or Queen Elizabeth wrote the plays, but also of those who long to tie Shakespeare down, to pigeonhole him in some profession or allegiance or character which would somehow explain away his disquieting genius. It's as if knowing what Shakespeare was like as a person would somehow relieve us from the obligation of understanding what he wrote.

So we have the 'lost years', in which he was allegedly employed as a schoolteacher in the country (Aubrey's *Brief Lives*) or as a soldier in the Low Countries (Duff Cooper's *Sergeant Shakespeare*). The battered old 'Theatre Edition' that I have in front of me argues, following the eighteenth-century Shakespearean Edmond Malone, that after leaving school Shakespeare was employed in the office of a local attorney – this on no stronger ground than that he had nice handwriting and there are more legal references in his plays than in those of his contemporaries. Surely the obvious answer is that, like anyone else trying to get into the theatre, Shakespeare spent his twenties learning his trade as prompter, scene-shifter and understudy – years lost only in the sense that there would be unlikely to be much record of them. For his later life we are offered the sour, money-grubbing capitalist of Katherine Duncan-Jones's *Shakespeare: An Ungentle Life* and Edward Bond's play *Bingo*. Well, it is always a mistake to underestimate how unpleasant great writers can be – though few of us would come out smelling sweetly if the only traces left of us were our dealings with the Inland Revenue and the local planning department.

The current favourite obsession is that Shakespeare was a secret Roman Catholic. Some of his Arden relations were undoubtedly recusants and several of the schoolmasters at Stratford Grammar were scholars who had contacts with the martyred Campion (so not just a bog-standard comprehensive then). Then there was William Shakeshafte, a player in service with the Catholic Hoghton family in Lancashire during the lost years. Could this have been the bard learning his trade under an alias (not much of an alias and Lancashire would not be very handy for dashing down to Stratford to impregnate Anne before zipping on to London to take his place in Lord Strange's company)? And there is the 'spiritual testament' of Shakespeare's father John, found hidden in the rafters of a Stratford house in 1737, full of references to Purgatory and ending with an 'Ave Maria'. Such testaments follow a form set down by Cardinal Borromeo and are said to have been brought to England by Campion in the 1580s. But three years ago, the scholar Robert Bearman produced evidence to show that English versions of these wills did not begin to appear until the 1630s, suggesting that John Shakespeare's one was an eighteenth-century fake. Father Thomas McCoog, the archivist of the British Jesuits, cannot see any evidence that links Shakespeare to the Jesuits at all. It remains possible that Shakespeare was a secret Catholic who had conformed in order to survive in those cruel chancy times, but if so, on the evidence of the plays he was such a secret one that the fact is no more important to Shakespeare as a writer than whether Glasgow Rangers' new signing is a left-footer in the religious rather than the football sense. For Shakespeare is not a religious poet as Donne, Milton and Herbert were, and he is not a religious playwright either.

Tragedies by their nature do not end in a redeeming, but was there ever such a bleak, nihilist play as *King Lear*? Dr Johnson declared that he could not bear to read the play through. Cordelia may be Christ-like in her forgiveness but she ends dead in Lear's arms and there is no resurrection. And when characters in Shakespeare do come back from the dead, it is because they were never dead at all. Cymbeline is not Lazarus. Nor is Hermione in *The Winter's Tale*; she has just been kept hidden away from her jealous husband Leontes and she returns with the extra wrinkles that she would have acquired in the interim. As for extracting from the plays any clue as to what Shakespeare thought about the Reformation, forget it. Which is why you will notice that what is common to the Shakespeare-was-a-Catholic obsessives and the Shakespeare-was-Marlowe/Bacon/Oxford/Queen Elizabeth brigade is that they draw their hidden messages or cunning acrostics from some bit of wordplay in the Sonnets or a minor poem like 'The Phoenix and the Turtle'. The plays themselves resist such fantastical interpretations, as does Shakespeare himself.

It is to undo all this that Professor A. D. Nuttall devoted his last book (he died in January). Tony Nuttall was a charismatic figure at Oxford, the son of a Herefordshire village headmaster and younger brother of the sixties guru-poet Jeff Nuttall, author of *Bomb Culture*. He aims to restore to us the depth and brightness of Shakespeare's thought, to undim him, like a good picture cleaner. And he has succeeded magnificently. The book starts unpromisingly with an introduction which tells us that one Oxford academic encouraged him to write the book and another one told him to stop 'when you find yourself writing about Shakespeare's essential Englishness'. But when Nuttall sets about his work, I immediately became entranced. He moves from play to play, at first in chronological order of their first playing or publication, later grouping them by theme, devoting no more than eight or ten pages to each, leaving out only a couple of duds like *King John* and *Henry VIII*. Each essay lights up some crucial moment or nub in the play, usually one I had not thought about and I could not wait to scurry on to see what he had to say about the next. Not since Harley Granville Barker has there been such an illuminating field guide to what Johnson called 'the great forest' of Shakespeare's work.

Nuttall contends that the greater part of this work is 'internally generated, the product not of Shakespeare's time, but of his own, unresting, creative intelligence'. Nuttall's Shakespeare won't stop still long enough to be pinned down. That is why he annoys some people. Shaw notoriously declared that 'there is no eminent writer I can despise as heartily as I despise Shakespeare, when I measure my mind against his', which tells us more about GBS's mind than Shakespeare's (Ralph Richardson once said that every time he did Shakespeare or Chekhov the part came out differently, but that acting Shaw was like running on tramlines). 'If we set aside technological advances like mobile telephones,' Nuttall argues, 'it is remarkably hard to think of anything Shakespeare has not thought of first, somewhere. Marxist, Freudian, Feminist, Structuralist, Materialist ideas are all there.' Christian apologists pounce triumphantly upon each little glimpse of religious allegiance, but, as Gary Taylor says, 'if Shakespeare has been the god of our idolatry for four centuries it is because he created scripture for an emerging secular world'. You want relativism, here's Hamlet: 'There is nothing either good or bad but thinking makes it so.' Freud, himself a passionate lover of Shakespeare, took inspiration from Hamlet's sexual jealousy of Claudius. For the dawn of introspection, see *Richard II*, passim. Or consider the debate between Perdita and Polixenes on plant-breeding in *The Winter's Tale*. Perdita says she cares not to gather slips of carnations and streaked gillyflowers because they are Nature's bastards, but Polixenes tells her that 'the art which adds to Nature is itself Nature' – pure Darwin.

From the unpromising terrain of *Henry VI, Part I*, Nuttall plucks these lines: 'One would have ling'ring wars with little cost; Another would fly swift but want the wings. A third think, without expense at all, By guileful fair words peace may be obtain'd.' There you have the choices in the Iraq debate: Rumsfeld's 'invasion-lite', shock 'n' awe, or UN mediation. Or take Henry V listening intently to the Archbishop of Canterbury going through the arguments for Henry's claim to the French throne. Directors fear that the scene may bore the audience and often play it for laughs, but we ought to be thinking of Tony Blair listening to the Attorney General before the war: 'May I with right and conscience make this claim?' – or do I need a dodgy dossier to legitimize my invasion?

Nuttall is persuasive too when it comes to convincing us about what Aristotle called 'plausible impossibilities' and 'unobvious decisions'. Would Lady Anne really have succumbed to Crookback Dick so soon after he had murdered her husband? Nuttall reminds us of David Niven confessing how sexually voracious he became in his grief after his wife's death. As for Richard himself on the night before battle seeing all the ghosts of the people he has wronged thronging round him, Nuttall tells us that the famously ferocious Dame Helen Gardner on her deathbed was visited by the ghosts of all the pupils she had failed and colleagues whose careers she had destroyed. An experimental psychologist of Nuttall's acquaintance is quite certain too that after the shock of having been violently blinded, Gloucester could easily be made to believe that he has fallen over Dover Cliff when he has merely toppled forward on to level ground.

Could Prince Hal in the Boar's Head be thinking aloud how well his riotous years will go down with the public 'when this loose behaviour I throw off'? Well, yes he could. Such cold calculations by ambitious young men are now familiar to us, Michael Heseltine at Oxford allegedly tracing on the back of an envelope his flight path to Downing Street. As for a riotous youth, these days every successful political leader needs to have inhaled a little.

Nuttall has a sharp ear for social nuance, pointing out that the Boar's Head scenes should not be played too downmarket. Falstaff, Bardolph and the rest are decayed military men, a little like Captain Grimes, and the mixture of posh and louche in the clientele requires Mistress Quickly to be given a touch of Muriel Belcher rather than Annie of the Rovers Return.

Shakespeare always returns us to earth, and to the city. The dukes driven out into the forest always go back. Celia and Rosalind toy with the idea of buying a country cottage together, no doubt pricing out local forest-dwellers, but return to South Ken, preferring hedgefunders to hedgerows. The beauty of Shakespeare's forests is that they are full of real mud and the milkmaid's hands are chapped from pumping at the cow's dugs and in winter Marian's nose looks red and raw and birds sit brooding in the snow. Shakespeare's pastoral is proper country, not a conventional daydream of 'when I was a child and it was all green fields round here'. In Shakespeare's Arden there is no pathos of distance, rather a poetry of presence.

Nuttall defends old-fashioned critics who were not ashamed to speculate how many children Lady Macbeth had and old-fashioned anthologists who liked to excerpt 'beauties' from Shakespeare. For the *dramatis personae* are not like types in a masque, they are characters with background. And from the first there are 'arias' and 'islands' in the plays, passages in which a character steps forward, sometimes out of character and sings – there is no other word for it – as Mercutio does in his Queen Mab speech, or the dying John of Gaunt, or Gertrude narrating Ophelia's death. He points out too how rapidly Shakespeare can change register, from the bitchy crosstalk of *The Taming of the Shrew* to Petruchio's heart-stopping lines:

> Kate like the hazel twig
> Is straight and slender, and as brown in hue
> As hazel-nuts, and sweeter than the kernels.
> O, let me see thee walk.

A critic who called Kate's speech in defence of wifely submission 'the greatest defence of Christian monogamy ever written' was none other than Dr Germaine Greer, who regards Katherina as uncommonly lucky to find Petruchio.

It is in an instant too that the backchat about Falstaff being too pissed to know what time it is provokes the old man to make his marvellous plea: 'Marry then, sweet wag, when thou art king, let not us that are squires of the night's body be called thieves of the day's beauty: let us be Diana's foresters, gentlemen of the shade, minions of the moon.'

Nuttall insists that what catches and holds Hal's affection, and ours, is not that Falstaff is just a charming old barfly but that he is, even in his ruined state, so blazingly articulate and intelligent.

But here comes the problem, which Nuttall candidly confesses. It is not that Shakespeare in, say, *Troilus and Cressida* is a Warwickshire innocent, insulated by a parochial culture, ineptly essaying a classical theme beyond his understanding. It is the modern reader who is commonly unable to match the sophistication of the Elizabethan dramatist.

For this reason there is a tinge of melancholy evident here and there in the book, a sense of coming too late on the scene. Nuttall takes on the task of showing us the full depth and complexity of Shakespeare's thought just at the moment when we are becoming incapable of absorbing most of it, like a tennis coach who only turns up after you have developed incurable tennis elbow. A great deal of the thought in the plays is simply too difficult for us to follow, partly for linguistic reasons. Nouns and verbs have changed their meaning; the use of prepositions has altered subtly too. Meanings are often highly compacted and further obscured by poetic locutions. Nuttall takes fifty-seven words to provide a modern paraphrase for the Fool's eight-word line in *Twelfth Night*: 'Words are very rascals since bonds disgrac'd them' – or, as they say in the City these days, you can't trust anyone's word since the lawyers moved in.

And if the reader is often nonplussed, the poor playgoer, who has no time to decode the knottier bits, is baffled. Ditto the actors. They shout or mumble out of sheer embarrassment when they don't understand what they are saying. Sometimes I yearn for a kindly Dr Bowdler who would iron out, this time not the obscenities, but the obscurities. Without a little help from somewhere, I suspect that directors will increasingly give up on the words, keeping only the plot and the songs, returning the plays to the condition of mere masques.

You can already see signs of this happening. In the 2007 production of *A Midsummer Night's Dream* at the Roundhouse (but originally created in India), the play is performed in seven Indian languages plus English (mostly rather broken). The actors flit up and round scaffolding, swirl and swaddle themselves in brightly coloured scarves and burst through paper screens to a rapturous reception from the audience. Now and then fragments of Shakespeare's words break through. The programme says rather severely that Indian audiences, let alone English ones, are not to mind if they cannot understand three-quarters of what the actors are saying, because their unreasonable expectation of monolingual drama arises not only from habituation to that mode, but also from the tyranny of literary studies dependent on the reading of books printed necessarily in one, 'pure' language, even more so when that language is the revered Bard's very own English.

I like those inverted commas round 'pure', suggesting that those who prefer to hear stuff in their own lingo are imperialist racist fascists. The director of the production, the gloriously named Tim Supple, concedes that 'the original text has a special quality, whether Shakespeare or Schiller.' That's nice of him. But, the Supple One continues, 'on the other hand, I can't accept the superiority of any language'. Not even a language you can understand? Ah well, these insubstantial pageants do fade. Still, the punters loved it.

THE GREAT VICTORIANS

The old view of the Victorians, put about by Lytton Strachey and his gang, and inherited by the next generation, was that they were stuffy, narrow-minded prigs. Legends of their prudishness appealed to our sense of having grown out of all that – the most famous, and most fatuous, being the myth that they draped piano legs to discourage indecent thoughts. To us now, the Victorians are beginning to look rather different: high-minded, yes, but open-minded too, ample-spirited, adventurous, confident that they could improve the world and themselves.

In fact, public authorities today devote quite a bit of time and money to restoring the great public works we inherited from the Victorians – the handsome city centres of Manchester, Newcastle and Liverpool, the amazing railway stations the size of cathedrals, the neglected city parks, the long choked canals. We are also starting to tackle the reforms of those institutions shaped by the Victorians which have gone slack – the police, the welfare state, the state schools. But how gingerly and ham-fistedly we go about it, compared with the electric energy and remorseless attention to detail of men like Peel, Palmerston and Gladstone.

Contrary to another part of the old myth, by and large the Victorians were anything but smug. The more we hear about them, the more respect we feel for their ability to confront the unwelcome and the unfamiliar. The career of Charles Darwin used to be told as a sort of biopic, the story of one man's fight to reveal the secrets of life in the teeth of public opinion. What strikes me, on the contrary, is how quickly the early Victorians took on board the general thesis of evolution and the insistence that man was part of that process. You have only to read the lines in *In Memoriam* about 'Nature red in tooth and claw' to see that Tennyson, writing before 1851 and so well before the publication of *The Origin of Species,* could assume in his readers some grasp of the purposeless, often brutal nature of evolution. Only a few of the thicker bishops, notoriously 'Soapy Sam' Wilberforce of Oxford, resisted the implications. No dogmatic materialist can have painted more grimly than Arthur Balfour the brief and doomed tenure of man's existence on earth. Walter Bagehot, the cocksure editor of the *Economist,* was anything but smug in his dire predictions about the future of democracy. He had too an unrivalled understanding of just how fragile the imposing institutions of the City of London were in reality. He even dared to ask whether Britain's Empire in India was sustainable in the long run, and whether it might not be better to begin to dissolve it in good time.

Nor should we lump together the Victorians as if every educated adult between 1837 and 1901 shared the same mindset. It is not hard to identify a late-Victorian doubt and pessimism which could no longer muster the old self-confidence. With the crumbling of certainty came a new frivolity and an elegant cynicism, from which those spoilt darlings of the Scottish Lowlands, Archie Rosebery and Arthur Balfour, undoubtedly suffered. Unleashed into the harder world of the new century, in which neither Britain's navy nor her industrial pre-eminence were unchallenged any more, such capriciousness was dangerous. For a single example, which was to have consequences up to the present day and beyond, look no further than the Balfour Declaration of 1917 – the last gasp of Edwardian nonchalance. It is hard to imagine Palmerston or Peel launching into such a wild promise without thinking it through.

SIR ROBERT PEEL:
THE FIRST MODERN

In Britain, modern politics starts with Peel. When William IV sacked Lord Melbourne and sent for Sir Robert, this was the last time a monarch dismissed his ministers of his own accord. When Peel replaced Melbourne again, in 1841, this was the first time a government had been overturned, not by the King, not by a vote in Parliament, but by a vote of the British electorate. Peel's manifesto to his electors in Tamworth was the first national election manifesto in British history. It was as beautifully vague as most manifestos since, but it sent a thrill through the newly enlarged electorate. They could sense that at last their interests and aspirations were to come first. The manifesto coincided with the growing use of the word 'Conservative' to describe the Tory party. And it was in these years too that Peel's confidant Francis Bonham took up his private desk at the Carlton Club, dressed in a long brown coat and carrying a large strapped book full of electioneering facts, figures and calculations, and Conservative Central Office was born.

Walter Bagehot, in his scorching essay, 'The Character of Sir Robert Peel', immediately grasped that here was the epitome of the new age. Peel was the ideal constitutional statesman, a man of

common opinions and uncommon abilities. According to Bage-
hot, Sir Robert was never in advance of his time. Unlike the
lightning that flashed from his Harrow contemporary Byron ('I
was always in scrapes at school, Peel never'), Sir Robert's 'opin-
ions far more resembled the daily accumulating deposits of a rich
alluvial soil ... You scarcely think of such a mind as acting; it
seems always acted upon.' In his most devastating attack on Peel,
at the Third Reading of the Corn Law Bill, Disraeli described
him as a 'burglar of other intellect ... there is no statesman who
has committed political petty larceny on so great a scale.' This
view of Peel remains influential to this day. Again and again, in
his light-footed, never less than readable Life of Peel, Douglas
Hurd repeats that Peel's was not an original mind, or as Gladstone
put it, he was not a far-sighted man but fairly clear-sighted. He
had changed his mind on so many things. As an absurdly young
chief secretary in Ireland, he had opposed Catholic emancipation
and been denounced by Daniel O'Connell as Orange Peel, not
just for his opinions but for the foppery of perfumed handker-
chiefs and thin shoes. Peel then believed that an honest despotic
government would be by far the fittest government for Ireland.
Few would have predicted his slow conversion to the belief that
Catholics should not merely have the vote but enjoy the fullest
part in Irish public life. The author of the act that returned Brit-
ain to the gold standard had originally voted against it. Again, he
had done everything he could to frustrate the Great Reform Bill,
then in the Tamworth Manifesto accepted it as a final and irrevo-
cable settlement of a great constitutional question.

Then there was corn. The ardent early protectionist became
the first great globalist, espousing free trade for Britain without
demanding anything in return from other nations. He who had so
long defended every tariff now confided to Prince Albert that he
had an immense scheme in view for removing all protection and
abolishing every monopoly. Like any twenty-first-century chan-
cellor, he now believed that we must make this a cheap country

for living and thus induce parties to remain and settle here. No wonder the Duchess of Richmond decorated her dining table with stuffed rats under a glass cover depicting Wellington and Peel. And John Henry Newman wrote from Oxford, 'It is not pro dignitate nostra to have a rat as our member'. There might be mega-ratting to come from Newman as from Disraeli, but it was Peel who was always to be remembered as King Rat. In vain, he protested that there was no dishonour in relinquishing opinions or measures and adopting others more suited to the altered circumstances of the country. The honesty with which he exposed his change of opinion, the factual power and fervour with which he defended his volte-faces only further enraged his contemporaries.

For the unforgiving Ultras, he was worse than a traitor to the good old cause; he split the party so that it didn't have a proper spell in power for the next thirty years. It is not the least irony of Peel's career that this pioneer of party politics should have been such a negligent practitioner of the art. Lord Shaftesbury complained that 'Peel has committed great and grievous mistakes in omitting to call his friends frequently together to state his desires and rouse their zeal. A few minutes and a few words would have sufficed; men would have felt they were companions in arms; they now have the sentiment of being followers in drill.' As Hurd points out, this is an excellent description of what goes wrong when prime ministers become too grand to cultivate their backbenchers; see Ted Heath passim, and Margaret Thatcher and Tony Blair in their later years.

In the recent spate of political biographies by leading politicians – Roy Jenkins on Gladstone and Churchill, William Hague on Wilberforce and Pitt the Younger – you get thrown in for your money a scattering of aperçus on the nature of political life and also quite a few comparisons between then and now. Lord Hurd is no slouch in this department, comparing Palmerston's gunboat diplomacy to George W. Bush's neo-colonial missionary zeal, and Peel's dislike of sentimental compassion masquerading as argument to Margaret Thatcher's. These comparisons do add enjoyment and sometimes illumination, but now and then they are a little forced. Yes, like Hurd's two political masters, Heath and Thatcher, Peel could be chilly and awkward in company. Yet the similarities are surely less striking than the great difference, which is that Heath and Thatcher are remembered for sticking to their guns, whereas Peel was notorious for, in Lord John Russell's words, being a very pretty hand at hauling down his colours.

Hurd acknowledges his debt to Norman Gash's superb two-volume Life and sometimes, for example when describing Peel's death and funeral, follows Gash almost word for word. There are occasional signs of haste. When Peel makes a bet with Lord Ashburton that he can pull off a John Macnab-style feat of shooting in a single day a pheasant, two types of partridge, both sorts of snipe, a woodcock and a wild duck plus a rabbit and a hare, Gash says he won 300 guineas, Hurd only 100. The larger figure gives the lie even more dramatically to the claim that Peel was nothing more than a puritanical prig. And where Gash tells us that Lady Floyd inveigled Peel to meet her daughter, his future wife Julia, by promising to find some Dresden ice pails for Peel's dinner service, Hurd says they were ice picks, not normally an item made in porcelain, otherwise Trotsky might have lived a bit longer.

But Hurd gives as vividly as Gash the sense of how odd Peel was, so cold outwardly, so affectionate and unbuttoned at home, the fondest of Victorian papas, apparently possessed of an imperturbable calm, yet not a redhead for nothing. He nearly fought two duels. Hurd does not quite convey the full bizarrerie of Peel's abortive shoot-out with O'Connell at Ostend. The news of the impending duel got into the newspapers and a warrant was issued for the arrest of both men. While O'Connell was arrested in London, the chief secretary for Ireland, who had already crossed the Channel, had to skulk about the Netherlands incognito for several weeks, but enjoyed the whole business, according to his friend Croker, 'as unaffectedly gay and at his ease as when we were going to Dover on our tour to Paris'. There was a generosity

and high spirits about Peel. He was generous to painters and poets
down on their luck, like Benjamin Haydon and James Hogg the
Ettrick Shepherd. He collected old masters by the score, including
Rubens's *Le Chapeau de Paille*, and had Julia painted in the same
get-up by Sir Thomas Lawrence. He built the most monstrous
of Victorian extravaganzas on the site of his father's old house at
Drayton, composed of, in Professor J. Mordaunt Crook's descrip-
tion: 'dull cupolas and Dutch gables, a Gothic porte cochère, and
a classical arcade, a Swiss lodge and French gates and an Italian
campanile. The gardens included a gaslit conservatory copied
from Frogmore, an Italian garden, an American pool, an avenue
of monkey-puzzle trees and balustraded terraces festooned with
winged cherubs and 209 marble urns.' Queen Victoria, who was
by now entirely reconciled to Sir Robert and no longer thought
him chilly and disagreeable, told Lord Aberdeen that Drayton is
certainly 'the most comfortable house I ever saw'.

By now Peel was enormously rich. His father, the first Sir Robert,
had employed 15,000 people in his mills, and Peel inherited from
him 9000 acres in Warwickshire and Staffordshire and an income
of £40,000 a year. He also inherited something of the mill-owners'
attitudes, opposing the Ten-Hour Bill for fear that reducing hours
would damage the industry's competitiveness. But he was second
only to Shaftesbury in his sympathy for the distress of the poor. If he
had not fallen over the Corn Laws, he would surely have moved with
his characteristic vigour to reinforce the measures he had already
undertaken to relieve the Irish famine. He would certainly not have
closed the food depots as Sir Charles Trevelyan did.

All his life there remained something provincial about him, not
least his slight Staffordshire accent. One snobbish observer noticed
that 'Peel can always be sure of an H when it comes at the begin-
ning of a word, but he is by no means sure when it comes in the
middle'. O'Connell was not the only one to think him a trifle
overdressed, if not on the Disraeli scale: his watch and chain were a
little too large. Greville records: 'I was never so struck as yesterday

by the vulgarity of Peel. In all his ways, his dress, his manner, he looks more like dapper shopkeeper than a Prime Minister. He eats voraciously and cuts creams and jellies with his knife.' Yet Carlyle, who was hard to please, found him congenial: 'clear, strong blue eyes which kindle on occasion, voice extremely good, low tones, something of cooing in it, rustic, affectionate, honest, mildly persuasive ... Reserved seemingly by nature, obtrudes nothing of diplomatic reserve. On the contrary, a vein of mild fun in him, real sensibility to the ludicrous, which feature I liked best of all.'

Carlyle, like almost everyone outside the ranks of Peel's immediate political opponents, sensed a kind of greatness in him. That greatness is hard to pin down only if we think of politics as a department of rhetoric, which was never Peel's forte. G. M. Young's sculptural analogy gives the clue: 'Like an able artificer, Peel always thought with his hands'. Anyone could pick off the shelf the idea of a professional police corps; it was what Peel made of it – the unarmed, modest, civilian force – that became immortal. Its founding principles are still enshrined in the code of instructions which every recruit has to learn by heart. There was a rare creative vigour in the way he turned bare slogans, whether financial or penal, into workable, living, enduring systems. In this he was truly original, perhaps the most original minister in modern British history. Douglas Hurd expounds Peel's achievements with lucidity, eloquence and not a little charm. Yet he never seems quite sure of how remarkable those achievements were.

Often underrated too is the strong-willed continence which runs steadily through all Peel's foreign policy, from the settlement of the furious boundary disputes with the United States to his last speech (in which he rebuked Palmerston's belligerence over the Don Pacifico Affair), the night before his horse threw him in Hyde Park, inflicting mortal injuries. It is easy to select damning quotations from Peel's letters and speeches for use today, for instance on the Afghan War: 'I fear the possibility of a terrible retribution for the most absurd and insane project that was ever undertaken in the wantonness of power.' Peel was an early opponent of imperial overstretch, exhorting successive viceroys not to annex the Punjab. But even he and his peacenik foreign secretary Lord Aberdeen were unable to check the remorseless expansion at the furthest reaches of what Peel called 'the overgrown empire', for as Hurd remarks, in these years the Empire was acquired not so much in absence of mind as in absence of communications.

What strikes one in foreign as in domestic policy was the relentless modernity of Peel's mind, his insistence on being guided by the latest facts. 'There is nothing like a fact' was his favourite maxim. It is in Peel's mind and in Peel's time that the dominant mode of British politics turns from the deductive towards the empirical. He more than any statesman of that period, perhaps of any period, clambered from one platform of understanding, to borrow Michael Oakeshott's phrase, to the next, without regret or recrimination on his side, for he was a forgiving man and made up almost all his quarrels. The Ultras repeatedly said that few tears would be shed for his passing. They were struck dumb by the outpouring of public grief that actually occurred, unequalled at the death of any prime minister except Pitt and Churchill, and perhaps not even by them. He had led the country through no great wars, he had stood consistently for no great principle, except the duty to elevate the condition of those who had no vote, but that was enough.

LORD PALMERSTON:
THE UNSTOPPABLE PAM

Under bare Ben Bulben's head was W. B. Yeats's chosen resting place. It was not Thomas Carlyle's. Passing through that bleak mountain landscape beyond Sligo during the years of the Famine, he exclaimed: 'Lord Palmerston's country – a dingy, desolate looking country. Would we were well out of it!' That was the last thing Palmerston could afford to wish for himself. He drew most of his income from his estates in Dublin and Sligo – £6100 out of a total of £7700. For those bleak moors were densely populated, wherever faintly habitable, by the descendants of the native Irish whom Cromwell had despatched 'to Hell or Connaught'. Two centuries later, they were still paying stiff rents to their absentee landlord on miserable plots too small to scratch a living from. It was said that no member of Palmerston's family had actually visited the estates until young Harry went there in September 1808 at the age of twenty-three. He was seized with a burning zest to improve the wretched lot of his tenants. He had a stone harbour built at Mullaghmore to encourage trade, planned 'a little manufacturing village', set up schools and fussed about their curriculum, planted bent grass to stabilize the sandy soil and Bordeaux pines too, which he recommended to O'Connell the Liberator for his seaside estate down the coast in Co. Kerry.

Above all, he was determined not to follow his more grasping neighbours in 'squaring' the land by amalgamating the holdings into viable units and evicting the surplus tenants. As late as 1837 – on the death of William IV when many leases fell in – Palmerston was still telling his agent that 'I have never yet acted on so cruel a system and shall certainly not begin now ... If any can be persuaded to emigrate voluntarily, well and good; but not a single creature shall be expelled against its will.' Yet Palmerston's racehorses and his mistresses and his rotten boroughs had to be paid for. By 1846, when the potato crop failed again (the acreage under potatoes in Co. Sligo had fallen from 50,000 to 3500), his estates were largely squared, and over the next year alone 2000 of his tenants had embarked for the New World, many of them, according to the emigration officers, 'in the most abject state of poverty and destitution, with barely sufficient rags upon their person to cover their nakedness'. Palmerston's agents claimed that the rations for the voyage had been adequate – and at least better than those issued by Lord Lansdowne's agents. Lord Palmerston had personally intervened to send puncheons of best Jamaica rum for the emigrants and, when the clergy complained, ordered that coffee and biscuits be sent instead.

When he visited Sligo ten years later, he found a green and prosperous land, with fat cattle grazing on lush grass and his tenants, probably fatter too and certainly far fewer in number, building their own houses and paying their rents on time. Rents from his Sligo properties had increased from £4467 in 1824 to £7370 in 1857. He had no legitimate children to leave these now smiling acres to, having married Emily Cowper only after she had been widowed, when they were both in their fifties. She had been his mistress, off and on, for thirty years. The stepchildren who became successively his heirs, William Temple and then Minnie Ashley, may well have been his own children. Through Minnie, the Irish estates and the far better-known Broadlands, in Hampshire, descended to Edwina Mountbatten (née Ashley). So when Lord Mountbatten set out with his family from Mullaghmore harbour for a fishing expedition on that pleasant August morning in 1979, he was reeling in the ghosts of the past as well as the lobster pots. In his fine life of Mountbatten, Philip Ziegler says, 'what had induced the IRA to decide that 1979 was a suitable year in which to kill a distinguished old man and his family may never be known.' But I don't think it's very hard to guess.

There have been many biographies of Palmerston – the most popular being those by Philip Guedalla and Jasper Ridley. Yet they all have a queer English bias and say little or nothing about Palmerston's experience of Ireland, the country from which he drew his title and most of his wealth, where he first saw poverty and saw the inevitability of Catholic emancipation and became a Liberal. In this new rich, thoughtful, occasionally slow but always rewarding biography, David Brown demonstrates clearly that John Bull's Other Island was also the other half of Palmerston. And he fills very nicely too that other lacuna in most accounts of Palmerston's career, his spell at the Home Office in Lord Aberdeen's coalition from 1852 to 1855. Because both Palmerston's contemporaries and his biographers were waiting to see which way he would jump on foreign affairs, especially on the Eastern Question, they paid little attention to what he was actually doing at the office. Yet it was here that Palmerston's domestic liberalism can best be seen in action. He introduced the Factory Act of 1853 which improved working conditions, especially for children, a Smoke Abatement Act and a Truck Act to entitle workers to cash wages rather than vouchers for the employer's shop. He took vigorous measures to prevent cholera, against the opposition of the water companies and local councils. He even tried unsuccessfully to pass a bill confirming the rights of trade unions. I am not sure why Brown describes this record as 'unremarkable'.

As always, Palmerston worked ferocious hours, though not as long as he had worked as foreign secretary, where he never left the office before 2 a.m. and was sometimes still there till five in the morning. He used to stand at a tall desk to stop him falling asleep. As Brown points out, 'Palmerston has long remained an elusive character: moving politically from Tory to Whig to Liberal; from reactionary eighteenth-century throwback to enlightened har-binger of late nineteenth-century democracy; the flamboyant and apparently disreputable society beau who was in fact a near teeto-tal workaholic.' By the time he reached the Home Office, he was still a Tory in his resistance to widening the franchise (indeed he briefly resigned over the question) and in his fear of public disor-der, but he was very much a progressive Whig in his belief in the education and welfare of the masses. In his teens, Harry had been sent to Edinburgh to live with and study under the philosopher Dugald Stewart. Other biographers have dismissed Stewart as a rather ponderous sermonizer, but it is clear that Palmerston really did inhale Stewart's belief in 'an almost divine advance towards improvement', and an equally rooted conviction that 'a great part of the political order which we are apt to ascribe to legislative sagacity is the natural result of the selfish pursuits of individuals'. The invisible hand of the market, the natural operations of free trade – these were what delivered the goods. Palmerston never wavered in his hatred of the Corn Laws and his belief in the ben-efits of free trade to the poorest classes. W. L. Burn, like other earlier historians, claimed that Palmerston lacked 'the sober, seri-ous, conscious thoughtfulness so characteristic of the age he lived into'; 'there was at the bottom of him a moral vacuum.' A. J. P. Taylor declared that 'very little has been written or ever will be about Palmerston's place in British political life, for it is an empty one'. He owed his success to public opinion and 'did not voice any great principle or idea'.

I think these sweeping dismissals derive from a caricature of Palmerston as his opponents liked to portray him, as a Regency roué overstaying his time, in Guedalla's famous phrase, 'the last candle of the eighteenth century'; or, in Disraeli's cutting image, as the old painted pantaloon with his dyed whiskers and false teeth, 'at best ginger beer and not champagne', flamboyant and superficial to the last. This is certainly not how he was seen by his contemporaries when he was young. His mentors, the Mintos and the Malmesburys, thought him singularly reserved for a young man, too afraid of committing himself even in ordinary life; there was a coldness and want of effect in his public speeches: 'he had too little spring for his age', Lord Minto wrote to his wife. At work, he was feared and ridiculed as a stickler and a pettifogger. In 1809, he became Secretary at War – a sort of ministerial quartermaster-general – and stayed there until 1828 without a glimmer of promotion, poring deep into the night over bread and forage returns, clothing expenses and claims by generals for often nonexistent ADCs. He was less like Young Lochinvar than the bureaucrat Blackhead in *A Dance to the Music of Time*. His energies in this period were also taken up with finding – and keeping – a seat in the House of Commons. This was in many ways a more laborious, certainly a more expensive business under Old Corruption than it was to be in the reformed House. The going rate for a borough seat could be as much as £5000. Palmerston managed to secure Newport on the Isle of Wight for £4000 on condition that he 'should never, even for the election, set foot in the place' – lest he should seduce the electors from their patron. Palmerston kept the deal so faithfully that in later years he could never quite remember the name of his first seat and referred to it as Newtown. Lady Malmesbury approved of this approach. She told Palmerston: 'At all events it is better to pay any thing, if you are to be in Parlt, than to court & canvass people for 7 years together' – an arduous business in those constituencies where every elector expected to be personally wooed by the candidate.

Even when finally settled in Parliament and in high office,

'Lord Pumicestone' was deeply unpopular with almost everyone. Greville said that at the Foreign Office he was detested as 'a bully, a blackguard and a coward'. George IV 'hated me', Palmerston claimed, and offered to make him first governor of Jamaica and then governor-general of India to get rid of him. Later, he had to resist several efforts to push him up to the House of Lords, in which as a mere Irish peer he had no seat. He himself admitted that in 1852 he could not go back to the Foreign Office because 'his general unpopularity in Europe unfits him for that post'. Queen Victoria said 'I never liked him' and moaned that 'if our dear Aberdeen was still at his post, the whole thing would not have happened' (the tangled affair of the Montpensier marriage).

Between them, either Aberdeen or Palmerston was either foreign secretary or prime minister almost continuously for the whole period between 1828 and 1865, an alternation in power longer and more unbroken than that of any other duo I can think of. They had been contemporaries at Harrow School. One anecdote had it that Palmerston triumphed over Aberdeen in a pillow fight; another that Aberdeen had locked Palmerston in a darkened room without a candle until Palmerston was heard pleading 'lighten our darkness, we beseech thee, O Lord'. No anecdote claimed that they had ever been friends.

In the public mind, and in their own, they stood for dramatically opposite styles in foreign policy: conciliation versus deterrence, appeasement versus bluster. The one thing they had in common was that they were both surprisingly poor speakers, hesitant and often rambling. Disraeli claimed that Palmerston's 'false teeth would fall out of his mouth if he did not hesitate and halt so in his talk'. Palmerston described Aberdeen as 'a good natured, easy tempered, apathetic and yielding man' and so soft on the French that he behaved like 'Under Secretary of State to Guizot'. Aberdeen supported Palmerston when he felt he ought to. Yet he could not disguise that he thought him incorrigibly reckless and could not abide the way Pam played to the crowd. When Palmerston urged that, for popular as well as strategic reasons, the British navy should be sent immediately to obstruct Russian forces, Aberdeen replied that in 'a case of this kind, I dread popular support'.

Palmerston was an indefatigable manipulator of the press. According to Cobden, he had 'made greater use of that means of creating an artificial public opinion than any minister since the time of Bolingbroke'. He would feed exclusive titbits to favoured editors in return for their support, and get them to insert pro-government articles, though he was well aware that they might publish a completely opposite piece tomorrow: 'though editors look to government for news, they look to their readers for money and they never can resist flying out upon popular topics'. In September 1846, he not only suggested to Lord John Russell that he send a few ships off the coast of Spain to restrain the French but added that 'it would do no harm at the Tuileries if any orders about fitting out our line of battle ships could be given in our dockyards, and mentioned in the newspapers, even if no active or real steps were taken to carry them into effect'. Even Alastair Campbell might have hesitated to go that far. It was certainly not the sort of spin that dear Lord Aberdeen would have countenanced.

Yet Brown's judicious treatment leaves us wondering how much difference in practice there was between their approaches to foreign policy. Aberdeen himself told the House of Commons in December 1852 that 'the truth is that for the last 30 years the principles of the foreign policy of this country have never varied' (admittedly he was trying to hold his fragile newborn coalition together at the time). Gladstone, always the peacenik in any cabinet of the period, testified that Palmerston and Aberdeen differed only in the sense that they represented 'distinct forms of the same principles connected with different habits and temperaments'. It is plausible to claim, I think, that there was an underlying consensus in British foreign policy throughout the Palmerston–Aberdeen years which kept the peace with great success until the Crimean War. The anti-appeasement camp claimed that this war too might have been deterred by an earlier show of force, but as with all such claims this is as unprovable as it is doubtful. Palmerston himself claimed that his overriding aim was 'not to bring on war, but to prevent war'.

Most of the episodes to which he had to respond in government were not of his own making – the Crimean War, the *Arrow* incident in Hong Kong (in which it was the British plenipotentiary Sir John Bowring who ordered the bombardment of Canton), the Indian Mutiny, the attempted assassination of Napoleon III, which led indirectly to the first fall of Palmerston's government on the grounds that he was too soft on foreign sovereigns. Aberdeen could be forgiven for finding it 'whimsical that the man who for so many years had reproached me for unworthy concessions to foreign powers, should have been overthrown in consequence of a similar accusation.' In fact, apart from the legendary Don Pacifico Affair, Palmerston despatched remarkably few gunboats in his career (and Aberdeen sent a couple himself).

And where the interests of Britain were not clearly engaged, he moved gingerly. When the American Civil War broke out, he tentatively supported the states-rights case of the South but mostly because he thought the South would win. When it became clear that it was losing, he switched support to the North, claiming that the abolition of slavery was now the crucial issue. He also feared that 'exiled Irishmen' might stir up war between Britain and the United States, that his former tenants might take their revenge. He was equally cautious in dealing with Italy. His heart was with the cause of Italian unity and independence and the expulsion of Austria, but to preserve the balance of power in Europe he needed Austria as a counterweight to Russia – 'I am very Austrian north of the Alps, but very anti-Austrian south of the Alps.' And so he really did not do much to assist Garibaldi.

The Palmerston that Brown shows us is a more cautious and self-aware operator, both more serious and more devious than the Flash Harry in his tall white hat and white trousers and blue frock coat with gilt buttons charging headlong at every fence. 'We must deal with things as they are and not as we would have them,' he said, almost as though reminding himself. Even in that famous five-hour speech defending his record against Anstey's motion in March 1848, he tempered patriotic fire with realistic calculation and moral judgment. Yes, the interests of England ought to be the shibboleth of every minister's policy. It was true too that 'We have no eternal allies and we have no perpetual enemies. Our interests are eternal and perpetual, and those interests it is our duty to follow.' But later in that same speech, Palmerston went on to explain that the policy of Britain was also 'to be the champion of justice and right: pursuing that course with moderation and prudence, not becoming the Quixote of the world'.

Brown argues that the wrenching of Palmerston's more flamboyant phrases out of the context of his overall moral realism has done some enduring harm to the practice of foreign policy. And I think he is right about that too. One still detects faux-Palmerstonian echoes in those calls for Britain to 'punch above its weight'. I caught a whiff of it in a *Times* leader when William Hague was foreign secretary:

The real issue for Mr Hague is not what he is saying but what he is doing. There is very little evidence that he is seriously engaged in the global conversations of the moment. On the prospect of peace in the Middle East, on climate change, on a plan for Zimbabwe, Mr Hague has been silent ... Diplomacy often depends on leaping on to planes and holding face-to-face talks, full of incentives and threats ... Mr Hague now needs to spend a little less time in Great Charles Street and Lincoln's Inn and define, not least by getting on more planes, the issues that he cares about. He then needs to start using the power that Britain retains in the service of the ethical values that he has articulated.

The Times, 16 September 2010

Lord Palmerston would have agreed with every word. Lord Aberdeen would not.

In this surely definitive biography, David Brown leaves us with a Palmerston who is more admirable, yet he does not make me like him more. Towards the end of his life, Pam basked in his unexpected new role as 'the People's Darling', but he never became truly lovable. There always clung to him some of that detachment which had struck people so unpleasantly when he was young. For all his celebrated love of women and racehorses and boxing, he seemed slightly inhuman. Even his amazing energy had a certain mechanical jack-in-the-box quality. When he died, he was not mourned as Peel and Wellington had been mourned or as Gladstone was to be. I do not think he ever wept much himself. In that, too, he was unlike Lord Aberdeen.

WALTER BAGEHOT:
MONEY MATTERS

There used to be a room in the National Portrait Gallery devoted to portraits of late Victorian sages by G. F. Watts. Inspissated in that painter's incurably muddy tones, they peered out from behind straggly beards and whiskers with sad, rheumy eyes – Matthew Arnold, Carlyle, Swinburne, William Morris, Leslie Stephen, Tennyson – giving off a steamy despair. They had heard the melancholy long withdrawing roar of faith, and they did not like the sound of it. Today relegated to a wall in a side room, these literary men seem to take second billing to the wall where the giants of Victorian science are gathered – Darwin, Huxley and Lyell, each whiskered too but each with an unmistakable half-smile playing about his lips. There's not much doubt which is the winning side.

Nowhere on either wall is space found for Walter Bagehot (1826–77). Yet G. M. Young, that hallowed chronicler of the Victorian age, came quite firmly to the conclusion that if you were looking for the Greatest Victorian, Bagehot was your man. There was no one else 'whose influence, passing from one fit mind to another, could transmit, and can still impart, the most precious element in Victorian civilisation, its robust and masculine sanity'.

Bagehot is not entirely forgotten – the NPG has a mezzotint of him somewhere – but exactly who or what he was is now a little fuzzy in our minds. A few stray bons mots about the monarchy, some connection with the *Economist* (which keeps his memory green in the pseudonym of a regular columnist) – that is as much as most of us can dredge up. What precisely was he great as: essayist, critic, economist, political analyst? Well, not really any of them under a rigorous definition of those trades, but a bit of each in a loose, agreeable way.

The simplest starting point – and also the ultimate answer – is to say what Bagehot undoubtedly was, thoroughly, professionally and ancestrally: a banker. His grandfather Robert Bagehot was a West Country merchant who shipped goods up the River Parrett under the name of the Somerset Trading Company. Robert's younger son, Thomas, married the niece of Samuel Stuckey, the founder of Stuckey's Bank, a sizable local house which had already swallowed up several tiddlers. Thomas rose to become vice-chairman, and so in due course did his son Walter, after serving a full apprenticeship in the Bristol counting house.

Even after moving to London with his wife, Eliza Wilson, Walter remained a key figure in Stuckey's. Eliza was the daughter of James Wilson, the owner-founder of the *Economist*, who also became Palmerston's financial secretary to the Treasury. Wilson, a genial, acute, hard-driving Scot, was then picked out to rescue the finances of India after the Mutiny of 1857, which he did with a sure touch by introducing India's first income tax. So successful was this that when he died of dysentery in August 1860, after only a year out East, all Calcutta turned out to mourn him – surely a unique tribute to a man famous only for inventing a new tax.

Wilson's death left his widow and daughters joint owners of the *Economist,* and Bagehot was pressed into service as the paper's editor and directing genius. But he never stopped being a banker. And his lifelong experience made everything he had to say about finance, in theory and practice, and about the herd instincts of the City of

London, as accurate today as when he took over the magazine a century and a half ago.

The Memoirs of Walter Bagehot is an oddity, for Bagehot left behind no memoir when his chronically weak chest finally undid him at the age of fifty-one. Instead, Frank Prochaska has stitched together this self-portrait out of the boxfuls of essays, letters and articles he did leave. These have been republished in multivolume editions three times, by Forrest Morgan in 1889, by one of the Wilson sisters, Emilie Barrington, in 1915, and finally by Norman St John-Stevas between 1965 and 1986. Prochaska chose to present Bagehot in the first person 'because I thought Bagehot could speak more vividly of his life and mind than I could as an intermediary in a conventional biography'.

I rather sympathize with Prochaska's self-effacement. So many biographies, after all, blur the subject by homogenizing the material; others elbow the subject aside to give the biografiend a bigger shout. As far as I can check, pretty much everything in this little book is direct quotation, with only minimal editorial linking. So you will probably get as good a picture of what Bagehot was like and what he thought from Prochaska's 200 pages as from St John-Stevas's fifteen volumes. Prochaska picks out the plums nicely, and the ripest and juiciest are usually Bagehot's remarks on the world he really knew from the inside, the world of money.

Happily, Bagehot tells us in his brilliant essay *Lombard Street*, 'banking is a watchful, but not a laborious trade'. Prochaska's version has 'arduous', which fractionally diminishes Bagehot's point, that sensible bankers do not need to put in excessive hours, still less to boast of them. They should have plenty of leisure for the library and the hunting field, because 'the modes in which money can be safely lent are not many, and a clear-headed, quiet, industrious person may soon learn all that is necessary about them' – advice which might have forestalled half-a-dozen bank crashes. Bagehot goes on elsewhere to give three warnings to investors, which pretty much exhaust the subject: 'Have nothing

to do with anything unless you understand it, divide your invest-
ments, and be wary of taking advice from others.' In a single
sentence, he waves away the delusions of derivatives, the folly of
putting all your eggs in one basket and the insidious temptations of
the financial adviser.

He points out too the most immediate threat which besets us
in the low-interest-rate environment of today, which is likely to
continue for some years to come: 'The history of the trade cycle
had taught me that a period of a low rate of return on investments
inexorably leads towards irresponsible investment ... People won't
take 2 per cent and cannot bear a loss of income. Instead, they
invest their careful savings in something impossible – a canal to
Kamchatka, a railway to Watchet, a plan for animating the Dead
Sea.' And how elegantly Bagehot describes the extreme fragility of
the financial system in his day and ours, where an inverted moun-
tain of credit teeters on a tiny base of cash. And how he mocks the
complacency of the money men:

> Again, it may be said that we need not be alarmed at the mag-
> nitude of our credit system or at its refinement, for we have
> learned by experience the way of controlling it, and always
> manage it with discretion. But we do not always manage it with
> discretion. There is the astounding instance of Overend, Gurney
> and Co to the contrary. Ten years ago that house stood next to
> the Bank of England in the City of London; it was better known
> abroad than any similar firm, known, perhaps, better than any
> purely English firm. The partners had great estates, which had
> mostly been made in the business. They still derived an immense
> income from it. Yet in six years they lost all their own wealth,
> sold the business to the company, and then lost a large part of
> the company's capital. And these losses were made in a manner
> so reckless and so foolish, that one would think a child who
> had lent money in the City of London would surely have lent it
> better.

For Overend, Gurney, read Barings, Lehman Brothers, RBS, Lloyds, etc. But Bagehot's fame never rested solely on the undoubted fact that he knew about money, knew so much that Gladstone relied on his advice and described him as for many years 'a sort of supplementary chancellor of the exchequer'. It was because his mind ranged far beyond the counting house, because he mocked the sluggish minds of City men, that his writings were so exhilarating and so popular. It is not because Bagehot was a brilliant banker that his name still has a quizzical resonance. It is because he was a brilliant journalist.

He was fully aware of what he was, alive to both his talents and his limits. When he was a boy, his parents had 'gently censured the haste and carelessness in my writing – and my tendency to criticise rather than get to the bottom of a subject'. He admitted that 'variety is my taste and versatility my weakness.' He could pick up any subject and give it a high bright gloss, leaving his readers confident that they now knew all they needed to know about it. They had been taken behind the scenes, they knew how much the show cost and what made it tick and how much it was really worth. Every page is full of bounce and *sprezzatura,* spiced with irony and liable to make you laugh out loud.

Two of his three best-known books, *The English Constitution* and *Physics and Politics,* were first published as articles in the *Fortnightly Review,* and they have all the fizz calculated to make a splash in that sort of journal. His pieces are never weighed down by punctilious analysis, dulling qualification or anxious quotation. Only in *Lombard Street* are there any statistics to be found, but that is because *Lombard Street* is about a serious subject, the only really serious subject, money. 'My great concern,' Bagehot confesses, 'was to avoid seeming dull, in the manner of the detached historian imprisoned in his tower, insensitive to the immediacy of the encircling world' – a confession which might stand as the journo's credo. And Bagehot is never dull. Prochaska claims that 'if he is not the "Greatest Victorian", he is the Victorian with whom you would most want to have dinner.'

Well, perhaps, if you wanted to have an easy clubbable sort of dinner, a dinner you would come away from thinking that the Victorians were really decent chaps, not unlike us. But if you wanted a dinner that you would remember for the rest of your life, would you not prefer to dine with, say, Carlyle, or George Eliot, or Dickens, or Ruskin, or Tennyson, or even Gladstone? There might be torrential monologues, harsh tirades, uncomfortable silences, but at least you would have experienced a force of nature, you would have trod the slopes of the volcano.

Bagehot, by contrast, tells us that 'a writer of genius, like a great man of the world, is distinguished by what I call "animated moderation".' In fact, 'success in life depends more than anything else on animated moderation.' Shakespeare, you will be relieved to hear, scores quite high on this: 'He is often perfect in it for long together, though then, from the defects of a bad education and a vicious age, all at once he loses himself in excesses.' If only he had been to a decent university, or better still worked in a bank. T. S. Eliot would have got high marks from Bagehot.

At least it looks as if Shakespeare was a healthy outdoor type. 'The passage in *Venus and Adonis* which describes a hare running through a flock of sheep to put the hounds off the scent could only have been written by a man who had been hunting.' The point is that writers must not be too bookish. 'So many poor books are written because writers have so little knowledge of the world outside their studies . . . the most perfect books have been not by those who thought much of books, but by those who thought little.'

Writers ought to mix socially with the people they write about. Full marks would have gone to Henry James for his heroic dining out, but *nul points* to Dickens. 'He knows the dry arches of London Bridge better than Belgravia. He excels in inventories of poor furniture and is learned in pawnbrokers' tickets.' But he had never penetrated the haute bourgeoisie. 'His delineations of middle-class life have in consequence a harshness and meanness which do not belong to that life in reality.' The Dedlocks and the Veneerings and Sir Mulberry Hawk are simply not like the people one meets. By the same token, Dickens's pictures of our higher institutions – the Court of Chancery, the Circumlocution Office – are overwrought and tend to excite futile 'discontent and repining'. Dickens's inveighing against what are the inevitable evils of life sets a 'pernicious example'.

The mission of a respectable periodical, as Bagehot sees it, is to make its readers feel at home. At the *Economist,* he tells us:

> Our typical reader is a businessman, banker or trader, who prefers statistics to abstractions and has little patience for padding. He is generally cool, with his own business to attend to, and has a set of ordinary opinions arising from and suited to ordinary life. He does not desire an article that is too profound, but one which he can lay down and say 'an excellent article, very excellent, exactly my own sentiments'.

On such first-rate principles the *Economist* has been conducted ever since, although few of Bagehot's successors as editor have stated them so frankly. Worldly men tend to applaud the judgment of other worldly men, and Bagehot's judgment has been much prized by his admirers. G. M. Young says in an essay on Robert Peel that 'Bagehot called him a second-class man, and Bagehot was not often wrong.' Peel lacked the inspirational qualities of Fox and the Pitts, of Gladstone and Disraeli, 'which is why no party has taken his memory into its care'. This is surely nonsense. Peel is a far more vibrant presence in Conservative politics today than any of the others, because he engaged with the modern world with a moral and practical seriousness that none of the others quite matched. Which is the reason the working men of London flocked to his house when he was dying.

The truth is that Bagehot was often wrong, and because he was a generous man, he often said so. He admitted that he had under-rated Abraham Lincoln and had been wrong to support the right of the Southern states to secede and form a slave-owning republic. By contrast, he thought at first that Louis Napoleon was an ideal leader, because 'the French just want treading down and nothing else – calm, business-like oppression, to take the dogmatic conceit out of their heads.' By 1870, however, he was telling the readers of the *Economist* that 'Caesarism has utterly failed in France'. He was scornful of twaddle about democracy: 'Of all the circumstances affecting political problems, by far the most important is *national character*.' It was 'the least changeable thing in this ever-changeful world'. Only a few years later, though, in *Physics and Politics,* he was declaring, with equal certainty, that 'a lazy nation may be changed into an industrious, a rich into a poor, a religious into a profane, as if by magic, if any single cause, though slight, or any combination of causes, however subtle, is strong enough to change the favourite and detested types of character.'

But surely *The English Constitution* still has something of value to teach us about the way we are governed. Its brilliance and charm have never ceased to attract later generations, and if Bagehot lives today, this little book is what makes him live. Yet those who have not previously read it or who come back to it after a long gap will, I think, be astonished by its relentless snobbery and its obsessive contempt for and fear of the lower orders. 'The masses of Englishmen are not yet fit for an elective government,' we are told. We need a visible symbol of personal authority in the shape of the monarchy, because 'the fancy of the mass of men is incredibly weak and can see nothing' without it. 'The lower orders, the middle orders, are still, when tried by what is that standard of the educated "ten thousand", narrow-minded, unintelligent, incurious.' So it is vital to preserve the mystery of monarchy, for fear of undeceiving the mob. 'We must not let daylight in upon magic' – itself a magical phrase which, unaccountably, Prochaska omits. Basically, the proles have to be conned into thinking that they are actually governed by the Queen herself, or they would not suffer themselves to be governed at all. Bagehot doesn't contemplate the possibility that, even among that educated ten thousand, there might be quite a few who would also find in the monarchy a symbol of their shared history and culture and hence see the Queen not only as the focus for their allegiance but also as the source of legitimate authority which is entitled to command their obedience. For Bagehot, all this is mere flummery which, by a happy accident of history, enables the middle class to get on with the actual business of ruling – the 'efficient' part of the constitution as opposed to the 'dignified' part, that distinction which is the book's most memorable legacy.

Bagehot shows little sense of or interest in constitutional structure. All he is interested in is power, and what he tells us – this is his groundbreaking insight – is that power resides with the majority in the House of Commons and nowhere else, and this is what is so good about the system, for 'the interlaced character of human affairs requires a single determining energy; a distinct force for each artificial compartment will make but a motley patchwork, if it live long enough to make anything. The excellence of the British constitution is that it has achieved this unity; that in it the sovereign power is single, possible and good.' Checks and balances are for the birds, or the Americans. Any separation of powers can only be a source of weakness. For Bagehot, writing in 1865, the agonies of the American Civil War had shown that republics were intrinsically weaker than monarchies. The vulgar and benighted Americans had persuaded themselves that their constitution was a work of providential genius, but in truth it was an outdated document which had turned out to be woefully inapplicable to modern conditions.

We don't have to wait for the twentieth century to see how short-sighted Bagehot was. Only two years after *The English Constitution* began to be serialized in the *Fortnightly*, Disraeli

managed to get the Reform Act of 1867 through, and all Bage-
hot's comfortable premises were overturned. He never revised the
book, but he did write a preface for the second edition of 1872.
And what a remarkable transformation of attitude we find in it.
Gone is the cheerful confidence of the high Victorian age, in
which science and reason would conquer all, and free trade and
Mr Babbage's calculating machines would bring prosperity and
leisure to an ever-expanding middle class. All at once we find
ourselves lapped in the apprehensive gloom of the later Victori-
ans. Bagehot's own high colour and high spirits seem to be fading
too. His health, never strong though he kept up a hearty front,
had been declining for years and he was carried off by pneumonia
in the spring of 1877. By the end, he seems to belong with the sad
sages in the Watts room. The modern world takes him aback, he
had not bargained for it and he doesn't care for it. That 'marvel
of intelligible government' which the English had had the luck
to stumble on was not turning out to be as robust as he thought.
He saw it as futile to imagine that the enlargement of the elector-
ate would improve the system. He didn't shrink from saying that
'I am exceedingly afraid of the ignorant multitude of the new
constituencies'.

But even these fresh apprehensions do not represent a settled
state of mind. He looks around a few years after Disraeli's thunder-
bolt and sees, to his relief and surprise, that 'Thus far, my fears that
the working classes would take all the decisions to themselves –
would combine as a class and legislate for their class interests – have
not been realised . . . In the main, things go on much as before. The
predominance remains as yet where it ought to be: in the hands of
leisure, of property and of intelligence.'

So Bagehot ends his sadly shortened life in a mixture of funk
and bewilderment. He really has no more idea than anyone else
how things are going to pan out. He can offer no rational prog-
nosis for the long- or even medium-term future of the British
constitution. This mental paralysis surely arises from his failure to

examine the structure and history of those arrangements with any sustained seriousness. What he offers us is a charming snapshot, coloured by his own prejudices and fears. *The English Constitution* is the first selfie. His confusion is compounded by the fashionable Social Darwinism that slips into his later writings, notably in *Physics and Politics*. It is surprising to see a man so proud of his cool and sceptical temper swallowing great gulps of Herbert Spencer. The fittest survive, the losers deserve to lose. 'The majority of the "groups" which win and conquer are better than the majority of those which fail and perish.' That is the way the world improves. We have to discard 'the mistaken ideas of unfit men and beaten races'. Bagehot has few tears to shed for the losers. 'I confess to having little compassion for the toiling masses of unknown men, whose lives are mired in misery and pain.' He attributes this to the terrible strains his mother's long-term insanity had placed on her only son. 'I sometimes feel that each of us is born with a measure of compassion, which is easily exhausted in this suffering world.' Bagehot can at least claim to have been a pioneer of compassion fatigue. This isn't just an unattractive way to look at the progress of the human race. It was also apparently contradicted by the experience of the 1860s and 1870s, for who were coming out on top but the lower classes, those very people who were 'clearly wanting in the nicer part of those feelings which, taken together, we call the *sense* of morality'? The unfittest were not only surviving but triumphing, and of course there were too many of them, for like many such pessimists, Bagehot worried about the overbreeding of the underclass.

It seems something of a mystery that Bagehot should endure as an icon of sagacity. No doubt his role as the founding deity of the *Economist* must have a good deal to do with it, not simply because of the worldwide success of that journal but because its prosperity enabled it to finance elaborate publication of Bagehot's work and because his editor St John-Stevas and his biographer Alastair Buchan were long associated with the paper. And the cocksure, worldly-wise tone of its columns is a living memorial to Walter Bagehot.

The one exception to the uncritical reception comes from a writer whose only connection with Bagehot was that he happened to live near his home town of Langport, Somerset. Prochaska doesn't mention C. H. Sisson's *The Case of Walter Bagehot* (1972) among the list of books he has consulted, but it is an acerbic and indispensable corrective to the excessive worship of the Greatest Victorian. Nobody could have been less like Bagehot than Charles Sisson, a modest, understated man equally distinguished as a poet and a civil servant. Sisson understood the deep springs of allegiance and the poetry of public service. No other critic has pinpointed the unconscious philistinism, the underlying money worship, the breezy swank which made Bagehot such a legend in his lifetime and such a warning to ours.

When people talk about the toxic influence of journalism, they generally mean the salacious intrusions and excesses of the tabloids. If he had been around today, Bagehot would have subscribed to Hacked Off. In his own time, he was grateful that 'our newspapers do not lift the veil of private life; they do not tell the inner weakness of public men or the details of their "habit as they live".' Thank heavens, for 'an incessant press dealing with real personalities would sicken its readers and would drive sensitive men from public life.' Alas, readers' stomachs and the sensibilities of would-be public men have turned out to be made of tougher stuff.

But the higher journalism that Bagehot did so much to pioneer is not without its downside. For again and again, it has turned out to be the higher journalism, as practised by, say, the *Economist*, the BBC and *The Times,* which has been deaf to the deeper passions of men and failed to grasp the enduring force of attachment to nationality and religion and the unquenched thirst for equality. The most potent resentments at work in Europe today are those provoked by inequality, mass immigration and the incursions of the European Union. And they are precisely those with which the elite media are most reluctant to engage. We can be sure, I think, that Bagehot too would have pooh-poohed these concerns as outdated prejudices of the coarse, contracted masses. He tells us, quite early on, that he had resolved as a young man 'to take this world lightly'. The trouble is that so many people will insist on taking it seriously.

LORD ROSEBERY:
THE PALM WITHOUT THE DUST

The schoolmaster William Johnson is remembered for three things, although not under that name. He wrote the most famous of all translations from Greek lyric verse, 'They told me, Heraclitus, they told me you were dead'; he wrote the words of the 'Eton Boating Song'; and in a letter to Francis Warre-Cornish, another Eton schoolmaster, he wrote of his pupil, the future Lord Rosebery: 'I would give you a piece of plate if you would get that lad to work; he is one of those who like the palm without the dust.' Ten years later, Johnson was sacked for fondling one pupil too many and changed his name to Cory. After his death, Warre-Cornish published his old friend's letters and journals. Unfortunately, the collapse of Rosebery's administration after only fifteen months was all too fresh in people's minds and Johnson/Cory's verdict stuck. No other prime minister in British history has surrendered power quite so limply, none more ignominiously except Anthony Eden after Suez.

Like Eden, Rosebery was a golden boy (both were made foreign secretary at the age of thirty-eight). Adoring crowds followed him throughout his career. Leo McKinstry in this excellent new biography makes a case for him being the first modern celebrity (but what about Nelson?). The music halls rang to the words: 'Nearly everyone knows me, from Smith to Lord Rosebery, / I'm Burlington Bertie from Bow.' His daughter Peggy's wedding drew crowds almost as big as for the Queen's jubilees. Thousands of spectators wore primroses as a gesture to the family name. The *London Evening News* printed its afternoon editions on primrose paper. Margot Asquith said that 'when the Prince of Wales went up the aisle, he was a nobody compared to Rosebery.' Until 1951 the Scottish football team would often turn out in primrose and rose hoops, the racing colours of Rosebery, who was their honorary president. Long after his ill-fated premiership, well-wishers from Edward VII downwards wanted him to come back and could not stop wondering what he would do next. In H. G. Wells's *The Time Machine*, one of the first questions the sceptical journalist asks the Time Traveller is: 'These chaps here say you have been travelling into the middle of next week! Tell us all about little Rosebery, will you?'

He had it all and was famous for having it all. As a young man touring America, he was said to have boasted that he had three ambitions: to marry an heiress, to win the Derby and to become prime minister (McKinstry can't decide whether this story is apocryphal – after all, Rosebery was supposed to have been speaking at the Mendacious Club in Washington). He overfulfilled his programme, winning the Derby three times and marrying not just any old heiress but Hannah de Rothschild, who brought him Mentmore, that vast treasure house in the Vale of Aylesbury, designed by Paxton of Crystal Palace fame on much the same scale and brimming with booty from Versailles and the Doges' Palace. According to Henry James, Hannah was 'large, coarse, Hebrew-looking, with hair of no particular colour and personally unattractive' (ah, the exquisite sensibility of the novelist), but he had to concede that she was good-natured, sensible and kind, and the twelve years she and Rosebery had together were the happiest of his life. She died of typhoid in 1890. Rosebery was never quite the same and never married again.

Was he gay? McKinstry doesn't think so; others do and go on about it, though without much reliable evidence, since the principal witnesses for the gay thesis are the notorious forger and fantasist Edmund Backhouse and the homophobe Lord Queensberry, who tried without success to rope him into the Wilde scandal. Rosebery might have married Princess Victoria, Edward VII's shy middle daughter, if her parents had not objected so violently – the only occasion on which he was found to be not grand enough. But then again he might not. My guess is that, in later life anyway, he would have preferred a book and a decanter to sex of any sort. Those who believe that hypersensitivity to personal criticism is proof of homosexual leanings have not met enough politicians. Apart from Mentmore, Rosebery also had Dalmeny, a Victorian Gothic palace on the Firth of Forth, plus the ancient fortress of Barnbougle in its grounds, which he restored and used as a retreat from his weekend guests (one weekend he appeared at Dalmeny only once, to fetch a penknife from the library); the Durdans, a much-loved low rambling lodge at Epsom for the racing; a town house in Berkeley Square; a fabulous villa on the Bay of Naples; and a couple of large shooting lodges in Norfolk and Midlothian. When his horse Ladas II was running in the Derby, he hired a special train to bring the colt and his attendants from Newmarket to Epsom. When the horse won, the crowd went wild. The next day at the Durdans Lord Rosebery stood on his head on the hearthrug.

In short, Rosebery was spoilt. Everyone said he was spoilt. Margot Asquith, who had once been in love with him, said: 'Selfish is too small a word for him. His selfishness is colossal ... He cannot get away from himself.' Rosebery wallowed in this reputation, challenging his friends to say whether they thought him a spoilt child and recording in his diary instances of his indulgences: 'Did a selfish thing for dinner. Drank some '48 claret alone.' At the same time, like many sybarites, he was drenched in self-pity, deploring the emptiness of a life of pleasure and, looking back, saw his existence as a dark tunnel. Simplicity of life was the only answer, but one not adopted at Mentmore, where, as that waspish paedophile Loulou Harcourt claimed, 'truffles seem to be treated here much as potatoes elsewhere.'

It was not just that Rosebery had always had his own way and 'never learned to obey', as A. G. Gardiner put it in his famous pen portrait. He also had a suspicious, prickly nature and bore grudges for an eternity. After Lewis Carroll reported him to the dean of Christ Church for bunking off a maths lecture, Rosebery refused to read *Alice in Wonderland* for nearly thirty years. Of these traits, too, he was well aware. In claiming (mendaciously?) never to have had the slightest ambition to be prime minister, he asserted: 'I realised long ago, in 1895, my unfitness for office. I am not sufficiently pliant, patient or accommodating.' He held a celebration dinner at the Durdans every year on the anniversary of the vote which brought his government down. The fact that his administration fell on such a trivial issue as whether the army had sufficient reserves of cordite (which it had) shows how feeble was its will to survive.

True, he had difficult colleagues: Gladstone by now querulous, rambling, half-blind, looking like a witch in his dark goggles, 'that crazed old man Merrypebble', as the Queen called him; Lord Granville, alternately known as 'Pussy' or 'Granny', whose bladder was so weak he had to have a chamberpot kept in the cabinet room; Sir William 'Jumbo' Harcourt, bullying, umbrageous, foul-tempered, egged on by his endlessly conspiring son Lewis, 'Loulou', when he was not chuckling over his collection of child pornography, said to be the largest in the country. Then there was the Queen, who in old age was less inclined than ever to acknowledge that she was supposed to be a constitutional monarch: 'I urged Lord Rosebery not to bring too many matters before the cabinet as nothing was decided there and it would be better to discuss everything with me and Mr Gladstone.' She repeatedly conspired with Lord Salisbury to unseat the Liberals. As for the speech from the throne, she refused point-blank to read out Rosebery's proposals for disestablishing the Church in Scotland and Wales. What a crew. But then cabinets are always full of duds and malcontents and intriguers, and any prime minister who hopes to survive must simply push on regardless. But Rosebery could do nothing regardless. The strains of office made his chronic insomnia insupportable without vast doses of morphine, not to mention draughts of porter in the middle of the night. Even then he could not sleep and would go for midnight drives, first by carriage and later by car, knocking up his chauffeur at all hours. It is piquant to think of those two drugged insomniacs, Archie Rosebery and Marcel Proust, simultaneously barrelling through the night, comforted by the moonlight and the scent of the blossom in the hedgerows.

McKinstry gives us painstaking (but never dull) blow-by-blow accounts of the endless manoeuvrings to persuade Rosebery to accept first the Foreign Office under Gladstone and then the premiership. Ambitious men who themselves would not have hesitated a nanosecond before accepting either office spent weeks trying to coax him to swallow his protestations of unfitness. Even in finally agreeing to serve as foreign secretary, he insisted on telling Gladstone: 'I have absolutely no experience of the Foreign Office, which I have never entered except to attend a dinner. My French is I fear rusty.' (This was quite untrue.) 'I have never had to face anything like what you would call hard work. I have no knowledge of diplomatic practice or forms and little of diplomatic men. And I am sensible of many deficiencies of temper and manner.' Never has British self-deprecation been taken to such extreme lengths. Why then did they all try so hard to get him, considering that he had never stood for election to the House of Commons, let alone sat in it? That remains the fascinating question, and in answering it McKinstry not only unravels the supposed mystery of Rosebery but also sheds a raking light on the impending death of Liberal England.

The first thing is that Rosebery was a terrific public orator. In cabinet or the House of Lords, he came across as nervous and pernickety. But on a platform before an audience of thousands, he blossomed. His strong melodious voice, his dark hypnotic eyes (all the more hypnotic after a hefty dose of Sulfonel), his air of mysterious gravity relieved now and then by a bubbling up of flippancy which the Queen did not care for ('in his speeches out of Parliament, he should take a more serious tone and be, if she may say so, less jocular which is hardly befitting a prime minister. Lord Rosebery is so clever that he may be carried away by a sense of humour, which is a little dangerous') – all this combined to produce an effect which never left the minds of the thousands who had queued for tickets to one of his set-pieces. Augustine Birrell added that 'a certain nervousness of manner, that suggested at times the possibility of a breakdown, kept his audience in a flutter of nervousness and excitement.' He might have been talking about Judy Garland.

Some of his old friends found his speaking technique stagey and contrived. Margot Asquith describes him 'waving his little short arms à la Gladstone, resting a very round waist across the desk and coming down with an almighty crashing fist on the words "Chinese labour"'. Lord Randolph Churchill warned him: 'Don't think you're going to terrify me with that poached-egg eye of yours.'

But most people thought him the most interesting speaker they had ever heard. McKinstry says that 'what was particularly sad about Rosebery's oratorical prowess was that he took absolutely no pleasure in it' and regarded it as one of the most tiresome chores of the political life. But surely this was one of his many affectations. He took enormous trouble over his speeches and never turned down an invitation if it suited his book. He could communicate with a mass audience in an almost intimate style that he could seldom manage with his peers. Like some men who are famous for being aloof and solitary (de Gaulle, for example), he positively loved crowds, rarely missing a Cup final and on the night of the Diamond Jubilee taking a four-hour bain de foule in the streets of Central London, delighting to be an anonymous celebrant. Rosebery was fascinated by the techniques he had seen in operation at the American Democratic Convention of 1873, and borrowed many of them when he persuaded Gladstone to stand for Midlothian and organized his campaign – for example, the whistlestop speaking tour from the back of an American-designed Pullman car. He insisted too that Gladstone's daughter Mary appear on the platform, another requirement that was to become standard in mass politics. He always loved the democratic vitality of the United States and on his return found England 'miserably smoky and narrow', because it was so class-bound.

This zest for the modern helped to give Rosebery his huge public appeal. When he became prime minister, he not only had Granny's chamberpot removed, he installed electric lighting in Downing Street (resisted by Gladstone) and insisted on typewriters being used for official correspondence (resisted by the Queen). His alertness to the coming thing was not mere gadget mania. He took the advent of democratic local politics with a seriousness his colleagues found hard to comprehend. He was as diligent a first chairman of the London County Council as he had been a lackadaisical prime minister, attending over 300 meetings in his first year of office. The dockers' leader, Ben Tillett, also an LCC councillor, remarked: 'he really made London government a living thing.'

Tories like F. E. Smith and Austen Chamberlain complained that Rosebery could never make up his mind completely on any subject. On the contrary, when it came to policy rather than politicking, Rosebery was usually consistent and often far-sighted. Although he was a confessed Liberal Imperialist, he had a decided view of the proper limits of Empire, and he was remarkably cool and resolute during his two brief spells as foreign secretary. British interests had to be defended and Britain's position made clear beyond any possibility of misunderstanding, but 'we cannot afford to be the knight errant of the world.' He did have a weakness for Cecil Rhodes and played a dubious role in the Jameson Raid – though not as dubious as Joe Chamberlain – but he had sense enough to see that imperial preference was a non-runner. At the same time, he never lost sight of traditional balance-of-power considerations in Europe. He was one of the very few public figures to come out against the Entente Cordiale: 'You are all wrong. It means war with Germany in the end!' Having an informed view of Germany's growing economic and military might, he began to warn of the horrors that such a war would bring long before it was on the public horizon. Is it fanciful to imagine that if Rosebery had accepted office in Asquith's cabinet and managed to stick it out, he might have steered Europe away from war? I fear it is, because Rosebery's prescience was inseparable from his independence. His unwillingness to compromise was the obverse of his freedom from wishful thinking.

But it was in domestic affairs that his prescience was most marked. He saw that no modernizing Liberal programme had any chance of success until the House of Lords was reformed – he wanted a mixture of life peers, hereditaries and ex-officio members not unlike what we have today. He came to believe that the old Liberal Party was drawing to its end, and years before the formation of the Labour Party feared that the elimination of liberalism would leave 'the two forces of reaction face to face'.

In his groping for what we would now call a Third Way between high-taxing socialism and laissez-faire Toryism, he was lured into some *sottises* that have become familiar. He began to hanker for an iron-willed dictator and a cabinet composed entirely of businessmen – though when he did come into contact with an iron-willed businessman in the shape of Alfred Harmsworth (later Lord Northcliffe) he found the experience discomfiting. Rosebery refused Harmsworth's peremptory instruction to deliver a series of ten big speeches against tariff reform, and so the press baron, in true Lord Copper style, went over to the other side and began boosting Chamberlain.

In his obsession with 'national efficiency', Rosebery also started
burbling about 'the need for a model race' to halt 'the physi-
cal degeneracy of our people' – a curious echo of his short-lived
father's only recorded effusion, 'An Address to the Middle Classes
on the Subject of Gymnastics'. Partly through his old acquaintance
Beatrice Webb, he dallied with the Fabians and even sipped at their
poisonous brew of eugenics. He had long believed that 'the over
and reckless production of children is debasing our race'. All this
came poorly from someone who was now conspicuously tubby
after a lifetime of truffles and claret. Edmund Gosse described
Rosebery, not yet sixty, in horrific terms: 'The flesh is so puffy and
thick on his cheeks, and his eye-orbits so deep, that it looks as if he
had a face over his face. His colour is unhealthy, a dull, deep red.'

But these lapses can perhaps be forgiven, when set against Rose-
bery's abiding virtue, which was to pay attention to the facts of
late-Victorian society and to consider the possible consequences
for public policy. Even though his actual time in office was so brief
and his official achievements so meagre, his influence on events
from the margin was considerable. By insisting as his price for
joining the government in the first place that there be established a
minister for Scotland, which almost nobody in the cabinet wanted,
certainly not Gladstone, he unleashed a long process of devolution
which arguably saved Scotland for the Union, just as Home Rule in
Ireland might have saved thousands of lives, though perhaps not the
British connection, if only the House of Lords had not stood in the
way. In the end, it was Rosebery's intervention in favour of Lloyd
George's People's Budget (which he actually detested) that saved it
and saved George V from having to flood the Upper House with
new peers. He was besides an untiring champion of better work-
ing conditions, the minimum wage and trade-union rights. After
he had successfully arbitrated in a miners' strike – the first cabinet
minister to attempt such a role – he was so delighted that he said
'this would have been a good day to die on.' His initial opposition
to the People's Budget was much derided at the time. In opposing

a budget that raised income tax and death duties and introduced a land tax and a supertax on high incomes, was he not revealing his real allegiances, to his class and his unearned income?

Yet his anxieties about the ever-increasing role of the state do not seem quite so blinkered and selfish today, not least in education: 'the lesson of our Scottish teaching was "level up"; the cry of modern teaching is "level down"; "let the government have a finger in every pie", probing, propping, disturbing. Every day the area of initiative is being narrowed, every day the standing ground for self-reliance is being undermined.' Easy enough for him to say, who never had to rely on anything but a steady flow of rents and dividends. Yet just as with Gladstone, people felt that he was saying something that could make a difference to their lives, even if they were not always sure what it was. There was a serious vein in him which throbbed all the more thrillingly because it was encased in such a glittering carapace. He was a Scottish Kennedy or Roosevelt, without their hunger for office.

By the time he was sixty, he had taken to calling himself 'a well-preserved corpse'. But as hypochondriacs often do, he lived on to a good old age. In accordance with his wishes, he breathed his last to the sound of Cory's 'Boating Song' on the gramophone. Perhaps someone should have recited Cory's threnody for Heraclitus too. The line 'Still are thy pleasant voices, thy nightingales, awake' would have made a great epitaph for such a melodious insomniac.

ARTHUR BALFOUR:
A FATAL CHARM

On a cycling holiday in Scotland, A. C. Benson went to meet Arthur Balfour at Whittingehame. The prime minister was out practising on his private golf course. They saw him 'approaching across the grass, swinging a golf club – in rough coat and waistcoat, the latter open; a cloth cap, flannel trousers; and large black boots, much too heavy and big for his willowy figure. He slouched and lounged as he walked. He gave us the warmest greeting, with a simple and childlike smile which is a great charm.' Even across the width of a fairway, the author of 'Land of Hope and Glory' was already melting under the impact of A. J. B. Lord Vansittart, a junior at the Foreign Office when Balfour was foreign secretary, confessed that he found it 'hopeless to avoid devotion'. The secret of Balfour's charm was his nonchalance. Staying cool seemed to be his only rule. Vansittart thought that he viewed events 'with the detachment of a choirboy at a funeral service'. Almost alone among politicians, he was indifferent to what his colleagues, the public or posterity thought of him or his policies. He kept no diary, made no attempt to preserve his papers.

His sloth was legendary too. He seldom appeared before 11 a.m., though as First Lord of the Admiralty before the Battle of Jutland he did consent to be called at nine. As a young MP, it was only when his third session in the House loomed that he showed up, spurred on by his Aunt Georgie Salisbury's chiding that it was time to show some 'overt signs of parliamentary activity'. He claimed never to read the newspapers, made no effort to get to know his backbenchers or to frequent the Members' Dining Room and Smoking Room, and refused to stay on the front bench until the end of Question Time. In any case, he had such a wretched memory for names that he would not have remembered whom he had met or been listening to.

But he had an endless appetite for the lighter pleasures. He never refused an invitation and would play after-dinner games with the Souls deep into the night or would entertain them on one of his four concertinas. He was sports mad, startling Gladstone by turning up at Hawarden on his bicycle, missing lunch with the Kaiser in order to see the Eton and Harrow cricket match and throwing bread rolls with deadly accuracy at the Lyttelton dinner table. When in Scotland he liked to play two rounds of golf a day, to keep his handicap down to ten (about the same as Ian Fleming and better than P. G. Wodehouse). On the links at North Berwick, when he made a bad shot, he would turn away and gaze over the Forth and then turn round again, smiling. At times he sounds like a fully paid-up member of the Drones Club.

No one, after all, was better equipped to live a life of a sporting fainéant: he had inherited 180,000 acres at Whittingehame from his grandfather, a nabob who had secured the Admiralty contract for provisioning all ships of the Royal Navy in Indian waters. Yet A. J. B. led the Unionist Party for longer than anyone before him since Pitt the Younger. He was a minister for longer than anyone else in the twentieth century, even Churchill. He was the only Unionist invited to join Asquith's first war cabinet, and he continued in the government as foreign secretary after the coup that brought Lloyd George to power. Churchill commented sourly: 'He passed from one cabinet to the other, from the prime minister who was his champion to the prime minister who had been his most severe critic, like a powerful, graceful cat walking delicately and unsoiled across a rather muddy street.' Twenty years after Balfour had ceased to be prime minister, and by then in his late seventies, Baldwin sought him out to shore up his fragile government. He remained indispensable to the last.

Yet, if brutally summarized, the concrete results of his efforts can only seem pitiful. He fought three general elections as party leader and lost them all. The premiership he had inherited from his uncle, Lord Salisbury, almost as a family heirloom, lasted less than four years and ended in the Liberal landslide of 1906, the greatest electoral humiliation for the Conservatives until 1997. At that election, he became the only prime minister in the twentieth century to lose his own seat. Some, like Curzon, maintained that Balfour's sloth was partly a pose and that he was in fact a hardworking and capable minister. Yet with suspicious regularity his policies came to pieces in his hands or in the hands of his successors or even, as his ministerial career was so long, when the pieces were back in his hands again. His first impulses were often borrowed or dictated by more powerful wills than his own.

As Irish secretary, he obeyed to the letter the priorities of his Uncle Salisbury: 'The severity must come first. They must "take a licking" before conciliation will do them any good.' For the Irish, he became indelibly 'Bloody Balfour' as a result. Like many mild-tempered men, Balfour thrilled to the smack of firm government and was not averse to taking a hand in the smacking. No doubt something needed to be done to restore the rule of law as well as to meet the piteous plight of the peasants in the west of Ireland, but there was no need to say, as Balfour did, 'I shall be as relentless as Cromwell in enforcing obedience to the law' – a bit like George Bush describing the invasion of Iraq as a crusade. Balfour's land reforms in Ireland lived on after him; he claimed that 'the Ireland the Free State took over was the Ireland that we made.'

Yet the legacy of his insensitivity lived on too. At times, it seems, he simply did not think hard enough about political choices and their consequences. He did not have to fight for his own interests – his waspish sister-in-law Lady Frances Balfour said: 'Arthur's opportunities were all made for him' – and he found it hard to imagine that those less fortunate would fight for theirs. He told his sister Evelyn Rayleigh that 'his mind did not naturally turn to politics. He never thought about them in bed, which was the test.' Unlike the great platform orators such as Rosebery and Churchill, his speeches tended to be delivered spontaneously with little preparation, with the result that they were often too long and flawed by digression and tangled argument. He was unwilling to campaign for his own leadership or for his policies to be seen in a better light. After the Battle of Jutland, the Kaiser was quick to declare a German victory, although it was the German fleet which had fled, never to venture out again. The First Lord of the Admiralty declared nothing at all. Only after several ambiguous official communiqués was there a more forthright and upbeat report, drafted at Balfour's request by his predecessor Winston Churchill. One may disapprove of spin, but there are limits. Balfour's teacher at Eton, William Johnson, author of the 'palm-without-the-dust' dissing of the boy Rosebery, described Balfour as 'fearless, resolved and negligently great'. The sting is in the 'negligently'.

Balfour (1848–1930) and Rosebery (1847–1929) were nearly exact contemporaries. They were both huge landowners in the Lothians, both hypochondriacs, famously charming, subject to fits of indolence, lovers of motor cars and all modern gadgets, believers in popular democracy and votes for women – though decidedly odd in their relations with them. Naturally, they hated each other. When Rosebery became prime minister, Balfour said that he was unaware of any particular quality that Rosebery had demonstrated save a talent for self-advertisement. Rosebery said that Balfour had done wonderfully well 'for an amateur politician'. In 1911, Balfour cautioned the Palace against awarding the Order of Merit to Rosebery. Five years later, Rosebery bitterly opposed Balfour's OM. It is perhaps over the top for R. J. Q. Adams to subtitle *Balfour*, '*The Last Grandee*', with Rosebery lurking up the Firth of Forth getting steadily fatter and redder in the face, while Balfour remained lithe and bonny on his thirty-six holes a day. But Adams gives us a worthy companion piece to Leo McKinstry's *Rosebery*, just as readable and equally sure-footed on the politics – he is the biographer of Bonar Law and a historian of British domestic and foreign policy from 1890 to 1945.

Balfour: The Last Grandee may perhaps lack the intimate charm of Max Egremont's biography of 1980, which first untangled the scant skeins of Balfour's love life, but in its lucid, generous and unobtrusive fashion, it offers readers everything they need to form a judgment on this baffling character. Adams's reluctance to be censorious may lead the reader to make that judgment sterner than it would have been. One of Balfour's grounds for despising Rosebery was that he regarded himself as a serious philosopher and writer, while Rosebery was merely a lightweight fatally addicted to the vulgar pleasures of the turf. Balfour presented himself as a curious mixture of Bertie Wooster and Bertie Russell.

Certainly, no British prime minister has been more at the centre of a genuinely intellectual circle. His brothers-in-law were Lord Rayleigh, who became head of the Cavendish Laboratory and won the Nobel Prize in Physics, and Henry Sidgwick, the Cambridge philosopher who with his wife Eleanor Balfour founded Newnham College. In 1896, he joined his brothers-in-law, along with James Bryce, G. K. Chesterton, R. B. Haldane and Sir Oliver Lodge in founding the Synthetic Society, which, in an age of waning faith, set out to contribute towards a working philosophy of religious belief. A decade earlier, several of the same cast had joined Balfour in founding the Society for Psychical Research. While claiming to be sceptical about the ectoplasm and the furniture-moving, Balfour never lost his taste for séances and lapped up messages from the astral plane. On his deathbed, he was happy to receive Mrs Willett, his brother Gerald's favourite medium, who immediately announced that the room 'was full of presences' and two days later made contact with the spirits of several departed Souls of whom Balfour had been fond, especially May Lyttelton. Mrs Willett told Balfour that May had sent a message: 'Tell him he gives me joy.' Balfour murmured that he was profoundly impressed. Compared with all this, Tony Blair's fear that he might be thought 'a nutter' for taking an interest in religion seems rather tame. Yet one wonders how deeply committed to any of it Balfour really was. In his writings he could be eloquent about man's desolation in an indifferent universe. The famous passage in his *Foundations of Belief* still makes you shiver:

> Man, so far as natural science by itself is able to teach us, is no longer the final cause of the universe, the Heaven-descended heir of all the ages. His very existence is an accident, his story a brief and transitory episode in the life of one of the meanest of the planets ... after a period, long compared with the individual life, but short indeed compared with the divisions of time open to our investigation, the energies of our system will decay, the glory of the sun will be dimmed, and the earth, tideless and inert, will no longer tolerate the race which has for a moment disturbed its solitude. Man will go down into the pit, and all his thoughts will perish. The uneasy consciousness, which in this obscure corner has for a brief space broken the contented silence of the universe, will be at rest. Matter will know itself no longer. 'Imperishable monuments' and 'immortal deeds', death itself, and love stronger than death, will be as though they had never been.

This grim scenario was only a prelude to the argument already rehearsed in his *Defence of Philosophic Doubt* and his opening paper to the Synthetic Society: that natural science on its own could not explain or underpin man's sense of morality, beauty and reverence. Yet he conceded so much to evolutionary processes – their ability to generate altruism, for example – that his faith in a First Cause seems a bit pallid and residual. It sustained him, nonetheless, as an easy-going communicant in both the Presbyterian and Anglican Churches all his life. If there was a fundamental pessimism lurking beneath his blithe exterior, it does not seem to have troubled him much. He was happy whistling in the dark.

There was, though, a rather unnerving contrast between his appetite for dwelling on large speculative questions of philosophy and religion and his rather cursory attention to questions of long-term political and economic strategy (as opposed to short-term tactics, at which he was as adroit as he was on the putting green). As a young man, he liked to claim that he was prey to hopeless indecision and could never decide whether to descend from the first floor by the left or by the right of the two great staircases of his London house. What was so damaging was his affectation that political decisions might ultimately matter just as little. When his party was torn apart by the dispute over tariff reform, he infuriated both factions by making it clear that he did not care much either way. When it came to Lloyd George's People's Budget of 1909, Balfour was initially prepared to accept that the House of Lords for the first time in two centuries might throw out a budget that had been passed by a huge margin in the Commons; then he energetically sought to resolve the ensuing crisis by inviting their lordships to back down. The budget he had denounced as unconstitutional suddenly seemed to be constitutional after all, and it was the lords themselves who were behaving unconstitutionally.

This ability to see both sides of the question but to see nothing important in either of them could result in his announcing contradictory aims in the same sentence without a blush, for example in the so-called 'Valentine Letter' of 14 February 1906 to Austen Chamberlain, in which Balfour asserted that 'the establishment of a moderate general tariff on manufactured goods, not imposed for the purpose of raising prices or giving artificial protection against legitimate competition, and the imposition of a small duty on foreign corn, are not in principle objectionable.' But what other purpose or result could these new taxes conceivably have? Not surprisingly, this facing-both-ways didn't even succeed in warding off his prime fear, that of splitting the Tories. 'I cannot become another Robert Peel in my party,' he moaned. Well, the party split anyway, and unlike Peel, Balfour had achieved nothing.

In the same way, the declaration for ever associated with his name, which derived from his long-standing friendship with Chaim Weizmann, contained irreconcilable contradictions within its final wording: it called for the 'establishment in Palestine of a national home for the Jewish people', but at the same time, Edwin Montagu and Curzon, who knew what they might be in for, were to be placated by the rider that 'nothing shall be done which may prejudice the civil and religious rights of existing non-Jewish communities in Palestine, or the rights and political status enjoyed by Jews in any other country.' Balfour saw no looming conflict, and even ten years later, having in the meantime been cheered by Jewish settlers in Jerusalem and rescued by French cavalry from an angry mob in Damascus, he still maintained that 'nothing has occurred during that period to suggest the least doubt as to the wisdom of this new departure.'

As for Ireland, in 1916 Lloyd George said that in the cabinet 'Bloody Balfour' fought for the new settlement 'as if he had been a Home Ruler all of his life'.

Even when he saw clearly, he seldom saw steadily. 'If Constantinople fell,' Adams imagines him reasoning when it was first suggested that the slaughter on the Western Front could be shortened by a diversion to the East, in particular by an attack on the Dardanelles, 'who would then possess it and control the Bosporus? For that matter, would a campaign to topple Turkey, or a successful Russian assault in the East, really "finish the war"? Might it not be "regarded as merely subsidiary", inflicting its wounds but leaving Germany undefeated and the Western Front essentially as it was?' Yet, little by little, more passionate advocates like Churchill wore him down, and by the end of the tragic venture he was the last man in the cabinet arguing against the evacuation of the Gallipoli peninsula.

He accused his successor as prime minister, the Liberal Sir Henry Campbell-Bannerman, of being a 'mere cork, dancing on a torrent which he cannot control'. But the same could just as well be said of himself. After following Balfour through some of his serpentine manoeuvres, one often feels like echoing Campbell-Bannerman's exasperation: 'The Right Honourable Gentleman comes back to this new House of Commons with the same airy graces – the same subtle dialectics – and the same light and frivolous way of dealing with great questions. I say . . . enough of this foolery.'

It was impossible ever quite to pin Balfour down. He was as flirtatious and elusive as Cherubino. In his youth he had always been a pet. To Randolph Churchill and the young bloods of the 'Fourth Party', he was 'Postlethwaite'; to the Souls he was 'Adored Gazelle'. Charm he had in abundance, but more than charm he would not give. In responding to (and returning) a love letter from Mary Elcho (née Wyndham), he said: 'I do not regret that I said nothing in my last epistle of the kind which perhaps you wished. Such things are impossible to me.' Echoes here of his contemporary Henry James, allegedly, to Hugh Walpole: 'I can't, I can't.' In another letter, he wrote: 'Whether I have time for *Love* or not, I certainly have no time for *Matrimony*.' He was, nonetheless, expected to marry May Lyttelton, and was described as being 'staggered to the last degree' by her death from typhoid at the age of twenty-five. Yet there is no hint in any of his or May's letters of any such attachment or plan. He was often deeply upset by the death of his friends, and was always glad to hear news of them from the Other Side.

Naturally, he was said to be quite sexless. Beaverbrook said: 'Balfour was a hermaphrodite. No one ever saw him naked.' Not quite true: though he usually dictated in his dressing gown, he would sometimes do so in his bath. For most of his adult life he enjoyed what was at the least an *amitié amoureuse* with Mary Elcho, but she wrote sadly after thirty years of it: 'I'll give you this much, tho, for although you have only loved me little yet I must admit you have loved me long.'

There are stray hints in their correspondence, always from her side, that they had paddled a little further together, perhaps in an unorthodox direction. In November 1911, just after he had resigned as party leader, she wrote: 'It seems to me a pretty tribute that upon yr attaining yr liberty a certain (white) slave should also be liberated. What think you?' In 1905, after seeing a play about a finishing school, she wrote: 'It reminded me, not that it in any way resembled it, of our school – the one I have aptly named and rather wittily named "the finishing school" – certainly, in many respects you gave that poor young girl a "liberal education" and left no regions of her little body! unexplored, after that night there will have been few surprises left for her.' Two years later: 'I must send you a valentine tonight . . . the Valentine objects are somewhat obscure – to the left is a birch rod, to the right a brush and a tin of squirting grease (smells of peppermint).' Perhaps we'll just leave it there.

It is not surprising, in view of her weird lover and her faithless husband, that Mary consented to be thrown to the ground in the most straightforward manner by the poet-lothario Wilfrid Scawen Blunt, her cousin twenty years her senior, who was leading Mary and her children on an expedition into the desert. As Irish secretary, Balfour had had Blunt jailed for nationalist agitation. Knowing of A. J. B.'s tendresse for Mary, the old goat may have derived extra satisfaction when he crept into her tent. Balfour was scarcely likely to compete with the words Blunt claimed he had whispered through the tent flap: 'It is the voice of my beloved that knocketh saying open to me, my sister, my love, my dove, my undefiled, for my head is filled with dew and my locks with the drops of the night.' I do think, though, in view of the track record, that Adams is being a little charitable when he protests that the Souls 'only occasionally lapsed (within the group, at any rate) into actual adultery'.

In the end, I am afraid, the charm is all that remains. On coming to the end of Balfour's almost interminable public life, I cannot help feeling a little like Anthony Blanche after going round Charles Ryder's exhibition: 'Charm is the great English blight. It does not exist outside these damp islands. It spots and kills anything it touches. It kills love; it kills art' – and it's not too good for Scotsmen either.

OUR STATESMEN

M arble and bronze are hopeless materials for the job. To model modern British statesmen, you need some fleshly substance. That latex foam they use for the *Spitting Image* puppets might be appropriate, with its rude, bungy, punchable quality. Anyone who looks into the outstanding political figures of the past century must be baffled by the complaint that the colour has gone out of politics. What bounders and bon viveurs most of them were. Lloyd George and Mosley and Eden were insatiable adulterers, Mosley in particular being an Olympic swordsman in every sense. Asquith and Roy Jenkins were not far behind in that department. As for their other appetites, twentieth-century statesmen – Asquith, Churchill, Healey, Jenkins – downed Homeric quantities of booze between them. Heath's gluttony, especially in his latter years, demanded Gillray's pencil. Macmillan, one of the few prime ministers to make even a pretence of piety, was at the same time no flincher from the glass, which is not surprising since he belonged to half-a-dozen West End clubs and virtually lived in them.

Perhaps we should forgive them their indulgences, for to be a British statesman throughout the twentieth century was to be on the receiving end of history. 'Events, dear boy, events' was Macmillan's famous, possibly apocryphal reply to someone who asked him what was the most important thing in politics. What a battering they all took. Several – Asquith, Churchill, Macmillan – made a fine show of being imperturbable, or unflappable as Supermac was described in his heyday, which was a terrific performance because he had undergone long-term treatment for depression and continued to throw up before making a big speech in Parliament.

The onslaught of hostile and untamable forces was relentless: the Irish Question which had bedevilled British governments since the 1870s and was to resurface no less bloodily in the late 1960s, the recurrent industrial unrest that boiled up in 1911 and lasted another seventy-odd years, the implacable rise of German militarism segueing into the rise of fascism, the implosion of the Liberal Party, the venomous quarrels within the Labour Party, which split twice within the period (and could well do so a third time), the communist threat at home and abroad. Two world wars, a general strike, a seemingly endless economic depression, or rather series of depressions between the wars, the virtual bankruptcy of the United Kingdom after the Second World War, and, partly as a result, the headlong break-up of the British Empire. These were huge and mostly terrible events which no individual politician could hope to master. Often all that could be done was to rescue as much as could be rescued from the debris and put a brave face on it.

Like many people who write about politics, I used to be pitiless about the inadequacies of our masters. But I now feel more inclined to salute the courage and charm with which these men usually met what was coming at them, their resourcefulness when they were so short of real resources, although I continue to log their absurdities and self-deceptions.

Then almost at the end of the period, a quite different character pops up: a woman to start with, puritanical by nature, with none of the ordinary vices, lacking in natural charm or much in the way of humour, lacking too that easy sociability which had sustained most of her predecessors, above all, more tenacious than they had dared to be and unwilling, as they had not been, to admit that history would get the better of her. She was lucky of course. She came along at a time when the overweening pretensions of the trade unions had exhausted public patience and the Soviet Empire was beginning to fall apart from within. Even so, her conspicuous triumphs – the Falklands and the miners' strike – were close-run. And from the beginning to the end of her time in office, half her colleagues were longing to see the back of her. What can be said is that she made the most of her luck, which is all that anyone can do. But I think it fair to say that the men who came before her were dealt poorer hands and played their cards as best they could.

MARGOT, ASQUITH
AND THE GREAT WAR

The Prince was walking up and down in silence. He caught me by the hands and said: 'Oh! say there is surely *not* going to be "warr" (pronouncing it like "far"). Dear, dear Mrs Asquith, can we not stop it?' (wringing his hands) ... 'I do not understand what has happened. What is it all about?'

Millions of people then and ever since have shared the bafflement and anguish of Prince Lichnowsky and have asked the same questions. If the Kaiser's ambassador to London, a warm Anglophile, felt so impotent and overwhelmed by events, no wonder the lightning onset of the Great War has remained the historical question of the last hundred years. Or rather questions, for following on the heels of 'How did it start, and why?' comes 'Could it have been prevented? – and if so, by whom?', 'Who was to blame?' and, for the British anyway, 'Could we have kept out of it?'

No other event has generated such an endless line of huge books, some reaching back to the Franco-Prussian War, others obsessively going over the last few days leading up to the declarations of war on 3 and 4 August. The pace of events is so hurtling, the outcome so tragic, that for all their length most of these books are impossible to put down, and accordingly tend to be received as magisterial masterpieces, although their conclusions may be utterly different from one another. The question is never laid to rest. The hunt goes on for the smoking gun, the killer fact (these often deployed metaphors being the worst possible in the circumstances).

Margot Asquith kept a diary for forty-seven years, off and on, starting when she was twelve years old. Yet it is only the two and a half years from July 1914 to Asquith's fall in December 1916 that Michael and Eleanor Brock have chosen to publish. Even within this period, they tell us, they have excluded most of her musings on her family, as well as lists of many of the guests she entertained so frenetically. On the other hand, the book is plumped out by the editors' introduction of 116 pages, mostly sketching the domestic and international background to the crisis and occupying nearly half as much space as the diary extracts themselves. Margot's journals too, it seems, are to be conscripted into the hunt for the truth about the war.

At first sight, this is an odd approach, for the Brocks never stop pointing out how ignorant she was, how crass, how deformed by snobbery (she insisted on Asquith shedding the last traces of his Yorkshire accent). Nor do they claim that she possessed an instinctive judgment to make up for her lack of formal education (she spent most of her youth on the hunting field, where she acquired her distinctive broken nose). She has no idea that Britain's army is only a third the size of Germany's, she thinks the war will be over in a year, then when it isn't, she bets Kitchener that it will be over in another six months. Like her husband, she fiercely opposes conscription, then admits she was wrong. In April 1916, she offers the bizarre reflection: 'I wonder if we have not got too big an army.' She sees no political future for Winston Churchill with his 'noisy mind' and childish egotism, and doubts whether Lloyd George will ever become prime minister (three months before he topples her husband). In fact, she starts a new volume of the diary at the end of July 1916 by claiming that

'Henry's position in the country and in the cabinet is stronger than it has ever been.'

Despite or partly because of all her defects, the diaries never cease to entertain, and they turn out to be remarkably enlightening too, if not always in the advertised way. Margot Tennant had always possessed the self-confidence and judgmental sweep of someone born to great wealth and social prominence. Her family were pioneers of chemical bleaching. The Tennant plant outside Glasgow was the largest chemical works in the world at the time, and its towering chimney was a famous landmark, known as Tennant's Stalk. Until her marriage at the age of thirty to the widowed Herbert Henry Asquith, she was proudest of her role as leader of the Souls. She thought that, for all their academic brilliance, Asquith's children by his first wife, Helen, were poor successors to her own coterie:

> The clever group of nowadays is very inferior to my clever group called 'Souls'. They are sexless and soulless, and so disloyal that they only hang together by a thread of mutual love of gossip and common capacity to say bright things, read bright and blasphemous novels, modern and very moderate poems (which crop up like weeds every day); and an unimpulsive, uninspired, dry desire to go against authority under the name of anti-cant.

Margot was a goose, but she was a hissing goose. While her judgments may not always be acute, they are almost always sharp. Of Mary Curzon, for example: 'The latter a very good type of decorative West End furniture – beautiful, silly, idle, and wonderfully, *amazingly* dull; always *saying* she is a fool and never minding it; never getting accustomed to her beauty, therefore never really interested in anything and with little or no power of admiration.' Mrs Asquith's arrogance is often staggering. She treats being the prime minister's wife as a sort of high constitutional office. When the Zeppelins raid London, she sends for the commissioner of the

Metropolitan Police to give her a personal report. When the government is under fire in the newspapers, she instructs the director of the government press bureau to make plans for suspending *The Times* and the *Daily Mail*. Her loathing of the reptiles rivals that of a later Downing Street consort, Denis Thatcher. 'I hate all journalists – it's a vile profession. Nothing is sacred; even corpses are copy.'

Her social energy and curiosity are so beguiling that at times one regrets the editors' exclusive focus on the war and begins to wish that they had listened to Margot's musing that it is possible that her 'children and great-grandchildren ... would rather read about the war in proper books, and hear from me of the kind of clothes and manners, foods and amusements of society than the perpetual political crises'.

Anne de Courcy's *Margot at War* is lighter in tone and lacks scholarly pretensions or apparatus. But it conveys Margot's milieu with a nice touch and takes time away from this enclosed self-regarding world to give us vivid and sharp vignettes of the harder times being experienced by other classes. De Courcy too records very well Margot's tortured jealousy, not only of her husband's dalliance with Venetia Stanley but of his daughter Violet's almost incestuous passion for her father. Not that Margot had any real grounds for complaint. She had, after all, been flirting with Asquith while Helen was still alive. He wrote to her: 'You have made me a different man and brought back into my life the feeling of spring time' – just the sort of stuff he wrote Venetia twenty years later. Margot quickly came to believe that Helen was 'no wife for him. She lives in Hampstead, and has no clothes.'

Yet Margot is anything but smug about herself. 'Hurting people's feelings seems to be my prevailing vice ... I am haunted by what Mama always said: "Dear Margot! She *never* improves."' She knows why she annoys people so much: 'Irritability, plus a very keen tongue, gets on other people's nerves, I find, and bores them ... It is really nerves and a devouring energy: I have several skins too few.' She was quite aware of how mocking her stepchildren were behind her back.

Nor has she any illusions about her fellow Edwardians. Her diatribe against the modern age in December 1914 anticipates almost everything that George Dangerfield was to describe two decades later in *The Strange Death of Liberal England*:

> There are a great many *very* rotten people in the London or England of today. This war has caught us at our worst. The Church never had less influence than it has today. Art is down – meaningless, grotesque pictures (cubists, Futurists, etc); invertebrate, washy, pretentious music (Debussy etc). Law is set at defiance – suffragettes, Carson's army (lives threatened, churches and gardens burned, pictures in galleries torn; the gentry of Ireland, the Court and the West End encouraging, advertising, promoting and expecting 'civil war'); the army cajoled, and here and there bribed, Field Marshals signing covenants against the King's Government, Generals asking for guarantees (Gough in the Curragh row). Politicians losing all sight of truth and courtesy, hurling the foulest charges against their enemy and using the ugliest language; cutting, forgetting and trying to oust all their oldest friends; and Society so flippant, callous, idle and blasphemous as to ultimately arouse in the Denis dénouement a storm of indignation and letters of protest from complete outsiders.

It is significant that the comble of this catalogue should be the callous behaviour of the river party that had left Denis Anson to drown. The party had included Lady Diana Manners (later to marry Duff Cooper) and Margot's stepson and daughter-in-law, Raymond and Katharine Asquith. Two years later, when Violet and her husband 'Bongie' Bonham Carter were laughing about Lloyd George's behaviour, Margot was reminded of 'that same laughter that rung down the river the night of the pleasure-party steamer when Denis Anson was drowned (the spectators went to bed and the opera while their friend's body was floating and unfound)'.

To the ferocity of her opinions, Margot added an unquestionable courage. She lost no time in going out to Belgium in December 1914, and gives as good a description as any war correspondent of what she saw:

> The Belgian trenches look very amateur to my unaccustomed eye. They are like rabbit hutches ... The whole country for miles around inundated with sea water and the roads where they are not *pavé* are swamps of clinging nasty mud on each side. The only dry fields are full of the holes of German shells like a solitaire board ... the houses are all smashed – avalanches of brick and window frames standing up in the walls like dolls' houses – no inhabitants, but soldiers smoking or cooking in the open doorways of less ruined houses. Every church – and some beautiful – littered with bits of bombs and debris of broken stained glass and twisted lead ribbons – tops of tombs, heads of stone saints, all pell mell in the grass of the cemeteries ... The Ypres cemetery will haunt me till I die. No hospital full of wounded ever gave me such an insight into war as that damp crowded quiet churchyard. Most of the names scrawled in pencil on bits of wood were English; where the names had been washed off their little forage caps hung on a stick ... A Tommy was digging a grave. Two English officers with their caps in their hands were looking at a grave, just covered.

By contrast, despite her pleas and those of the C-in-C, Sir John French, it was not until the end of May 1915 that Asquith himself visited the Front – one more indication of how wrong his wife was when she claimed that 'Henry was born for this war.'

The Brocks repeatedly tug our attention to Asquith's hopeless incapacity as a war leader. He failed to set up a War Council until three months had passed, nor did he set up any sort of secretariat for reporting the decisions of cabinet. He resisted conscription until forced to give in by a public and parliamentary outcry. He resisted coalition too, dreading the prospect of working with the coarse and mannerless Tories almost as much as he dreaded the war itself. Even when coalition too was forced on him, he did all he could to keep the Tory leader, Bonar Law, off the War Council, sharing every bit of Margot's disdain for Northern businessmen although they both came from that background.

Worst of all, though he was famous for his mastery of the House of Commons and his subtle and unflappable chairmanship in cabinet, he was utterly lacking in drive. Even his adoring daughter Violet was obliged to concede in October 1915 that 'I have felt sometimes lately as if his clutch hadn't got in – as if the full force of his mind was not in it and driving it forwards.' (Is this the first recorded use of the clutch metaphor?) The unaltered tenor of Asquith's life during the war brings to mind Hilaire Belloc's quatrain on the Liberal election triumph of 1906:

> The accursed power which stands on Privilege
> (And goes with Women, and Champagne, and Bridge)
> Broke – and Democracy resumed her reign:
> (Which goes with Bridge, and Women and Champagne).

As the casualty lists lengthened, so did the card games and the PM's drives through the Thames Valley with one of his 'little harem', hands entwined under the rug, or worse. The Brocks, who also edited Asquith's letters to Venetia, describe their tone as that 'of courtly rather than carnal love', an *amitié amoureuse*. The letters seem rather more erotically charged than that. It would be amazing if a man of Asquith's appetites had not insisted on physical liberties, at least up to the limit of prudence. He was, after all, a notorious groper, not safe in taxis or anywhere else. Anne de Courcy points out that of the 243 letters he wrote Venetia in 1914, more than half were sent after the outbreak of war. Asquith spills out his heart and military secrets in equal measure. What still seems shocking is how many were written during cabinet meetings, the most notorious being that of 13 January 1915, written during the all-day meeting of the War Council at which Churchill revealed his plans for a naval attack on the Dardanelles.

The duty to amuse oneself did not slacken with the approach of war. When Sir Edward Grey went to Number 10 with Haldane and Crewe bringing news of the German declaration of war on Russia, 'he found the PM and ladies playing bridge – and Lord Crewe said it was like playing on top of a coffin. They waited till they had finished – about an hour.' The same code applied on the Tory side. When some MPs went to haul Bonar Law back to London from a Thameside weekend party in order to denounce the government for its failure to support France, they had to sit on a grassy bank and wait until the Tory leader had finished his set of tennis.

Then, there was the drink. Margot denounces F. E. Smith for drinking too much, 'which is always ruinous to anyone'. She cannot have been unaware that her husband was lightly pickled a lot of the time and on a couple of occasions too soused to wind up a debate in the Commons. Not for nothing did George Robey, the Prime Minister of Mirth, warble: 'Mr Asquith says in a manner sweet and calm, / Another little drink won't do us any harm.' Churchill certainly matched Asquith glass for glass, but it is seldom recorded that he was incapable. Drink only made his speech more belligerent and oracular; Old Squiff became incoherent. This was an indolent, pleasure-loving elite, a clique of easy-going procrastinators. Asquith's famous 'wait and see' might be taken out of context, but it expressed an essential truth about him. When war came he was genuinely grief-stricken, like almost everyone else, and until the last few days had hoped to keep Britain out of it, again like almost everyone else. For it is clear that, though the British public soon rallied to the cause, the vast majority, contrary to the old myth, contemplated the prospect of war with deep foreboding. The supposed upbeat view, that it would all be over by Christmas, where voiced at all, was mostly to keep people's spirits up.

There was one notable exception to this universal gloom. Churchill wrote to his wife on 28 July: 'everything tends towards catastrophe and collapse. I am interested, geared-up and happy.' Lloyd George recalled that when he and Asquith were sitting in desperate silence in the cabinet room waiting for the British ulti-matum to Germany to expire, the double doors were flung open, and in bustled Churchill to tell them that he was about to send tele-grams to every British warship informing them that war had been declared and that they were to act accordingly: 'You could see he was a really happy man. I wondered if this was the state of mind to be in at the opening of such a fearful war as this.' Churchill's joie de vivre was undiminished as the slaughter intensified.

Then, as later, he was anxious not to be thought a warmonger. But his actions could not be erased from the record. It was the First Sea Lord, Prince Louis of Battenberg, acting on the wide discretion Churchill had given him, who had on 26 July ordered the fleet not to disperse after its exercises off Portland; and it was Churchill and Battenberg's orders (not brought before cabinet) on 28 July to take up war stations, followed by full mobilization on 1 August.

Not surprisingly, those historians who believe that the blame for the war should be spread among all the Great Powers have Churchill as their Exhibit A for Britain. 'The truth is that Churchill succumbed to a temptation to frogmarch events,' Douglas Newton declares in *The Darkest Days*. Newton's close-focus examination of events in Britain over the week leading up to war has an overt polemical intent: 'This book is meant to unsettle. It attacks the comforting consensus.' It is a myth that war was irresistible. The larger truth of the tragedy of 1914 is that the economic, political and diplomatic systems across Europe were defective, and all the Great Powers shared in these systemic defects – the New Imperial-ism, Social Darwinism, economic nationalism, ethnically conscious chauvinism, a creeping militarism that looted national treasuries, weak international institutions and a new popular press that debased political culture and poisoned the popular mind. The whole system was rotten, and 'the blunders of the German elite' can't be made to shoulder all the blame.

In *The Sleepwalkers*, Christopher Clark deploys on a grander scale and over a much longer timeframe essentially the same argument. 'The protagonists of 1914,' he writes at the end, 'were sleepwalkers, watchful but unseeing, haunted by dreams, yet blind to the reality of the horror they were about to bring into the world.' What was Britain's share in this collective catalepsy? Newton points out that in the run-up to the war Asquith's cabinet had a majority opposed to intervention and that when war broke out, four of its members resigned (there might have been more if Asquith had not exercised all his manipulative charms to keep the cabinet together). Nowhere else in Europe were there any such resignations. This neutralist mood was widely echoed by the public at large and by many newspapers.

Newton argues that Asquith and Grey had supplied the first fatal link in the chain by their secret naval collaboration with France, which firmed up the Entente Cordiale and was taken by the French as an implicit commitment to come to their aid. All this encouraged the pugnacious Poincaré to bolster France's alliance with Russia. Accordingly, the Germans had some reason to feel 'encircled' and to conclude that a 'preventive war' was the only option if they hoped to remain a great power, let alone become a greater one. A similar argument is to be found in Niall Ferguson's *The Pity of War* (1998), where he offers a relatively benign counterfactual alternative: if the First World War had never been fought, the worst consequence would have been something like a First Cold War, in which the five Great Powers continued to maintain large military establishments, but without impeding their own sustained economic growth. Alternatively, if a war had been fought, but without Britain and America, the victorious Germans might have created a version of the European Union, eight decades ahead of schedule. What the Pan-Germans dreamed of, in those hectic years before 1914, was a *stiller Führer* of Mitteleuropa – an Angela Merkel before her time.

These are beguiling scenarios, but they in their turn deserve a little interrogation. Suppose, to start with, that Churchill had let the British fleet disperse and the German navy had nipped in and steamed up the Channel to support an invasion of Belgium and Northern France. Would the First Lord not have been found guilty of feckless negligence? Suppose that Grey had refused to make anything concrete out of the Entente, not even a few joint naval exercises with the French, and had thereby encouraged the Germans to think that Britain would stay neutral in any Franco-German war. Why would that have deterred the German High Command from planning a war on two fronts? Suppose Prince Lichnowsky had secured from Grey the guarantee he sought on Saturday, 1 August: that Britain would undertake to remain neutral if Germany gave a promise not to violate Belgian neutrality. This was the conversation reported by Grey to the British ambassador in Berlin in the famous Document 123, which non-interventionists such as Bertrand Russell made much of when it was first published and which is still made much of today. Grey refused to give any such promise: 'I could only say that we must keep our hands free.'

Was this a fatal missed opportunity? It doesn't look much like one. First of all, Lichnowsky had no authority to launch that kite. France and Germany had both already been asked to guarantee the neutrality of Belgium: France had agreed, Germany had not, and was no more likely to do so now that its troops were already moving up through Luxembourg. Newton and Clark make even more of a further thought floated by Grey to Lichnowsky that same Saturday: that Britain would be happy to stay neutral if France and Germany could stay facing each other under arms without attacking each other. For a few hours that evening, the Kaiser wobbled frantically, attracted by the idea of confining hostilities to the East, but Moltke and the rest of the High Command soon argued him off it. The preparations for war on two fronts had gone too far to be called off.

In any case, whatever the inconsistencies and ambiguities of his policy, Grey was right when he said that he was in no position to guarantee Britain's neutrality. Here the political facts that both the diplomatic and the military historians tend to underplay have to be taken into account. Asquith's biographers, Roy Jenkins and Stephen Koss, both casually assert that Asquith 'won' three general elections. In our modern sense, he never won one. Campbell-Bannerman was the party leader at the Liberal landslide of 1906, and Asquith's two elections of 1910 both produced badly hung Parliaments, with almost identical results: the Liberals and the Conservatives each had between 271 and 274 seats, and the Liberals continued in office only with the support of the eighty-odd Irish MPs and the forty Labour members. With his effortless Balliol superiority, Asquith carried on as if he had a majority of a hundred. But his only way of surviving was to keep the Irish on side by delivering the Home Rule Bill, against the deepest instincts of many of his own members. The Curragh Mutiny of March 1914 showed just how badly the country was split over the Irish issue, encouraging Lichnowsky and others to report back that the British army might even refuse to fight a Liberal war.

Asquith's government was incurably fragile. If Grey had openly declared Britain's neutrality, the government would surely have fallen as soon as the Germans crossed the Belgian border, let alone the French one. A coalition dominated by the Conservatives, but led by Lloyd George, would have taken over. This isn't a what-if. It is what happened just over two years later. So it is extremely difficult to see how British neutrality could actually have come about. Nor, even then, is it clear that Britain with its 'contemptible' army (to use the Kaiser's unforgettable epithet) could have been a key influence in deterring the major land war that was breaking out at the other end of the Continent. These exercises in alternative history don't really allow us to escape from the same old questions about underlying German intentions. For fifty years the scene has been dominated by the arguments of Fritz Fischer and his school: that ever since Bismarck the Germans had been dreaming of a Mitteleuropa under German military and economic supremacy, with boundaries enlarged to allow German settlers to occupy lands in the East. Poland, the Baltic States, the Ukraine, Romania and Belgium would all be vassal states, controlled by if not formally annexed to the Greater Germany. According to Fischer, these aims were held consistently throughout the First World War, and shared by the diverse actors – the erratic Kaiser, the fanatic Moltke and the supple Bethmann-Hollweg. Large parts of the programme were actually realized at and after the Treaty of Brest-Litovsk, as a result of the collapse of Imperial Russia and Germany's support for Lenin and the Bolsheviks.

The second, inseparable part of Fischer's thesis is that most influential Germans believed that their country's legitimate aims could be achieved only by war, because it was encircled by the early starters in the race for empire. There would, as Moltke put it, have to be a final reckoning between Teuton and Slav. Naturally, the politicians would have to decide the timing, and the diplomats would have to present it as a defensive or preventive war, but war there would have to be. Thus the Schlieffen Plan for the war and the September Programme for the peace belonged together.

In the past few years, a reaction against Fischer has undoubtedly set in. Recent historians (Max Hastings's *Catastrophe* is an impressive exception) tend to find the anti-German colouring exaggerated. Many of them revert to the old orthodoxy of the 1920s and 1930s that everyone was to blame, that in Lloyd George's words, 'the nations slithered over the brink into the boiling cauldron of war without any apprehension or dismay ... not one of them wanted war, certainly not on this scale.' They have become re-revisionists.

On the whole, the re-revisionists tend to walk round Fischer rather than try a direct assault on his monument. Clark says merely that 'such arguments are not supported by the evidence.' Newton pays tribute to Fischer, but asks 'Why should Fischer's searing indictment of corrupting imperialism, delusional militarism, and the recklessness and vainglory of right-wing elites be confined to Germany? . . . Such men stalked the gilded rooms of power across Europe.' Really? Was there no difference at all in character, intention and humanity between Asquith, Grey and George V and the Kaiser and his circle?

Ferguson at least offers a more interesting argument: that Germany's megalomania developed only under the terrible pressures of the war. Fischer, he says, can produce no evidence that 'these objectives existed *before* Britain's entry into the war . . . All that Fischer can produce are the pre-war pipe dreams of a few Pan-Germans and businessmen, none of which had any official status, as well as the occasional bellicose utterances of the Kaiser, an individual whose influence over policy was neither consistent nor as great as he himself believed.' Well perhaps, but isn't it striking that the moment these pipe dreams were turned into official policy, only a month after war broke out, they captivated the German nation? By December, pretty much every professor in the country had signed up to the Manifesto of the 93 in support of Germany's war aims, a document which Clemenceau denounced as 'Germany's greatest crime'. Is it really plausible that this general enthusiasm for a Greater Germany had no deep pre-war roots?

The re-revisionists slide away from Fischer's shadow rather too easily. As a result, their pictures of Germany's internal politics, both before and during the war, can seem a little under-coloured. Newton is of course concentrating on Britain, but even so the Kaiser's occasional appearances as a clumsy but sincere peacenik scarcely do justice to his unpredictable ferocity. In Clark's superb panorama of European politics, the German background seems relatively faint, certainly by contrast to his vivid description of the Serbs and their obsessive crusade for a Greater Serbia. In the case of the Balkan Wars, Clark does not try to make out that the faults were evenly distributed, or that 'nobody wanted war.' The Serbs wanted a Greater Serbia and they were hot to fight for it. Clark demonstrates beyond any doubt that the murder of the Archduke Franz Ferdinand was no random outrage, but an operation carefully planned by the higher reaches of the Serbian security service, certainly including its chief, the notorious 'Apis', and no doubt with a nod from the elusive, unstoppable prime minister, Nikola Pašić. The assassination had two aims, and it achieved both: to remove a peace-loving heir to the throne who intended to conciliate the Serbs inside Austria-Hungary, and to foment a big war in which the Serbs could hope to gain or regain huge swathes of territory and incorporate into Serbia millions of Slavs who at present didn't even think of themselves as Serbs. The cost was terrible: between 1914 and 1919, the Serbs lost more than 60 per cent of their regular troops, and more than a million people in Serbia died of war, typhus and Spanish flu. The reward was the lead role in the new state of Yugoslavia. The obsession with Greater Serbia continued to exercise its malign hold, culminating in the terrible wars of the 1990s – the fifth Balkan Wars by some reckoning.

So there was certainly one venomously aggressive power at work in Central Europe. Might it not be reasonable to conclude that there were two and that the collision between them was what proved so fatal? What set off the wider chain of consequences was the harsh pressure that the Kaiser put on Franz Joseph to lose no time in launching a major retaliation for the assassination of his nephew. If the Serbs don't look much like sleepwalkers, neither do the Germans. Both of them appear wide awake and full of purpose.

Douglas Newton concludes his brisk and highly readable narrative by declaring that 'nations going to war are very like each other. Britain's descent into war was marked, as elsewhere, by panic, manipulation, deception, recklessness, high-handedness, and low political calculation – and decisions made at a tearing pace.' Certainly that is true if you look only at the machinery:

the expiring ultimatums, the last-minute démarches which don't come off because they aren't meant to, the ambassadors receiving their passports, the carefully crafted statements in Parliament. But what ultimately matter are the underlying intentions and mindsets of those involved. Was there really an equivalence in belligerence? Do sleepwalkers weep as Grey and Asquith wept?

CHURCHILL'S CALAMITY:
DAY TRIP TO GALLIPOLI

On the way up Scimitar Hill, my grandfather spotted Fred Cripps, Sir Stafford's pleasure-loving brother, then a young officer, and said to him, 'What are you ducking for, Fred? The men don't like it and it doesn't do any good.' Fred lived to the ripest of old ages. My grandfather got to the top of the hill and, like most of his staff, was never seen again. Those few of his brother officers who survived say that he led his brigade the whole way up with a walking stick in his hand and a pipe in his mouth. He only stopped once, to light the pipe. Apart from the smoke of battle, an unseasonable fog had come down, and the Turkish guns had set the gorse aflame. In the circumstances, the pipe seemed a bit superfluous.

The orders given to the Bucks, Berks and Dorset Yeomanry were, I think, much like those given further along the hill to Colonel Sir John Milbanke, VC, who told his Sherwood Rangers, 'We are to take a redoubt. But I don't know where it is and don't think anyone else does either; but in any case we are to go ahead and attack any Turks we meet.' He did not come back either.

This was the last great battle fought on the Gallipoli peninsula and, in terms of numbers, the greatest of the whole campaign. When it was over, the Turks had been forced to bring up their last reserves, but the British had endured 5000 casualties and had not advanced at all. General Hamilton had already asked Kitchener for another 95,000 troops and been told in effect that the Gallipoli enterprise had had its chance. Alan Moorehead argues that the battle had been lost ten days earlier when General Stopford dallied so long after the first landings at Suvla Bay and so allowed Kemal (not yet Ataturk) to recapture the heights of Tekke Tepe and Chunuk Bair. Scimitar Hill was only a foothill. As so often before throughout that spring and summer, when surprise was lost, so was the battle. Again and again, the frustrated commanders muttered, 'If only the navy had arrived on time . . . if only we had not been starved of ammunition . . . if only we had got there half an hour earlier . . .'

Nobody described the dallying at Suvla more vividly than Churchill himself, the author of *The World Crisis*, that resonant, sulphurous apologia of a man who felt he had been unfairly blamed for the whole business and who, at political meetings ten years later, still had to endure shouts of, 'What about the Dardanelles?':

We may pause to survey the scene on both sides of the front this sunny August afternoon. On the one hand, the placid, prudent, elderly (like many of the British generals, Stopford was over 60 and he was also in poor health) English gentleman with his 20,000 men spread around the beaches, the front lines sitting on the tops of shallow trenches, smoking and cooking, with here and there an occasional rifle shot, others bathing by hundreds in the bright blue bay where, disturbed hardly by a single shell, floated the great ships of war: on the other the skilful German stamping with impatience for the arrival of his divisions, expecting with every hour to see his scanty covering forces brushed aside, while the furious Kemal animated his fanatic soldiers and hurled them forward towards the battle.

Sitting among the irises and the red and pink anemones by the cemetery at Hill Ten, I began to share Churchill's impatience, with all the fury of a non-combatant gifted with hindsight. How could such a huge landing force have taken so long to capture this low, scrubby mound? It all looked so easy in the dream landscape of this vast bay with its shimmering salt lake (dried out in the merciless heat of the summer of 1915) and the wide horseshoe of pine-wooded hills behind, dotted with the white stone of the cemeteries on top of almost every one. I began to feel that almost anything could have happened in this eerie, empty place and that much of the futile slaughter might have been avoided, perhaps even that my grandfather (a large, untidy, kindly man I am told) might have gone on living his guileless life. If only old Stopford had not been such a dud, perhaps the Allies really could have reached Constantinople, taken Turkey out of the war, relieved the pressure on Russia's southern flank and prevented the Bolshevik Revolution, just as Churchill said.

The anniversary of the landings on 25 April [1990] is to be the final remembrance for the handful of remaining survivors, drawing Margaret Thatcher and Bob Hawke to these still untenanted shores (preserved from the rash of coastal concrete as a national memorial park). But each anniversary revives once again 'the terrible ifs', the alluring might-have-beens that Churchill so brilliantly deployed in the defence of his own seemingly shattered career.

After all, was there not something lightweight, unsustained, frivolous even, about the way the Gallipoli campaign was waged, not least in the diaries and letters – bobbish, lyrical, facetious by turns – of Sir Ian Hamilton with his enchanting smile and his twinkling eyes? An insect bite had prevented poor Rupert Brooke from getting any further than Skyros, but his friends and his prose style were as ubiquitous as the insects. The natural beauty of the surroundings ennobled the stench of the trenches. 'It was a cobweb morning,' wrote Sergeant Hargrave of the 32nd Field Ambulance, recalling Stopford's Day of Rest, 'misty-thick, foretelling a steaming-hot day. Every sagebrush and wild thyme hassock festooned with spiders' webs heavy with dew.' Everyone who fought there or merely visited seems to have been moved to write like John Masefield, including John Masefield. Classical allusions came up with the rations; the windy plains of Troy were only a few miles across the straits on the Asian side. Some of the French troops stationed at Cape Helles at the toe of the peninsula excavated antiquities in their spare time, aided by the huge craters left by the shells of 'Asiatic Annie', the big Turkish gun across the water. Both Moorehead (1956) and Robert Rhodes James (1965) give marvellous descriptions of that strange heightened life, a mixture of terror, boredom, dysentery and exhilaration which has made the whole tragic adventure ring in the memory to this day.

How peculiar it all was – peculiar, to start with, that we should be fighting the Turks at all, when, with only a fraction more diplomatic nous before the war, they might have been on our side (a fact which may explain the absence of rancour after the war and the mutual respect during it). And peculiar too for the Balliol subaltern sunning himself on these banks of asphodel to see only a few hundred yards away men in his own regiment under heavy fire in their trenches or clinging like seabirds to holes scrabbled in the cliff, often using corpses as sandbags or treading on their squashy faces. Peculiar too it must have been to return from the most vicious hand-to-hand fighting of the entire war, biting, bayoneting, clubbing one's way a few yards forward only to be startled by pitiless enfilading fire and forced to scurry downhill again along the maze of gullies and on to the beach and splash into the sea to get away from the flies. Against the violent freshness of these contrasts, it is somehow all the more touching to read the same understated phrases in letters home as from any other British battlefield: 'We got fearfully cut up last night', 'it was most awfully disappointing for us at Anzac'. No wonder the Gallipoli campaign has produced two of the finest short histories of any campaign in British military history: Moorehead the better on the submarine battles in the Sea of Marmara and on the bizarre intrigues at Constantinople, Rhodes James the more intense, sharp and gripping on the actual fighting (though marred by a bitchy insistence on belittling Moorehead's research at every opportunity). Both manage superbly to balance the heroism against the horror, and to give just as full weight to the dash of the best commanders as to the lethargy of the worst.

There could be no accusations of sloth or lotus-eating at the middle of the three battlefronts, Anzac Cove. There, only a couple of miles down from Suvla, the jagged, sandy cliffs rear almost straight out of the sea. There is scarcely room for the little graveyard at the edge of the beach. This place – one of the most legendary in the history of warfare – is hardly a cove at all, no more than the faintest of indentations in the roughest, least hospitable stretch of the coast. It is amazing that men could ever have fought their way to the top of the ridge, let alone held their trenches for months against the enemy above them. The ground is so cramped, so precipitous, so seamed with deceitful gullies and crevasses that any kind of coherent military advance seems inconceivable. Those cheerfully designated landmarks of the fiercest fighting – Plugge's Plateau, Johnston's Jolly – are mere pockets of scrub and scree, crammed to this day with the bones and equipment of those who died in them. Yet all the fire and dash at Anzac Cove achieved little more than the lethargy and indecision at Suvla Bay. For all the reckless daring displayed at both, the Allied line never reached more than a mile or so inland, the great ridge which forms the spine of the peninsula was never controlled, the Turkish batteries were never silenced, and the Dardanelles were never forced. And when I gazed down towards Suvla from the top of the ridge, where Kemal had his headquarters, the ultimate failure of the Allies no longer seemed so surprising. What looked like a fairly easy stroll from below looked hellish, verging on impossible from above. Suppose the Bucks, Berks and Dorset Yeomanry had managed to capture the high ridge and fought their way on up the peninsula, might they not still, I wondered, have been intercepted by German reinforcements from the Gulf of Saros, or been cut to pieces by Turkish guerrillas in the cruel winter of the Thracian uplands (thirty men froze to death in a single trench here in the last days before evacuation)? Constantinople still seemed a long way off, 200 miles and more, in fact.

What the Cassandras had said at the beginning turned out to be the case. After all, Churchill himself, before he was seduced by the marvels of modern artillery, had told the cabinet in 1911 that the days of forcing the Dardanelles by warships were gone: 'Nobody would expose a modern fleet to such peril.' And had not General Callwell, the director of military operations, told Kitchener and Churchill the preceding autumn that, even with a force of 60,000 men, 'the attack is likely to prove an extremely difficult operation of war'? And had not Admiral Carden, the British commander in the Aegean, told Churchill that 'I do not consider the Dardanelles can be rushed. They might be forced by extended operations with large numbers of ships'? Carden and Callwell both meant to discourage Churchill. They little knew their man. The First Lord telegraphed back, 'Our view is agreed by high authorities here' (principally, it seems, the First Lord himself – he had not consulted the First Sea Lord, the 73-year-old Jacky Fisher, or anyone else who might turn out to be sceptical). 'Please telegraph in detail what you think could be done by extended operations.'

Churchill then used Carden's reply and the subsequent refinements of it to argue in *The World Crisis* that 'I did not and I could not make the plan' and 'the genesis of this plan and its elaboration were purely naval and professional in their character'. Well, from this distance in time, it looks remarkably like a bouncing operation and a wilful misreading of a hesitant 'might' (which is what Carden later confirmed he intended) into a gung-ho can-do.

If Churchill had not been at the Admiralty, it remains highly doubtful whether the Dardanelles plans would ever have been carried through on such a scale. There might have been a couple of naval bombardments of the straits, no doubt abandoned when they turned out to be as costly as the 18 March assault which cost the navy three battleships. No doubt several British submarines would have slipped under the Turkish nets at the narrows and wreaked the same havoc in the Sea of Marmara as the incredible Lt-Commander Nasmith. There might have been one or two commando-style raids on the shore batteries. But would there have been landings involving half a million men, and would it all have gone on for nearly a year and cost 50,000 Allied lives?

As John Terraine remarks, 'The peculiarity of the whole Gallipoli story is the number of times that the Allies came within inches of success; it is this, as much as anything, that makes its memory so poignant ... a series of "accidents" may be blamed for each successive failure. But can so many breakdowns, so similar in character, only be called "accidents"? Do they not seem to point to a chronic basic disorder?'

The most obvious weakness was the division of command. Even when General Hamilton and Admiral de Robeck were on speaking terms, they were often unable to get in touch with one another. And this misfortune was not merely a technical accident or the product of inter-service rivalry, it reached down to the very depths of the enterprise, which seemed unable to make up its mind whether it was to be primarily naval or military. To start with, the straits were to be forced by the navy alone. Then the army was to silence the batteries first; then in the dying stages, when evacuation was virtually a certainty, Admiral Keyes hatched dramatic plans for the navy to blast its way through to Constantinople.

But why did the politicians never agree on a sufficiently large combined operation? Why was it always too little, too late? This is surely the crucial question, though it does not seem to have been asked much. The answer is that to have contemplated, openly and candidly, an operation of the necessary size would have drained the Dardanelles of most of their attractions as an alternative to the horrific slaughter of the Western Front. To call this thing by its right name, it would have been an invasion of Turkey – a country which had been only reluctantly dragged into the war by German arm-twisting and was much better left to doze on under the decrepitude of Ottoman rule. And any fool could see that an invasion might well tie up an Allied army of half a million men and more, which is just what did happen later on in Salonica. Churchill himself wrote to Fisher in January 1915 that 'I would not grudge 100,000 men because of the great political effects in the Balkan peninsula but Germany is the foe, and it is bad war to seek cheaper victories and easier antagonists'.

Yet that is just what, with many hesitations and backtrackings, they were about to do. For all the cultivated sobriety with which the forty-year-old Churchill persuaded his older colleagues of the virtues of the scheme, there is no doubt that he – and most of them – saw the prospect as a with-one-bound-we-are-free operation, to be carried through at relatively modest cost against an inferior opponent. Only Hamilton, I think, had the grace to admit that he had found 'Mehmetçik' a tougher nut than the Johnny Turk of British mythology. And there is no mistaking, either, Churchill's belief that success in the Dardanelles would also carry him bobbing along on the crest of the wave.

'My God,' he said to Margot Asquith in January 1915, 'this, this is living history. Everything we are doing and saying is thrilling – it will be read by a thousand generations, think of that! Why, I would not be out of this glorious, delicious war for anything the world could give me – don't repeat that I said the word delicious, you know what I mean.'

Immediately after the Great War, it was this self-dramatizing, self-regarding aspect of Churchill's character that struck people.

He was seen as 'continually posing, almost strutting, for his portrait for posterity'. Dr Bean, the official Anzac historian, denounced Churchill's 'excess of imagination', his 'layman's ignorance of artillery and the fatal power of a young enthusiasm to convince older and slower brains' (Asquith, Kitchener and Balfour were all in their mid-sixties). But under the heavy pounding of Churchill's own rhetoric and with the horror of Flanders burning ever deeper into the memory, by the 1930s the conventional wisdom had swung round to accept, more or less, Roger Keyes's claim that 'the forcing of the Dardanelles would have shortened the war by two years and spared literally millions of lives'. Liddell Hart described the policy as 'a sound and far-sighted conception, marred by a chain of errors in execution almost unrivalled even in British history'. Churchill's glorious achievements in the Second World War gave this view a further lease of life. In the mid-1950s, Moorehead was still more inclined to blame the generals than the politicians.

But already the tide was turning against Churchill again, J. F. C. Fuller's considered verdict in 1956 was that 'Mr Churchill forced the Dardanelles card on the Government and the Government was incapable of playing the hand'. A. J. P. Taylor diagnosed the operation as an attempt to evade the basic problem that the Germans could be beaten only by a force of the equivalent size. Correlli Barnett surely gets through to the real point: 'Surprise might have won an initial success, but sooner or later the German reserves would have arrived and the Allies would have faced a similar situation as in the West. As the second world war proved, Europe has no "soft underbelly".' The 'Easterners' were just as much escapists as those who believed in a quick victory on the Western Front. Since the American Civil War, large wars between well-matched opponents have not been decided without mass slaughter: in the Great War on the Western Front, in the Second World War on the Eastern. That is the terrible truth which nobody wanted to face at the time and I don't think most people really want to face today since it involves accepting that the real donkeys were not the generals but the politicians and the public who insisted on unconditional surrender. So much easier to blame silly old buffers in uniform.

In a way, the trouble with Churchill in 1915 was not excess but poverty of imagination. He had not at that stage (but then nor had anyone else) much instinctive understanding of the terrible imperatives of a people's war. His mind still bore traces of the dash and jingle of the low-cost victories of nineteenth-century colonial warfare. Of course, nobody was quicker than he to grasp what Raymond Aron dubbed 'the technical surprises' of modern wars; the fighting begins with cavalry and ends with tanks and aircraft. But did he as yet see how people's wars could mobilize entire populations and engender that inexhaustible determination to carry on to victory even in so apparently debilitated a nation as the Turks? After all, the only enduring legacy of Gallipoli — apart from the memory of so much carefree expenditure of heroism — was the forging of a popular will on the Turkish side which led ultimately to Major Kemal becoming President Ataturk and the creation of modern fez-free Turkey. 'The key to Winston', Leo Amery remarked in 1929, 'is to realise that he is mid-Victorian and unable ever to get the modern point of view.' That defect became a grand virtue in 1940, when a certain lack of accommodation to modernity was what was wanted. In 1915, by keeping alive the tempting illusion that somewhere, somehow there existed a short cut to victory, Churchill was making it possible for the same errors to be committed on other Mediterranean shores in the next war.

In the end, it is hard not to agree with that erratic old fire-cracker, Jacky Fisher, who felt himself pursued by Churchill's quenchless advocacy like a man persecuted by a swarm of bees: 'You are just simply eaten up with the Dardanelles and cannot think of anything else. Damn the Dardanelles! They will be our grave!' As the minibus bundled us back along the peninsula to the long, weary road through the plains of Thrace, I began to feel the spell of the Dardanelles drop away and became once more convinced that the whole enterprise had been not only a mistake but a mirage.

OSWALD MOSLEY:
THE POOR OLD FÜHRER

It is thirty-five years since Oswald Mosley breathed his last at the Temple de la Gloire, the athletic frame which he had once so proudly flexed now sadly bloated, his piercing eyes shrunk to peepholes, the sinister moustache long shaven. It is seventy-five years since Churchill brought his serious political career to an abrupt end by interning him in Brixton jail. Yet Mosley never quite stops haunting us. He provokes questions that some people think have not been properly answered even now, stirs uneasy if fading memories, tickles up nightmarish might-have-beens. Was he a lost leader, a usable Lucifer who need not have fallen? Why did he go off the rails, or was he pushed? Did he ever come within touching distance of power, and if so when? Was he right about the Slump and how to cure it, and, by extension, right about the Old Gang blocking his path? Martin Pugh's publishers tell us breathlessly that 'this book demonstrates for the first time how close Britain came to being a Fascist state in the interwar years.' Is that a fact or just a pretty piece of hype? Does the lime-light that Mosley continued to hog show how powerful his hold was over the British people, or was it merely a reflection of the far more powerful and evil megawattage sweeping the Continent?

Stephen Dorril's intertwined biography of Mosley and British Fascism is exhaustive but easy-paced and entertaining, judicious – and damning. We shall not need another. He says pretty well everything that needs to be said, working his way carefully through all the claims made for Mosley and showing how far each one is hollow, misconceived or false.

It is not true, to start with, that Mosley, always known as Tom, entranced everyone from the moment that, as a war veteran of twenty-two, he was elected as the Conservative Unionist MP for Harrow, the youngest member of the House. On the contrary, something about him apart from his wealth and glamour instantly aroused suspicion. Beatrice Webb called him the most brilliant man in the Commons, but argued that 'so much perfection argues rottenness somewhere'. F. E. Smith, another unscrupulous chancer whom Mosley idolized, called him 'the perfumed popinjay of scented boudoirs'. His voice initially had a high-pitched note, and after he took voice lessons, 'its calculated changes in pitch sounded like a car changing gear'. Duff Cooper called him an 'adulterous, canting, slobbering Bolshie'. When Mosley switched over to Labour in 1924, his new colleagues were equally suspicious of him. Ernest Bevin thought him 'the kind of unreliable intellectual who might at any moment stab me in the back'. Attlee complained: 'Why does Mosley always speak to us as though he were a feudal landlord abusing tenants who are in arrears with their rent?' For Ellen Wilkinson, he was the Sheikh – 'not the nice kind hero who rescues the girl at the point of torture, but the one who hisses: "At last – we meet."'

It is worth noting, too, how soon the mockery in print started. Aldous Huxley's *Point Counter Point* was published in 1928 while Mosley was still a Labour MP. Yet Everard Webley, the leader of the British Freemen, in their green uniforms 'like the male chorus at a musical comedy', is unmistakably Mosley, very tall and burly, consumed with ambition and deliberately unpleasant: 'Many people, he had found, are frightened of anger; he cultivated his natural ferocity.' Nancy Mitford, although persuaded by her husband, Peter Rodd, to don a black shirt and gush in print on behalf of TPOF (The Poor Old Führer), was already marshalling the Union Jack Shirts for her novel *Wigs on the Green*. It was not until 1938 that P. G. Wodehouse brought on Sir Roderick Spode and his Black Shorts in *The Code of the Woosters*:

> 'By the way, when you say "shorts", you mean "shirts", of course.'
>
> 'No. By the time Spode formed his association, there were no shirts left. He and his adherents wear black shorts.'
>
> 'Footer bags, you mean?'
>
> 'Yes.'
>
> 'How perfectly foul.'

Spode, a huge man with piercing eyes and a moustache, can be brought to heel by the mention of the word 'Eulalie', because in private life he designs ladies' underwear under the name of Eulalie Soeurs. Mosley, it turns out, had a plan for a range of Blackshirt cosmetics which were to be marketed on a commercial radio station secretly controlled by himself.

Previous biographies have not, I think, fully brought out how nasty Mosley was in private life. He was, for a start, what might be called a hereditary blackguard. The Mosleys once owned the whole of Manchester (admittedly then not much of a place) and were plutocrats of the most unmitigated ghastliness. A Sir Oswald Mosley built the Manchester Cotton Exchange in 1729. His descendants helped to instigate the Peterloo Massacre and suppress the Chartists. Mosley's grandfather was at the forefront of the campaign against Jewish emancipation. Both his father and grandfather were dissolute pugilists who quarrelled violently, liked to punch the lights out of each other and refused to leave a penny to their eldest sons. Mosley's mother left his father because of his goatish infidelity, and Sir Oswald senior poured out a stream of vitriol when Mosley decamped to Labour.

Mosley himself was anally tight with money, raided the trust funds of his first wife, Cimmie, and their children, and refused to pay for his son Alexander's university education. He was also notoriously ruthless in his pursuit of women. Apart from dozens of other married women, he slept with his wife's stepmother, Grace Curzon, her sister Irene and, after Cimmie's death in 1933, her other sister, 'Baba Blackshirt' Metcalfe, who was married to the Prince of Wales's equerry, 'Fruity' Metcalfe. Poor Fruity was a faithful member of the British Fascisti and had to put up with being cuckolded not only by Mosley but by Count Grandi, Mussolini's man in London.

Somehow Mosley managed to make his adoring wife think that she was the one who was at fault. He lied, habitually and unashamedly, to men and women alike. He told her: 'To lead what we believe to be a moral life in our immoral society, some subterfuge is necessary if we are to retain our power to change society.' For several years he denied his marriage to Diana Mitford, which took place in Berlin in the presence of Hitler and Goebbels. He came clean to his mother and his children by his first marriage only when Diana was about to give birth.

He lied just as persistently about the source of his party funding, claiming under interrogation in 1940 that he had never received money from Mussolini and that 'my general directions were that no money should be accepted except from British subjects.' In fact, MI5 discovered that he had been receiving tens of thousands of pounds from Mussolini every year, totalling £234,730 – £8 million in today's money, Dorril computes – through secret accounts personally controlled by him. And when Mussolini stopped the flow, exasperated by the Blackshirts' pathetic lack of progress, Goebbels stepped in with handsome donations through a secret agent – £91,000 in 1936 alone. But Hitler, like Mussolini, always regarded Mosley as a second-rate imitator of his methods who had

no idea how to appeal to the British people. Mosley was com-
pletely dependent on these grants, which made him subservient
to Mussolini over Abyssinia, and then to Hitler over Czechoslo-
vakia. He was, to use the sort of language that he belted out from
the platform, the lackey of an alien power, in fact of two alien
powers.

He lied repeatedly over the British Union of Fascists'
anti-Semitism, claiming that he was not to blame for the vile out-
pourings of the *Blackshirt* as 'party journals were in other hands,
because I was often absent from London.' A. K. Chesterton,
Gilbert's cousin, whose views made G. K. C. seem philosemitic,
reminded him that he read the page proofs of every issue and if he
was out of London would check them over the phone. Phrases in
the *Blackshirt* such as 'the oily, material, swaggering Jew' and the
'pot-bellied, sneering, money-mad Jew' would have been specifi-
cally approved by Mosley. Interviewed by the *Jewish Chronicle* in
1933, he claimed that attacks on Jews were 'strictly forbidden'
in the movement. But only a few months later, the BUF was
attacking 'the low type of foreign Jew who is to the fore in every
crooked financial deal' and denouncing Jews as 'a cancer in the
body politic which requires a surgical operation'. In talking to
Nazi representatives (and in his rare meetings with Hitler), he
stressed that he would have to take drastic measures against his
Jewish opponents, though he was dealing with the Jewish prob-
lem in an appropriately English way.

Among those he considered his intimates, he was unashamed
about his tactics. 'A new movement must find somebody or
something to hate. In this case it should be the Jews.' Only
Mosley could have said this to Israel Sieff and then been surprised
when Sieff asked him to leave the house. His brutal tactlessness
amounted to a form of autism, and it is noticeable that the only
people who thought him a decent chap who might one day
save the nation were themselves semi-autistic individuals, press
lords such as Rothermere and Beaverbrook and writers such as

Wyndham Lewis and George Bernard Shaw. As late as 1968, the lugubrious Cecil King, Rothermere's nephew and then boss of the Mirror Group, planned to install Mosley as the head of a military-backed government, with Mountbatten as his second choice.

For short-term tactical advantage, Mosley was ready to say anything. In 1927, he was mocking the British Fascists as 'black-shirted buffoons, making a cheap imitation of ice-cream sellers' – which went down a storm with the Independent Labour Party rank and file, who elected him to Labour's NEC. As late as 1930, he was assuring businessmen that 'you'll never see in England people walking about in black shirts.' The following year, in presenting the New Party as a centre party, he assured *The Times* that he had 'no use for Fascism or anything else that comes from abroad'.

But only a year later again he was telling Bruce Lockhart that his new organization was to be 'on the Hitler group system: members to wear grey shirts and flannel trousers. Storm troops: black shirts and grey bags.' 'You must be mad,' Harold Macmillan told him when he heard the news. 'Whenever the British feel strongly about anything, they wear grey flannel trousers and tweed jackets.' Or that is what Supermac later said he said; he was rather anxious to make light of his own dabblings with the New Party.

The tendency to violence emerged quite early. When Mosley was returned as Labour MP at the Smethwick by-election in 1927, the campaign was described as one of the most unpleasant contests since the war: there was 'an atmosphere of violence and unrestrained personalities who surround Mr Mosley's political career'. When he was setting up the New Party, his first thought was to recruit stewards who were useful with 'the good old English fist', the 'Biff Boys', who were to be led by the England rugby star Peter Howard at a salary of £650 a year. Mosley declared at this point that there could be 'no corporate state without a private army' and openly referred to the New Party as 'the British equivalent of the Nazi movement'. Howard, who later decamped to work for Beaverbrook and then to lead Moral Re-Armament, described

Mosley as 'the most vindictive hater of anyone I know'. When I met Mosley thirty years later, the light came into his eyes at the thought of his dear old Biff Boys. He was, I suspect, only truly happy when he was haranguing a brawling mob, with a few girl-friends in fur coats rushing for the exit.

Robert Skidelsky, in his 1975 biography, attempted to mitigate Mosley's culpability by arguing that the violence was 'at least as much the result of Anti-Fascist demonstrators interrupting meet-ings or attacking Fascists'. In the original edition, Skidelsky said that Jews themselves 'must take a large share of the blame for what subsequently happened', and that 'a Jewish malaise of this time was to be obsessed by Fascism'. Dorril reminds us that, after strong protests, these remarks were toned down for the paperback edition, and Skidelsky later referred to 'my unduly benign treat-ment of his later Fascist phase'.

But it is not clear that even now Skidelsky has really got the hang of what Mosley was up to. The whole point was to draw out the enemy; and he didn't care how he managed it. Kay Fred-ericks, the Blackshirts' in-house photographer, recalled Mosley telling him after the Olympia rally to fake some pictures to give the impression that it was the Blackshirts who had been attacked. From behind the Labour Party, Mosley said in January 1933, 'will emerge the organised Communist, the man who knows what he wants; and if and when he ever comes out, we will be there in the streets with Fascist machine-guns to meet him.' But because the Communists were too weak and few (Party membership was only six thousand at the time), the only hope of stirring up revolution-ary violence on a large scale was to be flagrantly anti-Semitic, which could be guaranteed to provoke much more widespread opposition. It is thus not true that, as Skidelsky maintains, from 1932 to 1934 Mosley 'regarded the Jewish issue as more of a liability than an asset, a diversion from his main task'. On the contrary, it was, as Dorril says, 'not cynical political opportunism but a genuine, integral part of the movement'. Indeed, as the BUF shrivelled back into the East End (by 1936 nearly half its members were concentrated there), the anti-Semitic campaign was Mosley's only hope.

And it failed. The failure of all fascist movements and parties in Britain from the 1920s to the present day has been abject. Mosley's huge rallies never translated into votes. His commanding presence and by now resonant speaking voice might hypnotize, but they did not inspire trust. Though the violence provoked by Mosley's activities shocked the remarkably peaceable Britain of the 1930s, that too had its limits, and no one died as a result, as far as I can tell. The Mosleyites never got a single MP elected or even a single local councillor. They were infinitely less successful than today's BNP, who themselves are a fairly trivial menace. Even when standing for the New Party in 1931, as a glamorous ex-cabinet minister who had just resigned on a point of principle, Mosley finished bottom of the poll at Stoke. At the 1935 election, the BUF were so terrified of humiliation that they did not dare contest any seats but campaigned on the dismal slogan 'Fascism Next Time'. In subsequent by-elections they usually scored only a few hundred votes. The Fascist candidate at Hythe in 1939, Kim Philby's father Harry St John Philby, received only 578 votes. After the war, the Union Movement suffered much the same fate, campaigning largely against immigration. In his last contest, at Shoreditch in the 1966 general election, Mosley himself secured only 1127 votes (4.6 per cent). All seven nationalist candidates in this one-time BUF stronghold lost their deposits. As Dorril points out, 'the BUF was among the weakest manifestations of Fascism in Europe.'

Dorril never loses sight of what matters. There are a few repetitions. We are told twice that the Duke of Windsor said: 'Tom would have made a first-rate prime minister.' (In exile outside Paris, the Windsors and the Mosleys dined together twice a week, either at the Windsors' Moulin de la Tuilerie or at the Temple de la Gloire, a grand neoclassical villa whose name even Mosley saw the joke of.) And there are one or two errors, mostly when Dorril is hacking his way through the thickets of dim Fascist-leaning toffs. Unity Mitford's second name was Valkyrie, not Swastika; Lord Portsmouth was formerly not Lord Sydenham, who was dead, but Lord Lymington, a ubiquitous figure in Fascist circles of the 1930s, whose English Mistery movement advocated selective breeding and unpasteurized milk and regarded the decline of the feudal system as the greatest misfortune to have befallen the English people. Dorril also confuses those two frightful Fascist moneybags, Lady Pearson and Viscountess Downe. Mosley's headquarters, the Black House, cannot have been simultaneously in Chelsea and at 232 Battersea Park Road (in fact, it was next to the Duke of York's Barracks, not the Duke of Wellington's). There is also a little too much in the later chapters about the toing and froing of various undercover Fascist agents. This reflects Dorril's special interest as a writer on the intelligence services, but the reader can motor through these passages without missing much.

The only serious complaint about this fine book is Dorril's refusal to include proper notes. Dissatisfied readers are referred to his website, where it is difficult to pick up which reference belongs where, because the numbering system refers only to whole paragraphs. This might not be so bad if Dorril weren't inclined to fragmentary, unattributed quotes where it's impossible to tell who is speaking.

Martin Pugh's much shorter book is virtually error-free, just as lucidly written as Dorril's and just as pleasurable to read. It has, however, one whopping drawback: it proves, in abundant and often hilarious detail, the very opposite of the thesis it sets out to prove. The introduction starts by describing what is regarded as 'a comforting and widely held British view that Fascism is simply not part of our national story'. We are, he says, led to believe that

Fascism in interwar Britain was not just a failure, it was an *inevitable* failure. While it flourished in Italy and Germany, the British simply failed to see its relevance to them. In fact,

Fascism seemed fundamentally alien to British political culture and traditions; the British people were too deeply committed to their long-standing parliament, to democracy and the rule of law to be attracted by the corporate state, and they found the violent methods employed by Continental Fascists offensive. Fascist organisations arrived late in Britain and when they did they were easily marginalised by the refusal of conventional right-wing politicians to have anything to do with them. When the Fascist movement under Sir Oswald Mosley showed itself in its true colours in 1934 the government took prompt and effective action to suppress the violence and the paramilitary organisation. The outbreak of war in 1939 promptly put an end to the movement.

Alas, by the end of the book that is pretty much what I do believe, and believe a good deal more fervently as a result of Pugh's researches.

Fascism, he argues, was 'much more central to British inter-war history than has traditionally been appreciated'. 'Like other European countries, Britain had a pre-Fascist tradition, and consequently there is no reason, other than hindsight, for regarding Britain as inherently less likely to generate a Fascist movement after 1918 or for seeing British Fascism as a mere import from the Continent.' But we have only to read Pugh to see just what this pre-Fascist tradition amounted to. There is Lord Lymington, of course, and Rotha Lintorn-Orman, the Girl Scout known as 'Man-Woman', who actually founded the British Fascists, and Valerie Arkell-Smith of the National Fascisti, a transvestite who spent many years masquerading as 'Sir Victor Barker', and the vet Arnold Leese, the author of *A Treatise on the One-Humped Camel in Health and Disease,* who dominated the Imperial Fascist League. Pugh rather half-heartedly adjures us to take these double-barrelled dolts seriously, but even he has to admit that the British Fascists never attracted a politician of the first rank to lead them. Nobody much wanted to join what Churchill called 'the suicide club'.

Pugh points out that we can't say that Mosley was bound to fail just because he did fail. Yet counterfactual hindsight can be just as pernicious as confirmatory hindsight. Yes, if one or two things had turned out differently, Mosley might have got closer to power, but to make any such thesis plausible you have to compare carefully the weight of the evidence of what actually happened against the weight of your counterfactuals.

We are told, for example, that if the Slump had gone on longer, voters might have turned in desperation to Mosley. This is the argument advanced by Skidelsky and indeed in later years by Mosley himself. But there was no sign of it in the worst years of the Depression. Mosley made virtually no headway in the areas worst hit by unemployment. What is much more likely is that people would have turned to the Labour Party. There were clear signs of this at the 1935 election, and Gallup's early polls suggested that the 1940 election might have been a close-run thing had it not been cancelled.

Again, Pugh's contention that a prolonged General Strike in 1926 could well have destroyed Baldwin's government, and created the opportunity that Fascists were looking for, ignores the much more likely alternative that Baldwin would have been succeeded by a Labour government after a general election. Nor do I see how the crisis of 1931 could have brought Mosley to power, even if he had had a full-blown Fascist party ready for action. After all, his New Party was slaughtered at the polls that very year.

Pugh claims that the abdication crisis was Mosley's best chance: 'December 1936 was the closest Fascism came to obtaining a share of power in interwar Britain.' How, precisely? If the King had attempted to dismiss Baldwin and appoint as prime minister Mosley or some other member of the 'King's Party', the House of Commons would have erupted in fury and the King would have been dethroned in days. The King's 'sudden withdrawal' was not, as Pugh argues, an unlucky contingency that snatched Mosley's opportunity away. The King knew the rules, and he knew that the game was up. With each of Pugh's counterfactuals, there is an absence of any mechanical device to trigger the required sequence of events. In any case, Mosley was, as his own henchman Peter Howard defiantly remarked, 'the most unpopular person in England today'. When he was finally interned, Mass Observation took a poll and had never found such a high approval rating for anything. And when he was let out in November 1943, huge crowds marched to Trafalgar Square demanding that he be interned again.

While interned, he read Goethe, Winckelmann, Schiller, Aeschylus, Sophocles, Euripides, Plato, Aristotle and Freud – which shows that the redemptive power of literature has its limits, because he emerged utterly unrepentant. He told the *Sunday Pictorial* that he had not changed his ideas one inch. 'I do not retract anything that I have either said or stood for in the past.' And he hadn't. On launching the Union Movement at the end of 1947, he said that Jews would not be allowed to join and that a Fascist government would deport them from Britain. As for the Nazi concentration camps, the ruin brought about by our bombing was much to blame. 'If you have typhus outbreaks, you are bound to have a situation where you have to use the gas ovens to get rid of the bodies.' In his magpie way, he added to the old menu only his schemes for a united Europe and for worldwide apartheid. Indeed, it is doubtful whether he ever really shifted from the underlying programme on which he had been first elected in 1918, which he called 'socialistic imperialism': a mixture of state control, protection for British industry, imperial preference and immediate legislation 'to prevent undesirable aliens from landing; and for the repatriation of those who are now resident in this country'.

The one thing that can be said for his later tactical adjustments was that he had the wit to pick up a smattering of Keynes, and to see the need for going off the gold standard, so the recovery could begin with devaluation and cheap money. But in the end the Old Gang realized that too, or were made to realize it, and in any case

Mosley's gut instincts in favour of protection joined him up with the very forces that helped to deepen and prolong the Depression. Besides, he did not really understand the policies he had espoused, because he still thought that the Depression would go on for ever and was taken aback by the evidence of economic recovery across the South and the Midlands through the 1930s, as the housing boom gained pace and the new industries – plastics, radio, cars – found their markets. His economic prescience was decidedly limited.

The mystery remains why the academic world has this incurable inclination to magnify Mosley, for Pugh is far from alone in the tenor of his researches. Skidelsky had at least the excuse of being the authorized biographer. He felt honour-bound to establish what sympathy he could with his subject and hunt out any redeeming feature. Besides, he was dealing face to face with a couple of accomplished liars, who managed to find the most charming ways of denying the death camps: 'Darling, it was so much the kindest way,' as Diana said to Nancy.

But why should this insistence on the fragility of British democracy persist in the face of such abundant evidence not only of Mosley's nastiness, but also of his failure to inflict the slightest dent? Is it simply a desire to make our flesh creep, or is there lurking somewhere a sense of disappointment that the British electorate proved so damnably phlegmatic and preferred to potter along with Baldwin and Attlee? That if we had been ready to run greater risks, we might have achieved greater things? If so, it is not a disappointment I share.

ROY JENKINS:
TRAINSPOTTING LOTHARIO

When out canvassing, Roy Jenkins always had a clicker in his pocket to keep a tally of the people he shook hands with or spoke to. He had been an obsessive list-maker ever since, as a boy, he used to go down to Pontypool Road station to note down the train numbers. He shared with Gladstone the habit of dividing his diary into quarter-hour segments. Are such compulsions peculiar to liberal statesmen, like Thomas Jefferson's use of his primitive pedometer to record the remarkable distances he had walked? Perhaps political idealists feel some obscure need to nail down the minutiae of their existence in order to tether their cloudy ballons d'essai.

But Jenkins's conquests were by no means all political and platonic. You would not expect to find it recorded in this marmoreal memorial volume – and it isn't but Jenkins was that unusual combination, a trainspotter and a lothario. I mention his fondness for the company of women into his deepest old age only to colour up the bloodless collective profile here assembled by his fellow liberal worthies. Despite the editors' instructions to avoid hagiography, the impression conveyed is of a somewhat bland personality – 'agreeable' and 'civilized' to use his most favoured epithets. What strikes me in retrospect was rather the immensity of Jenkins's appetites – for statistics and public offices, for wine, women and gossip, for seeking out new places and new friends (and keeping old ones), above all for work.

After a serious heart-valve operation at the age of eighty, he knocked off 100,000 words of his Life of Churchill in a couple of months. Following his pigeon-waddle up and down the sandstone entries of Hyndland and Kelvinside or into the dining room at Brooks's, you were conscious of his enormous unappeased energies, revealed by the curious opening and closing of his fists as he walked, like ratchets waiting to be connected to some larger cogs.

Among the prickly tribe of politicians his capacity for self-mockery stood out. He took genuine delight in Craig Brown's parodies of his absurdly orotund public manner. He even professed pleasure when Tory wags founded a Roy Jenkins Appreciation Society to celebrate his foibles. 'All first-rate politicians are figures of fun: better to be a figure of fun than not a personality at all,' he would say. Like Curzon, his predecessor as chancellor of Oxford, he came to relish the legends of his own snobbery: for example, that when asked at Oxford where he came from, he had replied 'the Marches'.

Like Curzon, he could be cold and dismissive to people who were neither socially conspicuous nor his constituents. But he was kind at heart, family-fond and forgiving of all his enemies except Dr David Owen. On his tombstone it could be written 'he wanted everyone to have a good time'. The only contributions in this rather lacklustre volume that give the reader much idea of what Jenkins was like as a human being come from the two political journalists, Robert Harris and Alan Watkins. Elsewhere the vivid phrases tend to come mostly from Jenkins's own pen, in particular from his memoir *A Life at the Centre*. It is there that he describes Jim Callaghan lurking 'like a big pike in the shadows' in the declining years of Harold Wilson's leadership; there too that he recalls how listening to Wilson default on his support for entry into the EEC 'was like watching someone being sold down the river into slavery, drifting away, depressed but unresisting'. And who could improve on his verdict on his failure to become prime minister: 'I may have avoided doing too much stooping but I also missed conquering'? One essay that does, however, capture Jenkins's political character pretty well is David Marquand's account of his last days in the Labour Party.

Rightly, Marquand endorses Richard Crossman's enraged accusation that, far from being urbane and passionless, Jenkins had become the Bevan of the Right, an eloquent, mercurial, vulnerable Celt, who would follow his principles even if it meant wrecking the party. Jenkins did not see himself as an intellectual in politics in the sense that Crossman and Anthony Crosland did. Of the PPE he had taken at Oxford he inhaled only the political history. He was a prudent chancellor of the exchequer without showing much interest in economics or devising any innovations such as Geoffrey Howe, Nigel Lawson and Gordon Brown have left us. Nor did he offer much in the way of a reasoned political philosophy. His biographies give wonderful accounts of the political life of the time, from Gladstone and Asquith to Attlee and Churchill. Yet in none of them do you gain much sense of the inner life of his subject, still less of the underlying currents of society and thought.

What he offered in his own political life was passion. In his G. M. Young lecture, he quotes Viscount Goschen as saying of the Duke of Devonshire, 'he is, like myself, a moderate man, a violently moderate man'. Jenkins himself could have been so described too. It was certainly passion which blazed throughout his two spells as home secretary, especially the first. No doubt the laws on homosexuality and abortion would have been reformed sooner or later; stage censorship would have disappeared, as would corporal punishment in prisons and something like the Race Relations Board would have been set up, whoever was home secretary. But that all these things happened in such a brief space of time, with so little fuss and in a form which has endured more or less to this day, is due very largely to Jenkins's wholehearted support, his mastery of the House of Commons and his sheer executive zest. He really was the godfather of the 1960s. Without him things would have been different, just as without his unyielding determination to take his supporters through the lobbies to support British entry into the Common Market the whole project might have failed once more – and, who knows, perhaps failed for ever.

In the same way, other presidents of the European Commission might have made token efforts to relaunch the project for a single currency. Other disenchanted Labour moderates were toying with the idea of a breakaway party. But only Roy Jenkins had the inbuilt self-confidence to go for it – the self-confidence of one born into the aristocracy of the South Wales mining community.   In areas that didn't much interest him he could be as unreliable as any other politician. He ratted on Barbara Castle's efforts to reform the trade unions, though he had the grace to feel badly about it afterwards. In fact, he seems to have stayed strangely aloof from the greatest struggle of post-war British politics, to revive the exhausted economy. But when he cared, he fought and he won. Tony Blair gladly acknowledged him as the John the Baptist of New Labour, just as Jenkins looked on Blair as his political heir. It is ironic that only a few months after his mentor's death Blair should have begun to blame the sixties for all the social ills of our time. Just the sort of irony that Jenkins would have savoured.

DENIS HEALEY:
THE BRUISER AESTHETE

The day Denis Healey was born, Virginia Woolf recorded in her diary that 'it was not actually raining, though dark.' Mrs Woolf was not to know it, but she was condemned to haunt Mr Healey for the rest of her days and into the Beyond, appearing and reappearing in the long windings of his biography like a Grey Lady at the end of the corridor: 'Virginia Woolf, a writer who never fails to refresh me ... Virginia Woolf has been as much an unseen presence during our years at Alfriston as Yeats was when we were living at Withyham.' When Yeats took up dabbling in the occult, did he have any idea where he would finish up being an unseen presence? Nor is he the only poet to be hovering in the Healey ambience: 'Emily Brontë's poems have a unique resonance for me.' Mr Healey also saw 'more than a touch of Jane Eyre' in Alice Bacon, Labour MP for Leeds South East (though he seems to have failed to spot the uncanny likeness between Mrs Barbara Castle and Tess of the D'Urbervilles). Among mere male literary figures, Ibsen, Chekhov, Montherlant, Malraux and Stendhal all get high marks. While on the military staff in Bari, he scurries to buy up the works of Croce, and 'Italian translations of Nietzsche and Unamuno, who were more to my taste'.

It should not be thought, however, that Mr Healey is a mere literary superman. He keeps on bumping into pale young men who turn out, later on, to be the Duke of Norfolk, or Lord John Hope, or Jack Profumo or Bill Cavendish-Bentinck. He dines at Buscot with Lord Faringdon and Lord Berners, he goes to Glyndebourne with the Christies and the Gibsons. When he declared in his spur-winning speech at the 1945 Labour conference that 'the upper classes in every country are selfish, depraved, dissolute and decadent', he presumably knew what he was talking about, and by the 1970s he must have had some inside knowledge of 'the howls of anguish' from the rich which he predicted would follow Labour's increases in income tax.

Sometimes, on the other hand, the pale young men turn out to be Zbig Brzezinski or Helmut Schmidt, or, if not so pale, Steve Biko or Henry Kissinger. But in most cases, the principal feature of these items from the small-world department is their bare, unadorned nature. The point of the anecdote about meeting Peggy Ashcroft when young, for example, is not that at that period she hated acting and wanted to be a physiotherapist. It is, quite simply, that our hero met her.

There is, in short, nothing that Mr Healey has not read, nowhere he has not been, no one he has not met – except a good editor. For, alas, the fruits of these far-flung travels, these rare encounters, these great literary experiences are not always as plump or ripe as they might be. There is too often a leaden touch, a faint echo of the essay on 'What I Did in the Holidays': 'Greece itself was an inexhaustible revelation – the people, landscape and art were all infinitely more exciting than I had expected.' 'My most unforgettable experience in Poland was my visit to the concentration camp at Auschwitz.' Chou En-lai was 'the most impressive political leader I had ever met.'

The Impressive Political Leader class turns out to be pretty crowded. President Ford strikes him as 'decisive, shrewd and helpful', as well as 'an exceptionally nice and decent man'. Pierre

Trudeau was 'one of the most attractive and enigmatic public fig-
ures I have met', with 'exceptional charisma'. As for the Kremlin,
it seems to be chock-a-block with leadership qualities. Khrushchev
was 'one of the half-dozen greatest political leaders of this century'.
Malenkov he describes in words which he himself says might have
been said thirty years later of Gorbachev: 'obviously quick intel-
ligence and subtlety – parried all questions with wit, moderation
and adroitness . . . replied with a twinkle.'

Yet, on second thoughts, this book might have been less utterly
endearing, less repeatedly thought-provoking than it is if all this
stuff had been cut out. Perhaps a decent proofreader would have
been enough, one who knew how to spell Iain Macleod and Lydia
Lopokova, who could check that it was Eric Hammond, not
Neil Kinnock, who said that the miners were like the men in the
trenches – 'lions led by donkeys' – and that it was Jeremy Thorpe
and not 'a Tory backbencher' who said of Macmillan's sacking half
his cabinet, 'Greater love hath no man than he who lays down
his friends for his life.' I suspect too that when Mr Healey speaks
of his (infinitely embarrassing) 'supporting roles in sketches for
Morecambe and Wise and Virginia Wood', he means Victoria
Wood – perhaps the shade of Mrs Woolf was jogging his elbow
again. Alas, the Eric-and-Ernie-meet-Leonard-and-Virginia show
remains unperformed. I could also have done without the shower
of old Churchill anecdotes. In a couple of pages, we have the
Plasterass joke, the Bossom joke and the joke about every cliché
except Please Adjust Your Dress Before Leaving – to be followed
a few pages later by 'this pudding has no theme'. Not quite up to
Nietzsche or Unamuno, even in an Italian translation.

But out of all this – and perhaps partly because of it – is built
up an unrivalled self-portrait, all the more vivid because so artless,
of a leading member of the governing class in post-war Western
democracy. Healey responds instinctively to the vibrations of
the spirit of the times. I do not mean that he is a time-server or
placeman. On the contrary, there have been few more dedicated,

energetic and sincere public servants anywhere, no more fero-
cious executant of the contemporary imperative. True, he likes
office – no, that is an understatement, he basks in it, he glows.
I have never seen a happier man than Chancellor Healey in his
scarlet braces with a bucket of gin-and-tonic in his hand, holding
forth about Schumpeter. On one or two occasions, he says, he
threatened to resign, over the cancellation of the F-111 aircraft,
for example, but nobody took the threat very seriously, then or
now. He was and is a Government Man.

After his brilliant exploits as beachmaster at Anzio – described
here with a vivid exactness which, unfortunately, is not main-
tained elsewhere – he came out of the war with the conviction
that 'we must solve the problems of the peace by applying the
same planning techniques as we had used to win the war'.
Gradually, like everyone else, he becomes disenchanted with
planning. At the end of the Callaghan government, he exults
that not a single one of the planning agreements dreamed of by
Tony Benn is in operation, except the Farm Price Review, which
had been invented years earlier. He begins to detect a widespread
desire to reduce the role of government and make people more
self-reliant. In any case, government simply does not possess
enough accurate information to make all the decisions. He tells
us, not once but four times, that if he had had the right figures
for the Public Sector Borrowing Requirement he would never
have had to go cap in hand to the International Monetary Fund.
And so it was that our Denis set in hand the most vigorous prun-
ing of public expenditure undertaken since the Snowden era, far
more stringent and at-a-stroke than anything since attempted by
Mrs Thatcher. Similarly, it was also Mr Healey who, as minister
of defence, finally ended Britain's pretensions to be a world mili-
tary power. Yet only a year or so earlier, he was still reassuring
the Australians that it was right and possible for us to stay East
of Suez.

No other British politician has devoted anything like the time or the intelligence to mastering the technicalities of defence strategy or East–West relations. No other British politician has enjoyed anything like the same network of comrades in expertise built up over the years of attendance at Bilderberg conferences and Königswinter and Ditchley. Yet none of this seems to have enabled him to see much further than the ordinary insular ignoramus. Indeed, there is a strong case for saying that, although he will certainly be remembered as a formidable defence secretary, he was really better as a chancellor, despite or perhaps because of having never previously read the City pages.

He it was, after all, who laid or relaid the foundations of such capacity to manage the economy as his successors as chancellor have shown, namely, the introduction of cash limits on public expenditure and the consideration of monetary targets in some shape or form. Mr Healey is proud of having abandoned Keynesianism but likes to pretend contempt for 'punk' or 'sado' monetarism, preferring to call himself an 'eclectic pragmatist'. It would be simpler to call him a conservative chancellor, who erred on the side of prudence when his colleagues would let him.

By contrast, his much greater expertise on defence matters led him to go haring off into some strange wastelands, sometimes in company with Dr Kissinger, sometimes with the entire defence mafia. In fact, it would be difficult to think of a single fashionable notion, from the Rapacki Plan to 'non-provocative defence' (including the famous Maginot Line of slurry packed with explosives), which Mr Healey has not taken up in its heyday. Sometimes he is candid about the transience of his enthusiasms and his failure to foresee debacles like the Winter of Discontent. At other moments, he presents himself as a prophet amid a host of myopic pygmies.

Unfortunately, at some of the most interesting parts of his career, the light shed by this book becomes rather poor, as during a power cut on an autumn afternoon. When, for example, the forces of the Left are rampaging through the party, all we see of Mr Healey is a somewhat indistinct figure counselling the Gang of Four not to leave because 'Right-wing breakaways from Left-wing parties have never come to anything'. In the 'several hours' of private discussion he had with them, there is no mention of any possibility that he himself might join any new centre party. These discussions are firmly identified as having taken place in September 1980, while he was in the middle of standing against Michael Foot for the leadership. But the more interesting question is how close he came to joining the SDP after he had lost that contest. Some founding members of the SDP say very close indeed; some, that Edna stopped him. She certainly sounds the more tigerish of the two, from the few stray views attributed to her, unwillingness to hear a good word said of Mrs Thatcher, for example. Might he have become not only the best leader Labour never had – which he surely was – but also the leader of a new centre party which, with the addition of his weight, would have mustered a few vital extra percentage points needed to overtake Labour at the 1983 election?

All the evidence is, though, that Mr Healey is not by nature a resigner or a splitter. He is a man for the mainstream, and he is quite prepared to swallow his pride and wait for the mainstream to flow back in his direction again. Besides, he seems to lack that creative instinct, that nose for the future, which is to be found in other perhaps less gifted politicians – Iain Macleod, Rab Butler, Tony Crosland, Margaret Thatcher, even Neil Kinnock. He only sees the rabbit when it is already caught and skinned.

There is something artificial, put-on about his serious bullying persona, no less than about his eyebrow-waggling comic act. He says of his father, Will Healey, the son of a tailor from Enniskillen, that he never established that warm and natural relationship with his children, or even his wife, which he achieved effortlessly with his students at Keighley Technical College; 'too often he found it necessary to conceal his emotions behind a brutal facetiousness'. With his son, it sounds as if things turned out the other way round;

a remarkably happy and relaxed man at home, it seems, in public he exudes an off-putting sort of bogus menace.

Without wishing to venture where even Abses fear to tread, I was struck by the curious deadness of his account of his years in the Communist Party which lasted through the Nazi–Soviet Pact up to the fall of France. Almost any undergraduate who wanted to stop Hitler joined the CP, we are told. There was nothing to it. The experience seems to have been quite unmemorable. Virtually the only thing he tells us about his duties in the Party is that during one summer vacation he made 'a short stop in Paris to leave a message for a certain James Klugmann, who was organising aid for Spain'. Klugmann? The Comintern agent, the spymaster-general. What sort of message – a violet-scented envelope, a small flat package, a bizarre snippet of code – 'Badgers are sneezing in Nuremberg'? But that is all we are allowed to know. Not so much darkness at noon as a passing cloud at teatime.

It is as much from these flat, unhelpful passages as from the more ecstatic moments – like unexpectedly seeing Botticelli's *Primavera* in wartime storage at Montegufoni – that one gradually gets an impression of something suppressed, not harmfully but irreversibly, within Mr Healey. Is there somewhere in there a puckish Hibernian trying to get out of this great Yorkshire bullyboy? And is it because, through some stern exercise of the will the Puck never does manage to get out, that there is, despite everything, a sort of greatness about him?

HAROLD MACMILLAN:
LONELY ARE THE BRAVE

The first thing about Harold Macmillan was his bravery, and it was the last thing too. In the Great War he was wounded five times, at the Battle of Loos and at the Somme. At Delville Wood he was hit in the thigh and pelvis and rolled down into a large shell-hole, where he lay for the next ten hours, alternately dosing himself with morphine and reading Aeschylus. He wrote home on 13 September 1916 that 'the stench from the dead bodies which lie in heaps around is awful.' Only a fortnight earlier he had told his mother: 'do not worry about me. I am very happy; it is a great experience, psychologically so interesting as to fill one's thoughts.' In North Africa during the Second World War his plane crashed on take-off at Algiers and burst into flames. Macmillan scrambled through the emergency exit, then went back into the burning plane to rescue a French flag lieutenant – a fact he doesn't mention in his account of the incident in his memoirs or even in his diary. John McCloy, FDR's assistant secretary of war, described it as 'the most gallant thing I've ever seen'.

Macmillan wasn't one of those war heroes who in peacetime are mild and eager to please. He remained dauntless and daunting in politics. He despised Rab Butler for not having fought (he had a withered hand after a riding accident as a child), he sneered at Hugh Gaitskell for not having any medals to wear on Remembrance Day and he loathed Herbert Morrison, his first boss in the wartime coalition, for having been a conscientious objector in the First World War, calling him 'a dirty little cockney guttersnipe'. Macmillan's diary is spattered with abuse of other public figures, often tinged with anti-Semitism. He never hesitated to tell his colleagues or his superiors when he thought they were wrong. He was the only minister who dared to tell Churchill it was time to go, although it had been Churchill who brought him back from the political wilderness in 1940.

He was implacable and proud of it. When his son, Maurice, wondered why his own career had fallen so far short of his father's, Macmillan said: 'Because you weren't ruthless enough.' When Eden offered him the Exchequer, Macmillan did a Gordon Brown, insisting that 'as chancellor, I must be undisputed head of the home front, under you' and that there could be no question of his predecessor, Butler, being accorded the title of deputy prime minister. Barely a year later, after the Suez debacle, he was promising the American ambassador that, in return for 'a fig leaf to cover our nakedness', he would arrange not only the withdrawal of British troops from Egypt but also the replacement of Eden. When he sacked a third of his cabinet in 1962 after a run of terrible by-election results, this was entirely typical of his undeviating self-interest, although in that Night of the Long Knives it turned out he had been so sharp he cut himself, fatally.

Not surprisingly, throughout his life he was disliked by many and hated by quite a few. At Eton, he received thirteen blackballs in the election for the debating society. The following term, he received eleven. 'He is his own worst enemy: he is too self-centred, too obviously cleverer than the rest of us,' his fellow new MP from the North-east in 1924, Cuthbert Headlam, noted after a dinner with Macmillan. 'He never will let the other man have his say, and he invariably knows everything better than the other man.' This inability to listen gained him a reputation in clubland as a bore and banger-on, despite his undoubted wit and languid charm. In politics, the results of his not listening were frequently calamitous.

Not that he much minded being unpopular. For most of his life he essentially lived alone. His two brothers were years older, his father was away building the great publishing house. His mother, the bossy and possessive Nellie Belles from Indiana, took him away from Eton when he was only fifteen, fearing he was being exposed to 'unnatural practices'. J. B. S. Haldane, who was there at the same time, claimed that Macmillan had been expelled for homosexuality; but Nellie seems to have thought it was the school that was out of order, not her son. Being a strict Nonconformist, she was no better pleased when he formed a close affection for one of his tutors, Ronald Knox, who came within an inch of converting Macmillan to Catholicism. The war saved him from taking this step, which would almost certainly have prevented him from becoming prime minister. In his last letter to Knox before leaving for France, he wrote: 'I'm going to be rather odd. I'm not going to "pope" until after the war (if I'm alive).'

Volunteering for the war meant that at Oxford, as at Eton, he stayed only half the course, being 'sent down by the Kaiser' as he liked to put it. It seems peculiar in retrospect that he should have retained such obsessive loyalties to two institutions he spent so little time in. Nothing gave him more pleasure than being elected chancellor of Oxford, and he was disappointed not to become provost of Eton in 1965 after he ceased to be prime minister. He continually referred to the Fourth of June, often to people who had no idea that this was the school's great festival, or to those who pretended not to, like the Harrovian Field Marshal Alexander.

There was something strangely fake about his snobbish carry-on, almost as though he was trying to convince himself that he belonged. Some of his smoking-room metaphors were merely mystifying: for example, when pondering whether Cyprus should be granted full Commonwealth status after independence; should the island 'be the RAC or Boodles'? When Roger Hollis, the head of MI5, exulted to Macmillan that they had arrested the spy John Vassall, the prime minister complained that this was the wrong approach: 'When my gamekeeper shoots a fox, he doesn't go and hang it up outside the Master of Foxhounds' drawing room; he buries it out of sight.' To which Hollis might legitimately have replied that some gamekeepers had the sense to hang the vermin they had shot on the nearest fence to warn off other predators.

This clubman's chatter dates from his marriage to the Duke of Devonshire's daughter Dorothy in 1920: a giant leg-up socially but ultimately a disaster. They were both gawky virgins and for nearly a decade were happy, until Dorothy fell in love with Macmillan's fellow MP Bob Boothby and demanded a divorce, claiming that her youngest daughter, Sarah, was Boothby's child. From being regarded as a jolly sort, keen on golf and a dab hand at opening fêtes, Dorothy suddenly revealed unsuspected Wagnerian depths of passion, saying to Boothby: 'Why did you ever wake me? I never want to see any of my family again.' She had four young children at the time. Years later, Boothby described her as 'on the whole, the most selfish and possessive woman I have ever known'.

She did not get what she wanted. Macmillan's solicitor Philip Frere pointed out that divorce would be fatal for his political career and recommended a 'west wing-east wing' solution, traditional among the estranged upper classes who had houses large enough for the purpose. Until she died in 1966 – suddenly, of a heart attack as she was putting on her boots to go out to a point-to-point – if they were both at Birch Grove, Macmillan's house in Sussex, they would meet for dinner and then go their separate ways.

Macmillan remained haunted by the affair. In 1975, he went to see Boothby at his flat and asked, for the sake of his peace of mind, to know the truth one way or another about Sarah. In the unbearably painful conversation that followed, Boothby assured him that Sarah was not his daughter because he was always scrupulously careful in his affairs. What Macmillan did not know was that Boothby had just been presented with a tape recorder by the Royal Philharmonic Orchestra of which he'd been chairman for many years. Before Macmillan's arrival, he had been taping a Tchaikovsky symphony from the radio. He had turned off the radio but unwittingly left the tape recorder running on the floor behind a sofa. And so all the agony that Macmillan had poured out to him was on tape, and Boothby played it back to his new wife, Wanda, when she came in, with tears running down his face.

This is how D. R. Thorpe tells the story, eloquently and elegantly, as he does everything in this exemplary biography, which complements if it does not entirely supplant Alistair Horne's two-volume official biography; Horne is better on the military, Thorpe on the political and personal. At every juncture Thorpe presents the evidence in a scrupulous and equable style. He is charitable, just as he was in his earlier biographies of Selwyn Lloyd and Eden, both of whom had reasons to be resentful of Macmillan's behaviour. By not taking sides, Thorpe leaves readers room to come to their own judgment.

And if you want my guess here, I don't think that Boothby, that insatiable seducer of both sexes, left the tape recorder on by accident. I don't mean that he had it in for Macmillan exactly, although it is always hard to forgive those you have wronged, especially when you have been wronging them for years. It is more that Boothby, himself the ripest of old hams, would have been unable to resist the dramatic potential of the scene: the aged ex-prime minister with tears running down his face, and then a few hours later Boothby, the man of feeling, recalling the recalling with tears running down *his* face.

Thorpe tells us that Macmillan never looked at another woman. He dismisses the claim of Sean O'Casey's widow (O'Casey was a Macmillan author) to have had an affair with Harold at the time Dorothy first fell for Boothby. Quite out of character, Thorpe argues: Macmillan was straitlaced and not much interested in sex anyway. He was lost for words when JFK turned to him during a break in their discussions on nuclear arms at Key West and enquired: 'I wonder how it is with you, Harold? If I don't have a woman for three days, I get a terrible headache.' What is certain is that Macmillan was deeply lonely. He took refuge in West End clubs to an almost pathological extent: Pratt's, Athenaeum, Buck's, Guards, the Beefsteak, the Turf, the Carlton – he was in and out of them every day. A member of Pratt's calling in there one evening in the 1960s enquired whether there was anyone in that night. 'Nobody at all, sir, only the prime minister.'

His health, always fragile, gave way during his wife's affair. In the summer of 1931 he had a serious breakdown. There were rumours that he had attempted suicide. He was secretly admitted to the Kuranstalt Neuwittelsbach outside Munich. He recovered but had another bad collapse in October 1943, during an unexpected visit to London from his post in North Africa. He remained an intensely nervous figure, inclined to vomit before big speeches, which was why he always lunched alone before Prime Minister's Questions. The unflappable façade was an amazing effort of the will.

He had become MP for Stockton-on-Tees in 1924, and held the seat almost continuously until 1945 and, in old age, took his title from it. Stockton was (and in its centre still is) a handsome old market town, transformed when it became the birthplace of the railways and the centre of the iron and steel industry. By the time Macmillan appeared there, unemployment was more than 20 per cent and rising (what trade there was had shifted to neighbouring Middlesbrough). His principal loathing was not for the Labour Party, which he periodically thought of joining, but for the hard-faced men on his own benches, the industrialists who had done well out of the war – the Forty Thieves as they were known to Macmillan and his friends. They were mocked in return as 'the YMCA'. All his life, Macmillan retained a distrust of the City and 'the banksters'. He claimed in 1936 that 'Toryism has always been a form of paternal socialism'.

The family firm had published Keynes's *The Economic Consequences of the Peace* and *The General Theory* and done very well with them. If Macmillan never looked at another woman after Dorothy, he never looked at another economist after Maynard. Following Keynes's death in 1946, he relied exclusively on the advice of Roy Harrod, the great man's biographer and disciple. The single thought Macmillan took from *The General Theory* was: reflate at all costs. He got rid of not one but two chancellors – Peter Thorneycroft and Selwyn Lloyd – for refusing to expand demand fast enough. Not long after Lloyd's restrictive 1961 budget, Macmillan was urging him to prepare a reflationary budget for 1962; two days after his 1962 effort, Macmillan was already egging him on to let the brakes off in 1963. Lloyd's successor, Reginald Maudling, was bombarded with memos urging him to go for 'the big stuff – the national plan, the new approach, to expand or die'. Industrial production rose by 11 per cent in the year after the pliable Heathcoat-Amory's 1959 election budget – a completely unsustainable gallop.

Macmillan's obsession with expansion and his utter neglect of inflation were of course a reaction to the bitter experience of the North of England in the 1930s. But badgering chancellors to flood the economy with cash was no substitute for a carefully targeted policy to revive the decayed industrial estuaries of the Tyne, the Tees, the Mersey and the Clyde; sending Lord Hailsham up to the North-east in a cloth cap was an embarrassing afterthought, which only drew attention to the threadbare nature of Macmillan's economic policy. *The Middle Way* (1938), his most substantial and influential political tract, was, as Thorpe says, not so much a revolutionary piece of work as 'a confirmation of the new orthodoxy', and when after the war it was identified as the origin of the Tories' Industrial Charter, it was because the charter came to terms with the Attlee settlement in precisely the way Macmillan envisaged: nationalization, state planning, the leading role of the trade unions – all these things were to be accepted, because, to misappropriate a later mantra, There Is No Alternative.

For an undeniably clever man, Macmillan left remarkably little evidence of strategic thought in his voluminous diaries. The latest volume covering his years as prime minister does little to improve one's earlier impression of an agile but not very original mind struggling to survive from day to day. The enormous length of the diaries remains a problem. In his introduction, Peter Catterall tells us that 'omissions have, of course, had to occur to reduce the original text to less than half its length. It has been possible to achieve some of that by cutting out repetitions. To a much greater extent than in the first volume [covering Macmillan's cabinet years, from 1950–57], however, it has also been necessary to omit Macmillan's reading, social activities and family life.' This strikes me as precisely the wrong way to go about editing this particular diary, perhaps any diary. The spattering of dots that mark the omitted passages give the text an unsatisfying, wispy feel. Besides, large chunks of the political stuff have, as Catterall himself points out, already been published in the six volumes of Macmillan's memoirs. Indeed, long stretches of those memoirs consist of little but diary extracts. The value of having the diaries in their entirety must be to give us a rounded portrait of this strange, lonely, rather wonderful but also decidedly unpleasant man. Pepys without Mrs Pepys, the delicious Deb Willet or the visits to the play would be a far poorer thing.

The diary also contains gaps. Macmillan admits several times that during a real crisis such as Suez or Profumo his diary-keeping breaks down. Nor does he seem fully alert to his own memorable moments. All he says of his speech at Bedford in July 1957 is that it 'was well reported in the Sunday press, and I think helped to steady things,' omitting to record that it was in this speech that he uttered the immortal phrase about most of us never having had it so good. His Wind of Change speech he does not mention at all in a skimpy retrospect of his African tour of February 1960. Quite a few entries read like a summary of events drawn up by someone else. Not often do you get the feeling of being there yourself or of learning something new about how it went, as you do on almost every page of the Crossman diaries. Only the odd languid wise-crack convinces you that this is the real Mac. I liked his musing during the Cuban Missile Crisis on 'the frightful desire to *do* something, with the knowledge that *not* to do anything ... was prob. the right answer'.

What strikes the reader, above all, is Macmillan's obsessive preoccupation with foreign affairs to the near exclusion of the domestic and economic; a good 80 per cent of the diary entries, perhaps more, are concerned with overseas affairs. Pages are filled with the fruitless efforts to save the Central African Federation. Weeks are consumed with overseas visits to prepare the way for a summit, until, as Macmillan wearily concludes, 'everyone else has visited everyone.' The summit then collapses and 'all our plans are in ruins.' By contrast, it is not until March 1963 – after he has been prime minister for six years – that he publicly launches a campaign for 'the modernisation of Britain'.

When we see Macmillan at his best is undoubtedly during the war years, which were covered in a volume published separately back in 1984 (*War Diaries: Politics and War in the Mediterranean, January 1943–May 1945*). Those diaries were published pretty much entire and contain fine descriptions of North Africa as well as sharp pen portraits and nippy asides. And besides, they describe an extremely delicate and fascinating mission, told as deftly as it was executed. As ministerial representative at Allied Forces HQ, Macmillan had to devise his own peculiar role. The generals like Eisenhower who at first wondered exactly what he was doing there came to respect his panache, energy and ingenuity. His management of the political chaos in Italy and then of the war-ring factions in Greece was nothing short of masterly. Richard Crossman, then assistant chief of psychological warfare at AFHQ, concluded in a shrewd single sentence: 'I suspect it was in Algiers, where he could do all the thinking and take all the decisions while Ike took all the credit, that Harold Macmillan first realised his own capacity for supreme leadership and developed that streak of intellectual recklessness which was to be the cause both of his success and of his failure when he finally reached No. 10.'

It is thus a pity and an irony that of all Macmillan's service in that war the only bit that is much remembered is the tragic finale: the handing over of Cossacks and White Russians and Croats at Klagenfurt in May 1945. The appalling consequences of this decision – thousands of men, women and children were slaughtered by Stalin and Tito – remain a black and unforgettable chapter. The accusations against Macmillan personally became progressively more pointed in Nikolai Tolstoy's three polemics: *Victims of Yalta* (1977), *Stalin's Secret War* (1981) and *The Minister and the Massacres* (1986), which fingered Macmillan as part of 'the Klagenfurt conspiracy' and an accessory to mass murder.

After Macmillan's death in 1986, an independent investigation led and largely paid for by Anthony Cowgill concluded unequivocally that, in the words of one of his team, Christopher Booker (who had originally believed that Macmillan was culpable), 'Macmillan's part in the story was (a) marginal at best, and (b) that he actually knew very little about the Cossacks in Austria, apart from what he was told at the briefing at Klagenfurt airfield.' In *The Repatriations from Austria in 1945*, Cowgill concluded that Macmillan had nothing at all to do with the decision to send back the dissident Yugoslavs against their will. The general decision to repatriate to the Soviet authorities arose from cabinet decisions dating back to June 1944; it then became part of a quid pro quo agreed with Stalin at Yalta in February 1945. The operational decisions on handover were taken, he argued, not at Macmillan's meeting with General Keightley in a hut by the grass landing strip in Klagenfurt on 13 May, but at a military conference in Udine on 26–27 May, by which time Macmillan was back in England. Those who criticize the orders fail to take account of the chaotic and menacing circumstances of the moment. Tito's forces were threatening to overrun Carinthia and Venezia Giulia. The whole war could have reignited in the region.

This is the new consensus on the subject; and Thorpe subscribes to it. Yet, fair-minded as ever, he offers several pieces of evidence to support those who still believe that Macmillan was, at best, guilty of 'over-compliance'. In his diary for 13 May, Macmillan wrote: 'Among the surrendered Germans are about 40,000 Cossacks and "White" Russians, with their wives and children. To hand them over to the Russians is condemning them to slavery, torture and probably death. To refuse, is deeply to offend the Russians, and incidentally break the Yalta agreement. We have decided to hand them over.' The next day, 14 May, Keightley telegraphed Alexander, the commander-in-chief: 'On advice Macmillan I have today suggested to Soviet General on Tolbukhin's HQ that Cossacks should be returned to SOVIETS at once.' As for there being no final authorization for handing over either the Cossacks/White Russians to Stalin or the Croats to Tito until the conference at Udine on the 26th, Lieutenant-Colonel Robin Rose Price wrote in his diary on 19 May: 'Order of most sinister duplicity received i.e. to send Croats to their foes, i.e. Tits to Yugoslavia under the impression they were to go to Italy.' Thorpe does not quote the even more sinister sentence that follows in Rose Price's diary: 'Tit guards on trains hidden in guards van.' It is not unreasonable then to suppose that the essential decisions were taken, not at Udine, which looks more like a rubber-stamping, but during the two hours Macmillan spent on the airstrip at Klagenfurt. Whether other orders could have been given in the circumstances of the time remains debatable, but 'marginal' isn't quite the right word to describe Macmillan's role.

What he cannot be acquitted of is callousness. Which is shown by a curious coda to the miserable story. Macmillan's diaries break off (not to resume until 1950) when he flies home on 26 May to become air minister in Churchill's caretaker government.

Thorpe, like previous biographers, assumes that this was his final farewell to the mountains and lakes of Austria. But William Dugdale, in his recently published memoir, *Settling the Bill*, describes being deputed to organize a Fourth of June dinner in an orchard by the banks of the Wörthersee. Sixty or seventy Old Etonian guards officers were invited to sing 'Floreat Etona' and toast the Old Coll in slivovitz, along with the army commander, General McCreery, Field Marshal Alexander (who as an outsider made his excuses and left early) and Harold Macmillan. Nothing, it seems, would have deterred him from flying halfway across the ravaged continent to celebrate the two institutions he loved best, Eton and the Grenadiers. At the end of dinner, Macmillan was accosted by Rose Price, aflame with drink and an almost Homeric rage, and lambasted for ordering his battalion to send the Cossacks to their death. Dugdale records beautifully how Macmillan, a cigarette drooping from his lips, turned his strangely flappy hands (weakened by war wounds) outwards in that gesture we came to know so well and replied: 'How else are we to demonstrate our loyalty to Stalin and the Russians?' Thus, long before the controversy reawakened in the 1980s, Macmillan was made forcibly aware of the repugnance the orders aroused among the soldiers who had to carry them out. What is so striking is that he had no hesitation in returning to the scene of the crime only nine days later.

Again and again, one notices the callous insouciance, which, as Crossman spotted, was both his strength and his weakness, leading him to overcome, seemingly without effort, 'little local difficulties' that might have unhorsed more careful operators, but also drawing him into wildly optimistic miscalculations which generated terrible outcomes. Certainly the part he played at Suez seems to fit that description. As chancellor, he was desperately keen to establish that the Americans would back Britain in the use of force. He hammered home as forcefully as he could to Bob Murphy, his wartime comrade who had come to London on Eisenhower's behalf, that the government had decided to drive Nasser out of Egypt and that

Parliament and people were behind them. He told John Foster Dulles, the secretary of state, the same thing. 'We are committed to a peaceful settlement of this dispute, nothing else,' Eisenhower said at a press conference on 5 September. But Macmillan refused to believe this or to grasp the fairly obvious fact that all Ike cared about was being re-elected in November. In Washington at the end of September, Macmillan saw Eisenhower, Dulles and George Humphrey, the US treasury secretary. Yet he still could not grasp that, in Humphrey's words after the invasion, 'You'll not get a dime out of the US government until you've gotten out of Suez.' Roger Makins, Macmillan's private secretary, who took notes at the meeting with Eisenhower, was amazed by the rambling, unfocused nature of the conversation and thought Macmillan was wholly unwarranted in his subsequent optimism about American support. Ike was rambling on purpose in his typically devious way. Macmillan just failed to listen.

Macmillan's diaries break off again on 4 October 1956, to resume only in February 1957, which is when Catterall's second volume begins. In the introduction to the first volume, the editor tells us that another diary covered the missing months, but that Macmillan destroyed it 'at the request of Anthony Eden'. In his introduction to this volume, Catterall says merely that it 'appears to have been destroyed'. It seems more likely that, if it contained material embarrassing to Macmillan, he destroyed it himself. But in any case, his fatal contribution to the fiasco had already been made, in Washington in September.

Thorpe acquits Macmillan of the charges usually laid against him: that he was 'first in, first out', that he pushed Eden into a disastrous venture which he knew would fail, that he exaggerated the ensuing economic crisis and that he poured his energies into outmanoeuvring Butler for the succession. Fair enough, but Thorpe also makes light, much too light, of the secret collusion with the Israelis. Contrary to the long prevailing misconception, he tells us, the cabinet was informed of Lloyd's meeting at Sèvres with the French and the Israelis – which serves only to implicate the lot of them. Then he wheels on the historians Robert Blake and Andrew Roberts to argue that secret diplomacy and *suppressio veri* are necessary to the successful prosecution of war: in Blake's words, 'no one of sense will regard such falsehoods in a particularly serious light'.

This sort of unabashed realpolitik is undermined if not exploded by the final Suez despatch from the supreme military commander, General Keightley, last seen in Klagenfurt: 'The one overriding lesson of the Suez operation is that world opinion is now an absolute principle of war.' Where military action is undertaken for moral reasons, to right a wrong or to turf out a tyrant, any hint of deceit is fatal (see Iraq passim). The gravamen of the charge against Macmillan is different: namely, that he was the only British minister to talk to all the top Americans and that he completely and disastrously misread their intentions.

Which is much what he did again, as prime minister, in gauging whether de Gaulle was ready to let Britain into the Common Market. As late as their meeting at Rambouillet in December 1962, Macmillan still had high hopes that de Gaulle would yield to his suasions. They went for a walk in the woods, accompanied only by Philip de Zulueta, one of Macmillan's private secretaries. Macmillan insisted on talking in French and returned from the walk believing that the conversation had gone well. Again, the private secretary was not so sure. The next morning, de Gaulle explained, as bluntly as he could, that though he was in favour of Britain's eventual membership the time was not yet right. Macmillan was shocked and dismayed. Yet anyone with his head screwed on could have seen it coming. Reginald Maudling, then President of the Board of Trade, had forecast exactly this outcome eighteen months earlier, after the failure of the free trade negotiations in Paris. And Macmillan himself had had repeated meetings with the General over the previous two years at which de Gaulle had made plain his ingrained resistance.

If Macmillan's political vision was impaired, his eye for the main chance was undimmed. He was, quite simply, a magnificent intriguer, opaque when he had to be, brutally swift to jump through any window of opportunity, smashing the glass where necessary. Enoch Powell described the way Macmillan destroyed Butler's chances of succeeding Eden when they both appeared before the 1922 Committee after Eden had flown off to Jamaica as 'one of the most horrible things that I remember in politics' (and he ought to know). Macmillan saw off Butler again, just as effortlessly, in the race to succeed himself in 1963. In his usual charitable way, Thorpe acquits Macmillan of organizing Alec Douglas-Home's startling triumph. As in 1957, he argues, the parliamentary party would not have Rab Butler at any price, and Home was the candidate that fewest people objected to and so the one best qualified to keep the party united. Yet once again Thorpe provides us with the materials to come to a rather different conclusion.

Compared to his dithering over the preceding months about whether he should resign, Macmillan moved with great rapidity once his prostate trouble was diagnosed. Contrary to previous misconception, he was told by his consultant urologist Alec Badenoch before he resigned that he didn't have cancer. The reality was that he was desperately tired and was glad of the medical excuse to pack it in. He told Badenoch that the illness 'came as manna from heaven – an act of God'.

But he was by no means done for. Consider the calendar. The lord chancellor, Lord Dilhorne, had asked all the cabinet ministers at the beginning of September whether they wanted Macmillan to carry on and, if he decided not to, who should succeed him; all but three wanted him to carry on, nobody mentioned Home as a successor. October 4: Macmillan discusses possible successors with his son Maurice; again no mention of Home. On the night of 7–8 October he is taken ill. On the afternoon of the 8th he is diagnosed and in the evening taken to hospital. The next morning, the 9th, he talks to Home about the announcement of his resignation and raises, for the first time, the possibility that Home might make himself available. At the same time, Selwyn Lloyd sets about spreading Home's claims. By the 11th, Lloyd has converted Dilhorne and Martin Redmayne, the chief whip, and is walking along the prom at Blackpool with them, plotting what to do next. It is these two men who are to be responsible for canvassing opinion: Dilhorne doing the cabinet (for the second time), and Redmayne the Tory MPs. By Tuesday the 15th, it is agreed that these soundings should include three questions: who's your first choice, who's your second and who would you oppose? Then, after Lord Hailsham makes a fool of himself at Blackpool, a fourth is added: what do you think of Lord Home as leader? That same day, before the soundings are actually taken, Supermac composes what becomes known as 'the Tuesday memorandum' for the Queen. It is a dithyramb for Sir Alec, comparing him to the heroic Grenadiers of 1914 and lauding his qualities of judgment and selflessness. He also makes a note in his diary after another meeting with Maurice and the party chairman, Lord Poole: 'the basic situation was the same – the party in the country wants Hogg; the Parliamentary Party wants Maudling or Butler; the Cabinet wants Butler.' But what they all got, only three days later, was Home.

Almost at the end of his book, Thorpe tells us, though without giving a source, that 'Macmillan and Home both came in time to think that it might have been better if Rab Butler had become prime minister in 1963.' I would go a lot further. It might have been better if Butler had succeeded Eden in 1957, or even Churchill in 1955. The country would undoubtedly have been better governed. There would have been no Suez, no inflationary stampede, no botched attempt to join the EEC but rather a careful development of a European Free Trade Area. Social reform and economic modernization would have been pursued in a more serious and systematic fashion. It would have been a soberer time, without the showmanship with which Macmillan delighted some and repelled others. We would not have been told we had never had it so good; but we might have been better off.

Alas, the qualities required for being prime minister are not the same as those required for becoming one. Butler had all the charisma of an old flannel. Supermac in his heyday was a class act. In his later years the satirists got at him, and to the young he was a somewhat moth-eaten comic figure. Thorpe tells us at the end that 'Macmillan *was* a great prime minister for much of his time in Downing Street.' There is a certain desperation about those italics. What was his legacy, after all? Premium Bonds and the Beeching Report. Macmillan said of Eden, quite rightly, that he had been trained to win the Derby of 1938 but had not been let out of the stalls until 1955. If you change the dates slightly, you could say much the same of Macmillan. His best years were already behind him when he reached the top at the age of sixty-two. And somewhere at the back of his mind, I think he knew it.

EDWARD HEATH:
THE GREAT SULK

At the end of his official biography of Lord Mountbatten twenty-five years ago, Philip Ziegler wrote: 'There was a time when I became so enraged by what I began to feel was his determination to hoodwink me that I found it necessary to place on my desk a notice saying: REMEMBER, IN SPITE OF EVERYTHING, HE WAS A GREAT MAN.' At the end of his authorized biography of Edward Heath, Ziegler writes: 'He was a great man, but his blemishes, though far less considerable, were quite as conspicuous as his virtues, and it is too often by his blemishes that he is remembered.' In the case of Mountbatten, we were to understand, it was the charm, the deviousness, the sexual vanity, the manipulation of people and the rewriting of history that were in danger of blinding us to the genuine achievements. Heath's traits were almost the direct opposite: charmlessness, rudeness, sexual neutrality, rancour, an excess of candour and an unwillingness to budge. But these too we are to forgive, or at least put to one side, and see beyond to the solid body of achievement. The trouble is that in both cases Ziegler's relentless accumulation and presentation of the evidence diminish that achievement to near-invisible proportions. Mountbatten smashed up almost every ship he skippered, and as a strategic commander his ingenious schemes vanished into the air with alarming rapidity. And Heath?

Ziegler has not lost his silken narrative touch, nor his insidious but brilliant gift of making the best possible case for his subject while not hesitating to show him in the worst possible light. Only thus can a biographer who hopes to be authorized or official please the victim's family or executors while serving the cause of truth. This is a deliciously readable and unfailingly fair book, but I cannot believe that its subject would have liked it any better than he cared for John Campbell's 1993 biography, Heath's own copy of which is scrawled with angry marginalia – 'Nonsense!', 'No!' and 'Wrong!'

Campbell's book was less alluring in style, more detailed in its accounts of interminable negotiations, psychologically no less acute than Ziegler's, but above all more hopeful that history would judge Heath less harshly than his contemporaries did; indeed, that his reputation was already beginning to be restored. Heath, he wrote, was arguably the true Tory, and his 'lonely doom-mongering looks more prescient than he was given credit for in the heady boom years.' Campbell, writing after the collapse of the Lawson boom, thought that Thatcherism had ended in painful disillusion and that Heath had been 'a political Cassandra, very largely right but not believed'. Yet seventeen years later, there are few signs of any such restoration of Heath's reputation, and Ziegler makes scarcely any such claims. It was to Thatcher, not Heath, that Tony Blair hastened to pay court. And although the Con-Lib coalition made much of its determination to protect the poorest against the cuts better than they were protected in the 1980s, it was common ground that the reduction of the deficit must be given top priority even in a recession. The protests of Keynesians and vulgar-Keynesian journalists were no more listened to than the 364 of their brethren who wrote to *The Times* to protest against the 1981 budget. Ted Heath's angry shade remains unloved and unappeased.

Not since Achilles has a public figure been so notorious for wrath. The journalist George Gale spoke of Heath's 'angry will'. Yet the sources of this anger remain hard to get at. If it was some sexual hurt which made Heath so solitary and so horrible to women (though, as Campbell points out, he could be equally horrible to men – it was just that the women minded it more), then it must have been as obscure as the hurt allegedly suffered by Henry James, since nobody so far has convincingly explained it.

Ted's father and grandfather were convivial, easy-going men, rooted in their native Kent, fond of a drink and ready to pinch any passing bottom. On his eightieth birthday, Heath *père*, who had started life as a carpenter and later done pretty well as a builder in Broadstairs, was asked if he had any regrets and said: 'Yes, that the permissive society did not begin 50 years earlier.' Ted was fond of both of them and they of him. His mother adored him, and her early death distressed him greatly. But even she seems to have been in awe of her fiercely ambitious and gifted son. Once, when she went up to his room and suggested that he was working too hard and should come down and join the family, the ten-year-old Teddy replied: 'Mother, sometimes I think you don't *want* me to get on.'

At school, he was excused football and cricket on the grounds that they might damage his pianist's hands. Yet the force of his character was such that he was never bullied or teased as a milksop. On the contrary, he was popular in every milieu he passed through: Balliol, the army, the whips' office (it is a later invention that he was a notoriously harsh chief whip). His opponents in the Monday Club liked to identify Heath as the original of Widmerpool – Anthony Powell disavowed the attribution. In any case, Widmerpool would never have been able to lose himself in music or sailing, or to achieve such high standards in either. Rising to wartime lieutenant-colonel, Heath certainly impressed his superiors, but he remained genuinely liked by his messmates and his men too. The fact was that he was almost superhumanly competent and diligent, and it was no surprise when he passed top into the Civil Service after the war. In his attitude to the British people, he reminds me more of the Efficient Baxter vainly attempting to sort out Lord Emsworth's affairs.

Nor was he lacking courage. As an undergraduate, he visited the battlefront of the Spanish Civil War and only just managed to get out of Poland before war broke out. As an artillery officer, he fought his way through Belgium and Germany and saw men die alongside him. Ziegler treats Heath's six years in the army rather skimpily (Campbell is a little better), yet this experience surely generated the hatred of war and determination to avoid it at almost all costs which were so conspicuous in his later attitudes to conflict, and also cemented his view, already formed in the late 1930s, that the best hope was a 'United States of Europe . . . in which states will have to give up some of their national rights'. As an MP in the 1950s, he would declare in his plonking downright style that 'the nation state is dead. What has sovereignty to do with anything in the 20th century?'

From this belief he never wavered. It was the source both of his sole claim to immortality and of the undying loathing he incurred in a considerable portion of his own party. Ziegler shows very well the energy, resourcefulness and mastery of detail that Heath deployed both as Macmillan's minister for Europe in his first, unsuccessful bid to have Britain join the EEC and his later triumph as prime minister. It remains doubtful whether anyone else could have pulled it off. Yet, as Ziegler also makes clear in his unstressed, faintly feline way, the manner of the pulling-off remains at the very least questionable and at worst the cause of long-term public disenchantment not only with the European project but with politics in general.

Heath wanted to gloss over the popular objections, just as his hero Jean Monnet had, believing that the European project could get off the ground only if it was undertaken by the elites, with little or no reference to the people. Heath told Kilmuir, lord chancellor at the time of the Macmillan application, that 'in the modern world if, from other points of view, political and economic, it should prove desirable to accept such further limitations on sovereignty as would follow from the signature of the Treaty of Rome, we could do so without danger to the essential character of our independence and without prejudice to our vital interests.' In reply, Kilmuir warned that 'these objections ought to be brought out into the open now because, if we attempt to gloss over them at this stage, those who are opposed to the whole idea of joining the Community will certainly seize on them with more damaging effect later on.' To put it bluntly, they would be accused of having taken Britain in on a false prospectus.

Heath would later claim that he had all along said explicitly that 'the main purpose of the negotiations was political.' But quite what 'political' was supposed to mean he did not feel obliged to elaborate on, preferring to point out that any move towards federalism could only come about with the support of all members, so that concerns about sovereignty were misplaced. Ziegler puts it nicely: 'He did not seek actively to mislead the British public about his expectations, but he did not feel it necessary or desirable to spell out the full implications of British entry in any detail.' That seems to me at least *suppressio veri*, with a whiff of *suggestio falsi* too. There was also in Heath's manner what Robert Rhodes James, then a senior clerk in the House of Commons, diagnosed as 'an ominous note of thinly veiled intellectual contempt for those in his party who opposed the application'. Neither then nor later did Heath have much time for vox populi or for anyone who objected to his *grands projets* on grounds either of democracy or history. In old age, he developed a soft spot for dictators and was a fêted visitor to Peking and Baghdad, where they understood how to deal with dissent.

This indifference to popular sentiment was striking in the reforms of local government which he undertook in concert with his protégé Peter Walker. It is a pity that Ziegler doesn't mention these, though Campbell covers them well, for the Heath–Walker reforms show Heathco at its crassest. Counties like Berkshire, which had lasted for a thousand years, were to be axed or have their boundaries sliced. The total number of authorities was to be reduced from more than 1200 to about 400. Bigger was better, more modern, more streamlined. Historical loyalties were for wimps. As a fledgling journalist, I was sent to interview Walker in his Commons cubbyhole and remember how astonished he was that anyone should have qualms about such alterations. Walker recanted long before his recent death; Heath did not. Some but not all of their work has been undone. It is now, I think, widely acknowledged that what we need is not less but more local government.

Elsewhere, Heath's legacy did not endure nearly so long. When he came to power in June 1970 (much to the surprise of his opponents and most of his own side too), he inherited a bad and fast deteriorating situation in Northern Ireland. Unfortunately – an adverb one reaches for far too often in reviewing Heath's life – he totally failed to grasp the realities of Ulster politics. Ziegler is inclined to give him credit for ramming through the Sunningdale Agreement in 1973. After all, its terms weren't so dissimilar from those of the Good Friday Agreement twenty-five years later – the latter memorably described by the SDLP deputy leader Seamus Mallon as 'Sunningdale for slow learners'. Doing his best for his man, Ziegler declares that 'with the benefit of hindsight it is possible to see that he was right and that the Ulstermen were wrong.' But is it? The trouble with this posthumous rehabilitation is not simply that Sunningdale lasted only two months, before the pro-Sunningdale Unionists were obliterated in the miners' election that Heath had so suicidally called in February 1974. It was blindingly obvious that the Unionists would never accept the plan for an All-Ireland Council, which they regarded as a preliminary step to a united Ireland. A year or so later, Garret FitzGerald, the Irish foreign minister, was asked why they had not warned the British team that the All-Ireland Council was a step too far. FitzGerald, charmingly and not unreasonably, replied: 'We didn't think it was our business to tell the British how to negotiate.'

But what Ziegler also makes clear is that the Unionists really did have reason to distrust British intentions. At an informal meeting between Heath and Lord Rothschild, cabinet secretary Burke Trend and Heath's principal private secretary Robert Armstrong (who were both hugely influential in British dealings with Northern Ireland), everyone had agreed that 'the only lasting solution would lie in bringing about the unification of all Ireland.' The foreign secretary, Alec Douglas-Home, also believed that 'the real British interest would ... be served best by pushing them [the Unionists] towards a United Ireland.' How revealing the apposition between 'British' and 'them'.

The signing of the Good Friday Agreement in 1998 took place under completely different circumstances: the IRA had been fought to a standstill and had signalled that the war was over, and Blair had told the people of Ulster that he did not expect to see a united Ireland in his lifetime or the lifetime of anyone in his audience. The principle of majority consent was no longer a hurdle which might be dismantled twig by twig, but the foundation of a new settlement and understood as such by all parties.

What one can't help noticing from this miserable story – more than 2000 people were killed after the failure of Sunningdale – is the singularly unresponsive quality of Heath's mind. It is not true, as Enoch Powell claimed, that he shied away violently from anything resembling an idea. On the contrary, he espoused ideas with a passion he scarcely ever showed in human relations. But once an idea was lodged in his head, he did nothing with it; he allowed it no interplay with other ideas or other people. As a result, he had little aptitude for judging political risk or public reaction. It was not just that he didn't know what made people tick, he made no effort to listen to the ticking. His insensitivity has often been compared with Thatcher's, but until she was overtaken by hubris in her later years she retained a strong prudential sense of how far she could go and what she could get away with.

For the same reason, Heath's grandiose plan for reforming the trade unions ran into collision after collision until it finally expired into irrelevance. He seems to have given little thought to how union members would react to an abrupt scrapping of all the legal exemptions that had built up since Disraeli's day. It did not occur to him that a step-by-step process of whittling away the more indefensible privileges might have worked, as it did for Thatcher. In the same way, he never considered building up the European Free Trade Area by voluntary agreement, gradually extending its reach into other social and economic areas, such as freedom of movement for its citizens and reciprocal welfare benefits. There is a useful alternative model here in the shape of the European Convention on Human Rights, which over the years seeped into the language of our courts until it was finally enshrined in an act of Parliament. Some right-wingers still don't fancy it, but they can't complain that it suffers from a democratic deficit in the way that the European Union itself now clearly does.

Nowhere is this failure to think through the consequences of an idea more embarrassing than in the case of his economic policies: the free-market approach on which he won office and the prices and incomes controls he resorted to two years later, in the great U-turn from which he never really recovered. Ziegler makes it clear that Heath was never a wholehearted believer in 'Selsdon Man' – the phrase was a nifty minting of Harold Wilson's. All he was looking for was a distinct and attractive contrast to Labour's flounderings, and so he promised a 'quiet revolution', in terms which understandably convinced his right wing that he had come over to their way of thinking. By instinct, though, he preferred to control things rather than let them run free and endure the consequences. Indeed, he had hardly stopped denouncing the evils of Labour's prices and incomes freeze before he was designing one himself. It is characteristic that in this secret enterprise he should have relied not on his political colleagues, whom he mostly thought little of, but on the senior civil servants he found so much more congenial, notably Sir William Armstrong, the head of the Home Civil Service. Armstrong became widely known as the deputy prime minister before he went mad and lay on the floor of Number 10 raving about Communist conspiracies and had to be taken away.

A later generation remembers Heath mostly from the years of the Long Sulk. His graceless behaviour began before he was supplanted by That Woman (herself not the best of losers). His refusal to quit Number 10 after the February 1974 election may not have been quite as deplorable as Gordon Brown's later carry-on, which would have made a limpet blush. Heath, after all, had secured more votes nationally than Wilson and had only four fewer MPs. Yet his behaviour imprinted the image of a lousy loser which simply got worse and worse, despite all the efforts of his friends to stage a reconciliation.

It is tempting to assume that things might have turned out better for him if he had been better humoured or if he had been married or had a close confidant. Yet Ziegler points out that there were always plenty of friends, such as the redoubtable Sara Morrison, ready to tell him when his grumpy behaviour, and general refusal to show any sign of life, was damaging his own interests. Campbell argues that he was exceptionally unlucky in having to preside over a fevered period of union unrest and oil shocks. Yet the pattern of his failures seems too insistent to be entirely excused in this way. Time and again, he tried to mould all-or-nothing answers which came to pieces in his hands before the clay was dry. The underlying trouble strikes me as having been less one of temperament than of intellect, in so far as you can separate the two things. He simply lacked the agility of mind and the openness of imagination to play through the ramifications of a theme. He knew what he wanted to happen and he thought that this was enough to make it happen.

He was, ultimately, a solipsist. Nothing is more characteristic than that he should have left the bulk of his £5.4 million estate not to his brother's children, of whom he saw little, but to the Sir Edward Heath Charitable Foundation, the principal function of which was to house his papers and show his lovely house in the Close at Salisbury to the public. It has now turned out that there is not enough money in the kitty to carry out his wishes. This vision too has foundered on the hard and slippery rocks of reality.

MARGARET THATCHER: MAKING YOUR OWN LUCK

The first lesson that Batman learns is that 'the will is everything'. Disraeli and Schopenhauer said much the same. And in this crop of books about Margaret Thatcher, rushed out in the weeks after her death, it is the raw will that is celebrated. The titles of the two big Lives, the first volume of her official biography by Charles Moore, the former editor of the *Daily Telegraph*, and the single volume by her long-time ghost Robin Harris, bear the same title advertising her unbendable quality. The two slighter works, on her foreign policy by Robin Renwick, the diplomat who was at her side in Rhodesia, Washington and Brussels, and by Gillian Shephard, the former education secretary who has collected reminiscences of what she was like to work with, often from unsung Conservative Party officers and apparatchiks, both remind us of that unforgettable title first conferred on her by *Red Star*, the Soviet Army newspaper. She became the Iron Lady even before she became prime minister, by virtue of a fiery speech delivered in Kensington Town Hall less than a year after she defeated Ted Heath. She has remained the Iron Lady ever since, and that is how she will be, not unjustly, remembered.

Yet we need to clothe this naked will a little. Her tenacity had a peculiar character which, I think, conforms perfectly to Antonio Gramsci's famous formulation, 'pessimism of the intellect, optimism of the will'. Her assessment of the situation was always bleak and unvarnished. She had, as Renwick puts it, 'an absolute contempt for any semblance of wishful thinking' and 'an innate ability to get to the heart of any really difficult or unpleasant problem and not to try to wish it away'. She loathed politicians like Harold Macmillan whose instinct was always to smooth things over – a loathing which was returned with knobs on.

One of the reasons that she thrilled to the company of Keith Joseph was his gloomy tone. In the 'Notes Towards the Definition of Policy' which he presented to an indignant shadow cabinet (the echo of T. S. Eliot was beautifully appropriate to Joseph's message of decline), he argued that 'We made things worse where, after the war, we chose the path of consensus. It seems to me that on a number of subjects we have reached the end of that road.' They had promised too much and been guilty of 'subordinating the rule of law to the avoidance of conflict'. 'In short, by ignoring history, instincts, human nature and common-sense, we have intensified the very evils which we believed, with the best intentions, that we could wipe away.' No rising Tory star of the Macmillan–Heath generation could accept Joseph's indictment that they themselves might have been complicit in the debacle. It was all the fault of the 'Socialists', and if only the right chaps were back in charge, things would look up. Mrs Thatcher resisted all such Micawberish temptations, and indeed all suggestions that the road might be anything but hard and stony.

The 'economics of joy', as the economist Herb Stein described the policies of the carefree tax-cutters, were anathema to her. She was deeply sceptical about détente too, being convinced that 'we are losing the Thaw in a subtle and disturbing way'. From the start, she was equally sceptical about the practicability of monetary union in Europe. On the very day she arrived in Number 10, she responded to a memo from the cabinet secretary suggesting an open-minded approach to such schemes: 'I doubt whether stability can be achieved by a currency system. Indeed it can't – unless all of the underlying policies of each country are right'. The fortunes of the euro thirty years later suggest that there is no getting round this uncomfortable truth. Nor did she welcome even the most astonishing success at face value. When the Berlin Wall fell, she was quick to point out that the break-up of empires was always a time of danger. She really did act out Kipling's 'If' (her favourite poem, as it was the nation's) and attempt to treat triumph and disaster as equivalent impostors.

Yet at the same time she had an ineradicable belief that 'we (or rather I) shall overcome'. She attacked head-on R. A. Butler's belief that politics was the art of the possible: 'The danger of such a phrase is that we may deem impossible things which would be possible, indeed desirable, if only we had more courage, more insight'. In refusing to accommodate herself to the inevitability of decline, she found herself at odds with virtually all her colleagues.

In her obituaries, the word 'divisive' was much deployed. This is pussyfooting. She was loathed, and usually despised too. Jim Prior, her first employment secretary, said 'She is, of course, completely potty. She won't last six months', and later asserted that 'she hasn't really got a friend left in Cabinet'. Her supposed allies also moaned about her behind her back. Willie Whitelaw called her 'that awful woman'. Even the courtly and cunning Lord Carrington was driven to explode to her principal private secretary, 'Clive, if I have any more trouble from this fucking, stupid, petit-bourgeois woman, I'm going to go'. (He later said that he would never have used such language, though it is not clear which particular epithet could not have passed his lips.) It was Carrington, too, who, on storming out of a meeting in the cabinet room about the EEC budget without looking where he was going, collided with a Doric pillar and exclaimed, 'My God, I've hit another immovable obstacle'.

At most, four of her first shadow cabinet had voted for her. Despite repeated purges, pretty much the same was true of her last cabinet when it came to the crunch. As for the Civil Service, the upper reaches of the Treasury and the Foreign Office found her alien and unappealing from the start. They were Heathite to a man, distrustful of the free market, wedded to prices and incomes policies and to greater European integration. Only lower down were a few potential kindred spirits emerging – Peter Middleton and Terry Burns in the Treasury, Charles Powell and Robin Renwick in the Foreign Office. Nor were outside assessments any more favourable. Although very taken with her, Henry Kissinger told President Ford in 1975, 'Soames may be a big Conservative leader sometime. I don't think Margaret Thatcher will last'. Peter Jenkins, the *Guardian* columnist, wrote in December 1981 that 'a brief obituary of Thatcherism is now in order'.

Partly, but only partly, this was because of her eccentric and overbearing manner of doing business. John Hoskyns, a businessman who had made a fortune in computers and who became the first head of her Policy Unit, despaired of her lack of any strategic sense. After a couple of years of working with her, he sent her one of the rudest memos a prime minister can ever have received from an understrapper:

> You break every rule of good man-management. You bully your weaker colleagues. You criticise colleagues in front of each other and in front of their officials. They can't answer back without appearing disrespectful, in front of others, to a woman and to a Prime Minister. You abuse that situation. You give little praise or credit, and you are too ready to blame others when things go wrong.

Even her most loyal of ghosts, Robin Harris, concedes that 'in matters of man management, she was, by common consent, hopeless – alternately chaotic and domineering, timid and abrasive.

She was a notoriously bad chairman'. He also accuses her of being a naive and hopeless picker of ministers. This is surely an unrealistic criticism. She was, after all, operating in a parliamentary democracy. Her cabinet had to be vaguely representative of the parliamentary Conservative Party, or there would have been even more hell to pay. All she could do – which she did – was to keep her most ham-fisted enemies as far from the levers of economic power as possible.

But there is no getting away from the fact that her behaviour towards her colleagues was in the end to prove a fatal flaw. She could and did sweep out the old wets at regular intervals, only to find herself drenched with a shower of Blue Chips off the same block – Chris Patten, Kenneth Clarke and William Waldegrave instead of Christopher Soames, Ian Gilmour and Whitelaw. Much more serious was the attrition rate among her allies, who were less easy to replace. One by one, they limped off the pitch, bruised and affronted: Geoffrey Howe, Keith Joseph, Leon Brittan, Nigel Lawson, Norman Tebbit, John Biffen – consoled only by their CHs, a recurring suffix which an uninformed observer might have mistaken for some obscure religious order, the Confraternity of Humiliation.

There is, however, a counter-argument which I think Moore glimpses but Harris doesn't. If she had been a 'good' chairman, she would, time and again, have found herself summing up the sense of a meeting wholly against her inclinations. When she was so heavily outnumbered, disruption was the only answer. It was essential, as Stephen Potter would have said, to 'break flow'. Interruption, Repetition, Digression – these were the only tools for getting her own way. When all these techniques failed, railroading decisions through smaller hand-picked committees and fixing the agenda were necessary resorts. It was the style of government that Michael Heseltine complained of when he stalked out of the cabinet in the Westland crisis. Harris finds plausible justification for Thatcher's behaviour then, but over a wider field than the helicopter business,

Heseltine was not without reason to complain. In fact, a prime minister who does not exploit her mastery of the cabinet agenda, which is one of her relatively few weapons, is probably not doing the job properly. In Thatcher's case, her disruptive style sacrificed collegial harmony to getting things done. It is notable that, when she had confidence in the men in charge, as she did during the Falklands War, she was content to leave most things to the military, herself providing martial spirit on a heroic scale but not attempting to meddle in matters she knew she knew little or nothing about.

Lord Renwick confirms this impression in his absorbing accounts of the negotiations he himself was involved in – the Lancaster House talks on Rhodesia, the stormy Budget negotiations in Brussels, and the transition from apartheid to democracy in South Africa – and of his colleague Sir Percy Cradock's collaboration with her on the handover of Hong Kong. In each instance, he depicts a demanding but entirely rational boss, eager to test any argument to the limit but seeking a stable and realistic solution rather than being pushed to it when her ranting had run its course. The freshest part of his account is of the encouragement she gave F. W. de Klerk and the steady pressure she exerted for the release of Nelson Mandela. Of course, the sanctions on investment imposed by the US Congress and the change of heart within the Dutch Reformed Church were far more significant factors, but Renwick shows that, when she was not faced with sullen and obdurate opponents, she, too, was someone to do business with. Mrs Shephard's accounts of Mrs Thatcher's encounters with unfamous cogs in the political world supplement this picture on the domestic front, reminding us in particular that, uniquely among recent Conservative leaders, she came from the heart of the Conservative party and was at her happiest in the company of its members. She wrote of her first visit to a Conservative Party conference at Blackpool in 1946, that she was 'entranced'. As Moore drily comments: 'This is perhaps the only recorded occasion when anyone has used that word about a Conservative Party conference'.

Her critics accused her of the illusion of omniscience, that as Hoskyns put it, 'she didn't know what she didn't know'. Hoskyns, while paying full tribute to her guts, determination and lack of pomposity, complained that 'she is quite limited intellectually. The problem is that she is unaware of the fact that other people's intelligence may be superior to her own'. I'm not sure that this is correct. Rather, she was inclined to hero-worship those intellectuals whose views coincided with her own. Out of her notorious handbag at one time or another, she would pull Lord Radcliffe's Reith Lectures, Hayek's *The Constitution of Liberty*, Beveridge's report on social insurance and that speech wrongly attributed to Abraham Lincoln which declares that 'you cannot strengthen the weak by weakening the strong'. She would read anything that was recommended to her: Popper, Burke, Schumpeter, Adam Smith, Dostoevsky, Koestler. It is quite true, though, that she was not an intellectual in the sense of relishing the free play of thought. Every excursion had to be subordinate to her driving purposes.

But where did these driving purposes come from? Caroline Stephens, her redoubtable social secretary for almost all her time in power, used to tell new secretaries, only half-joking, that 'The first thing you have to bear in mind is that Mrs Thatcher is a very ordinary woman'. If so, the first mystery that any biographer has to address is how did such an ordinary woman become Britain's first woman prime minister, and hold power for eleven years and leave such a lasting mark on the nation, rather than more brilliant and idolized characters such as Barbara Castle and Shirley Williams. If the answer lies in the will, we have to track down the ultimate origins of that will.

Mrs Thatcher herself was quite clear on the subject. 'All my ideas about Britain were formed before I was seventeen or eighteen.' The answer lay in Grantham, and the grocer's premises at

No. 1, North Parade, above which Margaret Roberts was born and lived her life until she went from Kesteven Girls Grammar School to Oxford. When she came to write her memoirs, it was, as with many people, her earliest memories of home and school that flooded back. The later stuff had to be extracted with some pain by her two ghosts, Harris and John O'Sullivan, the former *Daily Telegraph* journalist, who added a refreshing *allegrezza* to the end product, which is now reissued in a single volume compressed and edited by Harris.

Yet there is a strange reluctance on Harris's part to accept Grantham as the clue. He dismisses the place as 'a somewhat dreary town in the East Midlands, itself one of the more dreary regions of England'. Well, one could quarrel with that description: the town has ancient coaching inns and a glorious parish church with, according to Simon Jenkins, 'the finest steeple in England' (Ruskin swooned when he saw it), and it lies in gentle country between Belvoir Castle and Belton Hall. Pevsner rightly says that there is even a touch of Vanbrugh about the Wesleyan chapel in Finkin Street where Margaret Roberts worshipped and her father Alfred preached every alternate Sunday when he was not carrying the gospel to the surrounding country. It is true that she herself said that 'it was a great thrill to come to London. In Grantham it was like swimming in a very small pool: you keep bumping into the sides' – and in later life she did not go back there much. But then this is true of many ambitious young people in a hurry. It does not mean that her upbringing did not leave an indelible mark upon her; still less, as Harris claims, that at the deeper level of her being, she may have reacted against her upbringing more than she reflected it.

He deduces 'the lack of impact which Methodism had had on her religious outlook' from the fact that she did not seem to know her Bible very well and had little interest in theology. This is, I think, a dubious linkage. Methodism was never about theological learning. It thrived, in David Hempton's phrase, 'on the raw edge of religious excitement'. For the Methodist, the ideal Christian life was one of ceaseless cheerful activism. Margaret Thatcher's obsession with self-improvement and her hatred of wasting time were signs that her Methodist roots were still very much alive in her; ditto her unquenchable hopefulness and the strange sense of exaltation that she radiated. If she was not much good at forgiving, nor was John Wesley.

E. P. Thompson's blistering attack on Methodism in *The Making of the English Working Class* contained an internal contradiction. If Methodism was such a miserable creed, why did it produce such active, cheerful souls and come to generate the British Labour movement? But Thompson's scorching rhetoric did succeed in obscuring the virtues of Methodism at its best, so that even today it seems difficult to persuade people that such a queer creed could have had much to do with the nurturing of a Margaret Thatcher.

Moore sets out to rescue her, as did Bishop Richard Chartres in his brilliant oration at her funeral, from the misunderstanding of her notorious remark in the interview she gave to *Woman's Own* that 'there is no such thing as society'. He points out that in her 1977 Iain Macleod Memorial Lecture, she argues that self-interest was not the antithesis of care for others, because 'man is a social creature, born into family, clan, community, nation, brought up in mutual dependence'. Similar messages can be derived from the semi-sermons she gave at St Lawrence Jewry, the City church, and to the General Assembly of the Church of Scotland. But these were texts largely prepared for her by others, notably Alfred Sherman, the capo of what she called her 'awkward squad'. Her actions show less of a Burkean enthusiast for the little platoons. She steadfastly opposed the efforts of Geoffrey Howe and Nigel Lawson to retain some support for marriage when independent taxation of husband and wife was introduced. And she remorselessly squashed the independence of local government through rate-capping, nationalization of the business rates and, ultimately and fatally, the poll tax. She believed in strong but limited government and a strong individual, with nothing much in between. One's duty towards one's neighbour entailed compassion and kindness to others, and her efforts to bring succour to widows, wounded soldiers and anyone who might be lonely or depressed were unremitting. But ultimately she believed in personal salvation unaided by sacrament or intermediate institutions. And in this, too, she was Methodist to her bones.

Harris paints her childhood as a grim one and advises us not to take at face value the recollection in her memoirs and in earlier interviews of the *douceur de vivre* she experienced at the cinema or the odd musical, for such events were rare in her Spartan adolescence. This picture is undercut by a lucky discovery that Charles Moore made of more than 150 letters that Margaret had written to her elder sister Muriel between the end of the 1930s and the beginning of the 1960s. The letters, which had been lying unsorted in bags in Muriel's attic, not only cast doubt on Harris's assertion that, being four years apart in age, 'the sisters were never close'. They also refute the assumption that she never had much fun. The young Margaret wishes she could have danced like Ginger Rogers, loves the Laurence Olivier–Joan Fontaine film of *Rebecca*, thinks the latest Deanna Durbin flick 'rotten', but says that *Quiet Wedding*, starring Margaret Lockwood, with screenplay by Terence Rattigan, was 'an absolute scream. I laughed more than I have for months'. Even when she gets to Somerville, most of her letters are not about politics but about the underwear she has just bought.

The letters also disprove the line taken by previous biographers and followed by Harris that, until Denis came along, she had had no romantic friendships with men. This was never likely with such an undeniably pretty girl at Oxford where the sex-starved men were knee-deep and just back from the war. In Somerville Hall, she might be belittled as a humourless Midlands chemist, but she was not short of admirers. One of them, Tony Bray, wept when he was reminded of their walk-out sixty years later.

These letters are important not just because of their *Brief Encounter*-style charm but because they dispel the illusions that Margaret Roberts was some kind of freak. They do not, I hasten to add, transform our picture of her into a sweet, easy-going type. Her comments on her boyfriends are as tart as were to be her comments on her cabinet colleagues.

When she agrees to see Tony Bray a couple of years later, 'more to let him see how I've changed rather than to see him!', she remarks afterwards that 'I quite enjoyed seeing him again for a short time – it satisfied my curiosity – but he's a weird-looking chap to cart around the place!' When Denis Thatcher hove in view, he fared no better, being described as 'not a very attractive creature'. Nor did he improve for her on nearer acquaintance: 'I can't say I really ever enjoy going out for the evening with him. He has not got a very prepossessing personality'. (They were to be happily married for sixty years and she was irremediably shattered by his death.)

But her most remarkable dalliance was with Willie Cullen, one of a group of energetic Scots farmers who had come down to Essex to escape the agricultural depression in Scotland – not unlike Donald Farfrae in *The Mayor of Casterbridge*. Margaret is boundlessly patronizing about him: 'He has a kind of naïveté that only Scotsmen can have – the funniest part is that although I have been introduced to him twice, I can never catch his name and still don't know it! . . . He speaks with a frightfully Scotch accent. I'm afraid he's going to be an awful nuisance'. Then she has a brainwave: 'I showed him the snapshot of you and I [grammar, Miss Roberts!] together – and he said he could scarcely tell the difference so I should think we could easily substitute me for you' (she meant 'you for me' – Kesteven Girls Grammar School has a lot to answer for). Clearly, the bucolic if canny Willie will not do for her, but he might do for Muriel who has just broken up with her current boyfriend. Margaret urges Muriel to come and stay with her to meet Willie. 'By the way, he will never become your brother-in-law though I have big hopes that he may be mine one day!' Which he does. It is a plot out of a Hardy novel, except that it ends happily. But there is no greater testimony to Margaret Roberts's ability to get her own way than her effortless marrying-off of her elder sister (herself a fairly strong-willed character) to get rid of the incomprehensible Willie. The handover was delayed only because he gave her a very nice black-calf handbag and out of decency she had to go out with him a while longer.

Moore's touch is as sure in retailing these enchanting early days as in recounting her grim struggles to replace Ted Heath and to stamp her principles on the crucial budgets of 1979 and 1981 which were to set the country on its fresh path. Mrs Thatcher's capacity for cunning and caution is well displayed as much in her readiness to succumb without fuss to the first miners' strike, which the government was unprepared to withstand, as to fight with ruthless tenacity Arthur Scargill's decision to call out a national strike without a national ballot in the spring of 1984, by which time her previous energy secretary, Nigel Lawson, had coal stocks piled high. Both Moore and Renwick tell the story of the Falklands in brilliantly nuanced detail, demonstrating Mrs Thatcher's willingness to go to the tolerable edge (and probably beyond) in diplomatic negotiations and her agony at the thought of all the young lives that would be lost. Nobody who reads these pages could ever again think of Margaret Thatcher as heartless.

Moore's is, quite simply, a marvellous biography, and when the succeeding two (or possibly three volumes) are published, it will take its place alongside the monumental multivolume Lives of earlier great prime ministers – Moneypenny and Buckle's Disraeli, Morley's Gladstone and John Grigg's Lloyd George – while being more entertaining than any of these. It is hard to find anything much to quibble with: it was Clement Attlee, not Enoch Powell, who first popularized the phrase 'the enemy within', and surprisingly in relation to communist infiltration into the trade unions, much as Mrs Thatcher was to use the phrase. Harold Macmillan rose to stardom after building 300,000 houses a year, not 300,000 council houses, although in the early years of that Tory government the vast majority of houses built were indeed council houses – a strange thought in the light of subsequent history. Nor would I go along with Moore's proposition that 'she generally eschewed what she would call "personal remarks"'. Only seven pages later, he has her referring to Roy Jenkins as 'Shaky Jowls'. And her descriptions of her cabinet enemies are memorable: Jim Prior 'the false squire'; Michael Heseltine – 'every talent except brains'. But in general, Moore's estimate of her character, actions and achievements is unfailingly just and thoughtful but never uncritical, and his book can safely be recommended to readers who have no smidgen of sympathy for the Iron Lady as well as to her unswerving fans.

Look here upon this picture and on this. Talk about Hyperion to a satyr. While Moore is always keen to be fair to every side in the argument, Robin Harris has Old Vitriolic as his permanent font setting. Yet nobody could be better qualified for the task. As well as writing a history of the Conservative Party, Harris worked for Thatcher in one way or another ever since 1985, writing many of her speeches, intimately engaged in advising her on policy, and, most importantly, coaxing a full set of memoirs out of someone who was constitutionally averse to writing so much as a memo, preferring to scrawl straight lines (Good) or wiggly lines (Bad) under or beside other people's words, interspersed with the occasional 'No!' Indeed, the wayward lollop of her handwriting seems better suited to her gossipy letters to Muriel than to affairs of state. Those two volumes of recollection are an indispensable resource, gracefully written, self-serving, of course, but with the arguments for and against her views fairly and accurately reported. They are as well worth reading as the biographical works under review and much better history than the previous biographies published.

It is as though these Herculean efforts have drained Harris's resources of tolerance. His *Not for Turning* offers us the dark underside of the memoirs, and it is irresistible reading because the brilliance of Harris's gift for narrative has not deserted him.

The book administers a monster dose of catharsis, provoking pity, fear and horror in more or less equal measures. We are familiar with other periods of friction in High Politics – the war between the Bevanites and the Gaitskellites, the unending tussle between the followers of Peel, Russell and Disraeli, not to mention the misunderstandings between the Montagues and the Capulets. But in Harris's account, these are all fleeting tiffs compared to the war between the Wets and the Dries. There is scarcely a minister in any of Margaret Thatcher's cabinets who is not denounced as weak, devious, conceited or disloyal – or all of the above. Mrs Thatcher herself, although supposedly the heroine of the drama, is repeatedly ticked off, for 'her alternatively cloying and abrasive performances', for being 'unimaginative', 'incapable of forgiveness', of utterly lacking the logical, scientifically trained mind she was so proud of and on the contrary being remarkable for her 'feminine logic'. Almost all her choices of minister are denounced as 'transparently unsuitable' (it would be unmanly not to mention here that this reviewer's appointment to her staff is fingered in a footnote, no doubt rightly, as 'another of her mistakes'). His account of the manoeuvres leading up to her fall is as savage an indictment of individual and collective treachery as I have ever read.

But even this passage palls beside his account of her last years, which spill over the final hundred pages of the book. In this connection, Harris argues that 'no true portrait of her can be drawn that omits the dark reality'. He spares us nothing: her heavy drinking, her shouting matches with Denis, her wild suspicions of his infidelity, the cruel effects on her short-term memory of her succession of strokes, until she could no longer string a sentence together, although she was still capable of being wounded when her daughter Carol published a description of her dementia. Harris criticizes 'the intrusive and distasteful elements' of the Meryl Streep film *The Iron Lady*. Yet it is hard to see how his own account can escape the same indictment. By comparison,

Kingsley Amis's account of the indignities of old age in *Ending Up* is a drawing-room comedy.

More distressing than mere mental decay and mortality (in which, as Bishop Chartres reminded us, she really was One of Us) is Harris's account of the way that 'in her old age Mrs Thatcher's thought processes became cruder and her vituperation about the Europeans more intemperate'. Increasingly she hobnobbed with the more unsavoury characters knocking about the world stage – Augusto Pinochet, Franjo Tudjman of Croatia, Aslan Maskhadov, the leader of the Chechen rebels, and President Nazarbayev of Kazakhstan, 'the sort of wily authoritarian figure she understood'.

Harris's own lenses become a little blurred too. He conceives a driving hatred for Geoffrey Howe, for whom he had once worked until Howe made a flippant remark about the Falklands War. Howe, he says, was 'raddled with bitterness', but it is surely Harris's own bitterness which leads him to deny the credit that Howe genuinely deserves for the budgets of 1979 and 1981 (ditto with Nigel Lawson, who, for all his errors over monetary policy, will go down as one of the great tax-reforming chancellors). Nor is it true of Howe's resignation speech that 'its legendary qualities have been bestowed in retrospect'. Those mild, hesitant closing sentences were electrifying at the time, and anyone hearing them knew instantly that Thatcher was finished. It certainly is not true that, if she had gained a couple more votes in the leadership contest, she could have sailed on regardless. You cannot mislay the support of nearly half your MPs and hope to survive for long.

One may feel, as I do, that it would have been better if the general electorate had been given the chance to dismiss her, but one must understand the motives of those MPs who feared that they would be dismissed along with her. It was the same fear that animated those who supported John Redwood's 'no change, no chance' leadership bid five years later (Harris worked for the Redwood campaign) – and indeed the same fear that impelled those who voted for Thatcher to replace Heath. Politics always was a blood sport with no protected species. And it is simply bad history to dismiss in half a sentence John Major's triumph in the 1992 general election, when he totted up more votes than Mrs Thatcher did in any of her three victories.

Despite or perhaps even because of these blemishes, I cannot conceal my feeling that Robin Harris's *Not for Turning* approaches the condition of art. It is as compelling in its unrelievedly black and venomous fashion as the novels of Céline or Thomas Bernhard. Anyone who thinks that, in the modern politics of nudge, soundbites and focus groups, all passion is irretrievably spent has got another think coming.

NOTES AND REFERENCES

Introduction: The Amphibious Mob
Albion: The Origins of the English Imagination, Peter Ackroyd (Chatto)

VOICES IN OUR TIME

Kingsley Amis: the craving machine
Spectator, 11 November 2006
The Life of Kingsley Amis, Zachary Leader (Jonathan Cape)

Alan Bennett: against splother
Spectator, 22 October 2005
Untold Stories, Alan Bennett (Faber & Faber/Profile)

Muriel Spark: the Go-Away Bird
Spectator, 15 August 2009
Muriel Spark: The Biography, Martin Stannard (Weidenfeld & Nicolson)

V. S. Naipaul: no home for Mr Biswas
Spectator, 5 May 1984
Finding the Centre: Two Narratives, V. S. Naipaul (André Deutsch)

Hugh Trevor-Roper: the Voltaire of St Aldate's
Spectator, 15 July 2006
Letters from Oxford: Hugh Trevor-Roper to Bernard Berenson, edited by Richard Davenport-Hines (Weidenfeld & Nicolson)

W. G. Sebald: a master shrouded in mist
Spectator, 26 February 2005
Campo Santo, W. G. Sebald, translated by Anthea Bell (Hamish Hamilton)

John le Carré: spooking the spooks
Spectator, 23 September 2006
The Mission Song, John le Carré (Hodder & Stoughton)

Elias Canetti: the God–Monster of Hampstead
Spectator, 23 July 2005
Party in the Blitz: The English Years, Elias Canetti, translated by Michael Hofmann (Harvill Press)

John Osborne: anger management?
Spectator, 6 May 2006
John Osborne: A Patriot for Us, John Heilpern (Chatto & Windus)

Professor Derek Jackson: off the radar
London Review of Books, 7 February 2008
As I Was Going to St Ives: A Life of Derek Jackson, Simon Courtauld (Michael Russell)

Germaine Greer: still strapped in the cuirass
Times Literary Supplement, 19 March 1999
The Whole Woman, Germaine Greer (Doubleday)

EARLY MODERNS

Rudyard Kipling: the sensitive bounder
Spectator, 3 November 2007
Kipling Sahib: India and the Making of Rudyard Kipling, Charles Allen (Little, Brown)

George Gissing: the downfall of a pessimist
Spectator, 8 March 2008
George Gissing: A Life, Paul Delany (Weidenfeld & Nicolson)

Virginia Woolf: go with the flow
Spectator, 23 April 2005
Virginia Woolf: An Inner Life, Julia Briggs (Penguin/Allen Lane)

Arthur Ransome: Lenin in the Lake District
London Review of Books, 24 September 2009
The Last Englishman: The Double Life of Arthur Ransome, Roland Chambers (Faber & Faber)

E. M. Forster: shy, remorseless shade
Spectator, 19–26 December 2009
Concerning E. M. Forster, Frank Kermode (Weidenfeld & Nicolson)

Arthur Machen: faerie strains
Spectator, 29 October 1988
The Collected Arthur Machen, edited by Christopher Palmer (Duckworth)

Fred Perry: winner takes all
Times Literary Supplement, 26 June 2009
The Last Champion: The Life of Fred Perry, Jon Henderson (Yellow Jersey Press)

M. R. James: the sexless ghost
London Review of Books, 26 January 2012
Collected Ghost Stories, M. R. James (Oxford University Press)

Wilfred Owen: the last telegram
Wall Street Journal, 29–30 March 2014
Wilfred Owen, Guy Cuthbertson (Yale University Press)

John Maynard Keynes: copulation and macroeconomics
The Oldie, April 2015
Universal Man: The Seven Lives of John Maynard Keynes, Richard Davenport-Hines (William Collins)

DIVINE DISCONTENTS

Basil Hume: the English cardinal
Times Literary Supplement, 8 July 2005
Basil Hume: The Monk Cardinal, Anthony Howard (Headline)

The Red Dean
London Review of Books, 26 April 2012
The Red Dean of Canterbury: The Public and Private Faces of Hewlett Johnson, John Butler (Scala)

Charles Bradlaugh: the admirable atheist
London Review of Books, 30 June 2011
Dare to Stand Alone: The Story of Charles Bradlaugh, Atheist and Republican, Bryan Niblett (Kramedart Press)

Mr Gladstone's religion
London Review of Books, 17 February 2005
The Mind of Gladstone: Religion, Homer and Politics, David Bebbington (Oxford University Press)

The rise and fall and rise of Methodism
Times Literary Supplement, 27 May 2005
Methodism: Empire of the Spirit, David Hempton (Yale University Press)

IN SEARCH OF ENGLAND

Pevsner in Berkshire
Times Literary Supplement, 16 July 2010
Berkshire, Geoffrey Tyack, Simon Bradley and Nikolaus Pevsner (Yale University Press)

Oliver Rackham: magus of the woods
Spectator, 4 February 1989
The Last Forest: The Story of Hatfield Forest, Oliver Rackham (J. M. Dent & Sons)

The last of Betjeman
Spectator, 13 November 2004
Betjeman: The Bonus of Laughter, Bevis Hillier (John Murray)

Ronald Blythe: glory in the ruts
Times Literary Supplement, 1 January 2010
At the Yeoman's House, Ronald Blythe (Enitharmon Press)

The suburb and the village
Times Literary Supplement, 1 January 2010 and 25 December 1998
Wall Street Journal, 27 November 2010
The Freedoms of Suburbia, Paul Barker (Frances Lincoln)
Town and Country, edited by Anthony Barnett and Roger Scruton (Jonathan Cape)
Villages of Britain: The Five Hundred Villages that Made the Countryside, Clive Aslet (Bloomsbury)

Mark Girouard and the English town
Spectator, 2 June 1990
The English Town, Mark Girouard (Yale University Press)
Life in the Georgian City, Dan Cruickshank and Neil Burton (Viking)

SOME OLD MASTERS

Thomas Hardy: the twilight of aftering
Spectator, 19 May 1990
Thomas Hardy: Selected Letters, edited by Michael Millgate (Faber)
Hardy the Writer, F. B. Pinion (Palgrave Macmillan)
A Thomas Hardy Dictionary, F. B. Pinion (Macmillan)
Hardy Landscapes, Gordon Beningfield (Viking)

Charles Dickens: kindly leave the stage
Spectator, 8 September 1990
Dickens, Peter Ackroyd (Sinclair-Stevenson)

Samuel Taylor Coleridge: a wonderful leaper
Spectator, 11 November 1989
Coleridge: Early Visions, Richard Holmes (Hodder & Stoughton)

John Keats: what's become of Junkets?
Spectator, 20 October 2012
John Keats: A New Life, Nicholas Roe (Yale University Press)

Samuel Pepys: from the scaffold to Mr Pooter
Spectator, 28 September 2002
Samuel Pepys: The Unequalled Self, Claire Tomalin (Penguin/Viking)

Shakespeare at Stratford: the divine pork butcher
Spectator, 28 April 2007
Shakespeare the Thinker, A. D. Nuttall (Yale University Press)

THE GREAT VICTORIANS

Sir Robert Peel: the first modern
Times Literary Supplement, 28 August 2007
Robert Peel: A Biography, Douglas Hurd (Weidenfeld & Nicolson)

Lord Palmerston: the unstoppable Pam
Times Literary Supplement, 12 November 2010
Palmerston: A Biography, David Brown (Yale University Press)

Walter Bagehot: money matters
London Review of Books, 6 February 2014
The Memoirs of Walter Bagehot, Frank Prochaska (Yale University Press)

Lord Rosebery: the palm without the dust
London Review of Books, 22 September 2005
Rosebery: Statesman in Turmoil, Leo McKinstry (John Murray)

Arthur Balfour: a fatal charm
London Review of Books, 20 March 2008
Balfour: The Last Grandee, R. J. Q. Adams (John Murray)

OUR STATESMEN

Margot, Asquith and the Great War
London Review of Books, 8 January 2015
Margot Asquith's Great War Diary 1914–1916: The View From Downing Street, selected and edited by Michael Brock and Eleanor Brock (Oxford University Press)

Margot at War: Love and Betrayal in Downing Street, 1912–1916, Anne de Courcy (Weidenfeld & Nicolson)
The Darkest Days: The Truth Behind Britain's Rush to War, 1914, Douglas Newton (Verso)

Churchill's calamity: day trip to Gallipoli
Spectator, 14 April 1990

Oswald Mosley: the poor old Führer
London Review of Books, 6 July 2006
Blackshirt: Sir Oswald Mosley and British Fascism, Stephen Dorril (Viking)
Hurrah for the Blackshirts! Fascists and Fascism Between the Wars, Martin Pugh (Pimlico)

Roy Jenkins: liberal lothario
Times Literary Supplement, 22 October 2004
Roy Jenkins: A Retrospective, edited by Andrew Adonis and Keith Thomas (Oxford University Press)

Denis Healey: the bruiser aesthete
Spectator, 21 October 1989
The Time of My Life, Denis Healey (Michael Joseph)

Harold Macmillan: lonely are the brave
London Review of Books, 8 September 2011
Supermac: The Life of Harold Macmillan, D. R. Thorpe (Pimlico)
The Macmillan Diaries Volume II: Prime Minister and After, 1957–1966, edited by Peter Catterall (Macmillan)

Edward Heath: the great sulk
London Review of Books, 22 July 2010
Edward Heath, Philip Ziegler (HarperPress)

Margaret Thatcher: making your own luck
Times Literary Supplement, 5 June 2013
Margaret Thatcher Volume I: Not for Turning, Charles Moore (Allen Lane)
Not for Turning: The Life of Margaret Thatcher, Robin Harris (Bantam Press)
A Journey with Margaret Thatcher: Foreign Policy Under the Iron Lady, Robin Renwick (Biteback)
The Real Iron Lady: Working with Margaret Thatcher, Gillian Shephard (Biteback)

ACKNOWLEDGEMENTS

What a debt I owe to the Literary Editors who have indulged and encouraged me over the past thirty years: Mary-Kay Wilmers and John Sturrock at the *London Review of Books,* Mark Amory at the *Spectator,* Alan Jenkins, David Horspool, Lindsay Duguid and all my old comrades at the *Times Literary Supplement.* To their Editors in Chief, Mary-Kay herself, Peter Stothard at the *TLS* and Fraser Nelson, Matthew d'Ancona, Boris Johnson, the late Frank Johnson, Dominic Lawson, Charles Moore and Alexander Chancellor at the *Spectator* who have smiled on the publication and now the republication of these pieces I am no less grateful.

At Simon & Schuster, Suzanne Baboneau and Iain MacGregor have bravely supported this reckless enterprise and given valuable help in shaping it, with Jo Whitford deftly supplying the finishing touches. As ever, my agent David Miller has guided me with his unique amalgam of sympathy, sense and brio.

Perhaps the debt that I need most reminding of is the one I owe to the authors of the many and varied books discussed here. It is they who have been on the receiving end of my misprisions and pasquinades, who have innocently provoked my digressions and speculations, whose best stories I have pillaged and whose merits I have often underplayed or misunderstood. I would like to think that I have given them the credit they deserve, but I wouldn't bet on it.

PICTURE PERMISSIONS

INDEX

Abbott, Senda, 34
Abercrombie, Patrick, 238
Aberdeen, Lord, 322, 324, 330–1, 332, 334
Ackroyd, Peter, xiv, xvii, 272–3, 275–7, 278, 279–80
Adam Bede (Eliot), 206
Adams, R. J. Q., 362, 365, 368
Adie, Kate, 166
Adler, H. G., 42
Adler, Jeremy, 53, 55, 56
Akenfield (Blythe), 234, 235, 245
Alexander, Field Marshal Harold, 425, 433, 434
Allen, Charles, 90–1, 94, 95, 96
Almost a Gentleman (Osborne), 63
American Civil War, 332, 343
Amery, Leo, 397
Amis, Hilly, 4, 7, 8
Amis, Jaime, 4
Amis, Jane, *see* Howard, Elizabeth Jane
Amis, Kingsley, 4–11, 33, 67–8, 89, 464 (*see also individual works*)
   cruel streak in, 6
   drinking habits of, 5–6
   drug use by, 5
   generous nature of, 7–8
   Jane walks out on, 9
   Leader's *Life* of, 4
   marriages of, 7
   memorial service for, 6
   offence given in books by, 10
   panic attacks suffered by, 7

   and sex, 8–9
   types of book preferred by, 11
   writing style of, 10
Amis, Martin, 4
   at father's memorial service, 6
Amis, William, 6
Anderson, Benedict, xii
Angry Young Men, 2, 67
Anson, Denis, 376, 377
Archer, Lord (Jeffrey), 302
Arden, Mary, 306
Aristotle, 196
Arkell-Smith, Valerie, 408
Armstrong, Robert, 446
Armstrong, Sir William, 448
Arnold, Matthew, 152, 198, 335
Aron, Raymond, 397
Arthur Machen (Starrett), 131–2
Asbury, Herbert, 203
'The Ash Tree' (James), 146
Ashburton, Lord, 321
Ashcroft, Peggy, 417
Ashley, Minnie, 326–7
Aslet, Clive, 244–5, 246
Asquith, H. H., 134, 355, 369, 373–5, 377–81 *passim*, 383, 385
   and drink, 379
   edited letters of, 378–9
   general elections 'won' by, 383
   and Ireland, 383
   as war leader, 377–8
   and WW1 declaration, 379–80
   (*see also* World War One)
Asquith, Helen, 374, 375

Asquith, Katharine, 376
Asquith, Margot, 174, 349, 350, 353, 372, 373–9
  diary kept by, 373
Asquith, Raymond, 376
Asquith, Violet, see Bonham Carter, Violet
Atatürk, see Kemal, Mustafa
Attlee, Clement, 73, 104, 400, 461
Aubrey, John, 57
Auden, W. H., 20, 153, 228, 270, 281
Austerlitz (Sebald), 40–1, 42
Austin, Bunny, 141, 142–3
Auto da Fé (Canetti), 58
Aveling, Edward, 185

'Baa Baa, Black Sheep' (Kipling), 95
The Bachelors (Spark), 18
Backhouse, Sir Edmund, 350
Bacon, Alice, 416
Bacon, Francis, 74
Bad Blood (Sage), 39
Bagehot, Eliza, 336
Bagehot, Robert, 336
Bagehot, Thomas, 336
Bagehot, Walter, 159, 316, 335–47 (see also individual works)
  often wrong, 342
  on democracy and government, 342–4
  on France, 342
  on Peel, 318–19, 341
  parents' censure of writings of, 339
  Prochaska's 'memoirs' of, 337
  and Social Darwinism, 345
  transformation of attitude in, 344
Bagwell, Mrs, 301–2
Balcon, Jill, 8
Baldwin, Stanley, 93–4, 143, 360, 409
Balestier, Wolcott, 95
Balfour (Adams), 362
Balfour, Arthur, 121, 316, 358–68 (see also individual works)
  Declaration of, 365
  in intellectual circle, 362
  and Ireland, 360, 365
  and love and romance, 366–7
  and psychical research, 362–3
  and Rosebery, 361–2
  seat lost by, while PM, 360
  sloth exhibited by, 358–9, 360
  sporting interests of, 359
  Valentine letter of, 364–5
Balfour, Eleanor, 362
Balfour, Lady Frances, 361
The Ballad of Peckham Rye (Spark), 18
Ballard, J. G., 103, 237

Banks, Sir Joseph, 285
Barker, Paul, 238–42 passim, 247
Barnes, William, 233
Barnett, Correlli, 396
Barrack-Room Ballads (Kipling), 91
Bayley, John, 7, 54
Bean, Dr, 396
Bearman, Robert, 308
Beauvoir, Simone de, 82
Beaverbrook, Lord, 403
Bebbington, David, 192, 195, 196–7, 199
Beckett, Samuel, 296
Bede, Ven., xi, xiv–xv
Beerbohm, Max, 90
Beevor, Antony, 40
Bell, Adrian, 233, 235
Bell, Anthea, 40, 41
Bell, Clive, 108
Belloc, Hilaire, 378
Bellow, Saul, 11, 15
A Bend in the River (Naipaul), 25–6
Benedict XVI, Pope, 169
Beningfield, Gordon, 264
Benn, Tony, 419
Bennett, Alan, 2, 3, 12–17 (see also individual works)
  cancer suffered by, 14
  diaries of, 14
  and knighthoods, 14
  and mother, 13
  'national treasure' status of, 15
  plays of, 16
Bennett, Arnold, 110
Bennett, Jill, 61
Bennett, Lilian, 12, 13, 15
Bennett, Walter, 12
Benson, A. C., 147, 358
Berenson, Bernard, 15, 32, 33–4, 34–5
Berkshire, 211–17
  growth of towns in, 214
Berkshire (Tyak, Bradley, Pevsner), 211–16 passim
Berlin, Sir Isaiah, xv, 199
Bernadotte, Count, 37
Bernal, J. D., 172
Bernanke, Ben, 161
Berners, Lord, 213, 417
Besant, Annie, 181, 184–5
Besant, Rev. Frank, 181, 184–5
Bethmann-Hollweg, Theobald von, 384
Betjeman, John, xv, 69, 131, 135, 210, 211, 215–16, 217, 225–32, 253 (see also individual works)
  childlike qualities of, 231
  and modernist project, 229

on nostalgia, 229
paranoia experienced by, 228
and son, 231
Betjeman, Paul, 231
Betjeman, Penelope, 230, 231
Betjemann, Ernest, 230
A Better Class of Person (Osborne), 63, 65
Bevin, Ernest, 400
Biffen, John, 454
Biko, Steve, 417
Bingo (Bond), 307
The Biographer's Moustache (Amis), 5
Birkenhead, Lord, 173
Birrell, Augustine, 353
Blackhouse, Edmund, 350
Blair, Tony, 311, 320, 363, 415, 441, 446
Blake, Robert, 436
Blake, William, 229
Bland, Sir Simon, 64
Blunkett, David, 197
Blunt, Wilfrid Scawen, 367
Blythe, Ronald, 233–6, 245 (*see also
    individual works*)
Bond, Edward, 307
Bonham Carter, Sir Maurice 'Bongie',
    376
Bonham Carter (née Asquith), Violet,
    375, 376, 378
Bonham, Francis, 318
Booker, Christopher, 432
Boothby, Bob, 426–7
Born in Exile (Gissing), 98
Borotra, Jean, 140–1
'The Bowmen' (Machen), 132
Bowra, Sir Maurice, 32
Bowring, Sir John, 332
Boycott, Rosie, 81
Bradbury, Malcolm, 39
Bradlaugh, Charles, 164, 180–9 (*see also
    individual works*)
    editorial aims of, 181–2
    enters Commons, 186
    funeral of, 183
    oath taken by, 187
    prosecution invited by, 184
    republicanism of, 189
    teetotalism of, 181
Bradlaugh, Susannah, 185–6
Bradman, Don, 143
Braudel, Fernand, 37
Brawne, Fanny, 295–6
Bray, Tony, 459–60
Brecht, Bertolt, 57–8
Brian de Breffny, Baron, 20
Brief Lives (Aubrey), 57, 307

Briggs, Julia, 106–11 *passim*
Bright, John, 191
Bristol Channel Yacht Club, 10
Britain and the Beast (William-Ellis, ed.),
    238
The British Character (Pont), 56
Britons (Colley), xii
Brittan, Leon, 454
Brock, Eleanor, 373, 377, 378
Brock, Michael, 373, 377, 378
Brogan, Hugh, 115–16
Brontë, Emily, 416
Brooke, Rupert, 390
Brown, Charles, 290, 291
Brown, Craig, 413
Brown, David, 327–8, 331, 332–3, 334
Brown, Gordon, 161, 197, 414, 447
Browning, Robert, 290
Bruce Lockhart, Robert, 119, 120, 121,
    404
Brusiloff, Vladimir, 54
Bryant, Sir Arthur, 299, 303, 304
Bryce, James, 362
Brzezinski, Zbig, 417
Buchan, Alastair, 345
Buchan, John, 46–7, 159
Buck, Pearl, 53
Burdett-Coutts, Miss, 275, 276–7, 280
Burn, W. L., 328
Burne-Jones, Margaret, 96
Burns, Bishop Francis, 205
Burns, Terry, 453
Burton, Neil, 254, 255, 256
Burton, Richard, 8
Bush, George W., 50, 205, 320, 360
Butler, John, 173–4, 176–7, 178–9
Butler, R. A. 'Rab', 421, 423–4, 435, 437,
    438–9, 452
Butterfield, Herbert, 32
Buxton, Edward North, 222
Byron, Lord, 106, 319

Cable, Vincent, 191
Callaghan, James, 413
Callwell, Gen., 393
Camberg, Barney, 21
Camberg, Cissy, 21
Campbell-Bannerman, Sir Henry, 366,
    383
Campbell, John, 441, 442, 443, 444–5, 448
'Campo Santo' (Sebald), 42–3, 44
Canetti, Elias, 53–60 (*see also individual
    works*)
    'Diaries' of, 56
    England arrival of, 55

Canetti, Elias – *continued*
  generalizing habit of, 57
  'God-Monster of Hampstead', 54
  Nobel Prize won by, 53, 59
Canetti, Veza, 55
Caracciolo, Francesco, 163
Carden, Adm., 393–4
Carlyle, Thomas, 323, 325, 335, 340
Carr, John, 214
Carrington, Lord, 452
Carroll, Lewis, 351
The Case of Walter Bagehot (Sisson), 346
Castle, Barbara, 415, 416, 456
The Castles on the Ground (Richards), 241
Castro, Fidel, 175
Catastrophe (Hastings), 384
Catterall, Peter, 430, 435
Caute, David, 115, 174–5
Cavendish-Bentinck, Bill, 417
Cavendish, Lady Elizabeth, 230
Chamberlain, Austen, 354, 364
Chamberlain, Houston Stewart, xiii
Chamberlain, Joe, 355
Chambers, Roland, 115–17, 122
'The Character of Sir Robert Peel'
  (Bagehot), 318–19
Charles I, beheading of, 298, 300
Charles II, 300
Chartres, Bishop Richard, 458, 464
Chatwin, Bruce, 42
Chaucer, Geoffrey, xx
Chesterton, A. K., 403
Chesterton, G. K., 134, 135, 180, 362, 403
Chirac, Jacques, 57
Chou En-lai, 417
Christabel (Coleridge), 285
Church Principles Considered in Their Results
  (Gladstone), 192
Churchill, Lord Randolph, 181, 302, 353,
  366
Churchill, Winston, 53, 70, 174, 320,
  359–60, 361, 369, 373, 379, 380, 438
  (*see also individual works*)
  Jenkins's biography of, 413
  and Macmillan, 424
  and WW1, 380, 382, 389–90, 393–4,
    395–6, 397–8
The City Gardener (Fairchild), 255
Clare, John, 233, 234
Clark, Christopher, 381, 382, 385–6
Clark, Jonathan, xiv
Clarke, Kenneth, 454
Cobbett, William, 233, 238
The Code of the Woosters (Wodehouse),
  401

Coleridge, The Damaged Archangel
  (Fruman), 287
Coleridge, Samuel Taylor, 260–1, 283–9
  (*see also individual works*)
  drug addiction of, 285
  literary appetites of, 284
  military discharge of, 283–4
  and religion, 261
Coleridge, Sara, 288–9
Collected Poems (Hardy), 270
Colley, Linda, xii
Collingwood, R. G., 114
Collis, John Stewart, 233, 245
Colonel Sun (Amis), 10
The Comforters (Spark), 22
The Confidential Clerk (Eliot), 22
Conquest, Robert, 8
Conrad, Joseph, 47
The Constant Gardener (le Carré), 51
Cooke, Alistair, 172
Cooper, Duff, 376, 400
Coot Club (Ransome), 115
Courtauld, Simon, 73–4, 76, 77
Coventry, Sir William, 301
Cowgill, Anthony, 432
Cowper, Emily, 326
Cox, Harvey, 206
Cradock, Sir Percy, 455
Crawford, Jack, 139, 140, 143
Creighton, Anthony, 65
Crewe, Lord, 379
Crickhowell, Lord, 272
Cripps, Fred, 388
Cripps, Sir Stafford, 388
The Crisis in Russia (Ransome), 116
Cromwell, Oliver, 300, 325
Crook, Prof. Joseph Mordaunt, 322
Crosland, Anthony, 414, 421
Crossman, Richard, 414, 431–2, 434
  diaries of, 431
Crowds and Power (Canetti), 53, 59–60
Crowley, Aleister, 134, 137
Cruickshank, Dan, 254, 256
Crum, John, 178
Cullen, Muriel, 459, 460–1
Cullen, Willie, 460–1
Curriculum Vitae (Spark), 20
Curzon, Grace, 402
Curzon, Lord, 115, 121, 360, 365, 413
Curzon, Mary, 374
Cuthbertson, Guy, 152–4, 155

Damn You, England (Osborne), 68
Dangerfield, George, 376
The Darkest Days (Newton), 380

Darwin, Charles, 77–8, 172, 208, 310, 316, 335
Davenport-Hines, Richard, 34, 35, 157–8, 159–60
David Copperfield (Dickens), 94, 274
Davis, Bette, 142
Dawkins, Prof. Richard, 172, 182
Dawkins, Sir William Boyd, 171–2
Day-Lewis, Cecil, 8
de Courcy, Anne, 375, 378
de Gaulle, Charles, 436
de Klerk, F. W., 455
de Robeck, Adm., 394
Defence of Philosophic Doubt (Balfour), 363
Defoe, Daniel, xiii
Delany, Paul, 99, 100–1, 101–2, 103
Dettori, Frankie, 140
Devonshire, Duke of, 414
Diana, Princess of Wales, 14, 55
    funeral of, xvi
Dickens, Catherine, 278–9
Dickens, Charles, 150, 230, 260, 261–2, 271–82, 303, 340–1 (*see also individual works*)
    and Americans, 280
    in blacking factory, 273–4, 274–5
    oddity pursued by, 272–3
    and penal systems, 280–1
    and political activity, 280
    racist, selfish, money-grubbing, 279
    and religion, 261
    wife's separation from, 278
Dickens, John, 276
Dietrich, Marlene, 57, 142
Dilhorne, Lord, 437, 438
Dilke, Charles, 275
Disraeli, Benjamin, 190, 319, 329, 330, 343–4
Dombey and Son (Dickens), 273, 276
Dorril, Stephen, 400, 402, 405, 406–7
Douglas, Lord Alfred, 114, 131
    Machen's obituary of, 132
Douglas, Maj. C. H., 174
Douglas-Home, Alec, 437–8, 446
Downe, Viscountess, 407
Downing, Sir George, 301
Dugdale, Sir William, 434
Dulles, John Foster, 435
Duncan-Jones, Katherine, 307
Duranty, Walter, 118
Durrell, Lawrence, xvi
Duveen, Joseph, 34–5
Dzerzhinsky, Feliks, 120

Ecclesiastical History of the English People (Bede), xi
The Economic Consequences of the Peace (Keynes), 159, 429
Economist, Bagehot at, *see* Bagehot, Walter
Eden, Anthony, 348, 369, 424, 427, 435, 437, 438, 439
Edward VII, 217, 349
Edward VIII, *see* Windsor, Duke of
Egremont, Max, 362
Eisenhower, Gen. Dwight 'Ike', 431, 432, 434–5
Elcho, Mary, 366, 367
Eliot, George, 50, 206, 268, 340
Eliot, T. S., 20, 22, 25, 91, 112, 270, 281, 295, 340, 451
    'miserable creature', 54
Elizabeth II, 13–14
Elizabethan Architecture (Girouard), 214
Elton, G. R., xvi, xix
The Emigrants (Sebald), 39, 42
Ending Up (Amis), 11, 464
Endymion (Keats), 290, 296
England and the Octopus (William-Ellis), 238
English Civil War, 31, 38, 88, 293
The English Constitution (Bagehot), 339, 342, 343–4, 345
The Entertainer (Osborne), 68
Etzioni, Amitai, 197
'An Evening's Entertainment' (James, M. R.), 149
Eyre, Peter, 74

Fairchild, Thomas, 255
'False Dawn' (Kipling), 92–3
Far Off Things (Machen), 134
Faringdon, Lord, 417
Fascism, *see* Mosley, Oswald
Fearon, George, 67
Federer, Roger, 141
The Female Eunuch (Greer), 80–1, 85–6
Fenton, James, 228
Ferguson, Niall, 381, 385
Finding the Centre (Naipaul), 25–6
Fischer, Fritz, 384–5
Fisher, Lord (Jacky), 393, 395, 397–8
FitzGerald, Garret, 445–6
The Flight from the Enchanter (Murdoch), 54
Flush (Woolf), 106
The Folks That Live on the Hill (Amis), 10
Foot, Michael, 421
Ford, Gerald, 417, 453

Forster, E. M., 50, 88, 124–30 (see also
       individual works)
    critique of James by, 126
    enemies of, 124
    sexuality of, 127
Forster, John, 273, 274–5, 278
Foster, Norman, 239
Foundations of Belief (Balfour), 363
Fraenkel, Eduard, 32
Franz Ferdinand, Archduke, 386
Frayn, Michael, 240
Fredericks, Kay, 405
The Freedoms of Suburbia (Barker), 238
Freeman, A. E., 192
French, Sir John, 377
Frere, Philip, 426
Freud, Sigmund, 15, 146, 310
Friedman, Milton, 160
'Frost at Midnight' (Coleridge), 285
The Fruits of Philosophy (Bradlaugh,
       Besant), 184–5
Fruman, Norman, 287, 288
Fuller, J. F. C., 396
Fuller, Roy, 228

Gaitskell, Hugh, 424
Galbraith, John Kenneth, 159
Gale, George, 442
Gandhi, Mohandas, 183
Gardiner, A. G., 351
Gardner, Dame Helen, 311
Garrick Club, 5, 7, 8, 9, 68
Gash, Norman, 321
Gellner, Ernest, xii, 207
The General Theory of Employment, Interest
       and Money (Keynes), 158, 429
George IV, 330
George V, 356, 385
Gibbon, Edward, 35, 36
Gielgud, Sir John, 15
Gilbert, W. S., xiv
Gilliatt, Penelope, 61, 63, 65–6, 69
Gilmour, Ian, 454
The Girls of Slender Means (Spark), 18
Girouard, Dr Mark, 214, 249–58
Gissing, George, 88, 98–105 (see also
       individual works)
    autodidact, 99
    jailed, 100
    marriages of, 100, 102
    physical attributes of, 99
    and religion, 104
Gittings, Robert, 265, 292
Gladstone, William, 187–8, 189, 190–201,
       315, 319, 320, 331, 339, 340, 351, 352,

       354 (see also individual works)
    and Maynooth affair, 195–6
    and prostitutes, 198
    religious shifts in, 197–8
Goebbels, Joseph, 402
Gorbachev, Mikhail, 418
Goschen, Viscount, 414
Gosse, Edmund, 95, 267, 356
Granger, Derek, 67
Grant, Robert, 244–5
Granville-Barker, Harley, 309–10
Granville, Lord, 351
The Great God Pan (Machen), 133, 137
Greene, Graham, 50
Greenmantle (Buchan), 47
Greer, Germaine, 2, 3, 79–86, 312 (see also
       individual works)
    and housework, 84
    on imitating men, 83
    on Thatcher, 81
    readable style of, 81
Greville, Charles 323, 330
Grey, Sir Edward, 379, 381, 382, 383, 385
Grimond, Jo, 191
Grisham, John, 51
Guedalla, Philip, 327, 329
Guevara, Che, 175
Guinness, Alec, 64

Hague, William, 320, 333
Haig, Alexandra, see Trevor-Roper,
       Alexandra
Hailsham, Lord, 429, 438
Haldane, J. B. S., 148, 425
Haldane, R. B., 362, 379
Hamilton, Gen. Sir Ian, 389, 390, 394, 395
Hamilton, Hamish, 32
Hamlet (Shakespeare), 310
Hammond, Eric, 418
Handke, Peter, 42
Harcourt, Loulou, 351
Harcourt, Sir William, 351
Hardy, Emma, 265
Hardy, Thomas, 103, 233, 260, 261–2,
       263–70 (see also individual works)
    camera-eye technique of, 266
    cruelty and war hated by, 266
    and poetry vs novels, 269–70
    and religion, 261
    tidied-up character of, 264
Hare, David, 27
Hargrave, Sgt, 390–1
Harlow, Jean, 142
Harris, Arthur 'Bomber', 71, 72
Harris, Robert, 413

Harris, Robin, 450, 453–4, 457, 459, 462–5
Harrison, Maj. Gen., 260, 298, 299
Harrison, Nell, 100–1, 103, 104
Harrod, Roy, 33, 159, 429
Hart-Davis, Rupert, 34
Hart, Liddell, 396
Hastings, Max, 384
Hatfield Forest, 218–24
   and Forestry Commission, 222
   and National Trust, 222–3
Hathaway, Anne, 306
Hathaway, Bartholomew, 306
Hawke, Bob, 390
Haydon, Benjamin, 322
Hayek, Friedrich, 160
Hazlitt, William, 283, 284
Headlam, Cuthbert, 424
Healey, Denis, 369, 416–22
   as chancellor, 419, 420
   comedy supporting roles performed by, 418
   in Communist Party, 422
   as defence minister, 419–20
   and Gang of Four, 421
   literary choices of, 416
   public-expenditure pruning by, 419
   and Winter of Discontent, 420
Healey, Edna, 421
Healey, Will, 421
Heart of Darkness (Conrad), 47
Heath, Edith, 442
Heath, Edward, 212, 320, 369, 440–9
   Charitable Foundation of, 449
   early popularity of, 442
   and EEC, 443–4
   and ideas, 446
   and local-government reform, 444–5
   negative traits of, 440
   and Northern Ireland, 445–6
   and prices-and-incomes controls, 447–8
   and trade unions, 447
Heath, William, 442
Heathcoat-Amory, Derick, 429
Heber-Percy, Robert, 213
Heilpern, John, 62, 64–7
Heim, Bruno, 168
Hemingway, Ernest, 10
Hempton, David, 204–7 passim, 457–8
Henderson, Jon, 142
Henry V (Shakespeare), 311
Henry VI, Part I (Shakespeare), 310
Henry VIII (Shakespeare), 309
Herbert, George, 245

Heseltine, Michael, 454–5, 462
Hewer, Will, 304
Hewlett, Alfred, 173
Hewlett, William, 173
Hicks-Beach, Sir Michael, 187
Highways and Byways in Fairyland (Ransome), 122
The Hill of Dreams (Machen), 133, 134, 135–6
Hillier, Bevis, 226, 229, 230
Hirst, Paul, 243
The History of Man (Bradbury), 39
History of the Countryside (Rackham), 223
'History, Tradition and Modernity' (Grant), 244–5
Hitchens, Christopher, 182
Hitler, Adolf, 37, 76, 102, 402–3
Hobsbawm, Eric, xii, 240
Hobson, Harold, 67, 69
Hofmann, Michael, 58
Hogarth, William, xvi
Hogg, James, 322
Hogg, Quintin, see Hailsham, Lord
Hollis, Roger, 426
Holmes, Richard, 285–6, 286–7, 287–9
Holyoake, George Jacob, 182
Hood, Thomas, 277
Hope, Lord John, 417
Horne, Alistair, 427
Hornung, E. W., 99
Hoskins, W. G., 221
Hoskyns, John, 453, 456
Hough, Richard, 5
Hough, Thornton, 245
A House for Mr Biswas (Naipaul), 25
The House of Souls (Machen), 131, 134, 137
Howard, Anthony, 167–8, 169, 170
Howard, Elizabeth Jane, 7, 8, 9
Howard, Peter, 404–5, 410
Howards End (Forster), 126, 127–8
Howe, Geoffrey, 414, 454, 458, 464
Hubbard, L. Ron, 137
Hume, Dr Sir William, 166, 167
Hume, Basil, 164, 165–70
   becomes Archbishop of Westminster, 166
   monastic name taken by, 166
   and women priests, 167–8, 168–9
Hume, Mimi, 166
Humphrey, George, 435
Hunt, Leigh, 290–1, 291–2
Hurd, Lord (Douglas), 319, 320–1, 323
Hussey, Christopher, 216
Hutchinson, Sara 'Astra', 288
Huxley, Aldous, 60, 148, 400

Huxley, Julian, 238
Huxley, T. H., 147, 192, 193, 335

'Imitation of Spenser' (Keats), 291
Inadmissible Evidence (Osborne), 68
In Memoriam (Tennyson), 316
In the Year of Jubilee (Gissing), 98
Ireland, John, 131
The Iron Lady, 463
Isherwood, Christopher, 126, 128–9, 153
Islam, 207, 208

Jackson, Sir Charles, 72–3
Jackson, Derek, 3, 70–8 (*see also* Window
    affair)
    fascism of, 71, 76–7
    flees UK, 73
    and horses, dogs, 75
    marriages of, 74
    NoW inherited by, 73
    Paris exile of, 76
    and religion, 75
    socialism hated by, 76
    and twin brother, 73
Jackson, John, 304
Jackson, Vivian, 73, 74, 76
Jacobs, Jane, 239
Jake's Thing (Amis), 8
James II, 300
James, Henry, 10, 90, 95, 128, 149–50,
    268, 271, 340, 349, 366
    Forster's critique of, 126
    on Dickens, 272
James, M. R., 88, 144–51
    'almost incurably frivolous', 148
    candlelight readings by, 144
    on ghost-story settings, 145
    ghost-story survey by, 149
    and religion, 149
Jardine, Douglas, 143
Jardine, Penelope, 20
Jay, Douglas, 57
Jefferies, Richard, 233
Jefferson, Thomas, 241, 412
Jenkins, Peter, 453
Jenkins, Roy, 193–4, 320, 369, 383,
    412–15, 462 (*see also individual works*)
    appetites of, 413
    as chancellor, 414
    Churchill biography by, 413
    compulsions of, 412
    as home secretary, 414
Jenkins, Simon, 210, 457
Jessel, Sir George, 185
Joad, Cyril, 238

John, Augustus, 153
John, Elton, 95
John Paul II, Pope, 169
John, Poppet, 74
Johnson, Edgar, 275, 279–80
Johnson, Dr Hewlett ('Red Dean'), 171–9
    (*see also individual works*)
    properties and holdings of, 173
    'Red Dean' sobriquet of, 171
Johnson, Nowell, 172, 173, 175
Johnson, Dr Samuel, 308, 310
Johnson, William, 348, 361
Jones, Darryl, 145
Jones, R. V., 70
Jones, Thomas, 12
Jonson, Ben, 305, 306–7
Joseph, Keith, 451, 454
Joseph Stalin (Johnson), 177
Josselin, Rev. Ralph, 302
Joyce, James, 10, 20, 24, 48, 112, 148, 153

Kafka, Franz, 42, 58
Kangaroo (Lawrence), 237
Kaplan, Fred, 275, 279
Keats, Frances, 292–3
Keats, John, 152, 260, 261–2, 290–7 (*see
    also individual works*)
    Aeneid translated by, 291
    collected poems of, 291, 295
    epitaph of, 295–6
    and father's death, 292
    and laudanum, 294–5
    many fine biographies of, 292
    medical training of, 291, 293
    on food, 290
    and religion, 261, 293–4
    sexually transmitted diseases of, 294
    short stature of, 291
    tuberculosis suffered by, 294
Keats, Thomas, 292
Keats, Tom, 293, 294
Kee, Robert, 74
Keightley, Gen. Sir Charles, 432, 433, 436
Kemal, Mustafa, 389, 392, 397
Kennedy, John F., 57, 428
Kent, Bruce, 168
Kerensky, Alexander, 117, 118
Kermode, Sir Frank, 125, 126, 127, 129
Kersten, Felix, 37
Keyes, Adm. Roger, 394, 396
Keynes, John Maynard, 87, 148, 157–61,
    238, 410, 429 (*see also individual works*)
    dubious legacy of, 160
    heart problems of, 160
    on economics and economists, 157–8

as public servant, 158
sexuality of, 159–60
Khrushchev, Nikita, 418
Kien, Peter, 58
Kilmuir, Lord, 443–4
Kim (Kipling), 90, 91, 93
King, Anthony D., 240
King, Cecil, 404
King John (Shakespeare), 309
King Lear (Shakespeare), 308–9
Kingsley, Charles, 178
Kinnock, Neil, 418, 421
Kipling, Alice, 94–5
Kipling, Carrie, 95–6
Kipling, John Lockwood, 91, 94
Kipling, Rudyard, 89–97, 245 (*see also individual works*)
 and homoeroticism, 95
 marriage of, 95–6
 'most complete man of genius', 90
 neurotic habits of, 93
 newspaper work of, 91, 92
 parents abandon, 94
 wide reading of, 92
Kipling Sahib (Allen), 90–1
Kipling, Trix, 91, 94, 95
Kissinger, Henry, 417, 420, 453
Kitchener, Lord, 373, 389, 393
Klugmann, James, 422
Knight, Andrew, 168
Knox, Ronald, 425
Konstam, Phyllis, 143
Koss, Stephen, 383
Kramer, Jack, 142
Kristol, Irving, 207
'Kubla Khan' (Coleridge), 285
Kuhn, H. G., 73, 77
Kundera, Milan, 58

Labouchère, Henry, 186
Lady Chatterley's Lover (Lawrence), 51
Lamb, Charles, 287
Lane, Pamela, 62–3
Lansbury, George, 238
A Laodicean (Hardy), 266, 269
Lark Rise to Candleford (Thompson), 245
Larkin, Philip, 6, 8, 16, 33, 68, 228, 229, 256, 270
The Last Champion (Henderson), 142
The Last Days of Hitler (Trevor-Roper), 32, 37
Laver, Rod, 141
Law, Bonar, 362, 378, 379
Lawrence, D. H., 50, 60, 112, 128, 159, 237

Lawrence, Sir Thomas, 322
Laws, David, 191
Lawson, Nigel, 414, 454, 458, 461, 464
le Carré, John, 2, 46–52 (*see also individual works*)
 as Cornwell, 49
 ear for dialogue demonstrated by, 49
 teaching role of, 49
 undiminished anger of, 50
 women characters of, 47
Leader, Zachary, 4, 10
Leavis, F. R., 124
Lee, Laurie, 243
Leeper, Rex, 121, 122
Lees-Milne, James, 14, 228
Leese, Arnold, 408
Lefebure, Molly, 288
Lely, Sir Peter, xvi
Lenin, Vladimir, 87, 115, 118, 119, 121, 178
Leverhulme, Lord, 239, 245
Levi, Primo, 42
Levi, C. S., 31–2
Lewis, Sir George Cornewall, 193
Lewis, Wyndham, 404
Lichnowsky, Prince, 372, 382
A Life at the Centre (Jenkins), 413
Life in the English Country House (Girouard), 249
The Life of Kingsley Amis (Leader), 4
Lincoln, Abraham, 342, 456
Lindley, Sir Francis, 122
Lintorn-Orman, Rotha, 408
The Little Drummer Girl (le Carré), 51
'A Little Excursion to Ajaccio' (Sebald), 43
Lloyd George, David, 158, 183, 238, 356, 359, 365, 369, 380, 383, 384
Lloyd, Selwyn, 427, 429, 435–6, 438
Lockhart, John, 295
Lodge, Sir Oliver, 362
Loitering with Intent (Spark), 19
Lombard Street (Bagehot), 337–8, 339
Look Back in Anger (Osborne), first night of, 62–3
Looking Back (Osborne), 63, 67
'Lost Hearts' (James), 146
Louis of Battenberg, Prince, 380
Luxmoore, H. E., 148
Lyell, Charles 335
Lymington, Lord, 407, 408
Lyrical Ballads (Coleridge), 287
Lyttelton, George, 34
Lyttelton, May, 363, 366

Macaulay, Lord, 193, 194, 196
McCloy, John, 423
McCoog, Fr Thomas, 308
MacDonald, Ramsay, 173
Macfarlane, Alan, 221
MacGowan, Gault, 28
Machen, Arthur, 88, 131–8 (see also
    individual works)
  and Golden Dawn, 134
  name of, 133
  poverty suffered by, 132
  and religion, 135
MacIntyre, Alasdair, 197
MacKenzie, Jean, 275
MacKenzie, Norman, 275
McKinstry, Leo, 348–9, 350, 352, 353,
    362
Maclean, Alan, 20
Macleod, Fiona, 131–2, 136–7
Macleod, Iain, 421
Macmillan, Dorothy, 426–7
Macmillan, Harold, 369–70, 404, 423–39,
    461 (see also individual works)
  cabinet sackings by, 418, 424
  chancellor of Oxford, 425
  and Churchill, 424
  City distrusted by, 428–9
  and Common Market, 436
  and Cossacks/White Russians handover,
    433, 434
  diaries of, 424, 430–1, 433, 435
  and foreign affairs, 431
  fragile health of, 428, 437–8
  public figures vilified by, 424
  Stockton title of, 428
  and Suez, 424, 430, 434–6
  Thatcher loathes, 451
  and Tolstoy's polemics, 432
  unpopularity of, 424–5
  wartime bravery of, 423 (see also World
    War One; World War Two)
  and wife's affair with Boothby, 426–7
Macmillan, Maurice Crawford , 425
Macmillan, Maurice Victor, 424, 437
Macmillan, Nellie, 425
Macmillan, Sarah, 426–7
Mahony, Rev. Francis ('Father Prout'), 277
Major, John, 14, 301, 465
The Making of the English Working Class
    (Thompson), 202–3, 458
Makins, Roger, 435
Malenkov, Georgy, 418
Mallon, Seamus, 445
Malmesbury, Lady, 329
Malone, Edmond, 307

'The Man Who Would Be King'
    (Kipling), 97
Mandela, Nelson, 455
Mann, Thomas, 294
Manners, Lady Diana, 376
Mansfield, Katherine, 110, 124
Mao Zedong, 37–8, 177
A Map of the World (Hare), 27
Margot at War (de Courcy), 375
'The Mark on the Wall' (Woolf), 111
Marquand, David, 414
Mars, Tim, 248
Marshall, Alfred, 157
Martin, David, 203
'Martin's Close' (James), 146
Masaryk, Jan, 36
Masefield, John, 114, 391
Maskhadov, Aslan, 464
Maudling, Reginald, 429, 436, 438
Maurice, F. D, 178
Mehta, Ved, 20
Melbourne, Lord, 318
Memento Mori (Spark), 18
The Memoirs of Walter Bagehot (Prochaska),
    337
Men and the Fields (Bell, Nash), 235
Metcalfe, 'Baba Blackshirt', 402
Metcalfe, 'Fruity', 402
Methodism, 202–8
  decline in, 203, 207
  'form of psychic masturbation', 202
Methodism: Empire of the Spirit (Hempton),
    207
The Middle Way (Macmillan), 429
Middlemarch (Eliot), 51
Middleton, Peter, 453
A Midsummer Night's Dream (Shakespeare),
    314
Miguel Street (Naipaul), 30
Milbanke, Sir John, 388
The Military Philosophers (Powell), 2
Miller, Terence, 213
Millgate, Prof. Michael, 264, 265
Milton, John, 306
The Mind of Gladstone (Bebbington), 192,
    195
The Minister and the Massacres (Tolstoy), 432
Minto, Lord, 329
The Mission Song (le Carré), 46–52
Mitford, Diana, 402, 411
Mitford, Nancy, 33, 213, 401
Mitford, Pamela, 74
Mitford, Unity, 407
Molière, 45
Moltke, Helmuth von, 383, 384

Monnet, Jean, 443
Montagu, Edwin, 365
Moore, Charles, 450, 454, 455–6, 458, 459, 461–2
Moorehead, Alan, 389, 391, 392, 396
Morris, William, 200, 335
Morrison, Herbert, 424
Morrison, Sara, 448
Mosley, Alexander, 402
Mosley, Cimmie, 402
Mosley, Oswald, 75–6, 369, 399–411 passim
 and abdication crisis, 409
 ancestors of, 401
 and anti-Semitism, 403, 405–6, 410
 and electoral failure, 406
 hereditary blackguard, 401
 jailed, 399, 410
  and released, 410
 'most unpopular person in England', 410
 'most vindictive hater', 405
 and New Party, 404, 406
 parsimony exhibited by, 402
 as womanizer, 402
 as youngest MP, 400
Motion, Andrew, 292
Mountbatten, Edwina, 327
Mountbatten, Lord, 327, 440–1
Mrs Dalloway (Woolf), 111, 112
Muggeridge, Malcolm, 114, 116
Mumford, Lewis, 237, 239
Murdoch, Iris, 54
Murdoch, Rupert, 38
Murphy, Bob, 434
Murray, Andy, 142
Murray's Berkshire Architectural Guide (Betjeman, Piper), 215–16
Mussolini, Benito, 57, 102, 402–3

Nabokov, Vladimir, 11, 44
Naipaul. V. S., 2, 3, 24–30, 48, 89, 103 (see also individual works)
 and father, 28
 and Hare play, 26
 and spirituality, 28–9
Namier, Sir Lewis, xv
Napoleon III, 332, 342
Nash, John, 234, 235, 239
Nasmith, Lt-Cdr, 394
Nasser, Gamal Abdel, 434–5
Nazarbayev, Nursultan, 464
Needham, Joseph, 38
'A Neighbour's Landmark' (James), 146
New Grub Street (Gissing), 98

Newman, Cardinal John Henry, 320
Newton, Douglas, 380, 381, 382, 385, 386
Niblett, Bryan, 183, 186, 188
Nicholas Nickleby (Dickens), 273, 280
Nicolson, Adam, 95
Nietzsche, Friedrich, 182
Niven, David, 311
Norfolk, Duke of, 168, 417
Northcliffe, Lord, 355
Norton, William, 225, 231
Not for Turning (Harris), 462–3, 465
Nuttall, Prof. A. D., 306, 309–11, 312, 313
Nuttall, Jeff, 309

Oakeshott, Michael, 199, 322
Oaten, Mark, 191
O'Casey, Eileen, 427
O'Casey, Seán, 427
O'Connell, Daniel, 319, 321
The Odd Women (Gissing), 98
'Ode to Autumn' (Keats), 290, 291
'Ode to a Nightingale' (Keats), 294
'Oh, Whistle and I'll Come to You, My Lad' (James), 146
Okri, Ben, 48
The Old Devils (Amis), 11
Ollard, Richard, 299, 304
On Behalf of Russia (Ransome), 116, 119
On Drink (Amis), 6
On the Origin of Species (Darwin), 316
The Ordeal of Gilbert Pinfold (Waugh), 22
Orlando (Woolf), 112–13
Ortega y Gasset, José, 60
Orwell, George, 98, 103, 104, 281
Osborne, Helen, 61
Osborne, John, 2, 61–9 (see also individual works)
 CND supported by, 66
 depression suffered by, 61, 64
 as Porter understudy, 62
 and religion, 69
 trade periodicals work of, 64
 Who's Who entry of, 63
Osborne, Nellie Beatrice, 64
Osborne, Nolan, 63
O'Sullivan, John, 457
Our Mutual Friend (Dickens), 272
Owen, Dr David, 413
Owen, Peter, 22
Owen, Susan, 154
Owen, Tom, 153
Owen, Wilfred, 152–6
 killed, 155

Owen, Wilfred – *continued*
  and mother, 154
  sexuality of, 154
  wit, realism and directness of, 152

Pakenham, Thomas, 34
Palmer, Christopher, 133–4, 136, 137
Palmerston, Lord, 190, 315, 320, 323,
    325–34
  and American Civil War, 332
  Commons seat of, 329
  five-hour speech of, 333
  at Foreign Office, 328, 330
  at Home Office, 327–8
  and Italian unity, 332
  and press, use of, 331
  as prime minister, 330
  as Secretary for War, 329
  Sligo income of, 325, 326
Party in the Blitz (Canetti), 53–4, 57
A Passage to India (Forster), 128, 129
Patten, Chris, 454
Pattison, Mark, 203
Paul, Leslie, 67
Pearson, Lady, 407
Peel, Arthur Wellesley, 187
Peel, Julia, 321, 322
Peel, Sir Robert, 187, 190, 194, 318–24
  Bagehot's view of, 318–19, 341
  generosity of, 321–2
  horse throws, 323
  Hurd's biography of, 319, 320
  and Ireland, 319
  and police force, 323
  public grief at death of, 324
  strong-willed foreign policy of, 323–4
  vibrant presence, 341
  wealth of, 322
Penn, Pegg, 302
Penn, Sir William, 302
Penrose, Roland, 56
Pentecostalism, 203
Pepys, Elizabeth, 260, 302, 303, 304
Pepys, Samuel, 260, 298–304
  dalliances of, 301–2
  failing eyesight of, 299
  imprisonment of, 302
  last years of, 304
Perry, Fred, 139–43
  Grand Slam success of, 141
  outrageous gamesmanship of, 140
  sportswear brand of, 143
  Wimbledon success of, 139
Perry, Sam, 140
Peters, Yakov, 120

Pevsner, Nikolaus, 210, 211–17, 228, 457
Philby, Harry St John, 406
Philby, Kim, 406
Physics and Politics (Bagehot), 339, 342, 345
Pinion, Dr F. B., 265, 267, 268–70
Pinochet, Augusto, 464
Pinter, Harold, 64, 68
Piper, John, 210, 215–16, 217
Pitt, William, the Younger, 320, 359
The Pity of War (Ferguson), 381
Plain Tales from the Hills (Kipling), 92
Playfair, Sir Edward, 227
Poetry Society, 22
Point Counter Point (Huxley), 400
Pond and Stream (Ransome), 122
Poole, Lord, 438
Pooley, Fred, 248
Pope, Alexander, xx, 259
Portsmouth, Lord, 407
Potter, Stephen, 11, 454
Pound, Ezra, 25, 269, 281
Powell, Anthony, 2, 10, 14, 77, 228, 442
Powell, Charles, 453
Powell, Enoch, 56–7, 437, 446, 461
Powell, Michael, 137
Powell, Philip, 212–13
The Prime of Miss Jean Brodie (Spark), 18
Prior, James, 452, 462
Prochaska, Frank, 337, 339–40, 346
Profumo, John, 417
Proust, Marcel, 48
Pryce-Jones, Alan, 230
Puck of Pook's Hill (Kipling), 245
Pückler-Muskau, Prince, 256
Pugh, Martin, 399, 407–10, 411
Pye, Henry, 213
Pyke, Geoffrey, 57
Pym, Barbara, 16

Queensberry, Lord, 183, 350
Quennell, Marilyn, 10
Quennell, Peter, 10

Rackham, Dr Oliver, 218–24
Radek, Karl, 119, 123
Raine, Craig, 228
Raine, Kathleen, 54
Randal, 8th Earl of Berkeley, 34
Ransome, Arthur, 87, 114–23 (*see also
    individual works*)
  as accredited British agent, 121
  and celebrity interview, 119
  and hero worship, 114
  as propagandist, 115–16, 119, 121
  and Russia, 115–16, 117–23

Ransome, Ivy, 117
Ratibor, Princess, 74
Rattigan, Terence, 68
Rawlings, William, 292
Rayleigh, Evelyn, 361
Rayleigh, Lord, 362
Red Dean, *see* Johnson, Dr Hewlett
Redmayne, Martin, 438
Redwood, John, 464
Renwick, Lord (Robin), 450, 451, 453,
    455, 461
The Repatriations from Austria in 1945
    (Cowgill), 432
'The Residence at Whitminster' (James),
    146
The Return of the Native (Hardy), 269
The Revolt of the Masses (Ortega), 60
Rhodes, Cecil, xv, 354–5
Rhodes James, Robert, 391, 392, 444
Richard II (Shakespeare), 310
Richards, Gordon, 143
Richards, J. M., 241
Richardson, Ralph, 310
Richmond, Duchess of, 320
Rickards, Jocelyn, 63
Ridley, Jasper, 327
The Rime of the Ancient Mariner
    (Coleridge), 285
The Rings of Saturn (Sebald), 44
The Rise of Suburbia (Thompson), 235
Roberts, Alfred, 457
Roberts, Andrew, 436
Robey, George, 379
Robins, Col. Raymond, 121
Rodd, Peter, 401
Roe, Nicholas, 291, 292, 293, 295
Rogers, Richard, 239
The Romantic Adventures of a Milkmaid
    (Hardy), 269
Rose, Jonathan, 127
Rose Price, Lt Col. Robin, 433, 434
Rosebery, Lord, 316, 348–57, 361–2
    crowds loved by, 353–4
    at Foreign Office, 352, 354
    and local politics, 354
    and Lords reform, 355
    and 'model race', 356
    oratorical skills of, 352–3
    as prime minister, 354
    properties of, 350
    sexuality of, 350
    spoilt nature of, 350
    three ambitions of, 349
Rosebery (McKinstry), 362
Rothermere, Lord, 403

Rothschild, Hannah de, 349
Rothschild, Lord, 446
Rowland, Tiny, 48
Rowse, A. L., 32
Rumford, Count, 254
Running, Arnold, 64–5
Rushdie, Salman, 48, 50
Ruskin, John, 273, 340
Ruskin, John James, 253
Russell, Bertrand, 56, 57, 148, 182, 382
Russell, Lord John, 321, 331

Sackville-West, Vita, 107
Sage, Lorna, 39
St John-Stevas, Norman, 337, 345
Saki, 92, 129
Salisbury, Lord, 351, 360
Sampras, Pete, 141
Sandwich, Earl of, 301
Sartre, Jean-Paul, 53
Scargill, Arthur, 461
Schmidt, Helmut, 417
Scott, Peter, 9
Scott, Sir Walter, xii
Scruton, Roger, 243, 244
Searching for Light (Johnson), 177
Sebald, W. G. 'Max', 2, 15, 39–45 (*see also*
    individual works)
    autobiographical wanderings of, 41
    car-crash death of, 40
    and famous people, 44
    on burial customs, 44
    recycling by, 44–5
    writing style of, 40
The Secret Glory (Machen), 135, 137
Sergeant Shakespeare (Cooper), 307
Seth, Roshan, 27
Settling the Bill (Dugdale), 434
Severn, Joseph, 291, 294, 295–6
Sewell, Fr Brocard, 134
Sex and Destiny (Greer), 80
Shaftesbury, Lord, 320
Shakeshafte, William, 308
Shakespeare: An Ungentle Life
    (Duncan-Jones), 307
Shakespeare, John, 308
Shakespeare the Thinker (Nuttall), 306
Shakespeare, William, xx, 16, 149, 261–2,
    305–14, 340 (*see also individual works*)
    appearance of, 305–6
    'Delphic lines' of, 306
    fertile mind of, 310
    linguistic difficulties concerning,
        313–14
    'lost years' of, 307

Shakespeare, William – *continued*
  and religion, 261, 308
  tomb and bust of, 305
Shannon, Richard, 193
Shaw, George Bernard, 119, 310, 404
Shaw, Norman, 239
Shelepina, Evgenia, 119–20
Shelepina, Iroida, 119, 120
Shelley, Percy, 152, 294
Shephard, Gillian, 450, 455
Sheppard, Rev. David, 66
Sheppard, Rev. Dick, 66, 178
Sherman, Alfred, 458
Shirley, John, 176
Sickert, Walter, 183
Sidgwick, Henry, 147, 362
Sieff, Israel, 403
Simenon, Georges, 98
Simond, Louis, 254
Sinclair-Stevenson, Christopher, 276
Sisson, C. H., 346
Sitwell, Dame Edith, 22
Six Weeks in Russia (Ransome), 116, 118,
  119
Skelton, Barbara, 74
Skidelsky Robert, 159, 405, 409, 411
Skinner, Mary, 304
The Sleepwalkers (Clark), 381
Smith, F. E., 354, 379, 400
Soames, Christopher, 454
The Socialist Sixth of the World (Johnson),
  175, 176, 177
Society for Anglo-Chinese
  Understanding, 37–8
Something of Myself (Kipling), 96
'Sonnet Written in Disgust of Vulgar
  Superstition' (Keats), 293
Sontag, Susan, 40
Spark, Muriel, 18–23 (*see also individual
  works*)
  begins writing novels, 18–19
  and 'condition of exiledom', 19
  friendships of, 20
  gay friendships of, 20
  hallucinations suffered by, 22
  London quit by, 20
  and Poetry Society, 22
  and religion, 22
  son's relationship with, 21, 22
  Stannard biography of, 20–1
Spark, Robin, 21, 22
Spark, Solly, 21
Speak, Memory (Nabokov), 44
Spence, Lewis, 136
Spencer, Herbert, 345

Spies (Frayn), 240
The Spy Who Came in from the Cold (le
  Carré), 47
Stalin, Joseph, 116, 123, 171, 177, 178
Stalin's Secret War (Tolstoy), 432
Stallworthy, Jon, 152
Stanford, Derek, 20, 226
Stanley, Venetia, 375, 378–9
Stannard, Martin, 20–1
The State in its Relations with the Church
  (Gladstone), 188, 193, 195–6
Steffens, Lincoln, 118
Stephen, J. K., 109
Stephen, Leslie, 335
Stephens, Caroline, 456
Stewart, Dugald, 328
Stone, Lawrence, 37
Stopes, Marie, 82
Stopford, Gen., 389, 390
Strachey, Amabel, 238
Strachey, Lytton, 148, 315
The Strange Death of Liberal England
  (Dangerfield), 376
'The Strange Ride of Morrowbie Jukes'
  (Kipling), 96–7
Studies on Homer and the Homeric Age
  (Gladstone), 192, 193
suburbs and villages, 237–48 (*see also*
  towns)
  and suburbanized villages, 240
  and suburbs' population, 238
  and villages' disappearance, 245
  and villages' dramatic change, 247
Summerson, Sir John, 227
Summoned by Bells (Betjeman), 228, 230
Supple, Tim, 314
Swallows and Amazons (Ransome), 115
Swinburne, A. C., 103, 335
Sykes, Sir Francis, 214

Tacitus, xi
Take a Girl Like You (Amis), 4
Talking Heads (Bennett), 16
The Taming of the Shrew (Shakespeare), 312
Tawney, R. H., 178
Taylor, A. J. P., 328, 396
Taylor, Charles, 197
Taylor, Gary, 310
Taylor-Martin, Patrick, 226
Tebbit, Norman, 454
Temple, Archbishop William, 173
Temple, William Francis, 326
Tennyson, Alfred, Lord, 193, 293, 316,
  335, 340
Ternan, Ellen, 278, 279, 303

Terraine, John, 394
Thackeray, William Makepeace, 260
Thatcher, Carol, 463
Thatcher, Denis, 375, 459, 460, 463
Thatcher, Margaret, 57, 81, 169–70, 320,
    390, 421, 441, 446–7, 450–65
  and Falklands, 461
  and Howe resignation speech, 464
  in *The Iron Lady*, 463
  Iron Lady sobriquet of, 450
  letters of, 459–60
  loathed and despised, 452
  and man-management, 453
  mental decline of, 463–4
  and miners, 461
  and monetary union, 451–2
  and poll tax, 458
  'quite limited intellectually', 456
  and religion, 457–8
  and South Africa, 455
  and trade unions, 447
Thomas, Dylan, 228
Thomas, Helen, 117
Thomas, R. S., 228
Thompson, E. P., 164, 202–3, 458
Thompson, Flora, 245
Thompson, F. M. L., 235
Thomson, Sir Basil, 121
Thomson, J. J., 159
Thomson, James, 181, 185
Thorneycroft, Peter, 429
Thorpe, D. R., 427–8, 429, 433–4, 435,
    437, 438, 439
Thorpe, Jeremy, 418
Tillett, Ben, 354
The Time Machine (Wells), 349
Tolstoy, Leo, 54, 281
Tolstoy, Nikolai, 431–2
Tomalin, Claire, 299–300, 301, 302–4
'A Tombless Epitaph' (Coleridge), 288
The Tongue Set Free (Canetti), 55
Toulouse-Lautrec, Henri de, 153
towns, 249–58 (*see also* suburbs and
    villages)
  and commuters, 253
  distrait air of, 251
  representative democracy in, 252
  and smog, filth and traffic jams, 254
Toynbee, Arnold, 32
Trend, Burke, 446
Trevelyan, Sir Charles, 322
Trevelyan, G. M., 218, 221, 238
Trevor-Roper, Alexandra, 33
Trevor-Roper, Hugh, xii, 2, 3, 31–8 (*see
    also individual works*)

facial features of, 33
and Hitler diaries, 38
letters of, 32, 34
    seen as masterpiece, 35
'Mercurius Oxonensis' byline of, 36
'missing' works of, 38
on Lewis, 31–2
and parents, 32–3
telling historical essays of, 36–7
Trevor-Roper, Pat, 33
Troilus and Cressida (Shakespeare), 313
Trollope, Anthony, 98, 176, 273
Trotsky, Leon, 116, 118, 119, 121, 123
Trudeau, Pierre, 417–18
Tudjman, Franjo, 464
The Turn of the Screw (James), 149–50
Twelfth Night (Shakespeare), 313
Tynan, Kenneth, 67

Ulysses (Joyce), 24, 112
Underwood, Edith, 101–2, 104–5
Untold Stories (Bennett), 13, 14, 16–17
Unwin, Raymond, 239
Up from Methodism (Asbury), 203
The Upsurge of China (Johnson), 177
Ure, Mary, 61, 66
Ustinov, Peter, 142

Vansittart, Lord, 358
Vassall, John, 426
Venus and Adonis (Shakespeare), 340
Victims of Yalta (Tolstoy), 432
Victoria, Princess, 350
Victoria, Queen, 322, 330, 343, 351–2,
    353
The Victorian Country House (Girouard),
    249
The View in Winter (Blythe), 234
'A Vignette' (James), 148–9
villages and suburbs, 237–48 (*see also*
    towns)
  and suburbanized villages, 240
  and suburbs' population, 238
  and villages' disappearance, 245
  and villages' dramatic change, 247
Vincent, Nicholas, xix
Vines, Ellsworth, 140, 141
Voltaire, 259

'Wailing Well' (James), 146
Waldegrave, William, 454
Walden, Ben, 69
Waley, Arthur, 54
Walker, Peter, 212, 444–5
Walpole, Hugh, 366

War Diaries (Macmillan), 431
Ward, Aileen, 292
Ward, Colin, 240, 242
Ward, Mrs Humphry, 192
Warre-Cornish, Francis, 348
Watkins, Alan, 413
Watson-Watt, Robert, 70
Watts, G. F., 335
Waugh, Auberon, 4
Waugh, Evelyn, 4, 5, 33, 302
  hallucinations suffered by, 22
The Waves (Woolf), 111, 112
We Didn't Mean to Go to Sea (Ransome),
  115
Webb, Beatrice, 116, 118, 356, 400
Webber, Melvyn, 248
Wedgwood, C. V., 57–8
Wedgwood, Tom, 283
Wee Willie Winkie (Kipling), 92
Weizmann, Chaim, 365
Wells, H. G., 110, 118, 126, 159, 240, 349
Wesley, John, 202, 204–5, 207 (*see also*
  Methodism)
West, Fred, 247
Wheatley, Dennis, 42
Where Angels Fear to Tread (Forster), 128
Whitelaw, William, 452, 454
Whiteley, William, 245
Whitman, Walt, 80
The Whole Woman (Greer), 80–6 *passim*
Wigs on the Green (Mitford), 401
Wilberforce, Bishop Samuel, 316
Wilberforce, William, 256, 320
Wilde, Oscar, 133
Wildenstein, Georges, 35
Wilhelm II, Kaiser, 102, 361, 382–3, 384,
  385, 386
Wilkinson, Ellen, 400
Willett, Mrs, 363
William III, 301
William IV, 326
William-Ellis, Clough, 238
William of Orange, xiii
Williams, Heathcote, 137
Williams, Shirley, 456

Willoughby, Maj., 301
Wilson, John Dover, 305
Wilson, Harold, 143, 202, 413–14, 447
Wilson, James, 336
Wilson, Stephen, 44
Window affair, 70–2
Windsor Castle, 217
Windsor, Duke of (formerly Edward VIII),
  406, 409–10
The Winter's Tale (Shakespeare), 309, 310
Wodehouse, P. G., 54, 92, 129, 401
The Woodlanders (Hardy), 269
Woolf, Leonard, 107, 109
Woolf, Virginia, 60, 88, 106–13, 158 (*see
  also individual works*)
  breakdown suffered by, 109
  as diarist and essayist, 110
  family of, 109
  and Healey, 416
  on Forster, 128–9
  on literary style, 111
Woolley, Janetta, 74–5
Wordsworth, Dorothy, 283
Wordsworth, John, 285
Wordsworth, William, 152, 283, 285, 287,
  288
The World Crisis (Churchill), 389, 393
World War One, 372–98 *passim*, 423
  declaration of, 379–80
  and Gallipoli, 388–98
World War Two, 396–7, 423, 431–4
Worlock, Derek, 169
The Worm Forgives the Plough (Collis), 245
Wormald, Patrick, xii
Wren, Matthew, 301

Yeats, W. B., 131, 134, 295, 325, 416
At the Yeoman's House (Blythe), 234, 236
Yevtushenko, Yevgeny, 11
Young, G. M., 323, 335, 341
Young, Loretta, 142

Ziegler, Philip, 327, 440–1, 443, 444,
  445–6, 447, 448